HYSTERICAL

HYSTERICAL

EXPLODING
THE MYTH
OF GENDERED
EMOTIONS

PRAGYA
AGARWAL

CANONGATE

First published in Great Britain in 2022 by Canongate Books Ltd,
14 High Street, Edinburgh EH1 1TE

canongate.co.uk

1

'Hysteria' by Kim Yideum, translated from the Korean by Soeun Seo,
used by kind permission of Action Books.

Excerpt from *Emotions: A Brief History* by Keith Oatley, published 2004.
Used with permission of John Wiley & Sons; permission conveyed
through the Copyright Clearance Center, Inc.

British Library Cataloguing-in-Publication Data
A catalogue record for this book is available on
request from the British Library

ISBN 978 1 83885 322 8

Typeset in Bembo Std by
Palimpsest Book Production Ltd, Falkirk, Stirlingshire

Printed and bound in Great Britain by Clays Ltd, Elcograf S.p.A.

For all of you – all of us – who have ever been called *too much*

I want to rip you apart with my teeth. I want to tear you to death on this speeding subway. Hey, you groping, hey, hey, hands off! Ripping, I'll shred any second. I want to scream, throw a fit, but I take my hand and push deep into my gut. Breathe. Deep. Don't fucking touch me. I said stop leaning on me. Driving me nuts, what the fuck? My leather's pulled taut, a fox or a wolf, something's about to pop. Flowing blood like a lunar halo, bloodstains that bleed through blue sheets, you think that's instinct? Because of the full moon? Shut your mouth. Truth-speaking woman, if you know the truth, keep it to yourself. This is the gospel of filthy humans. Periodic bleeding. Stomach cramps. I won't stop. I'm complicated as hell, but people try and try to get inside. I'm an insider, me. Not an outsider. You mumble even in your sleep. Sudden hemorrhaging. Blood flowing. A world with a big door. Closing, opening, repeat, repeat. A wheel that stops and stops as it turns. I need a new route, need to get out. I need a heavy-duty maxi pad. What to do with this passed-out fucker? With his hand in my coat, this fucker is talking in his sleep like he's reading a scribbled letter. I want to kill the motherfucker. But what if he's my lover? If only I could pick him up by the back of his neck with my teeth. I would leap off this train and sprint over the tracks. I would head to the darkest part of the night, my wild hair flapping. If only I could go to the sandy beach on the red coast, moonlit. There, beside the cool well that flows, I would lay him down. If only.

— Kim Yideum, 'Hysteria'
(translated from Korean by Soeun Seo)

CONTENTS

Section 4: Can Emotional Women Get Ahead?

PREFACE

Hysterical /hɪˈster.ɪ.kəl/ US /hɪˈster.ɪ.kəl/ Unable to control your feelings or behaviour because you are extremely frightened, angry, excited, etc.

— *Cambridge English Dictionary*

THE WORD 'HYSTERICAL' CARRIES A great deal of cultural baggage. By its original definition, hysteria cannot be attributed to men, as it is historically inherently linked to women's bodies – specifically, in Ancient Greek texts, to a displaced or 'wandering' uterus, which was thought to move around a woman's body causing emotional and sometimes physical disruption. Even in today's apparently liberal times, the word 'hysterical' is used in a highly gendered way.

In 2016, on his radio show on the Australian station 4BC, the journalist Steve Price interrupted and talked over the author and playwright Van Badham, and called her 'hysterical' as she tried to get a word in.[1] Badham replied: 'It is probably my ovaries making me do it.'

Kamala Harris, the first woman vice president of the United States, and first woman of colour in this position, has been known for her determination throughout her twenty-five years as a prosecutor, but the same doggedness and tough line of questioning used against Attorney General Jeff Sessions in 2017 were deemed reason enough to brand her 'hysterical' by former Trump advisor Jason Miller on CNN.[2] Although Miller admitted that both Sessions and Harris were abrupt and shouting, only Harris was called 'hysterical'.

In March 2021 in London, a young woman, Sarah Everard, disappeared while walking back home one night at around 9 p.m. This case caused social media to explode with women sharing stories of how they had been assaulted; of the stress and anxiety they carried every time they left their homes; of having to make strategic decisions about which path to take, where to walk or run, whether someone is a threat or not, and what to do in case they are stopped, attacked, assaulted, or worse. Reclaim the Streets marches were planned around the country.

In response to this, Marion Fitzgerald, a criminology professor at Kent University, said on BBC Radio 4's *Today* programme: 'I think I'm entitled to say as a woman, we shouldn't pander to stereotypes and get hysterical.'[3] Fitzgerald also asked women not to 'get this out of proportion'. A reminder, if it were needed, that the notion of hysteria is reserved for women – and used to silence them – by women and men.

The United Nations Population Fund (UNFPA) published a 'State of the World Population' report in early 2021 which revealed that nearly half of women from 57 developing countries do not have autonomy over their bodies in terms of healthcare, contraception and sex.[4] What is not mentioned in this study, but is also arguably true, is that women do not have autonomy over their feelings either.

Women are not allowed to express the whole range of emotions in case they are deemed hysterical or over-emotional. When women are seen as emotionally unstable, or irrational, they may also lose autonomy and agency over their own bodies. As we have seen in the recent case of Britney Spears' conservatorship, women can be quickly labelled as 'hysterical' and mentally unstable, and once this has happened, the label is not easy to shift. And while we might try to reclaim some of these stigmatised terms, it is impossible to push away completely the historical narrative that insists that hysteria is a natural part of socially constructed femininity and womanhood. It is an aide memoire of the constant fear that we carry with us of being pushed down if we stand up too enthusiastically.

A complex system of cultural and social practices through history has led to these dualities of men/women, rationality/emotionality being embedded as norms. This proclivity for binary thinking has also led to a tendency to believe that there are some innate emotional differences between all women and all men: that men are rational, and women are not. That women are emotional, and men are not.

In 1996, for instance, Virginia Military Institute (VMI) was engaged in a legal battle to resist admitting women into its classes, where only men had been allowed since its foundation in the nineteenth century. As reported in the *Chronicle of Higher Education*, one of the witnesses said that VMI was unsuitable for women because, 'compared with men, women are more emotional, less aggressive, suffer more from fear of failure, and cannot withstand stress as well'.[5] These stereotypes about women – and men – keep repeating again and again.

The idea that rationality and emotionality are opposing sides of a coin has become entrenched in our social and political structures. There was widespread criticism when Barack Obama stated during his 2008 US presidential campaign that he would look for empathic qualities in a judicial nominee, including one for the US Supreme Court, saying at an address to Planned Parenthood: 'We need somebody who's got the heart, the empathy, to recognize what it's like to be a young teenage mom, the empathy to understand what it's like to be poor, or African-American, or gay, or disabled, or old.'[6] Critics argued that empathic judging would not be impartial, that it would be emotional and irrational, and lead to favouritism. Obama's proposals were eventually dismissed on the grounds that emotions would interfere with objective and rational judicial decision-making. However, decision-making can never be separated from emotions.[7] Emotional empathy – a means of forming emotional connection with others – can be a key to impartiality as it allows judges to see perspectives dissimilar to their own experiences, and therefore bypass their unconscious biases. Emotions are not disconnected from reason. The duality of emotionality and rationality does not make sense, nor does the association of reason with men, and emotionality with women.

•

> It is better to dwell in the wilderness, than with a contentious and an angry woman.

> — Proverbs 21:19

It is easy, on absorbing these tropes from society, to accept as a given that men's and women's emotional responses as well as their experiences are systematically and universally different. The truth, however, is that there is no conclusive evidence of this. That hasn't stopped both the scientific research community and popular media picking up on any idea that suggests that male and female brains have evolved differently. We like complex studies and results distilled down into soundbites. We often don't have the patience or energy to absorb more, nor the resources or the will to dig deeper into the research. And so, we keep believing any media headlines that proclaim that women are more emotional.

We will see in this book that emotions are not associated with any specific region of the brain, and so it is unlikely that men and women differ in their internal experience of emotions. It seems more likely that individual, outward expressions of emotions are affected by social status, hierarchies and organisation. It is more likely that emotions are interpreted differently depending on specific cultural display rules and norms.

In our society there are 'feeling rules' which tell us how to feel in certain situations: happy when you graduate, or get married, or meet friends; sad when someone dies. Don't yawn and roll your eyes in front of a teacher, do not laugh when giving someone potentially bad news. Then there are *display rules*, the ones that tell us which emotions to show and to what extent, like the flight attendant who has to pretend to smile even when they are overworked and exhausted. We expect these emotional displays at times; we often demand them. And we will see throughout this book how so many of these feeling and display rules are extremely gendered.

It is worth remembering as we explore gendering of emotions that the separation of sex and gender becomes an issue when it comes to academic research into emotions. Sex is determined by our biology, while gender is a social construct and the identity we present to the world. But when people refer to gender differences, sometimes they mean sex differences, and vice versa. There is an assumption of standard biology across all men and all women. This topic is very emotionally charged, and the notion of gender has been misused and exploited so much that any study discussing sex differences is likely to be controversial. And, as ever, there are hardly any academic studies being done on transgender people, so we do not know reliably if their expressions of emotions, and frequency of suppression, change over the course of transitioning, how much fluctuation of hormones plays a role, and how any shifts are associated with their changing gender identity. We have to remember that, for most people, gender falls into a spectrum. No one is 100 per cent masculine or feminine, in the traditional stereotypical sense, but we are forced (both consciously and unconsciously) to choose behaviours that align with the identity with which we feel most affinity.

The notion that women are more emotional also seeps into the way nonverbal communication is interpreted. With the advent of social media's omnipresence in our lives, despite its anonymity and its bypassing the need to adhere to socially acceptable forms of communication,[8] the stereotype of women being the more emotional sex/gender[9] is so deeply entrenched that women are still perceived to be more expressive online, using more positive emoticons, capital letters, longer sentences and more punctuation marks, especially exclamation marks, which is interpreted as a marker for intensity and abundance of emotions.[10]

In a study in 2000,[11] the participants were given a list of 19 very specific emotions and asked to rate how many of these men and women experience. Emotions such as happiness, sadness, fear and sympathy were mainly seen to be associated with women, while anger and pride were seen to be associated with men. All participants, irrespective of their gender, thought that women experienced and expressed most of the 19 emotions, but were not perceived to experience anger, contempt and pride as much as men. These three emotions are associated with dominance and power. The emotions perceived in women are associated with vulnerability. Men were not perceived to experience any such emotions associated with powerlessness. When the same participants were shown photographs of men and women showing ambiguous emotional expressions, women were perceived to be more sad than men, and always less angry, even when it was the same face with various 'feminine' and 'masculine' adaptations (such as long hair).

These beliefs about people's emotional reactions based on their gender no doubt have huge implications for what roles they are considered fit to play in society. And these stereotypes determine what emotions one is allowed to express. People perceive angry women as being more emotional and less competent than angry men, while angry men are seen either to be passionate or having a bad day. Moreover, experiments show that people would pay an angry woman significantly less than an angry man and predict a less prosperous professional and personal future for her. So these gendered stereotypes affect the response of the person interpreting the emotion, and thus influence social communication and interaction, which will in turn have an effect on further emotional response and expression. Thus, it becomes a self-fulfilling prophecy where stereotypic-consistent norms are maintained in society. If men and women do not conform to these gender roles, they are likely to be punished and penalised for their transgressions.

Women worry more about social rejection: they feel the pressure to maintain a happy state even when faced with expectations and pressures. They prioritise other people's needs. There is a belief amongst some evolutionary psychologists that there is an evolutionary basis to this,[12] that because women were supposed to care for infants and other members of their group, they are designed to be pro-social, prioritising collaboration and cooperation. Women are *considered* 'emotional experts', more inclined to pay attention to other people's emotions than their own. Women are believed to be better than men at describing in a complex way the emotional reactions they would have to different life situations. Women are also more likely to rate themselves as being emotionally open, and a Dutch study mapping the perception of almost 6,000 Dutch people (31.9 per cent men) towards emotions showed that women are more strongly connected to their emotions and those of others than men.[13] How much of this is due to societal and cultural expectations and how much due to biology is something that is of huge interest to me and other researchers who do not agree with the essentialist view that there is an innate difference between men and women that determines their emotional experience and expression. We know that we internalise societal expectations, and through this book I want to highlight how the idea that women are more nurturing, patient, kind, empathetic and resilient is sown deep into their bones.

Men, on the other hand, receive constant messages from a young age that emotions such as fear or sadness are not 'masculine' traits. Boys have to learn to be masculine. They are told by society that they have to conform to a certain presentation of masculinity, which involves all the clichés – being strong, fearless and competitive, and basically 'not like a girl'. This involves detaching themselves from any so-called 'feminine' traits, and actively expressing their masculinity through chauvinistic behaviours and aggressive personas. The more a boy has to suppress his natural personality to develop this hyper-masculine persona, the more he is boxed in and less able to express his emotions.

So, men are reasonable and reasoned, while women are not. Women show emotion, men don't. Women are excitable, men are self-possessed.

Why are we not considering how the scrutiny of women's

emotionality (the observable behavioural or physiological components of emotion that act as cues to a person's inner emotional state) and the subsequent need to regulate their emotions might contribute to the perpetuation of gendered 'emotion norms'? Is it not likely that it is these social pressures that make women hypervigilant and good at reading other people's verbal and nonverbal emotional cues – because they need to be?

·

'Mr Bennet, how can you abuse your own children in such a way? You take delight in vexing me. You have no compassion for my poor nerves.'

'You mistake me, my dear. I have a high respect for your nerves. They are my old friends. I have heard you mention them with consideration these last twenty years at least.'

— Jane Austen, *Pride and Prejudice*

Art and literature have undoubtedly perpetuated some of these stereotypes, even when trying to disrupt the same norms. Women's nervous dispositions are rife in literature. Men, meanwhile, appear mostly in these same books as the epitome of stoicism, all nobly repressed emotion and moody stares – Mr Darcy in *Pride and Prejudice* being perhaps the most iconic of this stereotype. These male characters – from Edward Ferrars in *Sense and Sensibility*, to Oliver Mellors in *Lady Chatterley's Lover* and Gabriel Oak from *Far from the Madding Crowd* – are reserved creatures, uncomfortable with outward shows of passion and love, and readers are asked to associate their brusque and surly demeanours with appropriately suppressed passion, ardent devotion and smouldering love. Their female counterparts, meanwhile, swoon, cry and suffer nervous exhaustion. It is not just that women are considered hysterical or emotional, it is that emotionality is seen as a flipside to rationality, to reason and logic.

We see a version of toxic masculinity in today's films and media, much of which depicts a hyper-masculinity where 'men don't cry'. Boys are bullied in the playground and continue to be teased as adults if they don't conform to this kind of male ideal, and if they show any supposedly feminine emotions are called a 'girl' or 'gay', both considered the worst kinds of insults, of course. We do not see many angry women as protagonists unless it is a negative image, and they are labelled as villainous. Angry women do not appear much but when they do, they are more likely to be a monster, harpy or witch. In her book *Good and Mad: The Revolutionary Power of Women's Anger*, Rebecca Traistor writes: 'The best way to discredit these women, to make them look unattractive, is to capture an image of them screaming. The act of a woman opening her mouth with volume and assured force, often in complaint, is coded in our minds as ugly.'

Every Bollywood film I watched growing up reinforced the 'damsel in distress', with a soft-spoken elegant melancholy seen as a desirable quality in every leading lady, while the caustic, sharp, angry tongue was always associated with a harridan, a vixen or a shrew. Growing up in India, I saw the goddess Kali as an unlikely manifestation of female rage. On one hand this was empowering, an image of a fearless, multi-limbed woman carrying multiple weapons, but on the other, we see her with a prone man in front of her, believed to be her consort Shiva whom she has killed in a fit of rage. There is a message here, that her anger has made her unable to distinguish between friend and foe. Kali is interpreted as a symbol of death and destruction, guilty and embarrassed by her anger. It is also used to remind women that rage can be all-consuming and destructive.

This being said, we now regularly see examples of practitioners, often women, using their art to challenge the patriarchy in its depiction of their emotions. One example of the deconstruction of the tropes of female anger is artist Pipilotti Rist's *Ever Is Over All* (1997). This large-scale projection installation, filmed on a standard video camera, shows a woman dressed in a pale blue dress and red high-heeled shoes happily walking down a street. Accompanied by a dreamy, almost ethereal soundtrack and with a large grin on her face, she smashes the windows of cars using a metal flower while a female police officer salutes her as she walks by. The action seems to provide a cathartic release from the suffocating and conservative feminine image we are often shown by the male gaze. The Swiss artist's film is a joyful requiem to the traditional societal norms and codes of feminine good behaviour. There are not many examples of this further back in history. *Timoclea Killing Her Rapist* by Italian artist Elisabetta Sirani from 1659 shows Timoclea standing resolutely above her rapist, shown upside down, feet flailing in the air, inverting the hierarchy and toppling the patriarchy quite literally. It shows Timoclea's rage and fury at injustice, at being violated, at not being believed, and her fortitude. Here the female gaze, so very unusual in art, shows the power of a woman's rage.

In Beyoncé's music video for 'Hold Up', released in 2016, anger is similarly given a positive slant, with the singer walking down the road smashing the windows of a car, smiling and unapologetic, singing about an unfaithful partner; the message being that anger is not always a negative thing, especially in women, but can be positive, empowering and free us from systemic inequalities as well as cheating partners. Such depictions question the way anger has been displayed and accepted in the past, even though at the same time they can also perpetuate and reinforce the trope of an 'angry Black woman', and 'crazy ex-girlfriend'.

Since women are perceived to be more emotionally expressive than men, they are also expected to smile more, be agreeable and to hold in their anger and pain. Women are then criticised for not smiling enough because they are seen as stepping outside a stereotypical cultural and social norm. A quick Twitter poll reveals that 'Smile, it might never happen' or 'Cheer up, darling, it can't be that bad' are commonly heard phrases by women, whether it be on streets, public transport or in a bar. Men are rarely asked to smile. A 2019 survey of 520 women showed that almost 98 per cent had been told to smile at some point in their lives by complete strangers, and for more than 15 per cent this happened regularly, almost twice a week. Fifty-six per cent of the women had been told to smile by men in public.[14] A smile is a sign of a deliberate lack of anger, a sign of agreeableness. Women are given the message that their anger is 'ugly' and that no one will listen to them if they are angry. Women have to suppress their anger and are more likely to ruminate. Women's happiness has been declining for the past thirty years, both absolutely and relative to men, in much of the western world, but especially in the USA and the UK. Women are also likely to experience more depression compared with men.[15] They are still being told to smile.

Another quick anonymous poll I did online – more like a crowd-sourcing exercise than a scientific research study – from about 500 women highlighted the words that are regularly used for women showing emotions, especially anger: 'bitchy', 'bossy', 'hysterical', 'emotional', 'fiery', 'prickly', 'hormonal', 'premenstrual', 'impulsive', 'dramatic', 'temperamental', 'sensitive', 'shrill', 'unhinged'. Words can get under your skin. Words can have an effect on how we feel about ourselves, about how others see us, how we worry how others see us.

Even when emotionality is not being stigmatised, women are given advice on how to control and manage their emotions. Think of all the business articles and books that are aimed at helping women navigate their emotions so that they can succeed in life: *The Mental Toughness Handbook, Anger Management for Women: Master Your Emotions with This Step-by-Step Guide to Overcome Rage and Anxiety, Women's Guide to Managing Emotions* and *Emotional Intelligence for Business Women* are just a few titles I found with a cursory online search.

In internalising these long-standing attitudes and beliefs about 'feminine' and 'masculine' ideals, women can believe that to be successful they have to emulate the universal model of masculine emotionality and behaviours. In doing so, the 'masculine' model becomes the model of excellence, and men and women alike get forced once again into the binary model of male and female attitudes and behaviours, something apparently innate in all of us due to our biological sex. Any concept of 'femininity' and its behaviours and expressions – in the arena of career success and power – meanwhile are deemed inferior. The struggle for equality therefore cannot be untangled from the struggle to overthrow notions of femininity, otherwise there is an acceptance of the patriarchal hierarchy, where men have the power and agency, and the world is divided into distinct masculine and feminine emotions and behaviours. This is not the answer.

•

You will not see much of me and my personal story in this book, but it is all linked to my life and my work. I have always struggled with the norms around emotions, unsure of how much of myself to express, called 'over-sensitive', 'over-emotional'. I have been called 'hysterical' so many times. I am raising three girls. I come from a family of women, with three sisters. Often we laugh at ourselves: 'Oh, we are all a bit over-emotional like that.' We fight, argue, get excited, and then we make up, come together, immediately forgetting that there were ever raised voices. We feel too much, too intensely. I know I do. I try and temper it, but then it stays inside all bubbled up like a mighty cauldron, all the pressure building up ready to explode one day, drowning me in it. Because I don't know how to keep it all in, how to not show my feelings, how to not feel angry, to not feel love, empathy, frustration. But we are told that we need to think with our brains, not with our hearts. As if the heart is only to beat but not too loud. As if the brain only thinks and never feels.

I try and appear calm, cool, collected, even when I am in turmoil. I try and appear nonchalant even when I am ecstatic, overjoyed, euphoric. I try and take very deep breaths and moderate my voice and my expression even when I feel offended, when I feel angry and even when I am seething. I try and believe that this is merely my 'System 1' processing in my brain, my amygdala reacting to stimuli in an impulsive, rash, irrational manner. I just have to step back, take deep breaths, count down from ten to one to activate my System 2 processing, let the information pass on to the rational parts of my brain, and then maybe I will not feel as strongly. I have considered my emotionality a drawback and a limitation of my personality, a liability. Even when I believe that I have valid justification for feeling so, my outburst can be dismissed as 'You are just being emotional', and sometimes 'Oh, don't be such a child', as if being emotional should be reserved to children, in their toddler brains when they haven't learnt to use rules and consequences, or self-control. Infantilisation is often a means of control, of denigrating and discrediting valid opinions, and emotions are often seen as a way of losing and lacking self-control.

When I started researching emotions way back in 2004 because of my academic work in human-centred interfaces – looking at the way technologies could be made more aligned with human behaviours, cognitive processes and emotions – I quickly became embroiled in what Kristen Lindquist and colleagues have called the 'hundred-year emotion war'.[16] As I started researching this book, and writing it, at times I felt like I was drowning, going down various rabbit holes. When I spoke with Professor Gina Rippon, neuroscientist at Aston University recently, we discussed how emotions are formed as a result of the entanglement of social and biological reactions, but it is the biological basis of emotions that has always been regarded as more significant. And I was pleased to hear that she agreed with me that the social and cultural interpretation of emotion has not been paid as much attention so far. We continue to be emotional about emotions, deeply fascinated by how emotions are made, and why we feel the way we do. Are we really humans because we can feel, or is it because we can think? I know we keep sticking to this age-old debate between reason and emotionality, and to a Cartesian view of the world that states that *I think, therefore I am.* I genuinely believe that emotions are a key to our humanness, that *I feel, therefore I am.*

•

This book is about creating a more equitable landscape for all our emotions, an emotional topography which is not chopped up into little parcels, hemmed in by high fences based on our gender. If we want to figure out a more feminist emotional rhetoric, we need, of course, to talk about men too. Because a feminist landscape of emotions would be one where, irrespective of our gender, we are able to reclaim all of our emotions. In such a world, women are not suppressing their negative emotions, and exaggerating their positive emotions. And of course, this benefits men too: men are not afraid to show tears because it makes them look soft or because it threatens their masculinity.

Through this book, I will examine whether we have some basic emotions, and whether there are universal expressions of them. This is useful in understanding whether we all understand and express emotions in the same way, and if we can really interpret other people's emotions in a standard manner. I look at how language and embodiment are key to understanding and expressing emotions, and how emotions are a result of interaction between our culture and language, the way our bodies interact with the environment and the way we are perceived by the people around us. Emotions help to maintain the social organisation and hierarchies that we are accustomed to, which in turn affects the way we regulate and express our emotions.

This emotional subjectivity is really the key to understanding how emotions have become gendered and I hope you can keep this close while the rest of the story unfolds in the coming chapters. My hope is that if women aren't perceived as hysterical or given the message that it is unseemly and 'unfeminine' for them to be assertive and to show rage, they will be more able to question words and actions that cast doubt on the legitimacy of their emotions. My hope is that if we all understand and acknowledge that emotions are not grounded in our inherent biological differences, we would not set our expectations and acceptations in a way that is pre-determined by the gender norms in our society.

Whatever your gender, this book might make you angry. It made me angry writing it. Anger is OK. Or it might make you cry. That is OK too. You're allowed to do either or neither. Or both.

Section 1:

I FEEL, THEREFORE I AM

Is it really possible to tell someone else what one feels?
— Leo Tolstoy, *Anna Karenina*

1.

WHAT IS AN EMOTION?

The cry that we each utter in the first moment of our personal history as we are propelled from the womb into the world is an emotional signal. So, emotion is the first language of us all.[1]

WHAT EMOTION ARE YOU FEELING right now? And could you put a name to it? Would someone close to you be able to look at your face and be able to tell exactly what you are feeling right now?

As I write this, I feel some joy at getting closer to finishing this book, some anxiety over whether it will be good enough, some apprehension as to whether anyone will ever read it, a bit of anger that I cannot go to bed right now, a little sadness that I do not have my favourite snack in front of me, and guilt that I cannot spend time with my children, or that the house is so dirty as I prioritise writing. These are all overlapping feelings with no discrete, easily identifiable label that I can put my finger on. I have this feeling quite often as I am getting closer to finishing a book, that stage where everything has unravelled and it seems impossible to put it back together. There is a looming deadline and my heart is racing, and there is a growing dread, but also a joyful anticipation of the moment when I will click 'send' on that email to my editor with the final draft attached. I want to lie down under heavy blankets and never emerge. I want to just get on with it and finish it as soon as possible. I want to run away from this computer as far as I can. I want to be tied down to my desk so that I cannot escape. All of it at the same time. There is pride, fear, joy, anxiety. I become frantic, I am distracted. I know that I will suffer for it, but my mind also makes me procrastinate.

Are you agreeing with me? Can you feel yourself feeling the same fear and joy at times? Do you find yourself putting things off? This is the 'akrasia effect', where we act against our better judgement, feeding a part of our brain that thrives on immediate rewards rather than awaiting future rewards. Maybe I should follow Victor Hugo's example. In 1830, Hugo had to deliver a new book, but he had been procrastinating by working on other projects, entertaining friends, and finding any excuse to delay his writing. It all sounds too painfully familiar. And then he had to take drastic action. He asked his assistant to lock away all his clothes and leave him nothing but a large shawl to wear. He could not go outside any more, so he remained in his study and wrote furiously, and finished *The Hunchback of Notre-Dame*. Hugo did not have Twitter or Netflix, so of course locking away my clothes is unlikely to help me deal with this feeling right now. I don't have a word for it yet, so I find it difficult to explain this emotion to anyone else. I could try and break it up into separate emotions that we find easier to understand, but then it is all of it, and also none of it. Could I call it 'bookanxiety', or 'deadlineangst' or 'almost-there syndrome'? Or what about 'Dread of Looming Deadline (DOLD)'? That sounds like it could catch on.

If many of us start using it, would it become an emotion that we found easy to talk about and to understand in others? Once we have an acceptable name for it, would my brain anticipate this feeling, and be better equipped to deal with it? Would it become stigmatised or celebrated?

I could imagine, in 100 years' time, writers talking about 'angst of almost there but not quite' as DOLD, much like FOMO (fear of missing out) or Hanganxiety (the anxiety about a hangover) are becoming part of our language and culture to share a certain feeling that we have not found a way to put a label on, something that cannot be described by the set of basic emotion words that we have in English. For instance, now that I know of akrasia, it suddenly makes sense, and I also know that I can try to counter it with enkrateia, which is having power over ourselves, so that we can reduce the friction our brain encounters and have a more active and autonomic way of suppressing the feeling of lethargy resulting in procrastination. If I put a word to this set of overlapping feelings as I drag myself over the deadline, while at the same time the dead-line feels like it is rushing towards me, would my brain be better prepared for it next time? It is also possible that someone might do an experimental observation with a group of writers all working towards a deadline, with some people better equipped to manage the looming anxiety than others, and draw conclusions based on our social groups: that older writers do not feel as much DOLD as younger ones, or that women feel more DOLD than men, based on the results they get from 20, 30, 50 writers. And these could become part of our folklore: women writers feel more DOLD. There might also be some interesting results about whether DOLD contrib-utes to the success of the book or not. You see where I am going with this? That it is easy to draw conclusions about emotions related to specific groups in an essentialist manner if we really want to see such patterns.

The fact is that our feelings aren't just one discrete feeling but overlapping sensations. I could talk about it in terms of colours: I am feeling blue; I am seeing red. But there are various shades of blue, depending on the intensity of a particular feeling, and this fluctuates through the day as well. But we always want to put things into neat boxes, and our brains find it easier to deal with clear categories.

What really are emotions? And how are they formed? 'What do you understand by the term "emotion"? Are you able to sum this up in a few words?' I put this question to people of all genders through an anonymous online survey and of 155 people who responded, 80 per cent said that it was 'how we feel', with similar responses defining it as a 'feeling' or an 'expression'. The other answers included 'how we act' and 'how we behave'. This was not a rigorous experiment in any way. But it was interesting to see these responses from people who did not claim to be scientists, and with diverse backgrounds.

We use emotions in everyday language almost all the time: 'I am feeling emotional.' 'This made me very emotional.' 'Oh come on, don't be so emotional.' Or even (in social-media speak constrained by the character limit on Twitter): 'All the feels.'

It might appear straightforward, but the concept of emotion is slippery, so difficult to define, yet seemingly easy to recognise in others. We interpret so much from body language, from facial gestures, from the tone of someone's voice. But emotion remains a concept that has vague, ambiguous boundaries when we try to define it. Despite the length of time that we have been aware of emotions and their impact on our lives, a complete understanding of them remains relatively elusive. We might think that we have access to all information at our fingertips these days, and that we therefore make considered decisions based in reason and rationality, but if we analyse human behaviour closely, emotions continue to play a huge role in our decision-making every day.

·

The term 'emotion' seems to have been introduced in the *Oxford English Dictionary* sometime around 1580, but it wasn't until the nineteenth century that it was recognised as a category that needed to be formally investigated. In both the English and French languages around this time, and in philosophical thought, emotions were mostly interpreted as 'passion', and had an inherent connection with impulsiveness and moodiness, with capriciousness and fallibility. The Dutch psychologist Nico Frijda explains that the broader notion of emotions in the French language emerged in the sixteenth century as émouvoir, meaning to 'stir up', a word that has its roots in the Latin for migration, or 'moving to the outside'.[2] It implied that emotions made people go outside of themselves, and also impacted others around them. Even in these early conceptualisations of emotions, the understanding was that they were a threat to rationality, and this push and pull between sensibility and impulsivity was seen. So, while people created rational actions in a controlled manner, emotions or passions emerged in a rather haphazard, uncontrolled way, without our own initiative.

Ancient Greeks spoke of emotions as pathema (πάθημα), a term that referred to those feelings that tend to overwhelm rather than sustain an individual, such as passion and suffering. As far back as Aristotle, who lived around 380 BCE, emotions were defined as changing feelings that were both social and psychological responses to external stimuli in the environment, including other people's reactions and expressions and situations. Many post–Darwinists believed that emotions were set in stone, that they were biological phenomena common to people across the globe and cultural contexts. On the other hand, much recent examination of emotions has shown that they are fluctuating, shifting categories that cannot be mapped universally, as categories such as 'sand' or 'elephant' can be. There has always been conflict between constructivists (those who believe that knowledge is constructed not transmitted, and therefore our emotions are not innate but part of our learning process), and the more traditional positivists (who propose that emotions are genetically determined and relatively invariable responses).

Until the late eighteenth century, people felt 'passions', 'accidents of the soul' or 'moral sentiments' and explained them very differently to emotions. Most seventeenth- and eighteenth-century philosophers and thinkers preferred to use the word 'passions', which we now associate largely with intense desire for something or someone. Passions were considered to be raw states of emotion which often evoked a violent and agitated response, while 'emotions' and 'feelings' were calmer and more controlled, after those passions had been regulated and reflected upon. From the Latin pati (to suffer), for a long time passion was associated with suffering, and emotions with a state of passiveness. Scottish philosophers such as David Hume, and the French philosopher René Descartes were rationalising these terms, which in current usage they considered irrational.[3] Although there was no commonly understood vocabulary for emotions at the time, one of the significant developments was a growing understanding that emotions played a crucial role in generating and maintaining social order and cohesion. Descartes focused on love and generosity as the main emotions that affected social organisation, while the Dutch philosopher Baruch Spinoza proposed that emotions were also grounds for interpersonal conflict, and that some could be disruptive to social order. Emotions were not merely things we felt or directed at others, arising out of our mind–body interaction, but also beginning to be seen to play a role in regulating society.

In 1884 the psychologist and philosopher William James wrote an influential article in the journal *Mind* titled 'What is an emotion?', where he defined an emotion as something that accompanies a distinct reaction or bodily change; for instance if we do not laugh at a witty remark our state of mind is not an emotion, but it is if we do.[4] These changes could be internal, such as an increase in heart rate, an expressive behaviour such as scowling or laughing, or an involuntary action such as bodily convulsions, as long as there is a distinct perception of intent or animation in these expressions. In James's view, if we assess that a situation is threatening, but have no feeling of fear, then that is a dispassionate assessment of the situation devoid of emotion. The acclaimed contemporary philosopher Martha Nussbaum, who has worked on emotions for many decades, has written: 'Emotions are not just the fuel that powers the psychological mechanism of a reasoning creature, but they are parts, highly complex and messy parts, of this creature's reasoning itself.'[5] Both James and Nussbaum propose that our mental lives are tied up with our bodily states. We encounter grief and we cry. We feel rage and we also feel the flushing of our faces and clenching of our teeth. James believed that emotions could not be separated from our bodies and if they were, then this was cold-blooded, rational and intellectual. Once again, the duality between emotions and rationality was set out.

But as I trawl through a mountain of literature just from the last few decades, it becomes apparent that there is little scientific consensus on the response to this question. The aim here is not to have an exhaustive review on the philosophy of emotions, but to understand that the broader discourse in emotions has shaped much of our understanding of how women and men experience and express emotions.

•

In 1981, the psychologists Paul and Anne Kleinginna compiled 92 definitions from a variety of sources in the literature of emotion in order to try to create a common framework for understanding the notion of 'emotion' and emotional expression.[6] When these were categorised based on the emotional phenomena they emphasised, there were as many as 11 distinct categories found amongst the literature pertaining to emotion, with a broad array of definitions. In 2010, the American psychologist Caroll Izard spoke with 35 prominent scientists working in the field of emotions across four nationalities.[7] No historians or sociologists were part of this study. Only four were women, which shows two things: that there is an inherent gender imbalance in academia, especially in the scientific domain, and that therefore much of the work on emotions to date has been conducted from a male perspective. These 35 scientists expressed what they thought were the most important structural and functional aspects of 'emotion'. Most of them agreed that there is a process by which we capture information through our sensory system, and that we integrate this incoming information with the pre-existing data and knowledge in our brains to execute a response. There is a neural element to what is happening in the brain during this process, a phenomenological aspect where we are first attributing meaning to our experience in the real world in order to understand both it and other people's responses, and, then a process where we change our emotional expressions before they become evident to others. As expected, there was no consensus on how to define 'emotions'.

There have been attempts in the last few decades to understand emotions as a physical manifestation of neurobiological activity that is sensed by an organism. One suggestion is that there is a locationist framework that proposes that specific brain regions are linked to distinct emotional categories. The locationist view assumes that each emotion has specific motivations that drive cognition and behaviour, with each of these being biological and inherent in all of us. So although we know that culture and learning can shape emotions, we all experience the same basic, core emotions. These first-order emotions are something all children are born with, and they are key to their survival – and each of these emotions comes with its own set of stimuli, motivations, feelings, behaviours that can adapt and grow as we age and accumulate more experiences and memories.[8] The different emotions are assumed to link to very specific mechanisms in the brain and body, and one brain locale: for instance, the amygdala is the centre of fear, insula for disgust, orbitofrontal cortex for anger.

Then there is the psychological constructionist approach that purports that there are general brain networks related to a range of different emotions and thus emotions are not connected to specific physiological or psychological processes. There are no distinct neural circuits associated with the concepts of 'anger' or 'sadness'. William James had argued that 'the trouble with emotions in psychology is that they are regarded too much as absolutely individual things. But if we regard them as products of more general causes . . . then the mere distinguishing and cataloguing becomes of subsidiary importance.' James proposed that emotions were a result of more complex perceptions in people's minds as they made sense of a particular situation (such as being stuck in a traffic jam when late), and the resultant physiological response (sweaty palms or heart rate rising). They might assign a specific meaning to these situations and responses such as frustration or anger. But in James's view there was no point in identifying each of these individual varieties, as it would be similar to giving each shape of a rock on a beach its individual name. There are as many emotions as shapes of rocks found on a specific beach, all variations of a particular kind.

Researchers have proposed that emotions arise from the integration of various brain activities that happen concurrently in the brain stem, amygdala, insula, anterior cingulate and orbitofrontal cortices. Some of these are basic emotions which are unlearned and rooted in our evolution as humans, while there are emotion schemas – the rules learnt from our own individual experiences as well as the cultural norms and frameworks that we exist in – laid on top of these that are formed during our lifetime. This idea that emotions interacted dynamically with perceptual and cognitive processes was not new but was framed in terms of 'emotion schemas' which are believed to be an integral link between our emotion and cognition; the way emotions interact with our perceptual processes to shape our responses. The cognitive aspects of our schemas are affected by our cultural contexts, and the way we have learnt. We are all individuals and have different capacity to feel pain, hurt, anger, sadness. Our individual differences affect our emotionality too, irrespective of gender or race or class. Rather than a simplistic, all-encompassing model of emotions as a deep-rooted biological process hardwired inside us, schemas are shaped by our experiences, the images we see around us and words we hear; the way we judge and evaluate a situation and its context; the cues we receive from the person with

12

whom we are communicating; the non-cognitive processes of change in our neurotransmitters and hormones that can affect how some emotions are intensified at certain times. We might joke and create memes about the notion of 'hangry', but it is an interaction of changes in our hormone levels when we are hungry, and the compensation carried out by our neurobiological processes to intensify the emotion of anger, which creates this particular feeling. What is crucial to understand and remember is that when some emotion schemas occur frequently, or are suppressed and regulated regularly, they can become stabilised as personality traits.

The neuroscientist and author Lisa Feldman Barrett proposes a social constructionist view of emotions and rejects the idea of universal emotions. I spoke with Professor Barrett over Zoom one very wet afternoon from a small cottage in the middle of rural Ireland. The connection issues notwithstanding, we had a really fascinating conversation about essentialism and the problems in discretising emotions, the way we create boundaries and boxes for emotions, as well as the issues with the binary categories we assign broadly to things and people in the world. In her work Barrett explains how emotions are stereotypes that we implicitly project on other people.[9] We see what we feel. For instance, Barrett rejects the idea of a 'resting bitch face' and that it is a negative expression. In an experiment she conducted with psychological scientist Erika Siegel from University of California San Francisco, it was demonstrated that people perceived a neutral face as smiling if it was paired with some positive stimuli (even when unseen), and the same face as not smiling or even scowling if they had been primed with negative stimuli that shaped their own mental representation of the scenario.[10] If they were feeling negative, they were more likely to see the neutral faces as negative. We also know that the notion of a

13

'resting bitch face' is very gendered, assigned more to women even though scientific research has not shown any gendered difference.[11] Also as discussed earlier, women are asked to smile more than men, and men are less likely to be singled out for having an unsmiling facial expression.

We map our preconceptions onto incoming events by first anticipating a situation, and then preparing to act in response to it. Emotions are constructed out of such predictive models too. When our brain predicts that a situation or a person should evoke a certain feeling, say of joy or of anger, it creates a simulated model that in turn influences our perception, experiences and responses. For example, if you anticipate that reading this book will be a terrible experience for you, a simulation of that feeling would be created in your head, and what you experience through your various senses is that simulation. When you actually read this book, you are likely to have some unexpected perceptions too, perhaps of joy or surprise, and it is likely that you could change your prediction based on this incoming data. But Barrett proposes that you are more likely to moderate the incoming information to suit the prediction that you had already made. This is less cognitively taxing for the brain. So, if you had already decided to hate this book and to feel disappointed, you are more likely to modulate your emotions to conform to that internal, predetermined expectation.

Our mind–body interface gets punctuated by the relationship between our thoughts and actions. These are accompanied by neuro-chemical fluctuations, by the ups and downs of hormone levels, by neuro-musculoskeletal reflexes, by the viscerality of our bodies affecting our internal organs. Our movements and actions are detected, measured and stored – all core effects mapped into our brains as signals and symbols. These change and shift and cause the body's homeostatic barometer to oscillate, and its value to be measured. Meanings and values are assigned to these different core effects by examining the social context and using the database of prior experiences and knowledge, called the 'episodic memory networks' or the 'default networks'. These emotions can be attached to certain objects or not, i.e., we can feel emotions independent of any affiliations to our environment. We can feel tired, we can have a wildly pumping heart, blood rushing to our head, a weight on our shoulders, we can feel fear and be immobilised by it, or spurred into action to flee. All these have a stimuli but no direct affiliation such as finding a particular food delicious, or a painting beautiful. In this framework of emotions, rather than attempting to define emotions discretely as good or bad, negative or positive, a multi-dimensional array is conceptualised. The notion of categorisation helps us make sense of the world around us, to simplify it into a manageable mental map. This allows for certain shortcuts: it would be too cognitively taxing to react to every sensory stimulus we encounter, so our brain puts similar stimuli into groups, to which we attach certain meaning and associations. We optimise. In doing so within ourselves, we also form an idea of what kind of psychological and physiological reactions in others signify what emotion, and we predict these in a context-sensitive way.

None of these theories of emotion are perfect, and scientists accept and acknowledge this. What is significant is that emotions are underpinned by regulation and expression. As, over the last decades, more research has been carried out, it is increasingly acknowledged that emotions are learned to a large extent, and their response and expression are taught, not innate. In the last few decades, we have come to understand that our physical bodies and brains are malleable, and that there is no universal body. That regardless of biological sex, our bodies are largely shaped by culture, both in the ways we perceive ourselves and how others see us. The philosopher and gender-theorist Judith Butler says that our bodies are the sites of performance, and although Butler does not explicitly mention emotions,[12] in her work emotions are continually being redefined and recreated as 'a repetition and a ritual'.[13] So through these bodily performances, emotions are fabricated and reconstructed every time an act takes place, never in the same way. Bodies, performance and emotions are inherently interlinked and these rituals very quickly become part of our social and cultural practice, becoming coded into our individual and collective beliefs and attitudes.

Emotions are 'tailored'[14] or 'situated conceptualisations',[15] constructed from context. People process sensory input from the world around them, assigning it with meaning; these meanings are constructed from past experiences and memories, the patterns and templates that we carry inside our brain, in something like those visual matching games we used to play as children where we matched the cards to each other as fast as we could. So, the way our bodies and our senses interact with the world, and the way we are situated and seen in the space around us matters. The raw, visceral, somatic (physical) cues that we get from our environment, the way our bodies move and engage with the liminalities of the spaces around us, the way we are aroused or disgusted, feel pleasure or displeasure, the way our bodies feel comfort and discomfort, all affect the discrete emotions we experience and perceive in others. All of these matter in how we arrange the sensory stimuli into an array of signals that make sense to us, how our brain makes initial predictions about what kind of sensory activity it is and creates a mental representation of our embodied experience. I like the culinary analogy that Kristen Lindquist uses where she says: 'Just as gastronomic delights such as croissants, brioche, tarts, cookies, sauces, and puddings emerge from the combination of basic ingredients (flour, water, salt, etc.), we hypothesize that emotions such as anger, disgust, fear, happiness, and sadness emerge from the combination of more basic "psychological ingredients".[16]

•

Our emotions produce a potpourri of changes in us: sensory (we might feel our skin tingling with excitement); perceptual (we might perceive threat in a situation or environment); motor (we might become paralysed by fear); physiological (our hearts might beat much faster, our bodies heat up). All these changes in our bodies make us and others aware of an emotion's existence.

In 2014 a unique topographical, self-reporting experiment was conducted with 701 participants using an on-screen tool called emBODY, where they were shown two silhouettes of bodies alongside listening to emotional words and stories, and facial expressions showing specific emotions.[17] The participants were asked to colour the parts of the silhouettes on-screen that corresponded with their own bodily regions they felt were reacting to certain stimuli. The colours ranged from cool colours such as blue for sadness and surprise, and red for high-intensity emotions such as anger, fear and disgust. The emotions were also clustered according to negative and positive, with surprise considered a neutral emotional state. This experiment was conducted in Finnish and Taiwanese to test for cultural specificity. The more active emotions such as anger were associated with upper limb activity and sadness with more stillness in the limbs. The results showed that many of our feelings are associated with embodied states that we then use language to describe as emotional states. This is how we also make sense of the emotional states of others, by perceiving their bodily states and evaluating the visceral impact on us.

Twentieth-century French phenomenologist Maurice Merleau-Ponty suggested that our bodies are the existential medium through which we experience and engage with the world.[18] From imagined to real risks, from the stigmas that cannot be transmitted by touch, air or body fluids, to the ones that cross these boundaries, we shape our bodies in relationship with others. We imitate the actions and beliefs of others: yawning prompts yawning, smiling encourages a smile, or the possibility of it at least. A loop is created between the self and the other, and so it creates an intersubjectivity, a form of carnal communication from one body to another, where we see ourselves as others see us.[19] Essentially, we make sense of who we are and who others are through our embodied experiences, and we define our actions and states in ways that all fall under the umbrella term 'emotions'. In this way, when the respondents in my survey called emotions both 'the way we feel' but also 'the way we act', they were not far from how emotions have been understood and described by scientists.

2.

WRITTEN IN OUR FACES

IN 2013, THE SOCIAL MEDIA company Facebook realised that their range of emoticons could not convey subtle emotions. Of course, I would argue that reducing our broad range of feelings into symbols that aim to convey a fixed state associated with 'crying' or 'laughing' can be problematic, because not everyone expresses their emotions in the same way. I would also argue that the nuance of our feelings is lost in such icons, but then social media is not really the place for nuance, some might say. Anyhow, the designers at Facebook were perplexed as to how to convey subtle differences between emotions such as shame and remorse. Dacher Keltner, a psychology professor at University of California, Berkeley, was brought in to improve their emoticons. Keltner worked with an artist, Matt Jones, to translate some of the basic emotions and muscle movements that had been proposed by Darwin into emoticon-style drawings. The idea was to make the emoticons more expressive and universally recognisable by using the science of facial movements as the basis for these designs. As a sidebar, I still do not quite understand all the emoticons. I recently found out that I have been using an emoticon for laughing out loud quite a lot over on Twitter, which

19

in fact is an emoji for 'loud crying face'. Quite embarrassed by it, but I wouldn't know which emoji to use to express this shame!

Faces do tell a story; they just don't tell the whole story. But it is easier to assume that they do, that we can tell everything about a person from the way they show their emotions on their faces, because these are our first cues in reading a person. And then sometimes – often – we start assuming that the facial expressions of an emotion are a person's whole personality, whether they are a sad person, whether they have a 'resting bitch face' or whether they are just always smiling and are, therefore, a naturally happy person.

•

The jury is still out on what emotions are, whether they are illusions or concrete facts. But do we have a set of basic emotions that we all agree and identify with? We do not know enough yet. Although there is some consensus that anger, sadness and joy, amongst others, are emotions that we all experience to some degree, even if our expression of them might differ.

Aristotle included desire, anger, fear, courage, envy, joy, friendship, hate and jealousy in his cornucopia of emotions (pathē). The French historian Maurice Sartre writes that the ancient Greeks and Romans also included modesty/restraint. One of the most important Aristotelean texts on emotions is the *Nicomachean Ethics*, which defines pathē as 'feelings accompanied by pleasure or pain' and pretty much similar to desire, and one of the three categories found in the human soul along with 'states' (hexis) that consist of virtues and vices, and faculties. Pathē motivate actions, both external and internal, and were believed to be morally significant: right pathē in the right way, on the right occasion, and to the right extent. Stoics such as Cicero and Seneca did not tolerate pathē and this shaped so much of philosophy's later thinking on emotions. Like Aristotle, they believed that pathē or emotions existed as passive elements, and represented our moral failings, but were not really a part of ourselves. The Roman Stoics called them a 'perturbation of our mind and soul', connecting them to suffering. The absence of alien pathos was tranquillitas or even apatheia – apathy – which sounds negative to me. Apathy, ennui or a lack of interest or concern seems like a lazy way to live, a gloomy state of affairs where our minds and bodies are shut down to the world around us. The Stoics aspired to it. Cicero organised emotions into four basic categories: fear (metus); pain, distress, sorrow or sickness (aegritudo); lust, desire or appetite (libido); and pleasure or delight (Laetitia or hedone). Anger was a specific form of desire, a desire for vengeance.

Charles Darwin, who we know most famously for his *Origin of the Species*, also published the less well-known *Expression of Emotions in Man and Animals* in 1872, where he proposed that there was a shared evolutionary history that could be traced across not only all cultures, but all species, and that emotions were not unique to humans. They were biologically determined and innate, and much like other traits found in animals, they evolved, and adapted over time. Darwin argued that emotions were discrete modular entities – each with their own unique fingerprint, in a way – easily identifiable by their expressions, and not just over-lapping conceptualisations ranging in intensity and acceptability. He also suggested that our facial muscles worked together to create a set of core emotions. For example, when we widen our eyes or raise our eyebrows, he believed that these expressions had evolved to demonstrate our inner states and acted as common signals for people to understand and interpret if you were scared or angry. Darwin proposed that these instinctive facial expressions and body language were inherited and were a result of the process of evolution.

Darwin was a medical student at Edinburgh in 1826 when he first came across Charles Bell's book *Essays on the Anatomy of Expression in Painting*, and much of Darwin's work in emotions challenged Bell's creationist ideas of expressions as divine designs; that there were specific muscles that were designed for specific expressions. Bell had asserted that 'the design of man's being was, that he might praise and honour his Maker' and that humans had a peculiar frame of expression that was distinct from non-human species. Darwin disagreed.

He identified two main functions of emotional expressions: to regulate the emotional experience, and to communicate. Many believe that *The Expression of Emotions* began the science of psychology, and Darwin's ideas form the basis of the theoretical framework of 'basic emotions', where some facial actions evolved to express certain internal mental states and that all humans are born able to decode these expressions across all cultures. Darwin's universal theory of emotions supported his belief that humans had evolved from one common ancestor. This meant that he ignored the impact of culture or other social factors on emotions and emotional expression. Many of these ideas persist in certain fields of scientific enquiry where emotions are to a large extent accepted as a consequence of natural selection. But many of Darwin's methods were questionable, based on a very limited sample of his own upper-class English friends, observing his own infant son, born in 1839, and his dogs, Polly and Bob, and informal experiments at London Zoo holding mirrors and nuts up to the monkeys. He also relied heavily on the photographs of the French researcher and physician Guillaume-Benjamin-Amand Duchenne,[1] who was studying human facial muscles a decade before, discovering that human faces expressed at least 60 discrete emotions.[2] Duchenne placed electrodes on the participants' faces to isolate the muscles and the combinations used in different emotional expressions in a rather controversial contraption called a 'histological harpoon' (now known as the biopsy needle), which he even used on severed heads of executed criminals.

Papers stored at Cambridge University archives show that these experiments, which Darwin conducted at home during dinner parties, included asking leading questions about facial expressions, such as 'Is astonishment expressed through the mouth being opened and eyebrows raised?'[3] For instance, a photograph of a person with their mouth wide open was shown to guests around the dinner table. Darwin writes: 'I showed it to twenty-four persons without a word of explanation, and one alone did not at all understand what was intended. A second person answered terror, which is not far wrong; some of the others, however, added to the words surprise or astonishment, the epithets horrified, woeful, painful, or disgusted.' Even the 'experiments' he claimed to have conducted abroad to demonstrate that there were cardinal emotions universal to different cultures were mostly through second-hand observations from English-speaking friends and limited to one or two people. Darwin had set out to challenge and directly attack Bell's ideas of emotional expression, but his own ideas were constructed ideologically rather than deduced from scientific experiments.

Many evolutionary psychologists consider human emotions to be best adapted to the life our ancestors led in nomadic foraging bands. Primal emotions, such as fear, are associated with ancient primitive parts of the brain that are wired to react to threat and ensure survival. According to Darwin, filial emotions, such as a mother's love for her offspring, also seem to have evolved among early mammals as

23

instinctive traces of our evolutionary past. This perhaps created the idea of 'maternal love' that all mothers, in fact all women, are supposed to feel immediately towards children. We know that this is not true. Much of Darwinian theory is based in the belief that our temperament and our characteristics are innate and immutable. This after all supported his theory of evolution: if our emotions were learnt from our parents and our surroundings, and if we did not have universal expressions, then it would have been difficult to prove a shared evolutionary history and a common ancestor. And much of his research, although pioneering in its own right, was based in anecdotal data and was not tested with rigour until the twentieth century. Darwin also created a hierarchy of mental faculties, where he stacked rationality and reason at the top, and imagination, emotion and instinct towards the bottom. Any sort of emotionality, therefore, was paralleled to weakness and irrationality. From there it became perceived as a distinct extreme of emotion, equated to impulsivity or instability, where a person was quickly labelled 'too much', 'too extreme', 'too wild'.[4]

This idea of emotionality versus rationality was used to justify racist ideas and oppression. 'Savage' and primitive cultures were inferior in their emotional fervour, banging drums, having celebrations with intense emotions on display. Women with their emotionality were to be kept out of the public eye. Stiff-upper-lipped white men, especially from the upper classes, with their rationality, were born to rule and govern. This is what essentialism really is, and racist and sexist beliefs are based in these ideas that people have essential characteristics because of their membership of a certain group. The beliefs that some groups were more or less emotional started many centuries ago, and since then we have seen what was thought of as a 'civilising' process, a linear progression from emotion to reason, with education being used to teach people how to control their 'primitive' faculties and tame their emotions. We see especially in Europe and then in the Americas that this process was designed to make 'men' out of 'savages', that emotions were innate and designed in us biologically, but that they could be unlearnt and suppressed, and that the cultures or groups who controlled themselves more than others were more civilised.

Even though some of our emotional expression was surely determined by evolutionary forces, as so much of our minds are, all our emotions do not come with a blueprint. There is a large element of representative heuristics in Darwin's work.[5] For example, when he writes that frizzy (and permanently erect) hair is a sign of insanity, he is estimating the likelihood of an event by comparing it to a prototypical belief that already existed in his mind. I think that confirmation bias must have played a role in Darwin's interpretations too because he asserts that 'the eyes and mouth being widely open is an expression universally recognised as one of surprise or astonishment', quoting Shakespeare's *King John*, and *The Winter's Tale*: 'They seemed almost, with staring on one another, to tear the cases of their eyes; there was speech in the dumbness, language in their very gesture; they looked as they had heard of a world ransomed, or one destroyed.'[6]

•

This idea that the heart feels and the mind thinks underlies so much of the duality that has persisted through history. In his 1649 book *The Passions of the Soul*, Descartes defines six primary passions: wonder, love, hate, desire, joy and sadness. He famously said 'Cogito ergo sum', 'I think, therefore I am', thereby distinguishing body and mind as two separate entities, but at the same time proposing that even the body was not as certain as the mind, because we wouldn't be aware of our bodies until we had a mind to make sense of it. In 1890 William James proposed four basic emotions according to the bodily experience and expression: fear, grief, rage and love.[7] In the early part of the twenty-first century the American psychologist Carroll Izard proposed ten discrete emotions that could combine to produce more complex emotions: fear, anger, shame, contempt, disgust, guilt, distress, interest, surprise and joy. Izard labelled some emotions as positive and some as negative, both key to a person's development in early years, and subject to change with passing years. Joy and interest were classed as positive emotions, while love, attachment, guilt, contempt and shame were 'social' or 'self-conscious' emotions, instrumental in forming a sense of self. The negative emotions such as fear, anger and sadness Izard considers to have a short time-span, and to be expressed by distinct facial and bodily expressions. He quotes Homer's *Iliad* – 'A man who stumbles upon a viper will jump aside: as trembling takes his knees, pallor his cheeks; he backs and backs away' – as evidence of the physiological and facial changes that he believes always accompany emotions.[8]

The American psychologist Paul Ekman, one of the most influential psychologists of the twenty-first century, is a major influence on current research in emotions.[9] He proposed six basic emotions that we all have irrespective of our history and culture: anger, disgust, fear, joy, sadness and surprise.[10] He later included a seventh emotion, contempt, and mentioned embarrassment, guilt and shame as special cases, although cross-cultural studies did not conclusively show these as basic emotions.[11] Alternative models have proposed that pride be included because it is socially and biologically relevant.[12]

Ekman proposed that all emotions are psychological mechanisms, honed by our interactions with our fellow human beings to communicate to others what we are feeling inside, and our facial expressions in turn prepare us to anticipate what may happen around us and how we are going to react. These proposed taxonomies of emotions stem from a 'basic emotions model' where the categories then combine to form more complex emotions. Ekman refuted the idea that our basic emotions were learned from our culture or environment, but 'rather they are prewired responses to a set of stimuli that have affected our species for tens of thousands of generations'.[13] The basic emotions model is built on the premise that even though language shapes expression of some emotions, and language is socially constructed, emotions are not. Ekman also theorised that our facial expressions prepare us to anticipate what is to occur around us, and how we are going to react, that there are universal facial expressions across cultures and societies that represent these basic emotions.

According to Ekman, even when we try to hide our emotions, some of these will 'leak' as many of our emotional expressions are involuntary, and our micro-expressions will always give us away. He discusses the case of a psychiatric patient who he filmed when they had been hospitalised, and then again a few weeks before they were released.[14] The patient was considered fit enough to be given a weekend pass but then admitted later that they had lied about not being depressed and were indeed feeling suicidal. Ekman and his research colleague scrutinised the hundreds of hours of video recorded in the weeks before the patient was given a release pass, and eventually found a fleeting look of intense anguish on their face during the interview – only two frames out of twenty-four, 1/12 of a second – just before they covered it up with a smile. They concluded that even when people hide their emotions, there will always be some nonverbal leakage in the form of micro-expressions that would give their true emotions away. These micro facial expressions often last for no longer than ½ second,[15] and were first discovered by psychologists Ernest Haggard and Kenneth Isaacs in 1966 as they played back video footage in slow motion between psychotherapists and their patients.[16] Haggard and Isaacs did not believe that these fleeting micro-expressions were a sign of deliberately suppressed emotion as Ekman did. Instead, they considered them a sign of repressed emotion, i.e., those that we unconsciously avoid, that make us uncomfortable or that over-whelm us.

Considering these micro-expressions are not visible unless seen in very slow motion and scrutinised carefully over hundreds of hours, is it not possible that the eye sees what the mind wants to see? Representative heuristics can always play a role in such examinations where we keep looking until we find what we are really looking for. While the idea that we all have universal facial expressions for certain emotions has been disproved by many other scientists, what is interesting to me here is that even if our facial expressions do reflect some of our emotions, we can also hide them very well if we really intend to. Our expressions do not always match our emotional experience. Also pertinent to this examination of gendered emotions is *why* we regulate our emotions, and why we try so hard to hide our true emotional expressions. This is something we examine in more detail further on in the book. For a long time, though, scientists have assumed that we all have basic emotions and that these are universal. These ideas are grounded in the assumption that our emotions are innate, that they are governed by our biology, and so part of our personality. The ideas of gendered emotions also emerged from these beliefs.

The 2015 Pixar film *Inside Out* (which Ekman was a consultant on) used a similarly simplified framework of five emotions (joy, sadness, fear, disgust, anger) to show the inner emotional landscape and feelings of an eleven-year-old girl called Riley. Interestingly, two of Riley's emotions – anger and fear – are represented as male while the others are represented as female. The director Pete Docter said in an interview that 'it was intuitive. It felt to me like Anger's very masculine, I don't know why . . . Sadness felt a little more feminine . . .'[17] We will have to return to this later in the book.

Ekman proposes that emotions happen to all of us and we do not choose to experience them. He also believes that there are seven universal emotions that transcend language, culture and regional differences, and that these last for no longer than one hour at a time. If they last longer, an emotion becomes a mood. He carried out his experiments with people from 21 different cultures. In one study, participants from Chile, Argentina, Brazil and Japan were given the option to choose from fear, surprise, anger, happiness, sadness and disgust, and match them to facial expressions. Ekman showed them faces with posed expressions to observe if they would have the same interpretation of the emotions as their North American counterparts. This forced-choice format led to scepticism of how valid the responses were because the respondents were alerted to what the researchers had already decided.[18] The anthropologist Margaret Mead, who furiously rejected the idea of universality, protested that this could be because they had been exposed to magazines and media from America that would have affected their interpretations.

In response, Ekman travelled to Papua New Guinea in 1967 to carry out similar experiments with the Fore people from the Okapa district of the Eastern Highlands province. He believed them to be ideal subjects because they were isolated from the rest of the world.

Their responses, he believed – free of outside influence – would show whether emotional expression is universal. Ekman had no knowledge of their language, culture or politics.[19] He used a small set of flashcards showing what in his view were the representative facial expressions for the six basic emotions. The Fore did not have many words for emotional expressions, and used storytelling to find out what their facial expressions would be for fear, anger and disgust.[20] Ekman tried unsuccessfully to communicate with them through translators, and in the end left Papua New Guinea with just a sparse set of results that nevertheless formed the basis of his basic emotion model, a model that stated that even the slightest of emotions could be detected in faces.

The Fore people had not been able to differentiate very clearly between Ekman's photos depicting fear and surprise, and when their own facial expressions for these two emotions were shown to American people, they found it impossible to differentiate between the two. When the Fore people were asked what emotion the person with the 'sad' expression was feeling, more than 50 per cent said anger. Despite these discrepancies in the physical expression of emotions, Ekman insisted on his theory that facial expressions for different emotions were universally understood around the world, and this therefore supported the hypothesis that our responses to emotions are biological and innate.[21] He attributed the discrepancy in interpretation of the facial expressions to 'display rules' that he defined as the way universal emotional expressions are modified to suit a particular cultural context.

To prove that cultural display rules exist, Ekman showed Japanese and American students two types of films: one featuring body mutilation, supposed to induce stress, and the other more neutral, with nature and landscapes; one while being openly observed and another while not.[22] When the students were not aware of being observed the two groups showed no difference in their facial expressions in response to the films. But when they watched the films in the presence of a high-status scientist from their own culture, the Japanese students were seen to be masking their negative emotions much more than the American students. In other words, there were differences in their outward facial expressions while watching videos when they knew that they were being observed by someone in authority.

Criticism of Ekman's work has arisen from the fact that the photograph experiments were carried out with posed photos of emotional expressions using the Facial Action Coding System (FACS) that had been developed by Ekman himself in 1978, and considered universal by the researchers. This was a comprehensive catalogue of all facial expressions broken down into individual components of muscle movements called the Action Units (AU). Photographs were only used in the experiments if they accurately matched the muscle movements coded in the FACS, and so in a way they had inherent bias built into them: a circularity of argument.

In a follow-up experiment in 1989, David Matsumoto, one of Ekman's doctoral students, recruited 124 US-born college students from University of California, and 110 students of Japanese ancestry from University of Osaka in Japan.[23] A pool of photos was created using volunteer students based on the prototypical muscle movements of 7 basic emotions, coded in accordance with FACS, and the final set of 48 photographs with 8 each (2 men and 2 women across 2 different cultures) were selected ranging only from medium to high intensity. The observers judged each photograph on a 9-point scale for each emotion (0 if they considered it to be completely absent), and whether low in intensity. The results showed that the Japanese participants judged the emotions to be less intense compared to their American counterparts, irrespective of the ethnicity or gender of the person in the photograph. It was deduced that since Japanese people were more likely to mask their emotions in front of an authority figure, and public display of emotion is generally prohibited, it was more likely that they discounted any intense display of emotion. Personally, I find this counter-intuitive. It was also seen that the Americans gave highest intensity ratings to the extreme emotions of happiness and anger. The Japanese gave highest intensity ratings to the photographs that were supposed to represent disgust. The study was inconclusive overall in determining whether there were any distinct cross-cultural patterns of emotional evaluation based in universal facial expressions.[24]

Despite the various controversies and lack of adequate evidence, the theory that all emotions have universal facial expressions became a widely held belief for more than fifty years. One practical application was in the development of the lie-detection test used by the FBI, CIA, airport agents and other security departments in the USA. In 2007, Ekman developed a controversial training programme called SPOT (Screening Passengers with Observational Techniques) which included teaching security personnel in the US and the UK to monitor passengers using their facial expressions for deception, aggression and fear. SPOT has since been found to be racially biased and inaccurate.[25] These facial-recognition algorithms have trouble identifying darker skin and curly hair, which can be read as 'unidentifiable' and potentially threatening. There are graver implications of this theory for our technology, especially in Ekman's beliefs that there are micro-expressions such as tensing of lips or raising of eyebrows, even for a micro-fraction of a second, that can tell us about a person's intentions. Other researchers have been unable to replicate his work, which has raised red flags as to the universality of his facial coding system. SPOT has also not been tested under controlled scientific conditions.[26]

In their 1975 work *Unmasking the Face*, Ekman and Wallace V. Freisen suggested that emotional expression could even be used as a form of evidence in legal cases: 'The trial lawyer often can't trust the words of a witness or client. He needs another source, such as the face, to tell him how the person really feels.'[27] In many legal systems, reading the emotions of a defendant has hence become a part of a 'fair' trial. In a 1992 case, Justice Anthony Kennedy of the US Supreme Court insisted that a defendant not be medicated to stand trial as that would interfere with his true feelings, which were necessary to 'know the heart and mind of the offender'.[28] We know that legal systems are not without bias, and even when we think that judges are reliable arbiters, they bring many of their own implicit biases to the process; their adjudication of cases can be determined by their state of mind, and their previous experiences.[29] So even if emotional expressions were definitively proven to be universal across all cultures, nobody can be an impartial judge of anyone's emotional expressions.

•

Ekman's work in Papua New Guinea used strategies that alerted the participants to the response he was expecting from them, and some of the responses were influenced by the feedback-loop between the translator and the participants.[30] To explore this further, in 2011 psychologists Carlos Crivelli and José-Miguel Fernández-Dols, along with Sergio Jarillo, an anthropologist, travelled to the Trobriand Islands off Papua New Guinea's east coast, which has a total population of about 60,000. The Trobrianders had been isolated from both mainland Papua New Guinea and the outside world. Unlike

Ekman, Crivelli and Jarillo spent many months embedding themselves in the local culture and learning the local language, Kilivila, so that they did not need any translators for their study. They showed 72 young people (aged 9–15 years) a set of photos that had been used widely in psychological research with facial expressions and asked them to link these faces to an emotion from the list of six basic emotions that Ekman had proposed in the 1960s. Happiness was recognised readily. But other emotions gave very mixed results.

The faces that the Trobrianders found most confusing showed nose-scrunching and neutral expressions. Pouting faces also gave ambiguous results.[31] Most surprising was that gasping faces were matched (across gender) to 'anger' or to the social motive 'threat', as opposed to 'fear' or 'disgust', which researchers had predicted from previous anthropological studies.[32] At the same time, only a very small number from the group matched the scowling face to the predicted label of anger or the social motive of threat. The study therefore showed that, although there is some concurrence between Trobriander society and the western society where most of the emotion and facial-expression studies have been based, there is no universal emotional expression or recognition.[33] Crivelli and colleagues cite examples from other small-scale, relatively independent societies where the 'threat gaze' has been observed as a mechanism for grabbing attention, such as in the Maori's traditional 'haka', where gasping faces with protruding tongues are used to induce fear in rivals. This study showed that facial expressions for emotions are not standard across different cultures and societies, and are also a reflection of cultural rules and norms.

The overlapping and non-discrete nature of emotions in different cultures was also shown in experiments carried out by anthropologist Karl Heider with the Dani people of the highlands of Western

New Guinea, Indonesia. Heider was an anthropologist at the University of South Carolina at the time and had collaborated for a long time with Ekman. Dani people, much like the Fore population, did not have access to modern technologies and so were unlikely to have learnt their emotional expressions from television, magazines or the internet, and did not have words in their language for anger and disgust. The study found that their facial expressions and understanding of the difference between anger and disgust were also ambiguous.

In 2014, a team of researchers from the Institute of Neuroscience and Psychology at Glasgow University examined these six 'basic' categories of emotions with 60 white Caucasian western participants looking at computer-generated facial animations.[34] The participants confused wrinkled noses for both anger and disgust, while a raised eyebrow was perceived as both surprise and fear. This confusion is especially prominent in the early stages of an emotion expression, when it is not fully developed yet. The researchers suggested that human emotional expression is adapted for optimal performance and minimum error and the confusion with fear/surprise and disgust/anger shows that there are only four basic emotions which interact to produce more complicated emotions.[35] The team was the first to study the temporal dynamics of emotions by examining the range of different muscles within the face. They attempted to create a grammar of emotions by mapping the muscles involved in signalling different emotions, and the timeframe over which each muscle was activated. This 'generative face grammar' was used to collect the participants' perception of the facial expression they most associated with certain facial muscles.[36] In their 2018 study, with 40 observers in each of 2 cultures (western and East Asian) it was found that, while there was a common understanding between westerners and

East Asians as to how faces display pain, there was a significant difference in their ideas about the expression of an orgasm.[37] Pain and pleasure are experienced and expressed in different ways by people from different cultures (although it is debatable in this case whether 'western' is a culture, or 'East Asian' – a huge area that is comprised of many different cultures – can be homogenised into one single category).

Many of these cross-cultural studies have limitations. In one case, the researchers provided the participants with a context: they narrated a story including the sentence 'He is looking at something which smells bad', and gave the participants two or three facial expressions to match this with.[38] They are using experimental methods that allow them to make the notion of emotionality immediate and accessible to the participants before asking them to match the emotion to facial expressions that the researchers already consider universal. They are relying on a universal construct to prove that there is a universal language of emotionality, which seems to be a circular reasoning fallacy. The circulus in probando – circle in proving – begins with what the researchers are trying to end with.

•

Again and again, using a range of methods, it has not been possible to conclusively prove that we have a consistent and universal emotional fingerprint. I don't believe that I express anger in the same way in all different contexts. But more importantly, the way even my sister and I express emotions is very different. My husband goes quiet and usually becomes more silent than ever. I often explode and have a huge outburst which then calms down as quickly as it started. It is easy to assume that there is this basic difference between men and women, that our expressions of anger are different because

36

I am a woman, and he is a man. But my sister acts in the same way as my husband does when she is angry. She is a woman, and she is genetically related to me. We grew up in the same household, so it is not even just a matter of innate cultural differences. It is highly likely that we express anger in different ways because we are different people.

In my children's school, they have one of those stick-on boards where they select an emoji face that best expresses their feelings every morning when they first go into their classrooms. This is meant to develop an emotional intelligence in children, so that they become more aware of their feelings, and those of others around them. I think it is really a lovely idea. But then my five-year-old has refused to take part in it since the start of term. 'I am very confused,' she tells us, 'because I don't understand how that is a sad face,' she says, picking up an emoticon cut-out. 'How are you feeling right now?' her teacher asks, trying to prod her into selecting one of the faces. 'I am nervous and happy and excited,' she says. But, there is no face for it.

3.

ALL IN A NAME

As we talk about emotions and examine the search for basic and fundamental human emotions, it is worth considering how much 'terminological ethnocentrism' plays a role in how we assume that these English words can be used to map the mental constructs across all cultures and societies. What if there is no parallel word in Polish for disgust, as Anna Wierzbicka has pointed out?[1] Wierzbicka is considered one of the most influential and innovative linguists of her generation across a career that has spanned six decades. As we talk about joy or anger we are assuming that we all think of these labels and categories in the same way, that the western concept of what anger really is and how it is expressed is the definitive answer to the age-old question of whether there are any basic emotions. As we will see in this book, there really are no basic emotions, but through a process of negotiation we seem to have reached some sort of consensus on what these emotion categories represent, i.e., some kind of an essence of an emotion. I believe that there is nothing like a single entity for these emotions, a common phenomenon that these labels represent no matter what the context (gender, social, cultural and so on). If I don't have a word for anger, then am I really 'angry' or just feeling a spectrum of emotions, from sadness to not-so-joyful? If the researchers had been working in another language, would they have been able to define anger as a basic emotion?

Does language shape emotions, or do emotions shape language? It's a chicken and egg conundrum.

We talk in metaphors: shivers down our spine, guilt weighing us down, feeling empty inside. 'I am going to explode', 'I am boiling with anger', 'I am brimming with love', 'I am heartbroken.'

We use these metaphors to express and explain, to extrapolate what we feel inside in terms of the language we have available to us. A bride can get 'cold feet', or we might feel 'butterflies in our stomach'. Sometimes, we articulate emotions by making links to our bodily states.

In the English language, when we say 'anger', that could mean a whole lot of things such as indignation, outrage, frustration, desperation: all stemming from a basic emotion of anger, which is the simple label we assign to a spectrum of complex emotions. But when Cliff Goddard examined the Yankunytjatjara language of Central Australia he found that none of the words they use for anger directly map on to what we mean when we say 'This person is angry.'[2] The word 'mipanarinyi' means anger with a sense of grievance, 'kuyaringanyi' means someone is resentful, and 'pikaringanyi' means active hostility. Context played a huge role, rather than the generalised way we use anger here in English-speaking countries. In Malay, Goddard found that there is no direct equivalent to the English 'surprise' and that the words (terkejut, terperanjat, hairan) overlap in various meanings but have no clear core like the word 'surprise' in English.[3] Malay speakers on Twitter inform me that there are various slang words for different kinds of surprise in the language:

fuyoh, for instance, denotes wonderment, but when someone wants to signify approval and admiration; alamak does not have an implication of being impressed but more a dawning realisation and dismay ('Alamak, forgot Mom's birthday!'); the word bapak can often be added for emphasis and intensity, and bapak ah is an expression of envy wrapped up in disbelief.[4] So it would be wrong and ethnocentric to assume that Malay speakers do not experience surprise, it is just that they have more nuanced and complex expressions which are explained in different ways to those of English-speakers.

•

I know that in Hindi aaraam can mean rest and contentment, comfort and happiness all at the same time, while in English feeling content and happy can be two different emotional states. If our minds are a product of our culture and upbringing, then our emotions cannot be merely an inevitable product of our biology, but more dependent on the interactions between our language with our history and geography. According to Margrit Pernau from the Max Planck Institute of Human Development, emotions play a big role in South Asian rituals, especially in bhakti (Hindu rituals with focus on devotion and love), Sufism (a form of Islamic mysticism emphasising spiritual closeness with God) and Shia (Islamic rituals that include lamentations).[5]

In Indian philosophy, rasa is the human state of mind, what one experiences and then expresses. In Indian dance, rasa is the emotion that a dancer tries to evoke in a viewer in response to their movement or facial expression, called a bhava. The Sanskrit discourse on the performing arts, Natyashastra, written sometime between 200 BCE and 300 CE and attributed to Bharata Muni, identifies navarasas (nine emotions) which every dancer needs to learn to complete their training: Shringara (love), Hasya (happiness), Rudra/Krodha (exasperation or anger), Bheebhatsa (abhorrence), Bhayanaka (trepidation), Shanta (tranquillity), Veera (valour), Shoka/Karuna (dejection or pity) and Adbhuta (awe). The mythological story of Radha and Krishna – a beautiful love story between the Hindu Lord Krishna and his consort Radha – is often told to demonstrate all these nine rasas, through various rituals. For instance, when Radha is getting ready to meet Krishna in the forest, the ritual Shringara – expressing erotic or romantic love – is demonstrated through dance poses. In these stories, sexuality and spirituality are very much interlinked, so the notions of lust and love were not two polarised emotional expressions, and sexual desire was not separate from romantic feelings, which was itself a twelfth-century European Christian construct.[6]

•

Research undertaken with the Himba group from the Keunene region of north-western Namibia and Americans published in 2014 using 'minimal universality' – the idea that there are some basic universal emotions and people everywhere can infer something about others from facial behaviour – showed that the Himba people did not assign so-called 'universal' categories to emotions as the Americans did.[7] There was similarity, however, in how both understood upturned mouths and wide eyes as happy, smiling faces. In this experiment, the researchers showed that cultural and social context matter in how emotions are construed. The predominantly agricultural Himba community did not have access to any western technologies or media, and the emotional labels were delivered to them verbally in their own language. Anger, fear, disgust, sadness, happiness and 'neutral' were translated into their dialect of Otji-Herero as okupindika, okutira, okujaukwa, oruhoze, ohange and nguri nawa, respectively.[8]

41

The findings suggest that English-language categories may not reflect the categories most relevant for Himba participants during facial-emotion perception. The various analyses showed that the facial expressions for various emotions are not universally recognised in different cultures, especially if they are not proximate. The Himba people were more likely to consider facial expressions as indicative of a person's behaviour rather than linking them to discrete emotional categories and expressions. Facial expressions are therefore a code and signal for emotions but these are very much culturally sensitive and dependent on social context. Once again, we have to look beyond the canonical western model of emotions and facial expressions that we assume to be universal.

The five Chinese words nu, sheng/qi, nao (hua), fen and taoyan are all related to anger and anger-like feelings but do not have direct correspondence. On the Language Log website, sinologist Victor Mair talks about his favourite word for anger: shēngqì 生气, which literally translates as to 'generate qi' but also as 'get mad, take offense, become enraged, be pissed off'.[9] Qi is a mysterious word which is difficult to translate in English but can mean 'life force'. So rage in this context is action-oriented: to generate life force, a force for good. Mair also mentions another word for becoming angry: huǒdàle 火大了, which literally means 'the fire became big' or 'inflamed'. Fire can destroy but also create. Anger can also be a life force, generating energy.

Ning Yu from the University of Oklahoma has examined how body parts shape the perception and conceptualisation of emotions in Chinese by using a range of popular Chinese dictionaries. In a fascinating discussion, he explains how body parts and facial expressions are used to denote emotionality via external and internal organs.[10] These are very specific forms of emotional expression, more so than what is available in the English language. For instance, yan-shu mu-heng (eyes-vertical eyes-horizontal) translates as 'stare in anger or contempt'. Internal body parts also engage in emotional expression: dong gan-huo (move liver-fire) means 'get angry; flare up; fly into a rage'. Of course, some of the body parts and internal organs feature more heavily in the determination of emotions than others. The temperature, orientation and dimensions of body parts such as brows and eyes, bodily sensations such as feeling tongue-tied, or movement such as snorting through one's nose become part of defining and understanding emotion. Looking at Yu's very detailed explanation of how the different sensations and body parts intersect to form a whole corpus of emotions and emotional expressions, it is not easy to distil basic emotions. However, it seems that fear, sadness, anxiety and anger may be more universal than others. It is also evident that none of these emotional boundaries are very clear; in fact, they are constantly moving and overlapping. The engagement with emotions here is on a rather metaphorical level, with heat being connected to anger and anxiety, while fear, sadness and disappointment are cold emotions.

Most of what we know of people's feelings comes to us through external expressions and via language. When we name something, it becomes real, it becomes something we can talk about, interpret, analyse. We only make sense of the bodily sensations through the linguistic labels that we have on offer to us. For example, we know something is a table because we can describe it as such. And we then create a social reality from these interactions between our mind and our bodies, using self-fulfilling predictions to provide our body with what it needs to survive any unexpected scenarios. Emotions are concepts for things in the real world that we can only make sense of because we have words for them in our language. If we didn't know about anger as a concept, we wouldn't be able to create a neurological simulation for it and predict its occurrence, as we have seen in the Yankunytjatjara language of Central Australia.

Our ability to label our emotions can vary in different cultures. If I have no word for the Persian emotion of boghz, the knot in the throat that I feel just before deep sadness takes over and crying becomes inevitable, then how do I label it or describe it? If I feel lethargy at the onset of spring, but do not know the German word for it – Frühjahrsmüdigkeit – then I might just resort to imprecise descriptions of the core states, such as feeling low, sad, tired, angry, upset, and so on. None of these sum up the very precise emotion of feeling 'spring fatigue'. I can feel Schadenfreude at the misfortune of an enemy if I know the word, but can't if I don't because there is no similar word in English (or Hindi) for this feeling. If I don't have the words to describe an emotion, do I give it a different label, one which does not include the *cause* of the emotion that, for example, Frühjahrsmüdigkeit does – and therefore categorise it as a different malady altogether?

If we learn a word for a feeling, does that mean we can then experience the emotion and communicate it better now we have put a label on it? When we have a word for it, we make a nebulous feeling more concrete and immediate. When we find out that a friend or an ex-lover has 'ghosted' us, or when we are 'gaslighted', it almost feels like a relief to know that what we experienced was not imaginary but that there was a label, a descriptor for it. Sometimes when my children are mixing paints and ask me what that colour is, I have to find the nearest that I can think of, but often I will say that it is 'a little purple, but also blue', or that it is 'kind of yellowish blueish red', and we use such estimations every day when we cannot locate a fixed category for something. But if we did not have a word for the colour blue, how would we describe it to someone? I have often thought about this.

Concepts of emotion become anchored by the words we have at our disposal to describe them. Language is used to express emotions and emotional expressions are located in language, as much as constructed by it. It is useful and relevant to talk about emotions and understand the language we use around them: understanding emotions in others and those that we experience ourselves can help us build connections and understand differences between us. We associate meanings with our feelings, and we create a semantic space for our emotional experience when we talk about how we are feeling, with one core effective state for every experience, but with many hundreds of other semantic categories corresponding with other emotional states. Families of emotions may form in this semantic landscape, with clusters overlapping, so for instance anger is the prototypical label for many other categories such as frustration, rage, irritation, resentment, etc., much like our very own personal emotional thesaurus.

We often define one emotion word in relation to another, such as when I ask how you know you are feeling sad, you might say, 'I am feeling down, depressed, downtrodden, low', and so we create a semantic map with other terms that lie somewhere in this emotional space, interconnected to each other like a spider web. It can be one or more of these concepts and terms. It can be that your sadness lies closer to being low than depressed, but in the end these are also the mental constructs of these emotion concepts that you have in your brain. They are individual but also linguistically and culturally specific. Each language has some ready-made words for emotions too. This book is, of course, largely rooted in the English language. But even as we talk about emotion words – so-called anger or so-called empathy – we need to remember that these feelings are being talked about and understood in this way because we are using a certain language and a certain cultural context to interpret and articulate them. And the way we talk about emotions also tells us so much about a speaker's culture, and the way it is organised. Wierzbicka discusses the Polish word tęsknota, which is variously described as some sort of longing, yearning, hankering. In older Polish it was used to mean some sort of sadness, but with the partition of Poland in the eighteenth century and much of Polish literature being written in exile, it started to mean something more like nostalgic sadness, caused primarily due to separation from homeland. In this way, this emotion has its roots in and is reflective of Poland's history and national pride and identity.[11]

•

In the 1960s, anthropologist Robert Levy worked with islanders in Tahiti to develop a framework of 'hypocognition', the inability to communicate certain concepts due to a lack of necessary words to explain them.[12] This makes me think of the game Balderdash, in which players have to make up a definition for an obscure word – all definitions are read out, along with the correct one, and the players have to guess which is the true definition. The Tahitians that Levy worked with did not have a word for the notion of 'grief' and even when they experienced loss and death, they described it as feeling ill or sick. Levy suggested that those cultures that did not have adequate words to describe such feelings were not able to process them properly. Of course, as discussed earlier, such attitudes were rooted in colonial perspectives and eugenics, where there was an assumption of 'savagery' in showing negative or excess emotions.

In the 1960s, anthropologists Renato and Michelle (Shelly) Rosaldo went to live with the Ilongot, an isolated tribe in the rainforest of the Philippines notorious for headhunting and killing.[13]

This is a riveting story of how a word in their language, liget, came to be associated with rage and anger. Renato found that the Ilongot used this word again and again, especially when they played a voice-recording of an elderly and highly respected man from the village who had died during a headhunting celebration a few years before. The tribe members talked about the liget they were feeling, the feeling that wanted them to take a head again and again, to take a head and throw it away. Renato and Shelly could not understand how an emotion they would have described as grief was so riddled with chaos and violence, and why it was driving the men to kill. In an NPR podcast years later, Renato talks about the death of his wife Shelly, who fell off a 65ft cliff while on a hike, leaving behind their two small sons, and this strange emotion that he began to feel. It wasn't until he was driving along the Californian coast one day that he could finally understand what this emotion was. He writes: 'Immediately on finding her body I became enraged. How could she abandon me? How could she have been so stupid as to fall? I tried to cry. I sobbed, but rage blocked the tears. Less than a month later I described this moment in my journal: "I felt like in a nightmare, the whole world around me expanding and contracting, visually and viscerally heaving. Going down I find a group of men, maybe seven or eight, standing still, silent, and I heave and sob, but no tears."'

He had to stop the car and let out a howling roar, a wave inside him that was bursting out. He could finally understand what liget was. It wasn't just anger, nor was it grief. It was the chaos inside his body and a combination of both these emotions.[14]

I am not sure if this is gendered. Renato talks mostly about men who were driven to kill in this tribe, and we do not hear what women made of liget, whether they felt it to the same intensity or even if they expressed it. But what is clear is that an emotion is constructed through our social norms, its experience as well as expression can be culture-specific, and in a culture where we tend to show grief through quiet meditation and reflection, we find it difficult to express the howling rage that it can entail. But although Renato experienced some of the visceral rage that liget entailed, his was not exactly similar. He did not go out and cut off someone's head and hold a celebration (even though he might have felt like doing it). Because firstly in his culture the visible expressions of rage are not welcome, especially in grief, which is mostly associated with sadness, and secondly, headhunting is not celebrated. Liget wasn't just anger, a negative emotion that we are told to suppress, but associated with energy and productivity, something that the Ilongots channelled and focused their grief and rage in Renato's attempt to describe it in English was that he could feel a 'high voltage inside his body'. Language can limit our emotional expression and the way we associate values to these emotions, but also how we construct emotions too.

The anthropologist Jean Briggs recounts her experience of living with an Inuit family in her book *Never In Anger: Portrait of an Eskimo Family* that was first published in the 1970s.[15] Briggs mentions that emotions were for a long time considered 'infra dig', not a worthy subject of study, and much of anthropological work before then was focused on personalities, and not how emotions might be constructed as well as construed differently in different cultures. In 1963, Briggs arrived at the small, isolated community of only 20–35 people, calling themselves the Utkuhikhalingmiut (abbreviated as Utku) and living across an area of around 35,000 square miles. What is fascinating is that Briggs does not pretend or profess to have a detached observation of this community that she was living with, and that she also reflects on her own emotional behaviour and patterns as she incisively reports on the emotions of the Utkus. She talks about how she tries to conform to the emotional norms of this society but finds again and again that she falls back on her own learned emotions and tends to express her anger and frustration freely. Utkus do not have a concept for anger in the same way as we do in English, and they have a perception of 'outsiders' as unable to control their emotions, like a child or an animal. The Utkus did not react with anger towards other humans, often responding with 'too bad' when something awful happened that would infuriate Briggs. The leader was particularly controlled in his emotional behaviour, and his status was a product of the way he controlled his emotions. Emotional control in harsh conditions was the basis of their moral framework. The Utkus associated morality with emotions: a happy person was a good person, an angry person was a bad, out of control person.[16] Emotions are therefore also rooted in the contexts in which they are used, shaped by the context of the user and the listener, and the associations and memories of both.

In a wonderful example of emotional socialisation in the Utku community, children are allowed to scream, shout, take out their anger and hit their parents and adults until the age of six years or so. But during this time, the adults show them emotional regulation in the form of calmness and reason, and use storytelling and drama to act out the consequences of such behaviour in real life. Children learn emotional regulation by example and by understanding the consequences of their actions rather than through threats or scolding. As the children's brains are still developing in these early years, and more plastic, they are wiring their emotional impulses and building templates for emotional control by rewiring their angry impulses into another form of expression. This tells us not only about different responses to anger in different cultures, but also about how we learn emotional regulation and display rules from the context we grow up in, and how our brains get wired as we grow through these experiences and accumulate our memories. This is key to understanding how gender norms are constructed in our society.

In the 1980s the anthropologist Catherine Lutz undertook ethnographic work amongst the Ifaluk people of the Micronesian Caroline Islands, where she found a highly sociable matriarchal society that had four primary emotional expressions: fago (a mix of compassion, love and sadness), song (nuances of rage), ker (nuances of extreme joy) and rus/metagu (a mix of fear, anxiety and surprise). Lutz found that these emotional expressions were important for the Ifaluk community to maintain social dynamics and their sense of belonging. The community described these emotions in terms of their bodily sensations. One person told her: 'People who are "rus" run around . . . and their eyes aren't the same; they hold themselves [wrapping their arms around themselves as if cold] and sometimes their voices shake . . . we shake inside; our legs tremble as we walk, and we think we'll fall.'[17] The testimonies not only shatter the myth that there are some basic universal emotions, but also demonstrate the intermingling of corporeality and cultural forces in shaping the emotions and being shaped in return. In the Ifaluk community, the environmental pressures on the land and resources meant that cooperation and a deference to authority were essential for survival and stability, and so the emotion words reflected this social order.[18]

The use of emotions here rested on a network of associations; the word fago loosely translates as empathy, compassion or nostalgia, or even missing a dead person. Fago emerged as a connection between two people, and therefore a way of organising the society. This emotion was a reflection of their values, as kinship was fundamental to their culture and society. Over time, it had become a moral concept, and a general character trait. This can happen with emotion words. There is a morality associated with certain emotions, so some become good and others bad, even though all emotions are a result of events and interactions, and the way our bodies and minds respond to our interactions and the predictions we make of what is likely to happen around us. Fago was a form of cultural currency reflecting status and respect. Some emotions thus become status symbols. In a society that prides itself on empathy, compassion can become a form of moral and cultural currency. In the time of the pandemic, for instance, empathy became a social organising principle when other sorts of social norms were under threat, and a means of association and network, such as people setting up online community groups and helping neighbours with shopping, during a time when we were all isolating and physically distant from others.

Emotional expression plays an important role in maintaining social position. Ward Keeler, an American anthropologist, conducted field-work in Java in the 1970s that concluded that the notion of self is prominent in Javanese society, and emotions and emotional displays are aimed at maintaining the hierarchical positions in society.[19] One's social status matters more in Java than individuating characteristics; any loss of emotional control or awkward encounter does not just disrupt the public perception of one person but threatens the collapse of a whole social order by dissolution of many people's identities and positions in this carefully assembled informal power structure based in emotional restraint. Status is not something that can be changed, but it is essential in self-definition. There is a code of conduct and any transgression from it can make everyone look bad and disrupt the 'social performance'.

Similarly, in 1985, anthropologist Arjun Appadurai showed in his research in South India that expressions of gratitude, for which there is no straightforward vocabulary in Tamil, is subject to rules of subordination.[20] The way emotions of gratitude are expressed by those who are lower in the social-class hierarchy reinforce and maintain the subordination. The social codes have to be interpreted through a delicate interaction of lexical and nonverbal cues. Gratitude in most cases is considered an acceptance of permanent subordination, built on the idea of moral reciprocity (much more so than western society), and so there is a difference in how a farm labourer would praise the gift and generosity of a landlord, where a permanence of hierarchy is assumed, compared to how a family member would do so.

Other researchers have shown that Ilongots from the Philippines cannot articulate feelings of guilt and Inuits lack vocabulary for anxiety.[21] The perception that certain cultures lack appropriate words for emotions is, however, a very colonial way of examining the framework of emotions and feelings. Who can say that their way of experiencing and describing grief is inadequate just because they do not have a similar word for it? In Hindi, for instance, we have the word dukh (दु:ख), which encompasses a whole spectrum of grief and sorrow, with different valence (subjective worth), contexts and intensities. Does that mean that the emotions experienced and displayed are less valid or not as processed and sophisticated as in cultures with more words for the whole spectrum of loss? Or is it possible that sometimes hypocognition is deliberate in order to keep certain emotions and feelings private, and not obfuscate them with public knowledge and display? Kaidi Wu and David Dunning looked at how the notion of hypocognition acts as a censorship tool, making certain behaviours visible when we have the word for them, and rendering them invisible when we do not.[22] In their experiment, they asked participants from the University of Michigan if they knew what benevolent sexism was.[23] They used the concept of 'benevolent sexism' to see if people could put their finger on such behaviour around them when they could name it. People who were hypo-cognitive of this concept and did not know it, noticed instances of it much less than those who knew the concept. Not knowing a concept can make people blind to it. Governments and politicians can sometimes block access to concepts as a means of information control, and in hypocognising a concept they make access to it difficult. Internet censorship is one such control mechanism which restricts access to certain websites or information for moral, religious or political reasons. For instance, Professor Jed Crandall from the University of New Mexico has shown that the Chinese government can blacklist certain keywords as a way of control; examples included 'Dalai Lama', 'massacre' and 'democracy'.[24]

•

So language is what helps us make sense of emotions to a large extent; if one does not have a word or label for 'anger', these different expressions can be perceived as entirely different categories and explained and interpreted as such. The language is also constructing the meaning of emotions, as well as helping us represent them. Words can act as a sort of glue that holds different feelings together in one category. So we might interpret feeling a rising heartbeat, heat in our face and neck, sweat forming in our palms, eyes blinking, mind feeling fuzzy, as symptomatic of anger, or as a subset of this broader category which encompasses many different internal and external changes. Someone kicking, punching, shouting or even smiling can all be expressions of anger: they are different actions, but in a specific context they might all be perceived as anger. When access to a

53

particular emotion label or category is impaired or obstructed – for instance by repeating the word 'anger' many times leading to semantic satiation – people find it more difficult to match two facial expressions that both display anger.[25] Semantic satiation is when a word loses meaning and sort of disintegrates before our eyes, looking nothing more than a collection of letters if it is repeated too many times.[26]

anger anger anger anger anger anger anger anger
anger anger anger anger anger anger anger anger
anger anger anger anger anger anger anger anger
anger anger anger anger anger anger anger anger
anger anger anger anger anger anger anger anger
anger anger anger anger anger anger anger anger
anger anger anger anger anger anger anger anger
anger anger anger anger anger anger anger anger
anger anger anger anger anger anger anger anger
anger anger anger anger anger anger anger anger
anger anger anger anger anger anger anger anger
anger anger anger anger anger anger anger anger

This might also be representative of the impact of cognitive taxation on our interpretation of emotional expression in others. When our brains are too tired, our cognitive resources depleted, we can find it more difficult to interpret people's facial expressions and relate it in meaning to a specific label. Patients with semantic dementia – where neurodegeneration occurs in the left anterior temporal lobe (ATL) of the brain, which supports concept knowledge and emotional perception – were unable to categorise facial expression cards into distinct categories of anger, sadness, joy, disgust and so on, and instead assigned them into positive, negative and neutral feelings.[27]

Access to language about a certain emotion through priming makes the experience of such an emotion more immediate and accessible. The theory of constructed emotions proposes exactly this: that emotions are constructed and created in every moment through a combination of our present sensations and past experiences.

In an experiment with 108 undergraduate students, participants were primed with the word 'fear' by asking them to write a story about a fearful character.[28] They then listened to evocative, high-intensity and continuous music and imagined previous unpleasant experiences as the music unfolded. The participants who had been primed for fear reported their response to the unpleasant music as instances of being afraid. These participants were then tested for risk aversion through a questionnaire where they had to respond to hypothetical risky behaviours in the real world, such as 'regularly riding a bike without a helmet'. Those who had been primed for fear as a core affective state saw the world as more dangerous and threatening. The experience of fear could be created through the feeling and sensation, but significantly through the interaction of the core feeling with the conceptual knowledge of the emotion. These feelings only make sense, and are assigned meaning, when we affiliate with other people, either through their response, but also by the context that we are placed in, and the categories that we have access to.

What stands out in all the research so far is the shared belief that emotional expression plays an important role in social organisation, especially in maintaining social positions. Emotions and their elicitations and expressions work to maintain the dominance hierarchy. Emotions are related to social structures. It is useful to understand how an individual's position and status in particular societies impact which emotions are considered 'proper' for them, and how much they are forced to maintain these social bonds and interpersonal relationships through their choice of emotional suppression and regulation. We have talked about how emotions are formed and how we make sense of our own and other people's. I am less interested in the specific cultural effects in this book, and more in how structural hierarchies and social organisation affect emotional display rules and are shaped by our emotional expression. As a behavioural scientist, I am more interested in what emotions *tell* us than what they are, and in why we feel and act the way we do. Do we always act the way we feel, and if not, why not?

4.

I CAN'T. I SHOULDN'T. I WON'T

A *HARVARD BUSINESS REVIEW* HEADLINE QUIZZES provocatively: 'What are difficult emotions trying to tell you?'[1] An article in another business magazine, *Forbes*, asks women: 'Do emotions sometimes get the best of you at work? Use this.'[2] My first thought is that certain emotions have become labelled as 'difficult', especially when it is a young woman talking about it, as in the *Forbes* article. It goes on to ask: 'How can we better manage our emotions as individuals?' and this idea of 'managing' our emotions is something that we hear quite often. Not just about which feelings to express to others, but also how and when to do so.

Emotion regulation is 'a heterogeneous set of actions that are designed to influence which emotions we have, when we have them, and how we experience and express them'.[3] From early childhood, we are constantly told to manage and regulate our emotions. Women in particular learn from a young age that they have to smile and be pleasing, to be polite and gentle; that anger is not a good emotion; that any strong opinions and assertiveness will be labelled as 'bossy'. Men, meanwhile, are told as boys that it is only girls who cry, and that it is OK to rough-house. We all consequently use a number of strategies to manage emotionality, especially in public domains. Emotionality is the measure of a person's reactivity to a stimulus in the environment.

The psychologist James Gross outlines four stages of emotion generation, where we express our internal feeling states: first we encounter a situation that has some sort of emotional relevance to us; we pay attention to it because this is how it becomes a specific event for us; we evaluate and interpret this situation in terms of our own personal goals and our personal history; and we then generate a response.[4] Our personal histories assign meanings to different stimuli and tell us whether a situation has any emotional significance for us, and the response generated by an automated neural process could be an experiential, physiological or behavioural reaction.

Let us look at an example. A child sees a bear, is afraid and runs away. It is easy to understand why the child is afraid of the bear, and their bodily symptoms show this through a rising pulse rate and sweating. The evolutionary theory of emotion would tell us that fear is a survival instinct in the child to protect themselves and stay alive; it is an instinctive reaction that is a form of adaptation, and it leads the child to run away. It is an action the child takes in response to the fear. And how did the child come to associate the bear with fear, if not as a product of the culture they grew up in, of the memories of their ancestors? This message has become an indisputable truth for the child, and they decide that this is the appropriate emotional response in this particular situation.[5] The significance of emotions lies not so much in what we feel inside ourselves, but what we do in response to these feelings. This isn't to say that internal feelings are irrelevant, but that much of what we consider as emotions in others are just our interpretation of their emotional *expression* – i.e., the external demonstration of what they are feeling inside. It is difficult for us to say with certainty what people are feeling, unless they show it in ways that we can apply our preconceived templates to, and so we rely on our translation of their external expression of their feelings, using a combination of our internal rules and societal measures, both of which are interlinked.

We can sometimes avoid situations (such as avoiding a phone- or Zoom call) or choose specific situations that will support more desirable emotions.[6] We can also use distraction techniques to divert our attention to a less emotional situation. We also sometimes modulate our responses, pretend to agree or tone down our emotions to modify a situation's impact on others. This is suppression, where we try to avoid betraying our internal states. We might be feeling scared of or disgusted by someone, but we try not to show this in order to not cause offence. This process of suppression controls not only negative emotions but also positive ones, sometimes creating a significant inconsistency between what we experience inside and how we express it externally. This is why it is a maladaptive strategy. These are usually coping mechanisms we pick up at a young age which stop us from adapting to new or unusual situations. This sort of cognitive control over our emotions (such as suppressing anger when we have been betrayed or cheated rather than tackling the situation) is also emotionally taxing, and strongly related to depression. Modulating our emotions can sometimes require reappraisals – a sort of cognitive-change strategy – where certain cognitive control mechanisms, supported by rational parts of the brain in the prefrontal cortex, help us reframe situations, and assign new meanings to them.[7] 'It isn't really that bad', or 'He didn't really mean it' is something we can tell ourselves in order to reframe the situation and prevent the more intense emotional experience of having to engage with whether or not something was really that bad or that he did mean it. This is often how coercive control and abuse can carry on. In everyday life, we can reframe situations, such as telling ourselves that 'talking to new people is not scary' or 'giving a public talk is not life-changing' to shift our mindset and our response to that situation. In doing so, we can decrease activity in the subcortical emotion system of the brain, which can influence our physiological responses (such as increasing heart rate) and support how we express and experience emotions. This can help us regulate the intensity of emotional experience and expression. Not everyone is able to do this readily.[8] It is a form of emotional contortionism that requires a lot from us: to be hyper-aware of our environment, to anticipate potential triggers and prepare for them in advance, and to be mindful of our emotions as well as pre-empt the emotional rules of the situation or context that we find ourselves in.

Emotions can be regulated before or after they have been initiated. Often it is done in order to conform to cultural rules and practices, which are not always explicit. When emotion-display rules become embedded in our societies and communities, we can be trained to automatically dampen, neutralise, mask or fabricate our emotional reactions according to these context-specific values.[9] An example of an emotional-display rule could be that we are expected to smile in social situations, even with strangers. I accompanied my five-year-old daughter to the opticians for an eye test. She was suitably nervous, of course. But she is also very observant and was watching and listening very carefully. The optician commented: 'She's had a frown on her face since she came in.' I decided to ignore it as a one-off remark. But then he continued, 'Oh, at last, we finally see a smile. Why has she been frowning? She has been frowning all the time. Why is she so serious?' I could not take it any more. I had to say that it was really just her face, and that she wasn't frowning, and that she didn't have to smile if she did not feel like smiling. My child later wondered, 'Mummy, should I have been smiling?' Of course, I reminded her that she did not have to fake a smile, that she never has to smile to make anyone else comfortable. But I kept wondering how much it was her being a girl that shaped this optician's expectations. I can never know. But we know that expectations around women having to show nurturing and positive expressions – in this instance as a smile – seemingly become more heightened with age.[10] This is also how emotional–display rules and expectations are enforced from a young age.

•

Emotions are also regulated to pursue specific goals, when a person is aware of the desired state and the outcome it would achieve. These could be social goals (i.e., to maintain positive social relationships), or aimed at optimising the feeling of pleasure and minimising the feeling of pain.[11] We try and not get angry with our spouses in public situations; we try to moderate our responses even when we encounter microaggressions in the workplace. Most of our social goals are to avoid conflict and to make others feel better, to influence others and to keep up appearances, and when our emotional responses are ill-matched to a specific context, we often try and regulate them.

People who have to modulate their emotions for a long time regularly show higher anxiety than those who do not have to do this, and people with higher levels of anxiety show lower emotional control.[12] Suppressing our emotions can be incredibly bad for our health. As we have seen, emotions are a result of interaction between behavioural, experiential and physiological processes inside our bodies and brains, and so emotional regulation is not a straightforward process.[13] It often involves adjustment of aspects such as 'rise time' (the time taken for the emotion to become evident), magnitude, duration and intensity of an emotional response. The suppression of emotions often requires a high degree of cognitive load, because it involves quick self-reflection and self-correction while at the same time anticipating an event and our own response to it. This is therefore cognitively an expensive process. Even though we might decrease the external signs of emotion, this does not mean we decrease our emotional experience, or make the feelings go away, even though sometimes we can change the way we think during this process.

Research has shown that suppression of our emotions can also affect our cognitive functions, such as our memory of emotional experiences. In an experiment, 58 female participants, students ranging from 17 to 22 years, were asked to actively suppress their emotions of sadness.[14] The women were shown 18 slides in 3 sets of 6 each, for 10 seconds each, with scenes that elicited negative emotions, such as wounded men. After each slide, the participants had to rate how they had felt on a 7-point scale from 'not at all' to 'a great deal'. The behaviour of each participant was also measured on how they responded to each slide, such as whether they were actively averting their gaze or shielding their eyes to avoid looking at the negative scenes. To test whether this affected memory, they were asked to recall details from the scenes they had seen. It was seen that they performed worse on memory tasks compared to the group that did not suppress their emotions.[15]

Regulating emotional expression can also affect any subsequent cognitive tasks and intellectual performance due to depletion of resources during the management and regulation of emotions, especially if the emotions are high intensity. In particular, when we suppress our emotions during social interactions, we are unable to observe and capture as much information from the environment as we would have otherwise been able to. This information is used to make assessments and decisions about such interactions, and in the case of a lack of adequate information about new situations and people, we are more likely to resort to stereotypical thinking.[16]

Emotional suppression can also be a sign of overcompensating for negative prejudice towards a marginalised or traditionally stereotyped group. When heterosexual male participants watched a video of a gay couple with clear instructions to suppress their natural emotions (alongside a control group), the people who had low prejudice showed less positive emotion compared to the control group, while the participants who had indicated high prejudice (homophobia) in the pre-questionnaire showed higher positive emotion.[17] This group was overcompensating in their emotional regulation to try to hide their prejudice, but also in the process increased their desire to sympathise and engage with the stereotyped group. Emotional suppression can therefore sometimes mediate prejudice and inter-group relationships too, bridging the gap between in-group and out-group associations.

We are not passive slaves to our emotions, but active agents who regularly use a number of strategies to modulate our emotional expressions. Why we do this, and to what extent, definitely depends on the context. Structural hierarchies, social class, power and status play a role in determining a person's behaviour and emotion. The philosopher Bertrand Russell suggested in 1938 that power is an ultimate goal and the single most important element in the development of a society.[18] Power is also a 'basic force in social relationships'[19] and is never absolute but also socially constrained and conferred.[20] Status is often an outcome of power, but sometimes it is possible to have power without formal status in society (such as the Mafia), and it can also exist in the form of informal roles outside the traditional corridors of power that are legally recognised. The Nobel laureate John Harsanyi has proposed that social status is one of the most important motivating factors for social behaviour.[21] We also know that power influences stereotyping. People higher up in a social hierarchy are more likely to stereotype those who are marginalised and perceived to be lower in status.[22] Those with less power are more likely to be socially vigilant to social norms and rules and attend to the expectations and expressions of those with high power more carefully. This is motivated by rewards, as powerholders are more likely to help them achieve their goals. The reverse is not the case. Those with more power do not have to be so socially vigilant and are accustomed to being attended to.

The subordination or oppression hypothesis proposed by Marianne LaFrance of Yale University in 1997 suggested that the gender differences in nonverbal communication and expression mirrored the status differences between men and women in society.[23] Women are less powerful, hold lower status in society and are more vigilant than men. They are more accurate and perceptive in interpreting other people's emotional expressions and nonverbal behaviour because they need greater vigilance.[24] Returning to smiling, it has been observed that social power affects the propensity of a person to smile. Those with more power and higher status do not feel obligated to moderate their emotions as much as those below them in the hierarchy, and feel free to express their positive emotions only when they experience them. However, those with lower power and status can feel obligated to smile even when they are not feeling happy. Women might therefore smile more often than men in similar situations.[25] (This is culture- and age-specific too, which I discuss in later chapters). Power accords a certain freedom to people to act in more counter-normative ways, while those who feel powerless are more likely to experience intense negative emotions that they are more likely to suppress, and to adapt their behaviours as per norms and expectations.[26]

Members of stereotyped groups experience additional pressure when they are in situations and domains in which they are more likely to be stereotyped. This is called a 'stereotype threat', a hyper-awareness that their behaviour might come under scrutiny and be used to validate an existing stereotype.[27] This is the case, for instance, of women in mathematics and science classes, because there is a widespread stereotype that women are not as good at science and maths as men. Stereotype threat can cause anxiety while the person is under pressure to suppress any such negative thoughts and feelings, and 'down-regulate' their negative emotions. This is a huge burden on cognitive resources and depletes the executive functioning, including our working memory.[28] The process of reframing a negative stimulus in less emotional terms in order to down-regulate a negative emotional response is also termed cognitive reappraisal.[29]

In a study of 85 women students, physiological functions were mapped while the women suppressed their emotions, and the results showed a higher activation of their cardiovascular systems, even though the level of emotion they were experiencing was the same as the group that did not have to suppress their emotional expression.[30] The depletion of cognitive resources and impact on executive functions, with its associated detrimental impact on performance, can create the impression that women are not a good fit to a workplace, or position of authority, while also making the women feel anxious and in a state of high alert. It is no surprise that women are more likely to suffer from anxiety and depression. In England in 2014, about one in five women suffered from some form of mental illness, compared to one in eight men.[31] Globally, in 2010, the annual prevalence of depression was 5.5 per cent in women compared to 3.2 per cent in men.[32] Depression is more than twice as prevalent in young women than men (aged 14–25 years).

It is not just the suppression of emotions but also the modulation and regulation to accommodate emotion rules in specific contexts that is problematic. Twenty-five people between 18 and 22 years old, of which 13 were women, all native English speakers, were given an fMRI[33] examination while viewing negative and neutral pictures.[34] They were shown a picture on the screen as a priming mechanism: either with the word 'decrease' to encourage people to down-regulate their response, following which a negative image was shown, or the word 'look' as a non-regulation instruction, following which a negative or neutral image was shown. After they had looked at the picture for 8 seconds, the participants were asked to respond to the question 'How negative do you feel?' on a scale of 1 to 4 (1 being weak and 4 strong). Participants were also asked to describe loudly their own reinterpretation of the emotional aspects of the image to understand their cognitive strategy for down-regulating their negative emotional response (examples included 'It's not real', e.g., it's just a scene from a movie, they're just pretending, and 'Things will improve with time'). Signals from the amygdala and the prefrontal regions that are associated with control during reappraisal of negative emotions were mapped. Both genders self-reported as being equally effective in down-regulating their response to the negative images, but the neural response showed that women had less down-regulation than men in their amygdala response to these images. The men showed less activity in their prefrontal cortical regions, which are usually very active during emotional regulation. The results show that it is likely that men are more efficient than women at emotional reappraisal, because they are more expert at doing so and it comes naturally and automatically to them. It is also possible that women use more positive emotions than men and engage more of the ventral striatum, which is involved in reward-related emotional management.

Men and women were also seen to be using different strategies for regulating the negative emotions. While men were suppressing and down-regulating the negative emotions, women were trying to transform the negative feelings into more positive feelings. Women were seen to be using more cognitive resources to successfully manage any negative feelings, shown by higher activity in their prefrontal cortex regions, using positive refocusing as a coping strategy, but also because they were adapting their emotions to appear more positive. Men, on the other hand, did not feel the same pressure; they were seen to be doing any emotion reappraisal more automatically than women and with less cognitive effort. The researchers suggested that women depend on more conscious processes to modulate and regulate their emotions. This does not mean that they do not do it as effectively, or that they are not as good at controlling their emotions, but that it is more onerous for women to modulate their emotions as they have to balance many factors.

While there has been much focus in scientific research on men's mental health and emotional suppression due to gender norms – and justifiably so, when we have seen the disproportionate impact of suicide rates on men – there has been little research into the impact of emotional suppression and gender norms on women. Arguably the very reason that this has not received due attention in academic studies is because of the stereotypical narrative that women are more emotional than men. The view persists and percolates through academic attitudes as much as through popular sensibilities that women show their emotions freely, and therefore must not have any effects linked to emotional modulation and regulation.

Suppressing emotions is also detrimental to productivity and to mental health. A study in 2005 from the University of Aberdeen showed across three experiments that women who suppressed their emotions ended up more angry than the men who took part in the experiment, due to a rebound effect.[35] The rebound effect is when we are more likely to think of something with greater frequency if we are explicitly told to suppress specific thoughts or feelings ('Do not think of the monkey', 'Try not to feel angry'). Forty-eight undergraduate students between 17 and 22 years old were shown videos of cruelty to animals and of protestors during Apartheid in South Africa. They were divided into 3 groups of 8 men and 8 women, and instructed to express their emotions freely, or to suppress their emotions, or to substitute their anger with another emotion that they were assigned. Their emotional states before and after were recorded using a self-reported 8-point scale. Women who had suppressed anger felt even angrier than those women who had freely expressed their anger. When women had to remind themselves not to look angry, they verbally primed themselves to feel the very emotions that they were trying to avoid. Telling women not to be angry can cause them to feel that emotion more intensely. Men, on the other hand, felt angrier when they were asked to substitute the feelings of anger for happiness, compared to both women who had substituted and also the men in the 'suppression' and 'expression' groups.

Historically, kindness and empathy have not been valued in men, whereas stoicism, outward confidence and toughness have been – of which more later. Consequently, men tend to hide emotions that are not associated with their gender, ones that are deemed more 'feminine'. The consequence of this suppression seems clear: three-quarters of suicides are in men;[36] suicidal ideation has been linked to hyper-masculine ideals in young men aged 15 to 20 years old,[37] and in America, the Pan American Health Organization reports that 1 in 5 men in the country will not reach the age of 50 due to rates of suicides and addiction.[38] For similar reasons, in Zimbabwe between 2015 and 2019, more than 2,000 men died by suicide, compared to 500 women.[39] In 2019, the American Psychological Association laid out guidelines for psychologists working with men concerning the effects of gender role stereotypes, stating that 'traditional masculinity is psychologically harmful'.[40] But there is always pushback when traditional, well-established norms are challenged. In this case, Canadian-American psychologist Steven Pinker[41] and British cognitive neuroscientist Christian Jarrett[42] have asserted that people who repress rather than 'vent' have healthier lives, and that men who subscribe to masculine ideals of success and winning at any cost have the highest wellbeing scores. These assertions, once again, rely on biological determinism: that there is something inherent in men and women that determine their propensity to certain behaviours; that the notion of a 'gentleman' (i.e., the ideal of masculinity) is linked to stoicism and quiet strength and dignity.[43]

•

It is clear that cultural differences play a significant role in emotions. Culture influences how people behave. Emotional regulation is important for a sense of self, but also for social cohesion. And so the cultural context also determines the nature and extent of emotional regulation, with different cultures valuing and promoting different levels. Much of the research in this area so far has focused on the suppression of emotional expression rather than understanding the process of managing and regulating the internal processes. Cross-cultural investigation has been focused on independent versus interdependent cultures, where western societies are understood as valuing independence, whereas East Asian cultures, for instance, are believed to prioritise interdependence and emphasise values of obedience and conformity. Of course, these are broad generalisations, and individual differences will occur depending on personality traits such as impulsivity, hostility, shyness, agreeableness and so on. Differences will also depend on how closely a person identifies with their cultural group membership,[44] how much they value social rewards, and how motivated they are to preserve their interdependent cultural values that prioritise social harmony and relationships with others over solitary independence and self-identity.[45]

As we have seen, the marginalised groups that are more likely to be stereotyped are also more likely to use suppression of negative emotions compared to the members of groups that hold more power and status in society. Those cultures that are focused on hierarchy tend to value the unequal distribution of power and attempt to maintain these hierarchies. In such cultures, it is discouraged for lower-status individuals to assert their independent feelings and thoughts, and they are encouraged to self-regulate and conform with the norms, especially in their behaviour towards the higher-status individuals. In more egalitarian cultures people are encouraged to express themselves more freely, both negative and positive emotions.[46] Intercultural adjustment also requires more emotional regulation.[47] Immigrants are expected to adjust to a different culture quickly, and they are also likely to experience stereotype threat in these societies, especially if they are moving to a dominant culture from the global south. People who are able to regulate their emotions and develop adaptive strategies to the dominant culture are valued and considered a 'good fit' and a 'good immigrant': something that also pushes the 'model minority' myth.

Cultural difference seems to lead people to suppress or inhibit their emotional expressions more readily than to reappraise them by reframing or reinterpreting emotion-eliciting situations. Reappraisal is the way in which individuals interpret and frame an emotion-eliciting situation to change its impact on emotional experience, while suppression is the inhibition of emotional expressive behaviour. In a study published in 2008, 3,386 university students across 23 countries completed an Emotion Regulation Questionnaire (ERQ).[48] The ERQ is a 10-item scale to measure a person's tendency to regulate their emotions, where they self-report on a 7-point scale of 1 (strongly disagree) to 7 (strongly agree) to statements such as 'I keep my emotions to myself' and 'When I am feeling negative emotions, I make sure not to express them.' The results showed that those cultures that were steeped in hierarchies and attempts to maintain these social orders were more likely to have higher scores on emotion suppression and reappraisal.

Suppression was also negatively correlated with autonomy. While suppression can have some positive influence on the social level, it often has negative consequences on the individual level. Comparative studies between Hong Kong and the Netherlands have also shown that in eastern societies such as China and Japan, people use different strategies for suppression and moderation of their emotions – and do so more frequently than in western societies such as the USA, UK and Europe.[49] There has not been much gender-specific cross-cultural examination of emotion regulation. In a 2013 study, 384 undergraduate students from Miami and 380 from Seoul completed the ERQ and other questionnaires to report on their tendency to suppress anger.[50] These nationalities were chosen because in both countries reflective pondering and brooding in the form of rumination was associated with more depressive symptoms. No difference was found in the frequency with which emotion reappraisal was used, but the Koreans reported higher levels of rumination – especially brooding – and internal reflection compared to the Americans. Surprisingly, compared to the previous studies, there was not much difference found between suppression of anger between the two groups. Since this group was much younger and recruited solely from amongst university students, it is likely that the younger generation is expressing their emotions more freely even in traditionally collectivistic cultures in order to break away from societal norms and express their individuality. There was no gender difference found between the two cultures, with women suppressing their anger more than men in both cultures.

These cultural norms can be verbal or nonverbal, are often implicit, and can force individuals to amplify their emotions (show more happiness than they are truly feeling) or de-amplify (show less enthusiasm or grief than they are experiencing). Often it is done because the true expression of an internal mental state would bring discomfort to the intended audience. Therefore, in some ways, emotional expression often tells us more about the expectations and values of the person perceiving the emotions.

Many of these studies are self-reported and there may be more resistance to reporting the negative impacts of emotional suppression in certain cultures than in others. Also, these are broad generalisations based on relatively small samples, and there cannot be a direct correlation between a culture and a country, because of course a country such as the USA or the UK is diverse and multicultural. While we should definitely refrain from homogenising whole countries and forming cultural stereotypes, it is useful to understand how an individual's position and status in a particular society impact on which emotions are considered 'proper' for them, and how much they are forced to maintain these social bonds and interpersonal relationships through their choice of emotional suppression and regulation. And when we examine historical texts and documents carefully, we can see that many of these rules that motivate emotional regulation and management have a long legacy, one that has gradually become so embedded in our societal fabric that we assume that it has always been there.

·

None of these theories of emotions is perfect, and scientists accept and acknowledge this. It is not easy to define emotions, and to be able to do this we need to consider the experience of these emotions (feelings, or the internal states), the physiological responses, and the observable patterns or facial, vocal and bodily cues. What is significant is that emotions are underpinned by regulation and expression, and, as over the last decades more research has been carried out in the field, it is becoming acknowledged that all emotions are learned to a large extent, and their response and expression are taught, not innate. In the last few decades, we have come to understand that our physical bodies and brains are malleable, and that there is no universal body. That regardless of biological sex, our bodies are largely shaped by culture, both in the ways we perceive ourselves and how others see us. Bodies, performance and emotions are inherently interlinked and these rituals very quickly become part of our social and cultural practice, becoming coded into our individual and collective beliefs and attitudes. Regulation is therefore not suppressing but expressing. Emotions are not pre-cultural, they are a response to society and environment and not only biology. Emotions also have history.

So much of this discussion places emotions in contrast with reason, while also contrasting biology with culture, as if these are two different things. Our bodies are part of the culture, they are placed in it and our bodily experiences are shaped by the culture too. William James said way back in 1890 that the categorisation of feelings depended on the 'introspective vocabulary of the seeker', the vocabulary that is shaped by a person's language and culture, their physiological experiences and the way they remember these events.

The corporeality of emotions is something we tend to ignore in the western conception of emotions. Emotions are a conversation, a back and forth, and the way we see and understand them, the value and meanings we associate with them, is dependent not only on the person feeling, but also the person seeing these emotions. The context of both people matters, and this is why any interpretation of emotion, and the broader values we associate with them – good or bad, negative or positive – is so much rooted in the social context.

There is a feeling, an affect which is a physical reaction to a certain event, and then there is the way we label it an emotion depending on the language we have at our disposal, and this is how we make sense of our feelings. And this emotion helps us to react to a particular situation in a specific way, following our experiences and memories, the templates that we have (metaphorically) stored in our brains. The meaning that we assign to different emotions isn't like a to-do list that we make on paper, it isn't a concrete set of actions and interventions, but it is a sort of guide that our brain uses to know what to do with these feelings, whether to suppress them, regulate them, or what action to perform in response. It helps us understand the world in a specific way, while interpreting other people's emotions is key to understanding their motives. But because we find it easier to essentialise, we also attribute these emotions and feelings to people's inherent personality:

all women are emotional, all men are rational. We assume that the world is always a certain way, because it is less cognitively taxing to assume this. This is why we try and meet the expectations of others in our behaviours and responses because it is easier for us to know what to expect, it is more efficient for our brains to make the other people's behaviour more predictable, and so we conform to societal norms and expectations. This is also how we reduce uncertainty, by constantly gathering evidence and remembering what has worked before, and making predictions based on these past experiences.

Our personal beliefs and cultural norms and stereotypes can affect how we process information. Our personal beliefs can drive behaviour, but our actions are also guided by cultural norms that shape the patterns and stereotypes that we hold in our brains − stereotypes we might unconsciously activate when assessing new people and situations. Even when we might not endorse certain cultural stereotypes around race and gender, they are ingrained in our societal structures, and we are highly likely to be influenced by and subscribe to them in our evaluation of our own behaviours and those of others. We are still constantly trying to figure out what these social norms are and where this line is as we navigate everyday life.

This 'priming', or the awareness of social norms, can be related to everyday scenarios, so, for example, if someone fears being stereotyped as angry, they are more likely to feel and experience anger. The more we have access to these stereotypes, the more likely it is that we will construct these emotions. This could also give us some clues as to why women might feel angry in certain domains and situations, where they are already hyper-aware of being perceived as angry, or when they have already been called angry (or hysterical). It becomes a self-fulfilling prophecy that perhaps when women are perceived to be angry, they subsequently are.

Section 2:

HOW DID OUR EMOTIONS BECOME GENDERED?

Women should be used like chamber pots: hidden away once a man has pissed in them.

— Marsilio Ficino[1]

5.

CHAMBER POTS

'SO THAT YOU MAY UNDERSTAND that it is not natural to be broken by sorrow, you should consider that grief wounds women more than men, barbarians more than civilised and cultivated persons, the unlearned more than the learned.' Thus said Seneca, Roman philosopher and Stoic, in 40 CE, consoling Marcia, daughter of a prominent historian, who was grieving the death of her son.[1]

Seneca's three works of consolation are written more as his reflections on the universe and human condition than works offering solace. These essays in the Stoic tradition are written in the detached manner one would expect of the movement, which sees death as a return to nature, and not something to be feared. Seneca makes it clear that moderating the demonstration of sorrow and grief is more respectful to those who are alive; to carry emotion is human but to be consumed by it is disrespectful and a path towards self-destruction. In Seneca's view, women were more prone to grief than men, and women could be redeemed of their ordinary faults by holding on to their virtue.

Jean-Noël Allard and Pascal Montlahuc from University of Paris carried out an analysis of literary texts, epigraphic and iconographic documents, as well as rhetorical texts to understand how emotions have been written about by researchers of antiquity, and found that there hasn't been a huge amount of attention paid to them. This is because 'the ancients' did not always separate emotions from other moral qualities. However, even though there has been no explicit study of emotions, looking at their rituals and behaviours tells us a lot about the social norms of the time. It tells us how emotions were being expressed and which emotional expressions were considered suitable. Any institutional arrangements such as religion or politics tell us about how emotional expectations spilled into these domains and which values were considered important to uphold. The emotional shifts were not always clearly perceptible, and these developmental milestones often have to be extracted through secondary sources which documented private and public life through the times.

Much of Greek and Latin literature differentiates between manly and womanly emotions. In classical Athens, men who fought great wars, were wounded in battle, and who slaughtered many were celebrated as heroes. They are remembered and immortalised in literature and art. In Euripides's tragedy *Herakles* (first performed in 416 BCE), the hero, even while heartbroken and facing the deaths of his children, resists shedding any tears lest he be seen as less masculine. When he is overtaken by grief, Heracles describes himself thus: 'And pity me, for I am pitiful indeed as I lie sobbing and moaning like a maiden! No one living has ever seen me [a man] act like this before; for I have never groaned at my misfortunes till now, when I have proved to be a mere woman.' A mere woman.[2]

The binary notion of cowardice and courage as opposite poles, one being manly and one womanly, is also seen in how Cicero, Roman statesman and orator, describes Mark Antony, army general and fellow statesman. Cicero composed a series of 14 speeches in 44 and 43 BCE called the *Philippics* denouncing Mark Antony. Antony, a close relative of Julius Caesar, formed a political alliance called the Second Triumvirate after Caesar's death (the first having been founded by Caesar himself). While Mark Antony did not participate in the slaying of Julius Caesar, he did not condemn the action. Cicero addresses Antony in the second *Philippics*, mocking him for his cowardice: 'You did not reveal the plot; I thank you. You did not carry it out; I forgive you. Such an act required a man to do it [Virum res illa quaerebat].'[3]

In her monograph *Cowardice and Gender in the Iliad and Greek Tragedy*, Jessica Wissmann of the University of Cologne notes that 'cowardice' in Greek can often be expressed as 'anandria', which in its most literal sense means failing in being an 'aner', an adult male, one who is virile, the most idealised social norm for masculinity.[4]

Cowardice was 'unheroic' and deserved shame, humiliation and self-condemnation, while glory was the greatest reward. Hector confronts Achilles because he would feel ashamed (αἰδέομαι) if he ran away: 'Be men, my friends, and put pride (αἰδῶ) in your hearts. In the battle's fury think proudly of your honour (αἰδεῖσθε) in each other's eyes. When men have pride (αἰδομένων δ' ἀνδρῶν), more are saved than killed; but when they turn to flight, there can be no glory there or courage to resist.'[5] Cowardice, modesty, reticence (verecundia), jealousy (zèlotupia), timidity, desire were all feminine virtues (and vices), often placed side by side with more masculine virtues, set up as polar opposites.

During the early classical period, there was also a notion of public and private display of emotions, the latter considered more respectable. Men cried, reluctantly and in private, and this humanised them. Women's emotions were unconcealed and public, and therefore shameless and weak-willed. Women were seen to be 'enjoying moaning'; as Euripides says in *Andromache*: 'It is in women's nature to charm their ills by having them always at the tip of their tongues.'[6]

In ancient literature, the gendered polarisation of emotions appears to have become strengthened in the time between the *Iliad* and the *Odyssey*, both written around the eighth century BCE, with men being ascribed ever more capacity for control over their emotions, and freedom to express them.[7] Women were marginalised and ignored in the many historical records and epics, their narratives only coming through a male gaze and in fragments, even though – as the historian Natalie Haynes shows in her recent book *A Thousand Ships* – the Trojan War was as much a women's war as one of the men. In Livy's *History of Rome* this contrast between masculine and feminine emotions is very clear.[8]

'It was then that the Sabine women, whose rape had provoked the war, their hair streaming, their clothing torn, overcoming in their distress the timidity of their sex, did not hesitate to throw themselves into the midst of a hail of arrows, separating the combatants, in order to end the dispute. Soldiers and captains were at once touched by emotion. All was quiet, calm. Then, the leaders stepped forward to make peace.'[9]

Emotions belong to the women, who are distressed and usually timid, and courage is rarely seen in such women: the notion of heroism and bravery was restricted to the battlefield, while the qualities of fortitude and resilience commonly ascribed to women, who survived as captors or slaves and waited patiently for their husbands to return, were not seen as heroic, or worthy of being included in these narratives. Instead, women were firmly set at the lower rungs of the social hierarchy, shaping these historical discourses, written by powerful, important men, and also forever sabotaged by them too.

There are women like Helen of Troy who have been assigned powerful positions in historical narratives but merely as helpless scapegoats for wars fought by men. In Aeschylus's tragedy *Agamemnon*, there is a line: 'Helen of Troy, destroyer of ships, destroyer of men, destroyer of cities.' Helen, whose face 'launched a thousand ships', has been portrayed as the instigator of the Trojan War, the one responsible for the loss of all the Greek lives. In Shakespeare's *Troilus and Cressida*, the Greek commander Diomedes states: 'For every scruple / of her contaminated carrion weight, / A Trojan hath been slain.'[10]

Dualism has abounded in western philosophical thought since Plato and Aristotle.[11] In *The Symposium*, Plato suggested that man and woman were once two halves of the same creature, split by the gods, with complementary characteristics: when we find our counterpart, it will make us whole again.[12] Some historians have interpreted this as an egalitarian way to insist that men and women complete each other, but in fact it created a binary divide, with men and women at opposing ends of the spectrum (and also the binary categorisation that we have since based our society in); much as reason and emotion are often seen as a dualistic relationship. So, where emotion or thumos* exists, reason and rationality cannot stand. Aristotle deemed women to be lacking in deliberative faculties – the capacity to reason – and that by their very nature they were 'without authority' (akuron), unable to control their emotions as compared to men, which is why they deserved a subordinate role at home. In the political realm and discourse, emotion was maligned, seen as conflicting with rationality and calmness. There

---

* Greek word meaning 'spiritedness', associated commonly with anger or disposition to anger.

was dignity in restraint, in controlling emotions or 'gravitas'. Plato says in *The Republic*:

> We would be right, then, to take lamentations away from famous men, and leave them to women (provided they are not excellent women) and to cowardly men, so that those we say we are training to guard our land will be ashamed to do such things . . . Moreover, they must not be lovers of laughter either. For whenever anyone gives in to violent laughter, a violent reaction generally follows . . . So, if someone represents worthwhile people as overcome by laughter, we must not accept it, and we will accept it even less if they represent the gods in that way.[13]

Gail Holst-Warhaft examined laments from Greece as part of her doctoral study at Cornell University and suggested that hired female professionals called 'praeficae', who often did not know the deceased, did most of the mourning during a burial.[14] These were acceptable forms of emotional expressions as they were not directed by personal attachments and were therefore not vulgar. Although lamentation was a feminine practice, these hired mourners could employ strict codes of lamentations in their weeping and avoid the embarrassment of any public display of spontaneous emotions from the men and women of the family. Since most (if not all) texts from the time were written by men, they are particularly dismissive of women's emotional expressions, even during the funeral rituals, of their practices and of their visibility in public at such times. Women's intense emotions – letting their hair flow loose, baring their breasts, beating their chests – were seen as distasteful, especially as they could evoke similar emotions in men, and diminish their power.

There was also an element of power hierarchy in who was allowed to show certain emotions and what these emotions said about the person. Those with power were deemed to hold gravitas, and this reinforced their position and status, while those who were in the lower classes and held no positions of power, especially the men, were freer to succumb to their emotions because emotions were seen as crass and hence signalled their inferior status. And while it isn't possible to examine every piece of historical evidence, and there is some fluidity in how emotions were considered across space and time during this period, these examples show that emotions had different consequences for men and women based on their value to the society and state more broadly. For instance, in times of crisis, men with their rationality would be deemed a stabilising presence, while women with their irrationality were thought to potentially put other people, and even the state, at risk.

During this time, anger in particular was a status emotion, signalling the relative positions in society. Medea's fury would have unsettled the Athenians, while it also threatens her own social status. Aristotle considered that anger could only be expressed between equals or downwards in hierarchical relations. Whether or not you had permission to be angry depended on where one sat within the social hierarchy. This is really crucial to our understanding of display rules, even today. Courtesans and enslaved women, of course, could not be angry, but some men at the lower strata of society could be. As Maurice Sartre notes in his 2016 essay: 'Female anger, like that of a tyrant, is expressed by a degree of fury that comes close to madness', i.e., during classical times, women's anger signalled their lack of control and consequent incompatibility with public civic life.[15] Male anger was perceived as a source of strength, while women were excluded from political roles because of theirs.[16]

Seneca wrote: 'Thus anger is a most womanish and childish

weakness. "But," you will say, "it is found in men also." True, for even men may have childish and womanish natures.'[17]

Chaereas and Callirhoe, written in the first century and the earliest known Greek romance novel, has anger as its central narrative with both the male and female protagonist: Chaereas flies into uncontrollable rage, while Callirhoe remains passive, entirely incapable of anger, thus satisfying the ideal of how a woman should behave (even though surprisingly she is shown as highly intelligent and very rational, which were not considered feminine qualities).[18] In depicting her as the one who was in control of her anger, the Greek writer Chariton abandoned some of the stereotypes of women being weak and emotional, driven uncontrollably by their feelings, and seems an outlier against the more gendered views of the time. But even as he rejects these views, the depictions serve to reinforce the norms around women's anger, such as their susceptibility to succumb to irrational temper, much to their own detriment as well as that of others.[19] While Chariton's female protagonist resists the rising emotion, the other women in the play are not as controlled, and so reason and emotion are still being played against each other as opposing forces.

The Greek philosopher Plutarch, a priest at the Temple of Apollo around 100 CE suggests in his treatise 'On Restraining Anger' that women might be more prone to emotions such as anger because of their physical frailty: 'In the most delicate of souls, the propensity to cause suffering to others causes greater anger in proportion to their greater weakness. That is why women are more likely to be aroused than men.'[20]

In every society and culture there are arrangements of femininity and masculinity, rigid boundaries laid down around these norms. Masculinity, or femininity, is really a performance which is constructed through certain specific behaviours that are then interpreted as markers of an identity by others through a shared sense of social norms.[21] In his *Lives*, Plutarch's series of biographies, there is a recurrent characterisation of 'good' and 'bad' women where women are either loyal, virtuous and maternal (much like Homeric wives), or witches that reject their femininity and use their resources for their own selfish purposes rather than for the benefit of their husbands or the state.[22] For instance, Odysseus's wife Penelope, famously known for her fidelity to her husband, is categorised as a 'good woman'. Fiery, hot-tempered and non-maternal women meanwhile – such as the enchantress Circe or Cleopatra – were 'bad' and to be avoided by men and women alike. Both Cleopatra and Fulvia – Mark Antony's mistress and wife respectively – are portrayed as controlling, manipulative and uncaring, examples of how women ought not to behave.[23] In writing predominantly for a masculine audience, Plutarch was warning men of 'dangerous women' and advising how to manage them and their emotions.

In his essay 'Coniugalia Praecepta' ('Letters to a new bride and groom'), in *Moralia*, Plutarch considers the female audience[24] and lays out the feminine qualities of charm and seduction that women use to gain advantage with men, portraying women as having weak moral attributes, linked to weaker physical and mental characters: 'It's quick and easy to catch fish with poison – but then you'll have nasty, poisonous fish. And women who use charms and spells to entangle a man, controlling him through pleasure, will live with stupid, mindless, ruined men. It's like Circe: she couldn't enjoy the men she'd bewitched: she couldn't even use the men she'd turned to pigs and donkeys. But Odysseus! The one who kept his wits and could still think: she was crazy in love for him.'[25]

Women such as Cleopatra, Circe or Medea, whom Plutarch

decreed to be witches, represented the dangers of loss of male control. Medea in particular responds to the limitations set on women in this time in a vengeful way. When her husband Jason leaves her to marry someone else, she makes the decision to kill his new bride, along with her own children. This classical tale was first told by Euripides in 431 BCE. But Seneca then rewrote the story in a version that is both more sympathetic to Jason, and is used to teach a dramatic lesson about Stoic precepts, especially concerned with the 'pathos' (unhealthy emotion) of anger. Though the story of Medea and Jason is a tale of violence and murder, at its core it is a complex conversation about women's place in society, and the emotions that a woman is allowed to feel and express, questioning the normative beliefs around femininity and feminine emotions while demonstrating the consequences of male entitlement. What happens when a woman carries all the suppressed anger at injustice and patriarchy? What happens to this anger bubbling under the surface because women are supposed to be passive? When discussions about equality and rights of women are pushed off the table, then sometimes women do not have a choice but to act radically. I have so often wondered if this would have been written the same way if Medea was a man. Would we be reading about this in the same way? Would a man have felt so helpless that he was forced to take such a radical action, the seething fury that blinded Medea, the helplessness and desperation that stretched her, challenged her and ultimately forced her to kill her own children?

In writing the original *Medea*, Euripides was challenging the beautifully curated images that Greek society expected its audience to believe in, that aligned with its normative standards of what a woman was and how she should behave. The classicist Shirley Barlow argues that much of this 'subversive' play is about 'men's images of women'.[26] Forcing women to remain behind the scenes was a means for men to control them and neatly pack them into a single, ideal standard. Medea broke this perfect identity and forced the audience to re-evaluate their society. But even as this character challenges the patriarchal structures, and disrupts the traditional roles and images of women during this period, she also acts in accordance with the stereotypes: irrational, over-emotional, crazy.[27] When Medea is prepared to use physical means to achieve her revenge, she has stepped outside these gender confines, and is therefore not protected by the social rules any more. And, in overstepping these expectations, as Medea is perceived to be disempowering Jason and diminishing his masculinity, she becomes the symbol of the woman that every man fears. The same behaviour which might have been justified in a man becomes worthy of condemnation. While Achilles is worshipped and becomes 'godlike' in the *Iliad*, Medea is demonised, even though both are driven by revenge and anger. When Medea is assigned the qualities that were typical of a man during the period, such as valour and courage, being deliberate, clever and methodical, she is perceived as unfeminine. As Aristotle says in his *Poetics*: 'For a character [may] be masculine, but it is not fitting for a woman to be masculine or clever.'

A painting by Eugène Delacroix titled *Médée furieuse* presents Medea as the most maternal and loving woman. But these aspects of her personality have been gradually erased through history, with the focus primarily on her fury and rage. I talk about Medea at length here, because it is a story of rules that women have been bound by for a very long time, and how feminine and masculine ideals were imposed rigidly so that women could aspire to masculine attributes but they could not be *too* masculine, and even in showing masculine attributes of courage and valour, they could only be maternal, not heroic. Men could be determined and heroic, but in women it was perceived as hyper-emotionality and volatility: always vices, never virtues.

When we consider Roman and Greek antiquity, even though authors such as Euripides and Plutarch wrote sympathetic accounts of women, many of the ideas were strongly grounded in the Aristotelian idea that all humans are born with natural tendencies and emotions, and that no amount of education can change the basic characters to which men and women are predisposed. Even when women were shown to be embodying typically masculine emotions, this was done to mock them, and to show the absurdity of this non-conformity. In Aristophanes's *Lysistrata* (411 BCE), women aim to end the Peloponnesian War between the Greek city states by withholding sexual privileges from the men, the one thing they most desired. The text is seen as a subversive attempt to highlight the sexual dynamics during the time.[28] Although it's now performed as a protest play, at the time it wasn't feminist; even when women were showing agency and autonomy, it was considered so transgressive that it was seen as a comedic moment. In disrupting the norms, women became a subject of ridicule.

> LYSISTRATA: Calonice, it's more than I can bear,
> I am hot all over with blushes for our sex.
> Men say we're slippery rogues –
>
> CALONICE: And aren't they right?[29]

Women are caricatured to show intense emotions, and many of them reflect on how women would have been seen by men during that time. Broader social norms were still upheld, with women depicted as powerless during war while men were hailed as heroic. Men went out to protect their wives, and women did not participate in public life, even as they 'suffer it in more than double share', because 'first of all, bearing children and then sending them out as soldiers'.[30] As David Schaps, professor of classical studies at Bar-Ilan University writes: 'The women . . . sat on the sidelines as long as they were left alone.'[31] Even though Euripides subverts feminine stereotypes in the character of Lysistrata, she is different to other women, more 'masculine', and hence does not see herself as 'womanly'. As she says: 'Yes, I am a woman, but I have the ability to think / and I have pretty good judgment besides.'[32]

It begs the question as to why it was considered ridiculous and amusing when women tried to take up power in sex and relationships, when they showed interest in war and other public matters, when they showed emotions. These things were comedic for that time, and now seen as feminist because we all still believe that women do not have power in the real world, and that women's emotions, especially anger, are transgressive. So, although we interpret these historical texts from our vantage point as empowering, they are so relatable because these emotional stereotypes have persisted through the ages.

•

When the world was half a thousand years younger all events had much sharper outlines than now. The distance between sadness and joy, between good and bad fortune, seemed to be much greater than for us; every experience had that degree of directness and absoluteness that joy and sadness still have in the mind of a child.
— Johan Huizinga, *Autumntide of the Middle Ages*[33]

We know that power and agency are closely related, and these are also linked to influence. During medieval times, strong gender ideologies shaped the way authority was created, which emotions were deemed necessary, and which were allowed. But the study of historical resources has also to be understood within the framework of authority that men and women exerted. Most, if not all, sources that we have access to were written by men who had the power and privilege to write these records and document the times. So any references to emotions in those texts are through a male gaze. Even when sources don't explicitly refer to emotions, they can still tell us so much about how masculinity dominated the discourse.

Therefore, letters written by elite women of the medieval period are often a rich source of information about how women adapted the gendered codes, rituals and emotional expressions to access authority when it was not directly given to them. In the production of embroidered objects that had texts imbued with meaning, or through writing poems and letters, women could signal an assertion of power through their mediated emotional expressions. It was of course mostly men writing the major texts, but women – particularly elite, aristocratic women – were using the epistolary form, deploying the masculine forms of communication, to exert power and influence. Not many of these letters have survived. One such letter is from Aline la Despenser, Countess of Norfolk, sent to the Chancellor of England in around 1273. Women did not partake in official communication, so this was unusual. But Kathleen Neal from Monash University proposes that, while this letter was a masterclass in persuasion, using typical male rhetoric such as 'dear friendship', mostly only used between male associates, Aline had to disguise this and carefully stay close to the expected gender norms of appearing to be a decorous, obedient wife: a tight line to navigate.[34]

In embroidery, women were subverting the traditional notion of female docility by incorporating symbols and messages in their designs to process both positive and negative emotions. During this period, embroidery was not just for practical purposes but served a role in the performance of assigned femininity by virtuous upper-class women, fulfilling their role as dutiful and obedient wives and daughters. Most embroidery pattern books were authored by men, and in rejecting patterns (and sentiments) that were proposed by them, these women were exerting power and emotional authority, while treading the line between masculine authoritativeness and female passivity.[35] Many of the designs in embroidery and lace attributed to Mary, Queen of Scots, carried out in collaboration with Bess of Hardwick, reveal how she displayed her agency and emotions during her captivity, through subverting the designated patterns and in her use of colour to show grief and melancholy.

The medieval period in Europe, by comparison to the era of the Stoics, is seen as a period of veritable emotional incontinence. Johan Huizinga, in his history of medieval Europe, *Autumntide of the Middle Ages*, originally written in Dutch in 1919, claimed that 'Modern man has no idea of the unrestrained extravagance of the medieval heart.' Katherine Harvey from Birkbeck University writes that crying was ubiquitous, especially by religious men and women.[36] Curiously, the display of extreme emotions was accepted in religious women – 'mystics' – unlike their lay counterparts, because it was seen as a virtue and a sign of their devotion to God. Women were not allowed to engage in intellectual pursuits such as writing and interpreting religious texts, so they could only channel their religious fervour and closeness to God through their sensory experiences and through their bodies.

Even in war and defeat, women's public grief was seen, in classical times, as 'the city' being overtaken by pathos. There was a strict period of mourning for women, but it was only permitted if they were mourning their fathers and husbands. There also remained a difference between private and public emotions,[37] so that weeping in public even while praying was seen as insincere.[38]

In many of the texts from the period, men are seen weeping, especially bishops of the twelfth and thirteenth centuries during their religious devotions. Harvey mentions that bishops had to be seen to be crying, overcome at the intensity of their emotions for God, in order to be considered for canonisation. How could they be canonised if they weren't moved to tears by their devotion? There was a perceived link between tears and purity, and these texts show the bishops as having received the holy gift, because the ability to shed so many tears could only be granted by God. Tears were a sign of miracles and of the bishops' saintly nature. On the other hand, tears of self-pity were unacceptable. Saint-bishops were perceived differently to those who were not saints. For any form of emotion to be accepted, and their sincerity to be legitimised, it had to be accompanied by the right context and motivation, as well as appropriate behaviour. However, even as devotional tears were acceptable in some men and women, there were codes around crying too, and concerns about hypocrisy and inauthenticity. For instance, women's tears were still seen as a sign of manipulation; women were capable of setting a 'trap with their tears', for 'when a woman cries, she is striving to deceive her man'.[39]

Women and uneducated people and their uncultured ways of mourning were denigrated and worthy of contempt; while men, educated and civilised, grieved in a way that did not harm social cohesion or sensibilities. Men were not allowed to mourn for too long, especially men from the upper classes, where a strict code of morality and virtuous behaviour insisted on calm in the face of adversity. They had to take their mourning garment off eight days after the burial. The mourning garment was a ritualistic piece of clothing (sometimes jewellery or other accessory) worn through the ages in various cultures that made mourning visible.[40] Men's self-restraint was a matter of pride, and it was their duty to bear this pain.

Grief was a social emotion, and also a social obligation. Women were still held very much to Seneca's tenets, where there existed a fine line in these social-display rules, across which the same emotions could become irrational. While those who did not show any grief could be considered not pious or loyal enough (especially when a powerful man died), if they showed *too much* grief, they were labelled 'effeminate'.

The art historian Allison Levy writes that grief and mourning changed from 'ritual sound' to 'ritual silence', where women lost their role in mourning the dead, and were removed from the public sphere.[41] With the rise of Renaissance humanism, where the focus was on remembering the deceased, their wishes and achievements with dignity, rather than mourning their loss through tears, there was no place to express grief publicly. Women had to find other ways to mourn their loss. Many women from the upper classes wrote private consolatory letters, which give a useful record of their emotional experiences and the repressed nature of their existence. In the thirteenth century, Agnes of Assisi writes:

> I believed that there would be one death and life on earth with whom there is one conversation and life in heaven, and one burial would enclose those with whom there is one equal nature. But, as I see, I am deceived, I am anguished, I am abandoned, I am distressed on all sides. Oh my best sisters, grieve with me, I beg, lament with me, lest you sometime suffer such things and see that

there is no sorrow like my sorrow. This grief always tortures me, this weariness always twists me, this ardor always burns me. Because of this my anguish is everywhere and I do not know what I should do.[42]

These letters were probably dictated to scribes and only a few of them survive, which makes me wonder if most were seen as narratives of ordinary domesticity and hence not worth preserving for posterity. So much of our historical writing is dominated by men's words, and these few letters give us crucial insight into women's thoughts from that period.

Levy's research on widowhood in early modern societies also gives insight into how widows were seen in such patriarchal societies. Widowed women were perceived to be both sexually available and sexually experienced, so were difficult to categorise in the chaste and pious boxes that society had designed for women of the time. They were neither a virgin, under their father's control; nor a married woman, under the protection of their husband. At times, these women were even encouraged to behave 'like a man', be more aggressive to protect their children and property with no man to do it for them. But because they were not 'feminine' enough, they threatened men, notions of masculinity and the gender hierarchy. Even in widowhood, women were supposed to allay the masculine anxieties around their presence and the ambiguity of their status, because of course they stepped outside the traditional notions of acceptable femininity. They were also a threat to women, as someone to whom some of these rules did not apply, and could be seen as a sexual competitor and threat.

The portrait *Mrs Jane Cartwright*, now in Dulwich Art Gallery, was painted by John Greenhill in the 1660s, as commissioned by her husband, William Cartwright, dressed as a widow in black with a veil over her head – even though her husband was not yet dead. Jane died before her husband, but widowhood was imposed on her by her husband during their lifetimes. Historians and art critics such as Nigel Llewellyn have suggested that the portrait is not reflective of her emotional state, but his.[43] There was a sense of heightened masculine anxiety around this time associated with their place in the world, as women's rights movements were beginning to take root, and there was a simmering fear as to whether their status at the top of the hierarchy was secure or not. There was also a fear of being forgotten. This made Cartwright impose a desexualised image on his wife even before his death, recorded in his inventory as 'my last wifes pictur with a blacke vaile on her head'.[44] It was women's sexuality that undermined men's authority. It is this sexuality that was stigmatised in the way emotion codes were imposed, so that they had to adhere closely to values of chastity and purity. When the mourning rituals and laments, and women's dramatic displays of grief, were disrupted, it ruptured the power held by men in some ways, because women were not following the emotional codes and display rules prescribed for them. A woman that does not align with femininity threatens the foundations of masculine–feminine duality that gender hierarchies are built upon. As women's mourning was curtailed, men had to take on this role, and any aggressive form of grief, especially if done publicly, was seen as effeminate and threatened the cultural constructions of manhood.

•

During the Renaissance period, between the fourteenth and seventeenth centuries, all forms of public and domestic authority continued to be vested in men. Similar to the previous centuries, and particularly with the revival of Platonic beliefs, men were considered to be rational, and women driven by their passions. Men were bestowed with all capabilities of the mind: wit, intelligence, judgement, while women were seen to provide a balance to their intellectual proficiencies with their physical beauty. Women were supposed to epitomise passivity and obedience, and the feminine qualities of chastity, modesty, humility, patience, constancy and kindness. The social codes in Europe during this time prescribed that women should not be too clever or witty or speak up and argue. They were supposed to be looked at and admired for their physical beauty alone, and any kind of intense emotional expression was supposed to detract from their beauty. At the same time, they had to be virtuous and pious, and abstain from any sexual desires (besides that for her husband).

Women could not perform roles in public and political service (even though we see examples of royal women, such as Queen Elizabeth, who stepped out of these traditionally feminine roles). But the concept of moral virtue remained significant in determining the gender roles, and it would have been a scandal if women stepped out of their moral codes. In Elizabethan England in the latter half of the sixteenth century, married women had little independence and few rights. They had to exercise emotional control so that they could use their minds 'to the best of their abilities' and avoid any sort of foolishness.[45] Carroll Camden, an eminent Renaissance scholar, writes in his book *The Elizabethan Woman* that 'The beauty of woman is more praised and esteemed than any other beauty . . . [for] it appears to be the order of nature that what is lacking in one sex is supplied in the other, and since man is endowed with wit, judgement, and a mind almost divine . . . woman is given bodily beauty that she may be superior to man in this respect, and the only positive demand of the woman was that she should be beautiful'.[46] The American scholar Catherine Dunn confirms that for a woman during the period: 'Her behavior was carefully prescribed. She was to tend to her household duties industriously . . . she must be silent most of the time and not speak out or argue . . . [and] she must never be witty or clever.'[47] Women were trained to be obedient and docile, never speak out or express themselves. Those women who stepped out of patriarchal control, in either countering their husband or publicly voicing their dissent, were punished.

Mary Dyer was a member of the puritanical community in England which taught a strict moral code. She emigrated to Massachusetts in 1635, and gradually, under the influence of Anne Hutchinson, the defendant in the most famous of the trials aimed at suppressing religious dissent in the Massachusetts Bay Colony, she began practising the Antinomian ideas that salvation could be achieved by faith alone.[48] This was seen as a rejection of the religious puritanical ideas of the time that claimed that salvation could only be achieved by good actions and moral virtue. Anne Hutchinson had been tried and banished for rejecting the religious orthodoxy, and for her central role in the Antinomian movement, because she was seen to be stepping outside the gender roles prescribed for women, and for being too outspoken in her views. Mary Dyer had become a Quaker, and this was also seen as a direct rejection of the religious powers of the State that women were supposed to uphold, and she was executed for heresy in Massachusetts in 1660. Her husband had petitioned for her to be spared because she was mad.[49] Insanity was preferable to a wife who was outspoken.

Women in the Renaissance period were legally powerless too, particularly if they were married, and men in their lives held all constitutional power: women couldn't own, buy or sell property, act as witnesses or make wills. Many of the historical accounts from that period specify that women were the property of men and family (fathers, husbands and then their male children), and these beliefs trickled down from the highest classes in society to the lowest. Intellectually, women were considered to be quite limited, and they internalised this belief, that even if they were taught the same material, they would be incapable of learning it because of their inherent cerebral weakness. The literacy rate in Elizabethan England remained low for both men (30 per cent) and women (10 per cent),[50] despite the fact that religious texts were becoming more accessible to lower-class women, and women in general were encouraged to read the Bible in their homes for their personal introspection.

Jean Jacques Rousseau's *Emile (or, On Education)* from 1762 was an influential book that outlined the social and political order in western society, whereby women were to be confined to the private and domestic world, and there had to be a separation of the private and the public sphere.[51] He justified his beliefs by citing what he claimed were the physical, moral and emotional characteristics of women. Rousseau says: 'Sedentary indoor employments, which make the body tender and effeminate, are neither pleasing nor suitable. No lad ever wanted to be a tailor. It takes some art to attract a man to this woman's work. The same hand cannot hold the needle and the sword. If I were king I would only allow needlework and dress-making to be done by women and cripples who are obliged to work at such trades.' In another part of the book, Rousseau despairs of women who engage with literature: 'When women are what they ought to be, they will keep to what they can understand, and their judgment will be right; but since they have set themselves up as judges of literature, since they have begun to criticise books and to make them with might and main, they are altogether astray.'

Since there was a general consensus that the two sexes were inherently different, it was naturally accepted that they would harness and experience different emotions too, i.e., emotions were related closely to physiology.[52] Nicolas Malebranche, seventeenth-century French Oratorian priest and rationalist philosopher, acknowledged that there were many differences in the emotions of people according to their 'different stations in life'.[53] Some philosophers of the time suggested that these variations were because of differences in bodily compositions. Marin Cureau de La Chambre was a physician who advised and treated two French kings, Louis XIII and Louis XIV, in the early 1600s. In his most famous work, *Les Charactères des passions*, published 1640–62, he wanted to 'examine the passions, virtues and vices' and 'inclinations, temperaments and traits' of people.[54] There existed at the time a culture of divinatory superstitions, in which certain behavioural characteristics were associated with physical characteristics (metoposcopy). La Chambre refuted the idea that emotions could be read in the wrinkles of the face or in the pointedness of the nose. Instead, he proposed that individual behaviours and emotions were better reflections of our thoughts, and these were different depending on specific situations.

Like many philosophers and scientists of the time, La Chambre also tried to combine science and medical thinking with faith, and although he strongly rejected divinatory practices, he was a proponent of Aristotelian beliefs about the four temperaments in the human body. Much like Hippocrates before him, Aristotle had believed in liquid 'humours' in our bodies, essential to our survival, which determined our varying emotions and personalities. Hippocrates had proposed that our body fluids (or humours) were composed of different amounts of blood (warm and wet); phlegm (cold and wet); yellow bile (warm and dry); and black bile (cold and dry).[55] It was the composition of these four that constituted how warm or cold our bodies were, and an imbalance would cause disease.[56] La Chambre also discussed how humours in the brain could have a temperamental effect, and this explained why women, whose bodies were believed to be colder, moister, clammier, were more emotional. Women started life with lower temperature, colder in temper, and this persisted over their lives, although some older (and melancholic men) could be equally cold too. This view had held since early antiquity, when women were considered an imperfect copy of men. As Aristotle announced: 'Females are weaker and colder in nature, and we must look upon the female character as being a sort of natural deficiency.'[57] Aristotle's main proposition was that heat was the matter that determined the development of animals: the more heat an animal had, the more advanced it was.[58] Since women were considered inferior to men, it was naturally assumed that they would have a lower temperature. And so, women came to be associated with coldness and clamminess, and because of this, smaller and weaker than men.

Carroll Camden also writes that there was a widespread belief amongst scientists that 'It is heat which makes a man bold and hardy . . . but the coldness of woman makes her naturally fearful and timorous. And since women are weak physically, they must be weak morally and mentally.'[59] Consciousness and cognitive awareness were linked to temperature so there was thought to be a strong correlation between heat, gender and conceptions of agency.[60] Men were considered to be naturally hotter and drier than women, and so had a different temperament. Rationality was less cold and humid than irrationality, and waking consciousness was warmer and drier than sleep. Rationality belonged to men, irrationality to women. Activity to men, and passivity to women. Women were colder, melancholic, phlegmatic compared to men. And inherently more emotional.

Helkiah Crooke, court physician to King James I of England, wrote *Mikrokosmographia: Description of the Body of Man* in 1615, an extensive work explaining that to maintain the order of all nature, men had to be hotter because their bodies had to bear the weight of toil and labour, of work and decisions, and his mind had to be stout to withstand dangers.[61] A woman, on the other hand, would be driven 'out of her little wits' if she had to withstand the same heat. Men's bodies could withstand their temper, while women could not. Crooke insists that there is a difference between the wrath of a 'stout-hearted man', and the anger of women and other 'weak' minds: 'Anger is a disease of a weake mind which cannot moderate it selfe but is easily inflamed, such as in women, children, and weake and cowardly men, and this we tearme fretfulness or pettishness: but Wrath which is Ina permanens belongs to stout hearts.'

•

Through the sixteenth to eighteenth centuries, sentimentalism was on the rise, in writing and in art, where human sentiments were considered to underlie any moral evaluation, and aesthetic theory was also grounded in this gendered nature of emotions. Edmund Burke, the Irish political thinker and philosopher, wrote *A Philosophical Enquiry into the Origin of Our Ideas of the Sublime and Beautiful* in 1756. Burke, and fellow philosopher Immanuel Kant, believed that the beautiful was something that we desired and loved (but was weaker) and the sublime was something that had the power to destroy us but was worthy of our admiration (and was stronger). In this framework, feminine beauty was contrasted with masculine sublime, where the latter was much preferable. The boundless feminine imagination had to be regulated and controlled by the more orderly and rational masculine sublime. As Burke said: 'In the female sex, [beauty] almost always carries with it an idea of weakness and imperfection. Women are very sensible of this; for which reason, they learn to lisp, to totter in their walk, to counterfeit weakness and imperfection, and even sickness. In all they are guided by nature. Beauty in distress is much the most affecting beauty.'[62]

Clearly, much of what was being written was to justify the hierarchical relations between men and women. The cold temperature of women meant they should not be allowed the same emotional and behavioural privileges and sanctions as were allowed to men. Even when Crooke acknowledges that men's and women's anger arose from the same event or situation, the difference in their supposed biological origin meant that women's tempers were not easily controlled. Heat was a necessary condition to sustaining life, and so men, with their supposed warmer physiology, were essential to society, and biologically deemed superior.

To Rousseau, women were naturally passive and weak, and their modesty and sense of shame justified their oppression by the strong (men). Even when women were associated with beauty, they had to be weaker, fragile, small and soft to be seen as beautiful and pleasurable. In being beautiful, they could be loved but not admired. They were passive objects of beauty, imperfect in their nature, to be admired and suppressed by men, who were stronger and perfect. Women were also expected to satisfy the sexual desires of their husbands because in having sex, it was widely believed that women were made perfect as they then absorbed the longed-for 'heat of the male seed'.[63] Meanwhile, in this act, the man was made imperfect, because, in the words of Aristotle, 'it is the nature of cold to desire, and draw'.[64] And so, women were perceived to be all-taking – being giving wasn't seen as in their biology or temperament. This seems paradoxical because even as women were supposed to be caring and nurturing, to moderate their emotional expressions to be of value to their husbands and agreeable to God and society, it was not seen as an act of benevolence or generosity. It was merely expected of women due to their normative gender role and their temperament.

Women internalised these rules and expectations too. Addressing the troops at Tilbury during the Spanish Armada, Queen Elizabeth said: 'I know I have the bodie but of a weak and feeble woman, but I have the heart and Stomach of a King, and of a King of England too.'[65] In the process, she evokes the theory of temperaments which stated the inherent physiological differences between men and women, and the forced materialisation of an innate physical inferiority of women.

Similar gender norms applied in Italian cities during the Renaissance period. The Renaissance was a time of order and structure in most of Europe, but especially in Italy, and the social order was so arranged as to place men and women into two separate camps through clearly demarcated hierarchies and norms. Even though women outside the capital city of Florence, where societal codes were enforced more rigidly, could exercise their right to hold formal positions, there was always a fear of them becoming too powerful, and any such women were subject to intense criticism and gossip to undermine their status and authority. Humanism was on the rise, especially in Italy, as a response to the darker medieval times. The movement determined to revive the legacy of classical antiquity for a more engaging civic life, proposing that going back to Greek and Latin classics was all one needed to lead a moral and ethical life. A small group of liberal elites – mostly men – wanted to imbue the ruling class with the virtues of the classical period. There was a strong revived interest in Platonism, and attitudes grounded in a hierarchical structure of the universe. Strict gender roles and emotional codes were imposed, both formally and informally. Women had to be kept hidden away as prized possessions, responsible for safeguarding families' honour − and their own. During this time, the Catholic Church was dominant, the story of Eve and original sin percolated through the broader consciousness, and women were seen as responsible for men's fall.

The Book of the Courtier (*c.*1507), written by Baldassare Castiglione, Count of Castico, and member of the court of the Duke of Urbino, reported on conversations between court members on the attributes of an ideal courtier or lady of the court, and was translated and distributed widely across Europe, shaping many societal attitudes. The book was on the Vatican's index of 'Forbidden Books' for over 400 years because of some of the views on gender equality, which were considered controversial. One of the courtiers, Gaspare Pallavicino, says: 'Women are unperfect creatures, and consequently of less dignity than men.'[66] Women were classified as mistakes since nature (or God) always plans and aims an absolute perfection. When a woman is born, this was seen to be a mistake or defect, and contrary to nature's wishes. However, Castiglione challenged this and wrote: 'I say that everything men can understand, women can too, and where a man's intellect can penetrate, so along with it, can a woman's.'

Thus he questioned the commonly held view that men were far more intelligent than women. But at the same time, while proposing that men and women matched each other in intellectual ability, Castiglione warned women not to do 'masculine' things such as wrestle and play tennis. Women had to remain 'feminine' to be attractive and desirable. The duality of masculine and feminine ideals remained strongly entrenched, and while Castiglione's view was that women could be educated, they had to remain graceful, agreeable, charming, while also trying to be witty, good company, and spirited (but not too much). Many of the plays from the time, such as those by William Shakespeare that document lives in Italian cities, show women embodying these values, traversing these very thin lines between having the right sort of feminine expressions and behaviours, but not crossing over to any behaviours that would be considered inappropriate or masculine. Men, by contrast, are hot-blooded and passionate, conforming to an idealised masculinity. Jonathan Shandell, professor of theatre arts, classifies these masculine types of the period into five categories: the Chivalrous Knight, the Herculean Hero, the Humanist Man or Moderation, the Merchant Prince and the Saucy Jack.[67] Even though Shakespeare challenges some of the hegemonies with transgressive 'feminine' men and 'masculinised' women, with characters such as Desdemona showing that women could have better control over their emotions than some of the men, there are stereotypical gender roles and underlying themes of misogyny in his work. There is cautious progress in terms of gender equality, but one and a bit steps forward, and one step back.[68]

The ways in which emotion and gender were interconnected can also be interpreted from the art of that time. The idealised beauty of women was linked directly to their virtue and grace, and specific ideas of femininity. Florentine poet Agnolo Firenzuola, who lived between 1493 and 1548, said: 'The hair must be long and fair, of a soft yellow turning brown, the skin light and clear, but not pale: the eyes dark brown, large and somewhat vaulted, their sclera shimmering blue. The nose ought not be curved, as aquiline noses do not suit women; the mouth should be small, the lips round, the chin round with a dimple, the neck rounded and fairly long, the Adam's apple not protruding.'[69]

Shearer West, academic and art historian, argues that we cannot analyse art, especially portraiture, without considering gender politics.[70] Gender roles around the time were strictly grounded in male domination and female dependency. The portraits during these times showed men with wealth and political roles while the emphasis in women's portraits was on their beauty.[71] Women were also painted in more passive profile views, restrained and controlled. The art historian Patricia Simons, examining some of these paintings, shows that women only moved out of the profile position in the late 1400s, but even then, women were framed in windows, as if their view of the world was narrow and limited.[72] Such paintings tend 'to be views of women both older and less ostentatiously dressed than their female predecessors had been'. In this society, women's virtue and chastity were her most valued possessions, and lowered, averted eyes indicated her deference − an immodest woman looked straight at men in the street − and her fitness to be a good wife and mother. These portraits therefore show noble women as passive and passionless, gaze lowered, but aimed at evoking passion in the spectator. As the poet Robert Browning says in his poem 'A Face', the woman is reduced to the beauty of her face in profile:

> If one could have that little head of hers
> Painted upon a background of pale gold,
> Such as the Tuscan's early art prefers!
> No shade encroaching on the matchless mould
> Of those two lips, which should be opening soft
> In the pure profile; not as when she laughs,
> For that spoils all: but rather as if aloft
>
> . . .

•

Titian, one of the most prominent Italian Renaissance artists, was commissioned to paint portraits of Francesco Maria della Rovere, Duke of Urbino, and his wife, Eleanora Gonzaga in 1536. These two portraits, done at the same time, sitting alongside each other, give us clues to how men and women were seen, and what their emotional attributes were. While Francesco's portrait is rugged and 'emphasises his military exploits' with his glinting armour and shining helmet, his pose vibrant and active, Eleanora's by contrast emphasises gentleness and poise. In her case, the face does not really tell a story, as was the case with many of the portraits of women from this period. Women were not supposed to have a personal story to tell.[73]

Even though the broader view was that a painter's brush is phallic and not suitable for women, a number of women, such as Sofonisba Anguissola (1532–1625) and Lavinia Fontana (1552–1614), managed to break the mould to become artists, and trained other women. Many of them were mobilising their pain, trauma and experiences of violence to create artworks as a means of demanding justice, including Artemisia Gentileschi (1593–1653), who justifiably has received much attention recently. Gentileschi was raped violently at the age of seventeen by another artist and had to undergo a traumatic trial to prove her ordeal, including an excruciating physical examination and 'sibille', where cords were wrapped around Artemisia's fingers and pulled tighter and tighter together, eventually crushing them. Her 400-page testimony is still held in the State Archives in Rome. Her painting *Judith Beheading Holofernes* shows the biblical Judith along with her maidservant beheading the invading general Holofernes.[74] A contrast with Caravaggio's rendition of the same scene in 1599 shows us the difference between how women and men interpreted women's emotions. While Caravaggio's painting shows the horror on Holofernes's face, Judith's face is rather detached and passively looking away from all the blood, as if even in this act she has no anger or agency. Gentileschi's Judith is instead determined and engaged, active in this act of revenge. Vengeance was not a 'feminine' trait, and something that women of the time were advised against. These women artists made women their central characters, drawing from classical myths and literature, shedding light on the women who had been made invisible, or relegated to dark corners of history as mere victims. Their art tells us a lot about women's emotional repression during the time, showing emotions such as rage that women of their standing were not supposed to show in public spheres.

Men had power and control over their honour, and could seize it back, by rage and revenge, while women had no power over their own honour, and could never restore it themselves once it was taken away.[75] They would be labelled a 'fallen woman' for ever. These paintings pulsate with repressed desire and rage and subvert the classic social narrative of women being passive and having no agency. Women are shown in dominant roles, with muscular physiques, disrupting ideas of women's bodies being merely objects of sexual desire and sites of reproduction by showing them as weapons of destruction.

Women's anger would, however, count against them; it was seen to be more enduring and premeditated, and hence they often preferred to speak (and write) about anguish and despair instead. In Renaissance Italy, the feeling of being powerless was palpable in many of the letters that women wrote. As in earlier periods, women were often limited to exercising their agency and emotional freedom in the form of letters. In *A Corresponding Renaissance: Letters Written by Italian Women, 1375–1650*, Lisa Kaborycha includes fifty-five letters by women of different social status showing them trying to claim cultural currency, enter the public sphere and assert some power through these correspondences. While women were mostly educated, especially in the upper classes, and eloquent and persuasive, their positions outside the home were not considered legitimate, and their education was mainly to make them a good marriage prospect. Their gender restricted them from learning about anatomy and human form because of their inherent sensitive disposition. Writing these letters was also their way of exercising and expressing the emotions they were otherwise not permitted to express freely and openly. One letter of Lucrezia de Medici shows how she felt trapped in the roles that she was expected to play. Lucrezia was the older sister of Lorenzo de Medici, one of the most powerful Italian statesmen of the time, best known for his patronage of artists such as Botticelli and Michelangelo. She was married off at the age of thirteen for a large dowry and brought to her husband's house five years later. In one of her letters she says: 'Don't be born a woman if you want your own way.'[76] A few words that say so much.

•

In the London *Times* of 15 April 1737, an article titled 'Young Emotional Woman Caught in Scandalous Situation' details a scene where a young woman, 'Miss Roxana', was caught kneeling in front of her married lover 'begging for his affection' and promising to devote herself to him 'with greatest zeal'. She was arrested for misdemeanour and in the ensuing trial it was concluded that Roxana was suffering from a 'fit of passion' or hysteria due to excessive sexual desire. These 'excessive emotions' had led to the lack of submissiveness expected of women. This lack of docility was the cause of her shame.

Around this time, such incidents were rising, possibly as a way for women to rebel against the strict moral codes imposed on them.

Literacy levels were rising and more ideas of women's liberation were spreading across Europe and America, and there was a cry for more independence for women from some quarters. Women such as Mary Astell (1666–1731) and Mary Wollstonecraft (1759–1797) were writing about women's education and independence, arguing that women's reasoning powers were as strong as men's. In *A Vindication of the Rights of Women*, Wollstonecraft highlights the role that masculine society played in forcing women to become 'creatures of their emotions' because the patriarchy did not allow them to develop their intellects. She writes: 'Their senses are inflamed, and their understandings neglected, consequently they become the prey of their senses, delicately termed sensibility, and are blown about by every momentary gust of feeling.' This seems like a turning point, where we see a slow shift and eagerness to address these emotional imbalances, to recognise and acknowledge that women's emotionality might not be as innate as society had always made it out to be, but in fact even brought on by society.

As a result, there was also a rise in so-called 'conduct books'. These were written mostly by men, and primarily targeted young women, detailing extensive codes of expression and behaviour that would make them attractive for marriage. These conduct books were a backlash aimed at keeping women from becoming too independent, and destabilising the social structures. In one such book, *A Letter of Genteel and Moral Advice to a Young Lady* (1746), Reverend Wetenhall Wilkes wrote a set of directions, including the following: 'Honest pleasures are not inconsistent with true modesty, but an affected air of coyness and gravity is always suspected. When a young lady is praised for her merit, good mien or beauty, she should not reject such recommendations, with an angry look, or a scornful disdain, but receive it with ease and civility, if it is obligingly offered.'[77]

'Mien' here implies a person's appearance or manner, especially as an indication of their character or mood. Women were also advised by Wilkes to 'condescend to their weakness and infirmities, to cover their frailties, to encourage their virtues, to relieve their wants, to compassionate their distress, to forgive their malice, to forget their injuries, to do good to the slanderer, never be angry at a friend, not revengeful to an enemy'. In essence, women had to display their emotions in a way that appeased others, and they were taught not only how to act but also how to react to certain situations with moderate emotions. Anger was particularly harmful to women as it could 'get the better of your reaction, for by it, the external parts are not only deformed, but the whole frame of the internal consti- tution is disordered.'[78]

Between 1734 and 1808 the first German-language encyclopae- dias were published in 68 volumes and with more than 280,000 entries. In the sixty-third volume was a 35-page article on rage (Zorn). Much of it was dedicated to the rage of God, but about 30 per cent discussed the rage of man. While these entries weren't explicitly about men or women, the descriptions always alluded to men, because rage was associated with protecting one's honour and if a man did not react with suitable rage when insulted, then his masculinity was suspect. And therefore rage was considered a 'manly, vigorous feeling'.[79] Ute Frevert, a German historian at the Max Planck Institute for Human Development, describes this rage as an effect, something that empowers people and 'fills them with vigour'.[80] In an emotion, there is a more prominent displacement in internal and external organs and muscles, so that it is always accompanied by some expressive movements.[81] Psychologists call anger a 'sthenic' emotion (from stenos, meaning strong), one that can be highly mobilising, giving strength to a person; a rapid emotion where the expressions happen rather quickly. By contrast, the asthenic emotions are those that tend to weaken people's spirit and resources.[82] These are also sluggish emotions, such as sadness, melancholy and discontent (and so associated with women, who were colder, wetter and less energetic in constitution). The sthenic emotions through history were believed to be unavailable to the feeble and weak-minded, who were not able to make decisions for themselves. Women fell into this particular category. Women's nature made them prone to uninhibited lust and desire, attuned to empathy, soft and therefore easily mouldable in an image that was expected of them. While men could feel stronger emotions, they could temper them more easily too as they had reason and rationality, and a stronger will. Women on the other hand were a slave to their emotions and therefore it was advisable that they refrained from engaging in pursuits that could fray their nerves. Women were also seen as more fickle, moving very quickly from one emotion to another, and hence their emotions and feelings were never reliable nor to be taken seriously, as they were completely capricious in nature.

•

The prominent Scottish Enlightenment philosopher and historian David Hume discussed emotions at length during this period in his *Treatise of Human Nature* (1739). He groups them as perceptions of the mind but affecting behaviours and reasoning.[83] One of his significant propositions was that passions (a word he uses interchangeably with emotions) were the drivers for all our actions because without them we would not have any reason to act: 'reason is, and ought only to be the slave of the passions'.[84] Even though Hume challenged the obligation placed on women to preserve their chastity, he examined it from his view that the inflexibility and universality of societal norms did not serve any purpose, since they could not be applied to all women equally in all contexts. Although Hume does not address the differences between men and women directly, he does fall back on some of these stereotypes in his writing. In expressing gallantry towards women, he indicates that this is an indication of their inferiority: 'As nature has given man the superiority above woman, by endowing him with greater strength both of mind and body; it is his part to alleviate that superiority, as much as possible, by the generosity of his behaviour.'[85] This assumed gallantry, the idea that men had to be generous in their behaviour towards women, also indicates the presumed inferiority of women. His views on the innate natural inferiority of women, who were slaves to their natural passions, is a subversive form of bigotry too, merely disguised as a heroic attempt to free women from their second-class status in society. Women did not deserve equal treatment because their opinions mattered or because they were as intelligent as men, but because through their graciousness, a man could further confirm his superiority over women and justify the system of power within which such behaviours were constructed and assumed. His politeness and courtesy towards women is aimed at exerting his authority (and that of all men). Just in a more generous manner than most. Protective paternalism can be used to rationalise power differences between men and women in a more subversive manner and is deployed to maintain the gender hierarchies. When men's desire to show their support for women comes from a place of misguided gallantry rather than a genuine belief in equality, it is termed benevolent sexism.

While hostile sexism is explicit prejudice towards women, benevolent sexism appears to be supportive and positive but emphasises the feminine stereotypes, such as nurturing or maternal, or deserving of protection because of inherent weakness. Hume also justifies the prejudice against women as natural and not a sign of bigotry, and his list of feminine traits include: bashfulness, timidity, exaggerated affectionate nature; all signs of womanly weaknesses. The philosopher Christine Battersby, in her searing enquiry of the Humean woman, shows that while addressing the women, Hume adopts a 'sugary tone' to pay his respects, and that even his apparent support for women was 'patronising, offering advice, criticism, flattery'.[86] Women did not have any real power or agency, and the only agency that was generously afforded to them (by men) was in order to make men look better and more refined, to show that they did not believe in the archaic gendered rules of the dark ages.

We have seen through the previous discussion of emotionality in the classical period and antiquity that it was firmly established that there were some good emotions and some bad emotions. There were emotions deemed acceptable for some people based on their gender in certain circumstances but not in others, and then there were emotions that were acceptable to a certain degree, but if over-indulged in were deemed inappropriate or irrational. There was also a clear demarcation between private and public spaces, behaviours that were appropriate in one or the other, and therefore seen as private and public emotions. Emotional-display norms were set to uphold virtue. The desire to set men and women as polar opposites drove much of this gendered regime of emotions.

And even though we see a tiny shift in attitudes during the eighteenth century, the age of Enlightenment, with some women speaking out against these traditional notions, society once again began to venerate the stereotypically 'feminine' behaviours, such as generosity, warmth and kindness. The beliefs that women were trapped by their biology and innate emotionality, while men had the intellectual ability and rationality to rise above their biology became more ingrained. There is a broader assumption that during this period, women's status and position had a decisive break from the medieval past. However, as the prominent American historian Joan Kelly asked rather dejectedly and provocatively way back in 1976: 'Did women have a renaissance?'[87] And, when she replies 'no', we get a sense of how difficult it was for women to gain emotional agency, and how gender roles were still stuck in the dark, even in the age of Enlightenment.

6.

STATE OF HYSTERIA

WHILE THE HIERARCHICAL GENDER NORMS meant that women's minds were considered inferior and subject to the whims of their turbulent emotions, it was also considered that their bodies were just as frail and susceptible to their emotionalities. During medieval and Renaissance times, women's emotional states and their nervous disposition were perceived to be at the root of many of their physical ailments. The term 'hysteria' comes from the Greek word hysterikos meaning 'from the womb'. The legendary Melampus, a renowned mystic and healer, and cousin of Jason (of Jason and the Argonauts), linked women's madness and emotional outbursts to a lack of normal sex life in single, unmarried, sterile women and widows in particular. The lack of orgasms would lead to melancholy. When the young women of Argos (including the king's three daughters) rejected marriage, the gods punished them and caused madness. The women fled to the mountains, and their rebellion was seen as a sign of madness spurred on by 'uterine melancholy', a sadness of the uterus.[1] Unmarried women and widows – those assumed not to have a regular sex life – were seen as more likely to experience anxiety and hysterical outbursts: not only was women's value associated with marriage and domesticity, but their emotionality was also linked to their marital status. The treatment offered to women for this condition was to participate in orgies and have sex with young men.

Hippocrates, one of the most well-known Greek physicians of the classical period, and Plato talked about hysteria, and other ancient philosophers such as Aristotle, Galen and Euripides believed the uterus moved about in the body, colliding with other organs and causing a range of maladies in women. It was what made women different to men: a mystery, a conundrum, a peculiarity. It was a female malaise; their delicate disposition led to intense emotions, resulting in madness, anxiety, depression and even infertility. And on that premise alone, men were exempt from being hysterical.

In the late second century, one of the most renowned Greek physicians, Aretaeus of Cappadocia, spoke of the womb as 'an animal within an animal', an organ that 'moved of itself hither and thither in the flanks'.[2] In her 1965 collection of essays based on her lectures at St Bartholomew's medical school, Ilza Veith first explained how the word 'hysterical' came about in the Hippocratic treatises.[3] These treatises had long been considered a canonical text for medical ailments by physicians but have since been revealed as a mix of multi-authored texts based in flawed understanding of human bodies, particularly the female body. They use hysteria as a broad term for all sorts of female ailments (and non-ailments) arising from the movement of the uterus (hysteron).[4] The Hippocratic concept of hysterical behaviour in women spread out from Greece and Rome during the Middle Ages and became more of a permanent entity. The dualism persisted. Male bodies were considered to be warm and dry, signifying perfection. Female bodies, even though with the same organs and constitution as men, were different.[5]

Women were widely recognised as more vulnerable than men, inferior because of their physiological differences. However, these anatomical differences were also extended to more theological differences to reinforce the Aristotelian theories of male superiority. St Thomas Aquinas, the most well-known theologian of the Middle Ages, wrote in the mid-1220s in his influential work *Summa Theologica*, 'Woman is a failed man.'[6] Beliefs such as this persisted through the Renaissance and modern developments in medicine. Eighteenth-century French physician Joseph Raulin wrote in *Traité des affections vaporeuses* that although hysteria could affect both sexes, women are lazy and irritable, affected by their 'vapours' and therefore more susceptible. Women were also seen as closer to nature, more instinctive, and not capable of thought and reason that could enable men to 'transcend the body through thought, will and judgement'.[7]

The belief that women's physiology and intense emotional sensitivity were responsible for hysteria continued during the Middle Ages, and there was more interest in finding neurological and medical reasons for it. There were even a handful of notable women physicians who attempted to examine hysteria independently from the gender politics and prejudices of the time.[8] Trotula de' Ruggiero from eleventh-century Salerno is considered the first female doctor in Christian Europe, one of the 'ladies' of the medical school of Salerno.[9] She recognised in her most famous work, *De passionibus mulierum ante, in et post partum*, that women were more vulnerable than men to gender stereotyping, even though she was quite faithful to the teachings of Hippocrates, and believed abstinence to be the cause of many ills in women. During this time, women's intense emotions were also linked to demonic influences, and hysterical women could also be subjected to exorcisms. Hildegard of Bingen, in the early 1100s was another female physician who believed that melancholy and hysteria were defects of the soul and originated from evil, although she also attempted to balance out the gender imbalance by asserting that both Adam and Eve shared equal responsibility for original sin, and that men and women were equal in front of God.[10] Even though these women had claimed some power and status, they were operating in a typically masculine domain, and so their views were not independent of the culture and gender discourse that they were embedded in.

•

In the British Library is a little book, *A briefe discourse of a disease called the Suffocation of the Mother*, written in 1603, and believed to be the first English work on hysteria. It was written by Edward Jorden, a physician who gave testimony at the trial of Elizabeth Jackson in 1602. Jackson was accused of being a witch. Jorden had argued against the supernatural allegation, instead suggesting that Jackson was suffering from a natural disease called 'Passio Hysterica', or the 'Suffocation of the Mother', the word 'mother' here used to mean all women with a womb or a uterus, as motherhood was considered the natural destiny of women. Much of Jorden's philosophy was rooted in the Hippocratic tradition where the womb was assumed to move around the body, and lack of sexual activity created a 'congestion of humours' resulting in 'monstrous' symptoms such as 'suffocation in the throat, croaking of Frogges, hissing of Snakes . . . frenzies, convulsions, hickcockes, laughing, singing, weeping, crying.'[11] The women were also compared to cold-blooded species, slow and lethargic, prone to 'syncope or swounding'* and Jorden

---

* 'Syncope' literally means that the sound is coming from a distance; 'swounding' is fainting.

comparing the awakening of hysterical, fainted women to a snake emerging from hibernation: 'All the faculties of the body fayling, it self lying like a dead corpse three or foure hours together . . . without sense, motion, breath, heate, or any signe of life at all (like as wee see Snakes and other creatures to lie all the winter, as if they are dead, under the earth).'[12]

Even though Jorden stood up to defend women against accusations of witchcraft, he also characterised them as victims of their own failing bodies. He was ultimately unsuccessful: Jackson was hanged for being a witch.

In 1681, Thomas Sydenham, an English physician, wrote, 'Women, except for those who lead a hardy and robust life, are rarely quite free from hysteria.'[13] By the time Sydenham was writing, hysteria had long been considered an immutable fact, something inherently linked with the notion of femininity, and always construed as a 'woman's disease', stemming from the innate weakness in women's nature. Even as the Middle Ages came to an end and the Renaissance period began, with medical explanations emerging, there were some physicians who proposed that hysteria was a neurological ailment rather than a physical one, and it continued to be associated with an excess of emotionality.

Many physicians during the seventeenth and eighteenth centuries believed that hysterical behaviours presented as unattractive, noisy, emotional displays. The English physician William Harvey wrote in 1651: 'How dreadful, then, are the mental aberrations, the delirium, the melancholy, the paroxysms of frenzy, as if the affected person were under the domination of spells, and all arising from unnatural states of the uterus.'[14] Historians such as Mark Micale, Emeritus professor at University of Illinois Urbana-Champagne, argue that the symptoms of hysteria – the histrionics – became a 'caricature

of femininity',[15] developed under the cultural forces of male domination that pushed women into trying to adopt behaviours and
emotional expressions that were deemed more attractively feminine
so as to avoid being labelled 'hysterical'. It was grounded in sex-based
biological determinism, that there were inherent differences between
male and female natures, and in turn reinforced the duality of the
masculine/feminine emotions in the broader psyche.

Renowned German philosopher Georg Wilhelm Friedrich Hegel,
in his *Grundlinien der philosophie des rechts* (*The Philosophy of Right*,
1820), supports a view of the female mind as mystical and unreliable,
saying:'The difference between men and women is like that between
animals and plants. Men correspond to animals, while women correspond to plants because their development is more placid and the
principle that underlines it is the rather vague unity of feeling . . .
Women are educated – who knows how? – as it were by breathing
in ideas, by living rather than acquiring knowledge.'[16]

While Hegel argued that sensibilities or emotions should not be
seen in contrast to rationality, he could not escape the view that
women were inherently not as good as men, with activities such as
abstract thinking being beyond their capabilities. Another prominent
and influential German philosopher, Immanuel Kant, also laid down
these gendered boundaries of emotions, saying 'feminine ways are
called weaknesses'.[17] Men were considered dynamic and reflective,
whereas women were supposedly passive, with their interests confined
to pursuit of personal needs. Even when Hegel advocated educating
women, he proposed that only domains that did not require creative
imagination would be suitable for them, as they only excelled at
intuition and feeling, and not vision: 'When women hold the helm
of government, the state is at once in jeopardy, because women
regulate their actions not by the demands of universality but by

arbitrary inclinations and opinions. The status of manhood, on the other hand, is attained only by the stress of thought and much technical exertion.'[18]

Hysteria wasn't just a malady, an illness of the reproductive organs, but inextricably linked to women's innate temperaments. Of course, if we look at the medical texts and history of medicine and madness it is also very evident that most, if not all, were written by men, and doctors were all men too.[19] The French physician Auguste Fabre wrote in 1883: 'As a general rule all women are hysterical and . . . every woman carries with her the seeds of hysteria. Hysteria, before being an illness, is a temperament, and what constitutes the tempera-ment of a woman is rudimentary hysteria.'[20] Looking at hysteria through a lens of gender, many feminist historians, both men and women, have attempted to tease out how this disease was an illness of the powerless and silenced; and that as much as it was a disease produced by misogyny, it was also about how masculine ideals of emotional expression affected the attitude of the (mostly) male physicians towards the patients.

Much of the notion of hysteria was based on certain limits and boundaries that were imposed on emotional expression, and, as the physician Julius Althaus wrote in the *British Medical Journal* in 1866, it was the women who were not 'strong-minded', who had not acquired perfect control over themselves, who succumbed easily to these intense emotions.[21] Anything outside these acceptable bounds was quickly pathologised. Althaus proposed that women of all standing, and in any part of the world, could get hysterical, because any woman was liable to feeling strong emotions and anxiety, and being feeble-minded. In upper-class women, in his view, the lack of any honest work and their artificial lives could provoke them into irritability very easily, while for women of lower classes, their limited resources and grief could do the same. Women were considered so fragile and susceptible to imagination, that any exposure to the pain and disappointment in the real world could evoke strong emotions in them. One of the solutions he offered was to remove any painful emotions from the young woman's life, which often meant keeping them confined away from the world and its troubles.

Although hysteria wasn't really a disease but a reflection of how women's roles, expectations and desires were changing within deeply patriarchal structures, it was also about race and colonialism. While in men hysteria was understood to be of lower-class men with darker skin from minority ethnic communities, conversely, in women, the racialisation of hysteria was the opposite: it was seen as the preserve of white women.[22] It was a disease caused by 'overcivilisation' where the 'savages'[23] and the 'natives' were hypersexualised, reproduced easily, and had many children, and did not experience hysteria.[24] Bodies were seen differently, so the white bodies were nervous and weak, while the colonised bodies were hardy. The distinct anatomical differences that scientists purported to find between colonised and white women were used to prove that 'savage' women were immune from experiencing any gynaecological and obstetrical problems that white women experienced.[25] This perception meant that the supposed fragility and nervousness of white women made them the focus of much medical care, which has subsequently used them as a template, while the racist views that were promoted by eugenicists that darker skin was thicker and hence able to bear more pain, meant that Black women were used as medical subjects, their bodies mutilated and probed.[26]

The Black woman's body was seen as a peculiarity. Saartjie Baartman, known as the 'Hottentot Venus',[27] was brought to London in 1810 from South Africa and became a sensation in the Circus of Oddities due to her 'buttocks of enormous size and genitalia fabled to be equally disproportionate'.[28] Her body was stared at, displayed in circuses and private salons during her lifetime and then used for scientific experimentation after her death. She died in Paris in 1815, where she was examined and dissected by naturalist Georges Cuvier, who later wrote articles arguing that the form of her labia was evidence of the primitive sexual appetite of African women. Baartman's skeleton, brains and genitals were put on display at the Musée de l'Homme in Paris until 1974, when they were removed and put in storage; in 2002 her remains were repatriated to South Africa, where she was buried in the Gamtoos Valley.

There was an underlying fear that white women's infertility and reproductive maladies would endanger the self-professed superior race, as they sought education and employment and transgressed their gender roles by taking control of their reproduction. This notion of 'endangered whiteness' was closely linked to what was termed 'neurasthenia' in the early 1890s. This was a weakness of the nerves, associated with busy society women, i.e., white and upper or middle class. Their 'nerves' were caused by overpopulation and the stresses associated with urban pollution.[29] This would lead to a mass hysteria: what Laura Briggs, a feminist critic and historian, calls a 'whiteness of hysteria', where race and gender work together and against each other in framing these narratives of a hysterical woman. The whiteness of hysteria signalled the language of 'white genocide' supporters or 'race suicide',[30] the latter a eugenic term coined in 1900 by the sociologist Edward Ross which suggested a different birth rate between the desirable and the undesirable sections of society (the great replacement theory), whereby it became easier to rationalise the prejudice and discrimination, the disparity between white women and others.[31] It became an easily understood story. Whiteness was in danger and so hysterics were reserved for white women.

US psychiatrist George Beard also referred to neurasthenia or hysterics as 'the Central Africa of medicine', maintaining that hysteria was something to be pleased about, a small price to pay for the modernity that was leading to such nervous ailments.[32] In his view, the rising population of the civilised white people was countering the rise of the 'savage', which could only be a good thing even if it came at a cost. These eugenic views were widespread in western philosophical and scientific thought at the time. Similarly, Sigmund Freud would call female sexuality the 'dark continent': both backward, unknown and undesirable.[33] In many of his case studies, Freud recognises that the 'suppression of emotions' and 'emotion work' that women had to undertake by caring for others at the cost of their own well-being often resulted in hysteria, but 'women oppose change, receive passively, and add nothing of their own' and were governed by their reproductive functions.[34] Freud also shows his dismissiveness for any signs of intelligence in women, labelling these the 'harsher' side of a woman's personality, and argues that it is her 'benevolent care for others, her humility of mind and her refinement of manners, and not her intelligence which makes her a true lady.'[35] He insisted that women's 'mental liveliness', their intelligence and ambition was problematic, labelling it 'unladylike'.[36]

While also agreeing with Jean-Martin Charcot, one of the most influential neurologists of the nineteenth century, that hysteria was a psychological disorder rather than a physical one caused by a wandering womb, Freud believed that this psychological damage was a result of the trauma caused by an 'Oedipal moment of recognition' or 'feminine Oedipus'.[37] This is when young females become aware that they do not have a penis and perceive that they have been castrated. In the book *Studies on Hysteria*, written in 1893, he suggests that this causes women to develop a sort of 'inferiority complex', a form of internalised resentment towards other females and is displayed as an exaggerated emotional response.[38] The concept of the 'castrated female' and their associated anxieties are what cause the nervous disposition of women: always representing what is not there, and what a woman★ is lacking.

Freud admits that 'hysterical neurosis is nothing but an excessive over-accentuation of the typical wave of repression through which the masculine type of sexuality is removed and the woman emerges',[39] but rather than acknowledging that this was a social issue, a sign of the social and economic powerlessness that women faced, Freud's sexist beliefs motivated him to assign it to women's personal troubled histories and label it 'characteristically feminine'. This theory, of course, reinforces the shame that those of the female sex should feel in their own bodies, their genitalia always seen as an evidence of loss, always morally inferior and second class to male genitalia.

While Freud's work, and Charcot's before him, initiated an understanding of women's bodies and mental health, Freud was still operating within patriarchal constructs, where women's emotional distress, or their 'hysteria', was seen as their own fault due to their innate inferiority; as 'personal troubles' rather than a symptom of the larger social and historical context of systemic oppression within which women were expected to do this 'emotional work'; where they were expected to repress their emotions, and their intelligence was treated with ambivalence and derision.

The way that notions of hysteria have continued over centuries has been supported by men's continuing domination in medicine. In his book *Hysterical Men*, Mark Micale writes: 'The history of hysteria is composed of a body of writing by men about women.

★   Referring to cis-women here.

Until the penultimate decade of the nineteenth century, medical texts concerning hysteria were produced exclusively by men, men who assumed the status of professional observers, and the subjects about whom they wrote were predominantly female.'[40]

In the late nineteenth and early twentieth centuries the word hysterical became more politicised, with its use by the anti-suffragettes against women who were challenging the status quo, feminists who were speaking publicly against sexism and patriarchy. In a letter titled 'Letter on Militant Hysteria' written to *The Times* in 1919, British bacteriologist and immunologist Almroth E. Wright states: 'For man the physiological psychology of woman is full of difficulties. He is not a little mystified when he encounters in her periodically recurring phases of hypersensitiveness, unreasonableness, and loss of the sense of proportion.'[41]

All these women were seen as 'abnormal, threatening and repulsive', says Elaine Showalter, emeritus professor at Princeton University, in her essay 'Hysteria, Feminism and Gender'. Women were caricatured as a result of their passion to mock and discredit their protests, much like the recent caricature of Serena Williams shown as an infant with a dummy in her mouth throwing a tantrum, which was somehow found to be 'non-racist' by a press watchdog.[42] These women were told that they would over-work their brains, that their ambition and their intelligence would be their own downfall. Charlotte Perkins Gilman's novella *The Yellow Wallpaper*, published in 1892, is the story of a woman who loses her mind as a result of a 'resting cure', forbidden to work or even write a word until she is better. In the process of losing rationality, self-control and reason she gains power and insight into herself and her mind. It is the story of how women's own bodily experiences are overlooked by those in power, of men making decisions on the women's behalf. It is about coercion and benevolent sexism, where the female protagonist is made to believe that she is privileged to be looked after and cared for, to have the luxury to not work. And how women's emotionality can be their own downfall. The narrator in the book says: 'I take pains to control myself – before him, at least, and that makes me very tired.'[43]

•

'Hysteria' continues to be used to call someone over-emotional or wrought with anxiety. And it is still used to discredit women's experience today. Ask women whether they have been referred to as hysterical – or its more 'acceptable' contemporary equivalent, 'emotional' – and if so, when, and you are bound to hear many stories. I created an anonymous online survey and encountered some of the following from around 125 women:

A woman who has faced microaggressions in a workplace
A mother who knew her child was seriously ill and needed urgent medical attention but was dismissed
A woman who was in pain and was sent back home again and again by healthcare professionals, her discomfort deemed to be psychosomatic
A woman who was ignored in meetings, her opinions and comments dismissed, or seen as her being 'opinionated'

And the list could go on.

The linking of emotionality to the female gender can make women become cautious of expressing an opinion, or of appearing 'emotional' about being hurt, ignored, abused. Because then they are seen as unreliable narrators of their own lived experiences. Women's reactions are seen as unstable, out of context or disproportionate.

'Surely it isn't that bad' is what they are told if they feel hurt, upset, angry, frustrated.

Hysteria is a creation of the way women are treated, not a biological determinant of their femaleness. Until men stop telling women how to be, how they feel, and why they feel so, women will continue to either repress their true emotions, or they might choose to express them despite this, and make men (and the rest of society) uncomfortable. The long and dark history of hysteria is also a history of men in authority and power using women's emotions to diminish their own sense of autonomy by labelling them unruly, wild and unpredictable. And it is also the history of how women's emotions have been used against them to snatch any last vestiges of power they might hold over themselves and their own stories.

As an interesting aside, in the 1890s, Freud found that he had 'railway phobia', much like the modern fear of flying, but of trains. He concluded that this was because he had shared a sleeper compartment at the age of two with his mother and seen her naked. Not that this story has a particular relevance to an understanding of emotionality, but I find it fascinating as an insight into how women are often blamed for things – even in the most far-fetched way – that are really not their fault.

7.

WITCHES' COVEN

ALTHOUGH BEFORE THE FOURTEENTH CENTURY, witches and magic were to a certain extent regarded as a normal part of everyday life, and witches were only considered bad or good depending on the objective of their magic, the fear of witches became more widely pronounced during the medieval period. The (in)famous *Malleus Maleficarum* or the *Hammer of Witches* (1485) by Catholic clergyman Heinrich Kramer (and possibly Jacob Sprenger), the best-known treatise on witchcraft, transformed the view of a witch as a power who could make the gods submit to her wishes, into a woman controlled by Satan; one who created problems rather than solving them.[1] Kramer proposed that witchcraft was as criminal as heresy, and should be treated as such, with most heretics at the time burned at the stake. The title of the book shows deep-seated misogyny as it does not talk about wizards,[2] and therefore in treating witches as more evil also implies that evil originates in women.[3]

Men could be sorcerers, but this was seen to originate from a desire for power, and somehow was more acceptable as it aligned with the masculine ideals of the time. *Malleus Maleficarum* suggested that, because of the weakness of their sex, women were more susceptible to being taken over by demons. Reginald Scot, a country gentleman and MP from Kent, wrote in his 1584 treatise, *Discoverie of Witchcraft*, 'The cause why women are oftener found to be witches than men: they have such an unbridled force of fury and concupiscence naturally that by no means is it possible for them to temper or to moderate the same.'[4] Women also had 'loose tongues', were seen as capricious, with fluctuating volatile temperaments, and believed to be more lustful than men.[5] Kramer wrote: 'She is more carnal than a man, as is clear in connection with many filthy carnal acts.'[6] The historian Michael Bailey suggests that women deemed 'witches', or who chose to call themselves such, were most likely to be women who stepped outside the social codes and norms of their times, and who defied the appropriate feminine conventions that were set out for them.[7] This would include women who were seen as lustful and sexually promiscuous, emotionally exhibitive and manipulative. The woman's carnal nature made it easier for the devil to corrupt women's faith. The book reinforced the dualistic notion of the world that was set during the antiquities, with each positive pole having an opposite negative one: Mary and Eve, God and Satan, Men and Women.

Magic was innately physical, and so could be more easily connected to women who were perceived to be less intellectual than men. Men, on the other hand, were seen as more grounded in their minds with their rationality and reason. Sigrid Brauner, an acclaimed scholar of Germanic history and literature, showed that following the publication of this book, witches were targeted even more than before, because they threatened the perfect society.[8] Even if there is some doubt as to whether the book was adopted as a manual by the secular courts throughout Europe, the penalties associated with witchcraft became much more severe after its publication and through to the late 1700s, when the Age of Enlightenment shifted the focus back to empiricism and rationalism.[9]

The consequence of the demonisation of these women led to many being hunted down and burnt at the stake.[10] Louise Jackson, a professor of social history, in her extensive analysis of the 1645 Suffolk trials, where 124 women were tried for witchcraft, argues that these trials were organised state violence against women, a way to reassert male power over traditionally feminine spaces.[11] The history of witch trials is also the history of the enforcement of emotional norms, what Jackson refers to as a 'dark mirror to feminine quietude'.[12] They were a warning to women of what would happen if they acted in any way counter to their roles as dutiful wives and mothers, widows and pious virgins. Witches were identified by their negative emotions, and with the negative emotional impact on women of being suspected and accused of witchcraft, it was something of a vicious circle. Due to acute resentment of their position in society, the limits imposed on them, and a life of emotional and physical repression, some women were driven to act with 'unbridled passion'.[13]

The belief in witchcraft was also evidence of the paradoxical rules associated with women's emotions, where on one hand some intense emotional expressions, such as weeping, particularly in service of God, was a sign of their piety and could lead them to sainthood, while on the other hand excesses of other emotions such as anger led them to be labelled a witch. Historian Lyndal Roper suggests that in fact the unbridled passions so often attributed to the accused women might in fact have belonged to the accusers, those driven to frenzy to chase and hunt down these women. Ironic that the emotions were ascribed to the women when men behaved the way they did. Women were even pitted against each other because a witch countered everything that a stereotypically good woman was supposed to be, and so other women saw this as a threat to their place in society, and saw their femininity as under attack by these transgressions.[14] The women who accused other women of being witches were desperate to support their own virtue because they were fearful of being labelled as a witch too. Fear drives prejudice, but it also forces internalisations of social codes, making people think some behaviours are more natural to their gender than others. Women not only accused other women of hurting the feminine norms by their behaviour, they also blamed themselves if they acted in a subversive manner, with many hundreds confessing to being overtaken by the devil and evil spirits.[15]

These voluntary confessions have bothered many historians. Why did women confess to being witches? For some it was a form of reframing their identity as more than a mother and a wife, and reclaiming their emotions; and for some it was a source of guilt and shame because they were judging themselves by the standards set by men and found themselves lacking. The history of witchcraft is a story of how women have been considered weaker, and the strict moral and emotional codes they have had to adhere to. In overstepping any of these codes of conduct, they were seen as a threat to social cohesion and to femininity, and punished. By men, as well as by other women.

Many social codes around self-expression for men and women were similar in America and England from the sixteenth to eighteenth centuries, although there were more women creating educational opportunities for young women in America. While there are hardly any accounts of emotional expressions from young girls and women during this period since women lacked the resources or power to record their narratives, the scrutiny of gender roles is a useful tool to examine the emotional codes. Documents in the Stanford University Library archives show that 'bookish' women were contemptuously termed the 'petticoat pedants'. This social ostracisation and condemnation of women who were interested in books and more broadly in literacy and education had helped in keeping the standard of education for women low compared to men through the colonial period.[16]

The notion of shame and dishonour was sewn into the societal fabric, but there were also stories of women who were rebelling against these codes, choosing to have sex outside marriage and refusing to conform. These women made men (and other women) uncomfortable. They drank, they were unruly, and dressed provocatively. There were of course serious consequences to this. As the Protestant Reformation shook up Europe, witch hunts continued as part of the mass hysteria. One of the deadliest episodes in the history of colonial America, the Salem witch trials, was a series of hearings and hangings of people accused of witchcraft between 1692 and '93, just as this practice was coming to an end in Europe. Across America, many young women started having fits and screaming,[17] uttering peculiar sounds.[18] The accused were primarily women – mostly teenage girls – but Dorothy Good was only four years old when she was accused of witchcraft and had to stand trial. Bridget Bishop was hanged in 1692 for dressing exotically, drinking and marrying three times. Sometimes, simply expressing an opinion was enough to be accused of witchcraft. In his book *Escaping Salem*, British historian Richard Godbeer examines the case of two women, Elizabeth Clawson of Stamford and Mercy Disborough of Fairfield, both of whom were 'confident and determined, ready to express their opinions and to stand their ground when crossed'.[19] Reason enough, seemingly, to be deemed a witch.

•

A ballad written in 1615 says:

> Then was the Scold herself,
> In a wheelbarrow brought,
> Stripped naked to the smock,
> As in that case she ought:
> Neats tongues about her neck
> Were hung in open show;
> And thus unto the cucking stool
> This famous scold did go.[20]

The 'Scold laws' targeted women – angry women – who shouted loudly and quarrelled. Such women were called a communis rixatris, a common scold, one who broke the public peace with her anger. A federal judge explained in 1829: 'for our law-latin confines it to the feminine gender'. Sandy Bardsley, a British historian, suggests that this practice started in the late Middle Ages in England,[21] when more stringent efforts were made to punish any speech or action that disrupted the status quo, i.e., with women keeping to the domestic sphere, and being passive and quiet.[22] When colonists first arrived in the United States from England they took this law with them. If a woman was found guilty of behaviours that were 'unwomanly' (or suspected of being a witch), she would be dunked into water with her thumbs tied to her toes to cool her down. Punishment for a scold was to wear an iron mask over her head fastened at the back of the neck with a padlock, and a flat piece of iron that went into the mouth and constricted her tongue – something called a scold's bridle, a terrifying and dehumanising piece of equipment. If she floated, she was guilty. And was hanged. If she sank, she was cleared. But, of course, also dead.

Commentaries on the Laws of England, an influential treatise on the common law of England from around 1765 (also used as the pre-revolutionary source of common law by United States courts), stipulates that such a 'scold' be placed into a ducking (or a cucking) stool. Women were dunked into the river several times on this chair until they were cooled of their 'immoderate heat'.[23] Women were naturally assumed to be much colder than men, as discussed earlier, and any warmth in women was considered inappropriate and against their natural temperament. It was believed that women's fragility and weakness made them incapable of handling the heat.

In historian Alice Morse Earle's *Curious Punishments of Bygone Days* published in 1896 there are extensive accounts of scold trials and dunking across much of the western world. She writes of trials in Jamestown settlement in Virginia in 1626: 'At the time of the colonization of America the ducking stool was at the height of its English reign; and apparently the amiability of the lower classes was equally at ebb. Colonists brought their tempers to the new land, and they brought their ducking stools.'[24]

The last witch trial in America is believed to have happened sometime in the 1770s when Grace Sherwood, the Witch of Pungo, was ducked in the Lynnhaven river in Virginia. Sherwood is believed to have survived but there is some evidence that she might have then spent eight years in prison for her perceived offences before being released.[25] But more than a century later, in 1819, Jenny Lanman was convicted for being 'noisy and troublesome'. A constable flogged her over and over with a cowhide but 'he could not quiet her tongue, for the more he had whipped, the louder she had screamed, so he absolutely despaired of a cure'. She was ducked until she could learn to 'hold her tongue'. Anne Royall was one of America's most notorious early 'gossip girls', a satirist and social critic. She was also a widow who fearlessly criticised men in important public positions such as politicians, religious leaders and bankers. Sixty-year-old Royall was called 'brash' and 'aggressive' and tried in 1829 for being a 'common scold': a woman with a 'serpent's tongue'.[26] A ducking stool was set up for her but eventually the court ruled this punishment obsolete and fined her ten dollars: a cause of civil shame for Royall. These were public humiliations of women that came at a huge emotional cost for not only the women involved but also the bystanders. Incredibly, this law remained on the statute books in England and Wales until 1967, and endured in New Jersey until 1972, when it was finally removed for contravening the 14th Amendment to the US Constitution for sex discrimination.

The characterisation of women as witches was not a peculiarity of western societies, although there have been more extensive historical records of it in the UK and USA. In India, for instance, dayans, or witches, have been a part of the folklore since the fourteenth century. These malevolent spirits – always female, and called dakhini in Sanskrit – are mentioned in medieval Hindu texts such as the *Bhagavata Purana*, and the earliest record of witch-hunting (dayan pratha) is from 1792.[27] In the state of Jharkhand, which has one of the lowest literacy rates in India, witch-hunts have occurred as recently as 2021. On 28 March 2021, a 55-year-old woman suspected of practising witchcraft was beaten to death by locals in the Ranchi district of Madhya Pradesh. The National Crime Records Bureau confirms that between 1990 and 2000, 522 women were mercilessly killed (often first publicly paraded naked to shame them), accused of being a 'witch'. A total of 2,400 cases of witch-hunting were filed across the country between 1999 and 2012, but the majority go unreported.[28] Gender dynamics play a huge role in these deaths where men have an upper hand and all the power, and often single women and widows, some of the most vulnerable groups, are labelled witches in order to seize their land and property illegally, or to punish them for shunning any sexual advances. Caste is also a factor. Upper-class Brahmin men use accusations of witchcraft as an excuse to shame and kill Dalit women. Elsewhere, sub-Saharan countries have reported continued witch-hunts of women. Much like in the past, it is vulnerable women who have to pay a price for non-conformity.[29]

The Puritan notions of witches bolstered the belief that women were inherently sinful, and therefore susceptible to easy temptation (and damnation) by the devil. So, although society believed that men and women were equal in the eyes of God, they also believed that women got angry very easily and that women's bodies and minds were weak and vulnerable. In the witch trials, especially in the west, these women were portrayed as scheming, deviant and manipulative. But to be all this, surely, they had to be rational, reasoned and intelligent, qualities that were praised in men. Perhaps the threat of a woman who could not be silenced and was intelligent (almost as much as a man, or even more) was enough to cause mass hysteria and anxiety.

8.

HYSTERIA IN MEN

IN 1859, THE FRENCH PHYSICIAN and psychologist Pierre Briquet remarked in his influential treatise *Traité clinique et thérapeutique de l'hystérie* that 'We saw little hysteria in men because we did not want to see it.'[1] Briquet is referring to confirmation bias, whereby we look most for information that confirms our existing beliefs. It is easier for our brain to process this information, rather than actively take on new information that overturns our existing beliefs and attitudes, which is cognitively more taxing. Quite a progressive statement for the times in which he wrote.

Around the 1850s we start seeing research suggesting that men could be hysterical too, that there was at least 1 man for every 20 women[2] that would display symptoms. But male hysteria was perceived to be very different to that of a woman. Briquet presented a study of 430 patients, which included just 7 men, to show that hysteria was not linked to the uterus but to the brain.[3] His autopsy on bodies that had succumbed to hysteria did not reveal any lesions on the brain. Instead, the main factors associated with male hysteria were found to be lower social class, family history and other such situational difficulties based in socio-economic and cultural context.

Jean-Martin Charcot had worked for almost his entire career at Salpêtrière Hospital, one of the major Paris hospitals and a hospice with over 5,000 female patients. Most of his studies and experimental work was carried out with women in this institution. In 1882, he opened a special ward with twenty beds for men suffering from nervous disorders, which was expanded to accommodate fifty male patients just two years later. Charcot's work proposed that male hysteria, which he called 'grand ébranlement psychique' (great psychic shock) was completely different to how hysteria was expressed in women: it did not present as full-blown symptoms as in women, and it mostly emerged from trauma rather than the frailty or failing of their bodies. Men were not believed to display the attitudes passionnelles, the passionate phase, instead veering more towards sadness and depression.

Despite the fact that Charcot acknowledged that this was not just a women's disease nor caused by the wandering womb, and that not only men but also women could become sad and melancholic, he and his students could not be called progressives. Instead of trying to fight the ingrained gendered approaches to hysteria, they were trying to use the objectivity of science to prove that hysteria was a stable entity, that it followed definite rules and was universal in women, even though it did not reside solely in the womb as previously believed. One of Charcot and his students' arguments was that men have 'pseudo-ovarian zones' corresponding to the position of ovaries in a female body, lower down in the abdomen, and that this was likely to be the point where their hysteria originated: the 'hysterogenic' point. However, even in hysteria, men were more controlled, more stable, more tenacious; women were flighty, unstable, unreliable. Charcot wrote: 'In the male . . . the disease presents itself often as an affection remarkable for the permanence and tenacity

142

of the symptoms that characterise it. In woman, on the contrary – and that is without a doubt what seems to make the crucial difference between the sexes for those who do not know the illness well in women – what is thought to be the characteristic trait of hysteria is its instability, the mobility of its symptoms.'[4]

Male hysteria was associated with the body on the outside, while female hysteria was physiological. One was believed to originate because of physical work, the other due to the lack of it. In women, hysteria was also seen as a manifestation of intellectual overwork, or any attempt to tax themselves mentally. Quite a paradox. This also meant that, while in women hysteria was mainly associated with white, upper-class women, in men it was generally the opposite. It was believed that it was mostly working-class men who worked with their hands, and those from marginalised racial groups who were affected by hystero-neurasthenia, heightening the class divide.[5] While these were strong, sexually active men, which avoided male hysteria being labelled as effeminate, Charcot and other physicians of the time feminised it by immediately associating it with lower mental faculties. Middle- and upper-class men were perceived to be rational and controlled. In dissociating it from upper-class men who engaged in intellectual pursuits, who held the power, were sophisticated and existed in the upper echelons of society, it was associated with earthiness and with coarseness, with lack of refinement. Men with hysteria lay somewhere between upper-class men and women, who were also seen as unrefined because of their weaker minds and the biological process of child-birth. So, hysteria and hysterical behaviour became associated with a sense of animality for both men and women, a disease caused by weakening of the mind when an already weak mind could not tolerate the pressures put on it.[6] In this way, a hierarchy for masculinity was also imposed, with elite men forming a special class, immune from the disease of a frail mind. On one hand, this discourse acknowledged the privilege that certain men had over others which protected them from irrationality, but it also entrenched ideas that we have come more latterly to associate with toxic masculinity even more firmly.

Jan Goldstein from the University of Chicago looked at the admissions register of Salpêtrière and of Bicêtre, the adjoining asylum for men, for the two-year period between 1841 and 1842.[7] Of the 648 women who entered, only about 1 per cent were diagnosed as hysterical. However, just 40 years later, of the 500 women admitted, 89 (17 per cent) were diagnosed as hysterical (which has led to some historians marking the 1880s as the golden age of hysteria). Amongst the men admitted during 1841–43, no one was diagnosed with hysteria. The number had gone up to 2 in 1883.

Strong emotions had long been considered a threat to masculinity. As a backlash to the ideals of the Enlightenment, emphasising rationality and denigrating emotionality, 'Sturm und Drang' (storm and stress) was a movement that started in German literature and music between 1760 and 1780 that insisted on giving extremes of emotion free expression. The works created in this aesthetic were aimed at inspiring readers and audiences with extreme emotions. Johann Wolfgang von Goethe's novel *The Sorrows of Young Werther*, first published in 1774, is a book about a young man's intemperate emotional response to unrequited love, a man of 'sensitive and passionate temperament'. It led to the 'Werther effect' or 'Werther epidemic', with a spate of copycat male suicides in the latter part of the eighteenth century, and men were warned against such books.[8] Women in this book were characters of equal intellectual depth to men, of great determination and emotional depth, and Goethe subverts the stereotypical representations and understandings of women as passive and unagented. However, Werther is shown to treat them merely as objects, therefore also displaying some of the attitudes of men towards women in the society at the time.

For a brief time in Georgian England, in the eighteenth century, where class and gender ideologies were quite rigid and social mobility was not common, many upper-class men became comfortable with the idea of having a nervous disposition. Lower-class men were seen to be inferior (socially and morally), less delicate and commonly engaged in manual labour (especially with the Industrial Revolution). The upper- and middle-class men were keen to maintain the class divides and distinguish themselves from the lower classes. This meant that they were comfortable with displaying more refined and sophisticated sensibilities (rather than being weak and womanly) than their more working-class counterparts. Unlike in women, however, this made them more worthy of holding power and status.[9]

The discourse around hysteria was ultimately about patriarchy and power, and ensured that the position of (some) men as the voice of reason, rationality and knowledge was not threatened. Besides class, there was of course a racialised element to the study of hysteria as discussed earlier. In Britain during this period, for instance, it was suggested that male hysteria was particular to 'Latin men' (darker-skinned) and that Anglo-Saxon men were immune from it, a view intended to maintain the supremacy of white Europeans. A similar view was also professed in Germany around the middle of the nineteenth century as medical journals circulated theories and research that Frenchmen were more prone to hysteria. Slaves and indigenous populations in the colonies were also diagnosed with hysteria at a high rate by European and white American physicians to support the eugenic theory of a racial hierarchy being promoted at the time.

More broadly, the discourse around male hysteria ensured that the position of men as the voices of reason, rationality and knowledge was not threatened, and that male hysteria continued to be associated with shame, with the periphery and margins, with bodies that were not the norm, with 'womanish, homosexual or childish impulses', reinforcing stigmatisation and infantilisation of women and homosexuals, both seen as deviance from the heterosexual male ideal.[10]

•

Emotions have a gender or, if you prefer, gender determines certain emotions or the way they are expressed.

— Maurice Sartre[11]

It was only in 1985 that the term 'emotionology' was coined, which announced the arrival of a specific multidisciplinary study of the history of emotions.[12] William Reddy, a professor of history and cultural anthropology at Duke University, introduced the term 'emotives' in 1997 to understand how emotions were shaped through history by society and its expectations, but also by individuals as they understood and interpreted societal norms and sought different ways to express how they were feeling.[13] Much of the research into the history of emotions, especially the gendering of emotions, has been conducted by studying the language used to describe internal feelings, making ephemeral emotions comprehensible in a tangible manner. As we know, we often make sense of our emotions through the words that we have at our disposal. Without this language or external articulation of feelings, these inner states of emotion would not be understood. The 'emotives' or the external emotional expressions referred to in historical texts have played a part in shaping the current social reality.

Historians talk about an 'emotional turn' that occurred only about twenty years ago as studies in the history of emotion gained momentum and scholars and scientists started to focus on developing concepts and frameworks for a better understanding of human emotions.[14] History has been mainly the preserve of men of the middle to upper classes, and for so long emotions were considered by that group as irrational and a barrier to proper rigorous scientific scholarship and enquiry. So, emotionality wasn't something that was explicitly studied or written about. As Joanna Lewis, a historian from the London School of Economics said in 2020, 'Emotions were for the down-trodden masses and not worth serious study.'[15] There has been such an emphasis on objectivity in academic research that emotions were not considered a suitable subject. And as the historians Piroska Nagy and Damien Bouquet said in 2018: 'Emotions and feelings are guests who were invited late to the banquet of history.'[16]

From the dualism of early antiquity, to the medieval linking of emotionality with the womb, and then the neuroscience and biochemical myths (which I examine in the next section) that propound the flawed sex-based determinism that men and women are inherently different in the size of their brains or their hormonal and chemical responses, much of western culture has taken an irrefutable view that emotionality and womanhood are equivalent. This belief in the primacy of the man has persisted along with the association of emotional intensity to specific physiologies, where women are inferior to and weaker than men, and therefore more emotional.

Section 3:

BRAIN, GENDER AND EMOTIONS

She has [a] man's brain – a brain that a man should have were he much gifted – and a woman's heart. The good God fashioned her for a purpose, believe me, when He made that so good combination.

— Bram Stoker, *Dracula*

9.

SUGAR AND SPICE (IT ALL STARTS HERE)

> What are little boys made of?
> What are little boys made of?
> Snips and snails
> And puppy-dogs' tails
> That's what little boys are made of
>
> What are little girls made of?
> What are little girls made of?
> Sugar and spice
> And all things nice.
> That's what little girls are made of
>
> — Robert Southey, c.1820[1]

IN 1873, HARVARD PRESIDENT EDWARD Clarke argued against women's education on the grounds that their brains would demand too much blood, which would be taken away from their reproductive organs and stop them from developing properly and that would put their whole womanhood under threat.[2] In the same year, Clarke went on to publish 'Sex in Education, or a Fair Chance for Girls' where he asserted that identical education for girls was completely unwise, a violation of the laws of nature, because it would be a 'crime before God and humanity, that physiology protests against, and that experience weeps over'.[3] The belief that men's and women's brains work in different ways, that women's reproductive mechanisms shaped their behaviour and aptitudes, have continued to persist, and have shaped so much of the emotional stereotypes and the ideals of true 'womanhood' and 'manhood'. If we believe that this is indeed the case, that biology determines who we are as men and women, and how we experience and express emotions, then this should be evident from the moment we are born.

As children develop through their early years, they also learn to express emotions. Babies cry to get attention, to show distress, and to communicate to their caregivers that they are unhappy in some way. Infants as young as 4 months have been shown to discriminate between different emotions.[4] Babies have been found to stare at people's faces for different lengths of time, depending on what emotion they are showing (e.g., joy, anger, neutral expression), which is their way of showing preference. Babies are also seen to start to distinguish between facial expressions of emotions and vocal emotional tone. When shown two videos and one audio clip in an experiment at 5 months old, babies watch the video of the face showing the emotion that matches the emotionality in the audio clip that they are listening to.[5] By the time these babies are 7 months old, they can pick up even more subtle emotional information and do not even need the video and audio to match each other. What is clear from this experiment is that, from a young age, children are picking up emotional cues from the adults around them, particularly from their faces and voices.

As children's sense of self and identity develops, they also learn which emotions to use to get what they want, and to facilitate various social relationships.[6] By the time they are 2 years old, children are likely to be talking about their emotions such as 'I am happy' or 'I am sad'.[7] They can identify some of the emotions, such as happiness and sadness, from facial expressions, although they find it difficult to interpret emotions such as disgust and shame. Children even learn how to mask their emotions depending on their social context and expectations around them, such as learning to smile for a photograph, or not showing anger when they are with other adults besides their parents or carers. By the age of 5 or 6, children can identify more complex emotions in others. Most children have already been socialised to a large extent by this age, their reference groups expanding and widening as they come into contact with other adults and children outside their home, at school and in playgrounds.[8] Their desire to fit in and be like the other children around them and to please the adults in their lives grows, and so they also learn to mask and adapt behaviours according to the expectations of other adults. And children are learning social rules of behaviour such as being told to use their 'outside voices', so they adapt their emotional expressions according to their environment.

My 5-year-old is now more comfortable thinking about emotions in a multi-layered manner compared to last year (rather than discrete categories), as well as people's intentions and the impact on her: 'I am sad but also quite angry' and 'Your voice was not very kind, but I know you didn't mean it.' When we ask a child to 'smile' on meeting their grandparents or when their photo is being taken, we are telling them that a smile is an expression that is more palatable to others, that it makes them more comfortable, and that society associates an inner emotional state with a certain expression. The children are picking up these normative displays of emotions around specific people and situations every day. Their emotional landscape is becoming broader and more intricate, and their understanding of their own emotions as well as that of others slowly more expansive.

Any time I mention to people that I have twins, a horrified look appears on their face, followed by sympathy. Their next question is almost always 'girls or boys?' and then a sigh of relief that 'At least they are not boys.' Can you imagine, they all say with a laugh, reminding me that 'girls are calm and easy' while boys are a 'handful' and 'so loud'. It is a commonly held view that children express emotions differently based on their gender. Many biological theorists have believed that these differences in their emotional expressions are innate and shaped prenatally or develop due to genetic and hormonal differences, and that boys naturally have a lower ability to inhibit certain negative emotions such as anger.

Leonard Sax, an American psychologist and physician, proposed in his book *Why Gender Matters* (2005) that girls and boys behave differently because their brains are wired differently. He puts forward stereotypical beliefs about men and women to confirm the age-old attitudes that women are better in the domestic spheres ('Girls and women smell and hear more acutely than do boys and men, so that may explain female superiority in the areas of housekeeping and listening'), and boys make better leaders ('They are biologically predisposed to risk-taking').[9] In one of his proposals, Sax asserts that boys' and girls' vision differs greatly because of their biology: 'Every step in each pathway, from the retina to the cerebral cortex, is different in females and males' due to fundamental biological differences. 'Girls and boys play differently. They learn differently. They fight differently. They see the world differently. They hear differently.'

Yet in an extensive discussion of Sax's theories on his blog

'Language Log', Mark Liberman, professor of linguistics and computer science at University of Pennsylvania, shows that these conclusions are based on experiments conducted on the retinas of rats, not humans.[10] Rat retinas have been shown to have significant differences from human retinas, and caution is advised in projecting results shown with rats to humans.[11] Many of Sax's conclusions are also drawn from studies with tiny sample sizes, some as small as 19 children, with 9 boys and 10 girls to study between-group variations. This is like observing my children's class of 20 for an hour, giving them biscuits and cake, counting who eats what on that particular day and in that particular moment, and making grandiose claims such as boys only like biscuits and girls only like cake. This is what we call an over-interpretation.

Sax also concludes that boys do not develop emotionally as much as girls and that a 17-year-old boy is as emotionally immature and as uncomfortable with emotional expression as a 7-year-old girl.[12] In this small data set of 9 boys, there were only 3 that were older than 12 years old, not enough in any way to draw any reliable conclusion about emotional maturation. Also, the study that these conclusions were based on did not claim to be robust, saying: 'Results are preliminary and were obtained with a relatively small sample; conclusions based on these findings must be viewed as tentative until replicated with larger groups of subjects.'[13] Liberman has an extensive discussion about this on his blog where he explains the extent of over-interpretation when both sex and age are being studied and when the results are being used to determine what is 'natural'. Yes, there could be some differences between girls and boys and how they mature emotionally, but it is impossible to conclude so definitely from this study alone that any such differences are because of biology and not because of the moral and social codes that determine the way we live, and feel.

Researchers have not been able to find any consistent biologically based sex differences between girls' and boys' behaviour, and social-development theories propose an alternative – and more plausible – view, that children learn their behaviours through social-isation. Albert Bandura of Stanford University proposes that learning occurs by observing behaviours and their consequences and mimicking them, and that cognition and environment all interact mutually to shape behaviours.[14] This means that children can learn both by direct experience as well as by observing the behaviour of others. By being aware of the probable consequences of different actions and behaviours, children can modulate their responses accordingly.[15]

Bandura carried out an experiment with children aged 3–6 years from local nursery schools in Stanford, famously called the 'Bobo Doll Experiment'. The Bobo doll was an inflatable toy about 5 feet tall to represent an adult, and it sprang back when it was knocked over. There were 12 girls and 12 boys in the control group that did not engage with an adult experimenter, while the second group had 24 of each gender and out of these, half were interacting with a man and the other half with a woman. Children were tested individually so that there was no effect of their classmates' behaviour on their own. The third group had a passive adult, who sat quietly and played peacefully with the toys in the same room as the child. In the second group, after a few minutes, the adult – both man and woman – would start hitting the doll with a mallet and shouting at it for about 10 minutes while the child observed from a corner. Later, when left alone in a room with some toys and the Bobo doll, the results showed that children imitated adults and absorbed and replicated their behaviours very quickly. Many of them who had been in group two and observed aggression against the doll repeated the behaviour.[16] Boys were more likely to show physical aggression than girls, who showed verbal aggression.

When this experiment was repeated two years later with a video rather than an actual inflatable doll, the variations and responses were seen to be less significant.[17] It was also observed that children were less likely to imitate behaviours that they saw were being actively penalised and punished in adults, such as being reprimanded and given warnings not to ever do it again. So even though it is not clear how much of the aggression shown by children is due to imitative behaviour and how much to other social and cultural inputs, the impact of this experiment has been far-reaching. Although this experiment in itself did not look at between-gender effects, it has shown that from a young age, children learn by imitation of behaviours and emotions, and absorb the value judgements placed on them in different contexts to regulate their own behaviours.

•

There are two main categories of social norms: injunctive and descriptive, both comprising of explicit and implicit rules. Injunctive norms are the social norms that determine what people perceive that they *ought* to do (e.g., social or legal rules about how much a teenager *could* drink at a party). The descriptive norms are what *is*, or what people really do in a given social situation (e.g., how much a teenager really drinks at a party). People who violate the injunctive (or prescriptive) norms are often penalised. There are perceived (and potentially real) risks of punishment and the motivation of rewards related to injunctive norms that can guide people's emotional displays and expressions. There is an understanding of how certain emotions are rejected and disapproved of by others in society, and how that can affect social standing and position.

This is associated with certain intense emotions, especially negative emotions. Children learn these social rules from a young age through observation and being bodily embedded in the social and cultural context.

Gender has always been used as an organising principle for emotions, albeit implicitly. As I discussed in the first chapter, the way we conform to gender norms has always shaped how our bodies and behaviour are seen and evaluated. 'Sex-typing' is the stereotypical categorisation of people based on some kind of societal conventions of what is expected and typical of each sex.[18] Sandra Bem, a pioneering feminist psychologist from Cornell University, proposed the gender schema theory in 1987, which is grounded in situational appropriateness, demonstrated when our behaviours are reflective of our environment. We all are gendered in society, and the characteristics (sex-typed) that are associated with our gender are then conveyed to other people in our culture through schemas and symbols. A schema is a network of associations, a cognitive model and guide that we use to organise our perceptions of the world. The gender schema theory states that children learn their own 'adequacy as a person in terms of the gender schema, to match his or her preferences, attitudes, behaviours, and personal attributes against the prototypes stored within it'.[19]

These gender-coded behaviours create an intense polarisation in our society into 'masculine' and 'feminine', which we have seen repeated through history, and that we perpetuate by statements such as 'boys will be boys' that are grounded in ideals of masculinities.[20] This is where the phrase 'sugar and spice' emerges from, a persistence of duality from Aristotle's and Plato's times. Our motivation to conform to social norms emerges partly from the desire to not be disliked or punished by others, and from a yearning to belong to our social group.

Children start learning these social rules as their sense of identity associated with their own gender grows, and they want to fit in.

Of course, many children do not conform to gender stereotypes, but they become hyper-aware of being seen as rebellious, disrespectful or 'too much' (or not enough) with growing awareness of social norms.[21] The extent to which a child conforms to gender stereotypes depends on the choices that are on offer to the individual, how accessible these schemas about gender roles are to them, and how much penalty and disapproval they are willing or able to absorb from society. But in absorbing these roles as part of the schema, children modulate their behaviour to conform to our society's perception of what a man or a woman ought to be like, and in then performing these sex-typed roles, they confirm and reinforce the gender-based differentiation in our society. And so these myths about opposing masculine and feminine behaviours become a self-fulfilling prophecy. The gender schema theory disrupted the polarised gender view of society that has been so pervasive through history by questioning the assumptions that sex roles are mutually exclusive and opposite. The gender dichotomy becomes a guide from the moment a child is born. It is very readily available cognitively to children, and so they learn that this simplified model of maleness and femaleness has direct relevance and applicability to almost every aspect of their life, from what clothes they wear, colours they like, toys they play with and emotions they should or should not show.

Sandra Bem also created the Bem Sex-role Inventory (BSRI) in 1974, which consists of sixty different adjectives that are perceived as either masculine, feminine or gender-neutral/androgynous. In the BSRI, 'aggressive', 'assertive', 'dominant' and 'forceful' are associated with masculinity. 'Moody', 'sympathetic', 'compassionate', 'warm', 'tender', 'yielding' and 'childlike' are associated with femininity. It is generally assumed that if a person scores high on a masculine attribute, they would automatically score low on the corresponding feminine attribute (for instance, if a person is strong, then they are not weak). But BSRI assumed that a person could be high or low on both, and these are not mutually subjective attributes, but independent characteristics. Men and women do not lie on opposite ends of a gender divide; rather on a spectrum. Bem insisted on an androgynous view of people, whereby people are sometimes more masculine than feminine, and vice versa, and they move flexibly between the two (and should be allowed to). Although in saying so – and Bem admitted as much – there is still a view enforced that there is indeed a 'masculine' and a 'feminine'. In focusing on masculinity and femininity but not their production as a cultural construct, Bem asserted that androgyny reproduced 'the gender polarisation that it [sought] to undercut', that even in talking about non-binary or androgynous behaviours, we are forced to fall back on the masculine/feminine polarisation.[22] As long as we continue to believe in masculine and feminine polarisation, women will continue to be judged on how they look and act, especially in domains which have long been considered masculine. And similarly for men in a stereotypically feminine domain.

•

Most contemporary researchers have reached an agreement that gender socialisation begins at birth,[23] and parents and other adults can often implicitly and unintentionally impose a set of expectations on the child that are consistent with stereotypical gender traits.[24] This sets the context within which a child is raised, and responded to, and can become a major force in the child's development of their own sense of identity.[25]

As far back as the 1970s, there were a number of studies that showed that parents reacted differently to girls and boys as babies and toddlers, with boys handled more roughly before 3 months of age – with the presumption that they are hardier – and girls given more cuddles and physical forms of affection after 6 months of age.[26] In a 2010 study, parents were asked to describe new-born children and rate them on a number of adjectives solely based on the sex of the baby (they didn't really have any other information about the infants).[27] It was seen that girls were rated as softer, smaller, cuter and also surprisingly more inattentive than boys. We might argue a lot has changed in the last forty years, and parents are less likely to make these distinctions now, but we know that we all carry implicit biases and stereotypes. The forty pairs of predominantly Caucasian parents in the study rated new-born girls as finer featured, less strong, more delicate, and more 'feminine' than new-born boys. Thus, pre-formed polarised attributes are assigned to children as soon as they are born, before they've had a chance to develop their person-alities and express themselves.

In another study, twelve pregnant women and their partners who knew their child's sex were compared with twelve others who did not.[28] These parents were interviewed before and after receiving this ultrasound result, and after the birth of the child. Over the course of pregnancy, several differences emerged in how the parents perceived their child and talked about them according to their gender, but these differences became more pronounced after birth, when parents perceived girls to be smaller, less co-ordinated, quieter and weaker than boys – all traditionally 'feminine' attributes. It is clear that stereotypical knowledge about our gender/sex roles is acquired very early on, and from a very young age boys and girls are typically encouraged to make the divide between themselves and others in very different ways through different patterns of interpersonal inter-actions and socialisations. Both parental expectations and observations of their children's emotions can be loaded with gendered expectations. And this creates a loop where, when the child behaves as per the expectations (both implicit and explicit), they are seen to be conforming to some innate propensity to a certain behaviour.

By the time children are adolescents, they have already formed a very strong sense of self-identity that in most cases is consistent with the gender roles pervasive in our society. They judge not only them-selves but also others through this lens, although the effect of sex-role stereotyping is strongest between 3 and 14 years of age, and starts diminishing somewhat as they take on new information and form a stronger sense of self separate from their peer group. Children as young as 3 years stereotype other infants and children. Forty children from two diverse private schools in Southern California aged 3–5 years were shown a videotape of two 12-month-old infants, a boy and a girl who looked similar, playing with traditionally gender-typed toys, such as a puzzle, a doll and dinosaur.[29] All other factors were kept consistent. When the participating children were asked to label these videotapes with polarised adjectives such as big/small, nice/mean, quiet/loud, strong/weak, angry/scared, happy/sad, it was found that simply assigning a gender label such as a typically masculine name to one child and a feminine name to another elicited responses that were consistent with gender-role stereotypes in our society. The infant who had a stereotypical girl's name such as 'Lisa' with no other distinguishing characteristics was labelled small, quiet, weak, scared and sad. Gender salience – where gender becomes the signifi-cant attribute in assigning other characteristics – is shown to play a significant role in early child development.[30]

In terms of emotions, gender differences tend to become stronger from infancy to early teenage years, as children socialise more and develop a more enhanced gender schema to draw their normative experiences from. Context, therefore, plays a role in the way gendered emotional schema develop for children. Kay Deux and Brenda Major from University of California proposed what is known as the 'gender-in-context model' to emphasise the role of the context and observer expectations.[31] If gender differences and expectations are quite salient in a particular context, gender-related schemas can be activated, and children are more likely to negotiate their own identities in terms of the expectations of perceivers and situational cues. This is why children might regulate their emotions more with strangers than with parents, and this might explain the 'after school restraint collapse' that young children often experience with meltdowns at home after school, when they have been perfectly behaved all day. The pressure to regulate and manage their emotions as per expectations and norms at schools can be very cognitively taxing for young children.

Gender differences emerge more strongly when children are with their friends, particularly if the peer groups are very gendered.[32] From American children it was seen that the more girls played only with girls, the more closely they related to gender-stereotypical behaviours. In another study, 61 children (28 boys and 33 girls; mean age 4 years 5 months) were observed over 6 months.[33] Their type of play and choice of play partners was recorded. While at the start of the school year the play behaviours of boys and girls were almost alike, by the end of the six months, their behaviour had become more gender-typed. In this way, stereotypical gender rules, where boys play more rough and tumble,[34] while girls play more quietly in the 'home corner' at nursery or school, can often become expectancies.[35] This is more the case when gender divides are laid down implicitly in the form of words and actions by the teachers, or explicitly where children are regularly divided into girls and boys for classroom activities.

Stanford psychologist Eleanor Maccoby proposed in her influential book *The Psychology of Sex Differences* that rather than biological differences, environmental and parental influences play a more significant role in shaping gender differences.[36] Maccoby and her colleague Carol Jacklin did an exhaustive review of studies that showed no gender differences between children's behaviour at a young age, but found that many of the researchers had been unable to publish their findings because of publication bias. The outcome of research studies influences whether they are accepted and published by academic journals or not, and therefore there can be a tendency by researchers to exaggerate the statistical significance of their results in order to be published. Their analysis shows that infant boys and girls are very similar in responding to the same frustrating situations, showing emotions such as anger or crying. However, by just 18 months old, boys show more frustration than girls. This means that within a very short time, girls have learned to minimise the display of external negative emotions such as anger. This could be because they are becoming more aware of the implicit emotional norms for girls ('Girls don't get angry'), or it could be because they are acquiring more language and inhibitory skills than the boys. Either way, these gender differences have become significant within a period of 12 months. Certain emotions, like anger, are much more gendered and carry more 'feeling rules' (rules about when such feelings can be shown and to what intensity) in our society. Other emotions, like fear, did not show any such differences between girls and boys. But when parents were asked to report on the fearfulness of their children (3–13 years old), there was a small difference between girls and boys, with girls perceived to be showing higher fearfulness (e.g., of unfamiliar situations or sudden changes), showing that parental expectations influence the measure of emotional expression in a child.[37]

A meta-analysis of children aged 2–12 years did not show any significant differences between smiling across gender.[38] However, girls develop a proclivity to appease adults, and often smile to ease discomfort in others. Girls and boys show no significant differences in the amount they smile until they reach early teenage years, when girls start smiling much more than boys, and similar differences have been noticed between teenage boys and girls, and adult women and men.[39] Boys start to minimise their emotions as they grow older to appear more self-controlled, which also means that the biological theories about boys having less inhibitory abilities are not entirely accurate.[40]

Psychologist Ann Kring and colleagues have shown that in western cultures – especially Europe and the USA – there is an expectation on girls to be more emotionally expressive than boys, and display more positive emotions such as happiness, while internalising the negative emotions such as sadness, fear, shame and guilt.[41] The expectation is also for them to show more empathic behaviours as well as more smiley facial expressions. The stereotypical feminine expectations are to nurture closeness in relationships, and to be collaborative and accommodating. Surveys with adults have shown how more than 98 per cent of women reported being told to smile at some point, revealing societal expectations on women to be friendly and approachable; 15 per cent noted that this was more frequent than once a week.[42] A meta-analysis of 162 research studies shows that adult women and adolescent girls do smile more as they grow older, but results vary in different cultures and with age, and need further investigation.[43] The differences disappeared in the workplace when men and women were in the same professional roles, particularly with seniority.

An experiment in 7 countries[44] with 688 students showed that women tended to rate smiling faces in photographs as more honest than men,[45] and both genders rated non-smiling faces as less honest. While smiling faces are seen as more honest, they are also perceived to be more 'feminine'[46] than non-smiling faces especially by men.[47] Girls absorb these messages from a young age, and so are likely to smile more frequently than boys. When more than 16,000 photographs from school and college yearbooks in the United States, from kindergarten to adulthood, were analysed, it was seen that this difference in smiling was insignificant until the age of 8 or 9 years old, at which point the difference between girls and boys became increasingly significant.[48] Clearly this difference must develop between infancy and somewhere around this developmental stage in late childhood. By the age of 14 years, the difference between girls and boys became even stronger. However, recent research shows that some of these differences in emotional displays of boys and girls are manifesting at an even younger age, around 3 years old, and becoming more concrete by the age of 10.[49] This is likely to be because social media and advertising is becoming more ubiquitous, and children are more exposed to stereotypically consistent gendered images at a much younger age.

Cornell University researchers Brooke Erin Duffy and Urszula Pruchniewska termed this 'digital double-bind', where even when women are promoting their businesses, they have to try and conform to traditional notions of femininity on social media.[50] Young women in particular tend to get more likes and feedback when they replicate normative feminine signals in their Instagram selfies,[51] such as pouting faces or 'T-Rex hands', side-eye or the 'looking down giggle'.[52] An analysis of half a million statuses by Facebook in 2013 also found that there was a gender divide in the kind of things men and women posted about. Women write about issues personal to them as their main motivation is to maintain social ties, while men discuss social and political events.

Emotion socialisation for children happens both directly and indirectly through their early years. Parents and primary carers of course have a very important role to play, and emotions are often discussed with children while parents/carers play with, comfort and discipline them.[53] They use emotion-socialisation strategies to do this, adjusted as per the child's level of understanding and development. Emotion socialisation happens in all cultures to build emotional competence in children and to align them with the values of a particular community. More recently storybooks are also focused on developing these emotional competencies and capabilities in children, and often reflect the emotional norms of a society. In a longitudinal study with 315 Dutch-speaking families in the Netherlands, the four major emotions that parents tended to discuss with their children were anger, fear, sadness and happiness.[54] This study was undertaken solely with heterosexual couples. An 'Emotion Picture Book' was developed that showed eight drawings for anger, fear, sadness and happiness. Each emotion was shown twice: once with the context of the emotion such as a birthday party or a broken toy, and the second with only the face of the child (ambiguously gender-neutral). Parents were recorded reading and discussing these emotion books with their children and then the videos were analysed and coded for gender-labelling. Generally, parents were increasing the emotion talk with their children (especially second-born) around 2 or 3 years old. And both parents used the label 'boy' more often when talking about the pictures depicting anger, and 'girl' more often when talking about sad and happy pictures.

The focus of mothers on emotions in that study is consistent with another study, published in the *British Journal of Developmental Psychology* carried out with 65 Spanish parents that shows mothers were more likely to use emotional language when speaking with 4-year-old daughters than with their 4-year-old sons.[55] Before the start of the experiment, no difference had been seen in the emotional understanding of 4-year-old girls or boys. By the gendered use of languages around emotion by a key care-giver, the children were being given a message that emotions are more acceptable for girls than for boys, and that women talk more about their feelings. In fact, even at birth and until around 7 months old, infants are likely to hear more words from the primary female carer in their life than the primary male carer. So, based on the findings of these studies, in cases where a child is being brought up by a heterosexual couple, the infant is more likely to see emotions and hear words from the mother than from the father. In conversation with their sons (heterosexual) fathers were more focused on achievement, using active words such as 'win', 'top', 'proud', while responding more quickly to sadness and anxiety in their girls and asking them to be more careful when they attempted something risky.[56] Mothers, meanwhile, were seen to be more encouraging of positive emotional expressions in their children of either gender compared to fathers.[57] There is a tendency for both parents to encourage submissive emotions in girls and suppress any emotions that seem to cause disruption and disharmony. This can often lead to women developing self-blame and low self-esteem as they grow older.[58] Mothers also tend to elaborate more on emotions than fathers, which could be because women internalise the expectation to be more nurturing, and talk about their emotional experience with others, or because they often spend more time with children than the fathers.

These early socialisations can enforce gendered views of the different roles that men and women ought to play in the domestic sphere. And they are also an indication that the home and family frequently become a gendered domain where parents take on distinct parenting roles which are more likely to be aligned with socially accepted stereotypes of masculinity and femininity. Caregivers in schools can also reinforce these gendered emotions. In a study with 1,213 children aged 13–83 months old, where the teachers reported emotional expressions, girls were found to express more 'peaceful', 'calm' and 'neutral' expressions (all positive but passive emotions with little agency), while boys were reported to show more 'surprise', 'curiosity', 'anger' and 'frustration' (more agentic emotions).[59] This cycle will continue, perpetuating the myths of gendered emotions if we do not address the role that emotional socialisation plays in forming the emotionalities of children.

•

Children's self-esteem and sense of self are linked closely with their emotions. As children develop a circle of influence, they are also developing emotions such as pride, guilt and empathy; they are developing self-consciousness, because these emotions are strongly linked to the notion of 'me' and their relationships with others around them.[60] And so the children with positive perceptions of themselves and a strong sense of self are confident and more resilient, as well as more likely to perform better on literacy and numeracy tests. As more standards and rules are learned, emotions can either be considered 'bad' emotions or 'good' emotions depending on gender, and children can learn to hide them or be ashamed of them, which can impact their self-identity and self-esteem.

It is problematic that most studies on emotions have been conducted with children in western Europe and North America, which means that 96 per cent of research that we read in journals is based on only 12 per cent of the world's population.[61] Researchers commonly assume that there is little variation in humans across the globe and that we can use western, educated, industrialised, rich, democratic (WEIRD) people as a standard representation of the global population, while findings show that this is the least representative population from which to draw such conclusions, in both adults and children alike.[62] Most of the parenting studies are done on heterosexual couples too. A meta-analysis of studies showing gender difference shows that only about 2 per cent of these studies were in developing counties, and only about 10 per cent from any countries besides the United States, Canada or the UK.[63] Most other studies have been based in Australia, Finland and Germany. There have been some cross-cultural studies that show that in some cultures, such as in collectivist cultures in Asian countries, high-arousal positive states such as excitement and enthusiasm are valued more and hence most stories and parental expectations and behaviours would reflect that too. In other cultures, low-arousal states such as calmness are more valued and reflected in parental behaviour, and in this way children are socialised emotionally.[64] These are again of course generalisations and rooted in the individualistic/collectivist cultural dichotomies whereby it is proposed that individualistic cultures value personal and individual autonomy while collectivistic cultures value relational harmony at the cost of individual achievement. Any sort of generalisation such as this is harmful, and often rooted in how some non-western/Asian cultures are seen as 'alien' and fetishised.

Boys are encouraged (and expected) to show less of the more tender emotions, such as empathy and kindness, but also pain and distress. Since masculinity is associated with aggressiveness, assertiveness and individualism, and men are expected to protect their own and their family's honour, boys are also allowed to externalise and express some of the negative emotions such as anger and disgust more than girls, so that they can be seen to be pushing forward authoritatively.[65] Girls are encouraged to be more reflective and inward-looking than boys. However, boys show more gender-typed behaviours when they are with peers, which is an active strategy to self-present in a way that will win approval. In a recent study at Duke University, it has been shown that peer pressure and a threat of being seen as 'unmanly' also plays a huge role in young men conforming to toxic masculine behaviour.[66] 195 undergraduate students (of both genders) and a random group of 391 men, aged 18–56 were selected for the study. In the first stage, the participants were asked a series of questions associated with stereotypically gendered interests, such as questions on sports and auto mechanics for the men. They were then told if their scores were higher or lower than the average person of their gender. Women did not feel threatened by being seen as unwomanly. However, when men who received a low score were told that they were less manly than an average man, they expressed more aggressive tendencies (such as completing the word fragments 'ki__' as 'kill' and 'kick' or 'g__' as 'gun'). Research particularly in the USA shows that men are social-ised to respond aggressively (as per the cultural script of masculinity) when their manhood is threatened, in order to regain their threatened status.[67] Men in such cases responded with increased verbal sexual harassment towards the experimenter (especially if she was a woman),[68] and were more likely to choose to participate in an aggressive activity such as boxing rather than doing jigsaw puzzles after they felt their status as a man was precarious or being judged negatively.[69] For young boys and adult men, the pressure to be masculine and maintain their social status is significant in shaping their emotional expressions, particularly in western cultures. In fact, younger men's identity is more linked to social pressure than older men, and so they tend to be more aggressive in conforming to the masculine script.

A large cross-cultural study – one of its kind – looked at gender differences in physical and relational aggression across China, Colombia, Italy, Jordan, Kenya, the Philippines, Sweden, Thailand and the United States, in 1,410 children aged 7–10 years.[70] Prior to this, aggression had primarily been studied in America and western Europe, where research across Finland, Poland and the United States showed 8-year-old boys to be more aggressive than girls, but there is inconclusive data on relational and non-direct aggression. In this cross–cultural study, a survey was sent home where children were asked how often they had engaged in a series of aggressive acts in the previous 30 days. Relational aggression was measured as: 'excluding another child from a group', 'trying to keep others from liking someone by saying mean things about that person' and 'saying things about another child to make people laugh'. Physical aggression was measured on three indicators too: 'throwing something at someone to hurt them', 'shoving or pushing' and 'hitting or slapping other children'. Some of the data from children between 8 and 15 years old has shown girls to be more relationally aggressive than boys, and boys to be more physically aggressive. The results showed no significant gender differences in relational aggression in this age group, but boys were seen to be more physically aggressive than girls, which confirmed the results from some of the earlier studies. However, in Japan it was seen to be the opposite, and so the gendered nature of aggression as an emotional display is not very clear in young children. Children in China, Italy and Thailand were found to be more relationally than physically aggressive, while the opposite was true for Jordan and Kenya. There were no significant differences between their physical and relational aggression in four countries: Colombia, the Philippines, Sweden and the United States. Once again, the sample size from each country was relatively small and it is not ideal to generalise these results to the wider population, because there is likely to be variation within a population too.

Social and cultural factors have a significant effect on how emotions and emotionality develop, and also on gender stereotypes and norms. The risk of a particular kind of aggression developing in a young person is dependent on how normative and visible that kind of behaviour is within that culture, whether the culture is collectivist (prioritising needs and goals of a group over individuals) or individualistic, and whether it is loose (weak social norms and high tolerance for any sort of behaviour perceived as deviant) or tight. The idea that boys are naturally wild and aggressive, and that girls are but more manipulative, is ultimately based on long-standing myths. This also feeds into the 'mean girls' trope, and is based in essentialist beliefs that our brains are determined by our biology, that men's and women's brains are innately very different, and hence so is our behaviour.

Studies with children and adolescents in Japan[71] using a 'Children's Emotional Regulation Scale'[72] show that until the age of 12 there is no clear differentiation between emotion suppression (emotion regulation strategy to make certain emotions more manageable by lessening the intensity of display) and cognitive reappraisal (internal cognitive strategy to reframe the situation so that emotional experience is modulated and not just its expression). Suppression of an emotion happens before it can be expressed, while reappraisal can happen even before the emotion is experienced. The researchers suggested that young people do not have the necessary

173

neurobiological or cognitive capacities to regulate their emotions. As they grow older, by the time they are 18 their capacity to avoid negative emotions as well as find more strategies to manage their emotions in response to specific situations increases.

We are – often inadvertently – enforcing our ideas of what boys and girls should like, or what we believe they like. Rough and tumble, being more interested in outdoor and intellectual pursuits, are for boys, while softness, tenderness and cute baby animals are for girls. Girls are taught to look inwards, to examine and talk about feelings and emotions; boys to interact through rough play, through aggression and dominance of others, looking outside themselves at the broader world. It is as if we make this world so small for girls as soon as they born, drawing a line around them to say 'Look, this is yours and you have to stay within these lines.' In some ways it is worse because we are telling girls that actually this is what they want and need, and nothing more, until they start believing it, and think that there is somehow some innate choice in it. This is a message we give children through implicit actions and words, through the books that we present to them, through what they see around them in the roles that men and women play in their lives. They absorb, imitate, learn. And we then use them as examples of the differences we have enforced.

While we want our children to learn effective strategies to manage negative emotions, it seems sad that we learn from a young age that certain emotions are unacceptable, that we put on brave faces when we might be feeling fearful inside, and we give messages to our young people that some of what they are feeling is not important, nor valid to express in front of people. It also reflects how much of our emotional behaviour is linked to how we grow up, and where we grow up, no matter what our gender. Culture is not a static, nor a simple thing: it is complex and ever-changing. Nevertheless, looking at the meta-analysis of many of these studies, as well as the broader research in developmental psychology, it is very clear that children are learning emotional socialisation from a very young age. This socialisation is happening through the influence groups that they socialise with and aspire to fit in with (parents, carers, friends, etc.) and also through books, television programmes, social media and films. The gendered cues for emotions and behaviours exist all around them in different forms, through words and images like a smog. Our society rewards compliance and adherence to these social codes. These therefore become self-perpetuating.

10.

PINK AND BLUE BRAINS

G IRLS CAN REGULATE THEIR EMOTIONS more than boys so that they are more likely to sit still and pay attention. This is a widely held misconception. But no neuroscience studies so far have been able to show that self-regulatory mechanisms are more developed or active in girls compared to boys. Fifty years ago, neuroscientists started to track brain activity that linked reason to emotion. Research has shown that when viewing emotional movies, the amygdala, an almond-shaped structure in the brain also called the 'fear centre', exerts a 'positive influence' on the ventrolateral prefrontal cortex, which is involved in successfully remembering events and selecting a goal-appropriate response.[1] The amygdala also shows increased communication to other areas of the brain involved in memory during particularly emotive events. Most scientific studies agree that gender and emotion are interlinked in some way. But is it because men's and women's brains are different or is it that they have developed these regulatory mechanisms in their lifetimes due to social conditioning?

For a long time, it was believed that each hemisphere of the brain housed a specific emotion. Known as emotional cortical lateralisation, this associated the right side of the brain with most of the emotional expression and perception, with most of the emotional intensity being perceived by the right hemisphere too.[2] This led some researchers to believe that the right hemisphere of our brains stored facial emotions as icons or templates. There was also a widespread belief since the 1970s that one side of the face was more expressive than the other, and that it was a universal thing. This belief originated in the lateral dominance theories which proposed that our most important motor functions were controlled by the dominant side of our brain, such as handedness. This model was somewhat refined by the 'valence model' that suggested that hemispheric difference was more significant for positive and negative emotions.[3] The right hemisphere was believed to be specialised for negative emotions, and the left hemisphere for positive emotions. This model was then largely superseded by the 'approach–withdrawal model' of emotion processing that suggested that the left and right regions of the brain were processing emotions that elicit an approach or a withdrawal response respectively in humans in different social contexts. This, of course, overlapped with the valence model because most negative emotions such as fear or disgust elicit a withdrawal response, while the positive emotions such as joy and amusement are more likely to make people approach the source.[4]

As we've seen in the discussion in the previous sections, this classical view of emotions – that they are discrete categories and have an evolutionary basis and universally recognised expressions – is deeply embedded in our society and systems.

Much of neuroscience research has largely been focused on finding out whether there are specifically localised brain regions to separate emotion categories. As we saw earlier, the locationist theories propose that there are specific regions of the brain that relate to a discrete

177

emotion category such as fear, anger or happiness. A meta-analytic review of major studies in brain-emotion correspondence did not find any evidence of this.[5] It has long been believed that fear, for instance, is localised in the amygdala. In 1937, scientists Heinrich Klüver and Paul C. Bucy conducted experiments with monkeys where they removed the temporal lobes (the hippocampus and amygdala) and found that monkeys developed 'psychic blindness', where they lost the ability to be fearful of other species, such as snakes, that they would usually be threatened by.[6] However, later studies could not validate these results, and more recent studies have questioned whether fear can be so localised in one small part of the brain.

Dr Eliza Bliss-Moreau of the University of California-Davis conducted experiments with rhesus monkeys (Macaca mulatta) in the early 2000s. These monkeys had neurotoxic injections in their amygdala at only 2 weeks of age but were then raised by their mothers in their social groups rather than by scientists in the lab. The researchers tracked their behaviours for more than a decade, observing them in their social groups as well as with external stimuli such as toy snakes and videos. The researchers found that even though the monkeys who had amygdala damage had hypersocial tendencies in infancy, these behaviours normalised through the years, and became similar to those monkeys who had their amygdala intact.[7] Further studies by the team also showed that although there were some subtle differences in the sequencing of behaviours, these were more pronounced in animals who had their amygdala removed or lesioned later on in life. In humans, damage in the amygdala has led to impairment in processing social cues and facial expressions but it has not been clear to what extent this is linked to processing and expression of fear.[8]

The case of one patient, SM, is very well known. I first came across her in 2016 when I was researching neuroscience and bias.[9] Often referred to as SM-046, she is an American woman who reportedly did not experience fear. A carrier of the recessive gene that causes the very rare Urbach-Wiethe disease, she had neurological damage in her medial temporal lobes due to build-up of calcium deposits in the blood vessels in specific areas of her brain that affected her amygdala. On one hand, SM watched horror films with interest and excitement, showing no sign of fear, and lacked the ability to recognise social cues in facial expressions of other people, but on the other, she was found to experience panic attacks of greater intensity than neurologically healthy control participants. SM was also learning from her experiences, and was fearful of a visit to the doctor because of her memory of pain, although she did not label this as 'fear'. Ralph Adolphs from the Institute of Neurology at University of Iowa and his colleagues showed that in fact SM was not looking at the eye region of faces when judging emotions.[10] When she was explicitly asked to look at the eyes, she did not find it difficult to recognise fear. Moreover, she found it difficult to rate the intensity of emotions in facial expressions that show surprise and anger, both emotions that are often (but not always) depicted with wide eyes. It has therefore been suggested that her inability to understand fear was not to do with the damage in the amygdala but more likely to her problem in processing widened eyes that can sometimes be a cue for fear.[11] The results have shown that the amygdala is useful in tracking other people's gaze where other sensory cues are limited, especially in high-intensity environments.[12] This gaze-tracking is useful for survival, by predicting threat. In this way, the amygdala is less about fear-sensing and more to do with tracking reward and threat potential in unexpected situations. In a patient with amygdala damage, it was also seen that there was an impairment of the usual enhanced memory for emotional aspects of stories, thereby highlighting the role that the amygdala plays in consolidation of emotional memories.[13] These case studies have shown that there are no specific areas of the brain that act as localised emotion centres for specific emotions.

Rather than a two-dimensional view of this landscape of emotions, it is more likely that there is a gradient, ranging from valence to experience. So on one end is the valency (or intensity) of pleasure or displeasure and on the other is how much arousal or sensation a particular emotional experience causes. When we talk about the behavioural and psychological characteristics of emotions, and comparing intensity in one and another, we are doing so along a number of different dimensions. Johnny Fontaine and colleagues from Ghent University asked participants in three different languages – English (188), French (198) and Dutch (145) – to evaluate emotions in terms of bodily sensations, facial gestures and voice, subjective experiences, and emotion regulation, in a controlled web-based study.[14] Each participant was given 4 emotions randomly selected from a group of 24. They had to rate them on a 9-point scale from extremely unlikely to extremely likely. The results did not show any cross-cultural differences, which seems likely to be down to the fact that only Indo-European languages were used and all three countries are part of the western, European context. The sample participants only consisted of students who were asked the meaning of the emotion words in their culture, and not of their own individual experience. This study of course is based in semantic associations of emotions, and so more representative of linguistic conventions. Nevertheless, it has interesting implications for neuroscience researchers who are looking for a mapping of the subjective emotional experiences, and suggests that a more complex multi-dimensional space is needed to understand and to explain emotions and emotional experience.

The notion of gradients is also useful to understand how the brain processes incoming information, and maps the cortical topography. In 2019, the Italian team of Pietro Pietrini, Luca Cecchetti and colleagues carried out an experiment to test the hypothesis that our emotional states are encoded in a gradient-like manner in our brain.[15] These spatially overlapping gradients would code either the intensity or the significance. Twelve native Italian speakers were shown an edited version of the movie *Forrest Gump* and for the entire duration of the film they reported their feelings (using six 'basic' emotions: happiness, fear, surprise, sadness, anger and disgust) and the intensity of these feelings on a scale from 1 to 100. These emotional ratings were correlated with brain activity – mapped with fMRI – seen in another group of 15 volunteers who had been exposed to the same movie in an experiment conducted in Germany. The results showed that a broad emotional landscape exists in our brains, with several areas reacting and interacting to create specific physiological and psychological responses, and that a gradient of neural activity overlaps to create complex emotional experiences. The main activities were seen in the frontal gyrus, the occipital sulcus and precentral sulcus. It is not the case that happiness is represented in one cortical area and another emotion such as anger is represented in another. The right temporoparietal junction (TPJ) in the brain, which is associated with integrating visual, auditory and sensorimotor information, is seen to be involved in representation of subjective emotional experiences, activated for spatially overlapping emotional dimensions in a gradient-like manner, rather than for discrete emotions. The researchers introduced a new term, 'emotionotopy', to encapsulate the different overlapping gradients in the TPJ that encode the various emotion dimensions.

There is little research which gives clear and reliable evidence of how emotions are formed in the brain, and which mechanisms link parts of the brain to which emotions, and what kind of brain activity occurs during processing of stimuli and expression of emotions. There is also no consensus so far on how our autonomic nervous system (ANS) is activated and organised during emotion processing. There are researchers such as Barrett who have outright dismissed any emotion-specific patterns in our ANS, while others assert that there are specific ANS activities for different contexts, but many of these studies have focused on just a handful of emotions, and the sample size has been too small to provide any perfect answers. On the other hand, there are scientists who argue that specific autonomic activity exists for specific emotions and that it is crucial for the body to prepare a behavioural response to any external or internal stimuli.[16] The jury is still out.

Whether there are innate emotion circuits in our brain associated with discrete emotions or not is also grounded in the debate over whether there are some basic universal or natural kinds of emotions. We have seen how this idea is disputed. The methods that were used to extract these basic categories of emotions and universal facial expressions have been questioned as well as shown to not be universal when they interact with different physical and social environments. So, it is unlikely that specific parts of the brain correspond to specific emotions. It is more likely that there are several neural networks that are working together in fluctuating conjunction to create different emotional states. Over the last few years, evidence has been accumulating that different parts of the brain are activated in an interconnected manner to create overlapping patterns across different emotion categories – for instance, the insula is activated for both pain and pleasure.[17] However, even though there are many theories and experiments that have attempted to isolate the specific regions associated with emotional processing, there is still a lack of consistent empirical evidence of how each region works together as part of a broader emotional system in our brains. One thing is clear: no one single part of the brain constitutes a specific emotion.

•

At the Institut universitaire en santé mentale de Montréal and the University of Montreal, 46 healthy people (25 women, 21 men) participated in an experiment where they had to view images that could evoke positive, negative or neutral emotions.[18] Brain imaging was used to map brain activity, and hormone levels were also monitored. The dorso-medial prefrontal cortex (dmPFC, which plays a role in processing empathy, sense of self, social impressions and fear) and the right amygdala were seen to be most activated. The results showed that the women were more likely to have a strong reaction to negative images, but it was more significant that a higher testosterone level, irrespective of a person's sex, was associated with a higher sensitivity to these images, which resulted in more brain activity being seen on the imaging. The higher interaction of these two areas of the brain, mostly in men, but more generally in people with higher levels of testosterone, show the likelihood of a less analytical approach to emotions in people with lower testosterone, irrespective of their gender.

Testosterone has similar evolved functions in women's and men's bodies.[19] The ovaries produce both testosterone and oestrogen. While testosterone levels in men are generally higher than women – especially after the onset of puberty due to the testes secreting much more testosterone than is usually found in women – the standard limits defined for men and women do not take into account factors such as polycystic ovary syndrome (PCOS), adrenal hyperplasia, weight, menstrual phase and diet, as well as daily fluctuations. Sari Anders and colleagues from University of Michigan claim that because the difference in testosterone is presumed to be based in a sex difference, it is also presumed that it is a sign of maleness.[20]

There is also a misconception that the levels of testosterone are fixed and unchanging and based only in innate factors. But in our culture, as men are pushed into powerful positions, while women are discouraged from showing power and authority, these gender socialisations (both external expressions and internalisations) can lead to changes in 'normal' testosterone levels in men and women. If men are engaging in such testosterone-fuelling behaviour more often, and women are curbing these behaviours to conform to social norms, then this gendered behaviour also modulates testosterone. Masculine stereotypes increase testosterone more than feminine. Competition in particular is considered to have an evolutionary advantage and so, as men are encouraged to engage in more competitive behaviour more often, or be more aggressive and authoritative (to wield power) while the same behaviour is discouraged in women, this has an impact on testosterone levels. And this is likely to result in more testosterone in men. Experiments with actors engaging in stereotypical masculine and feminine behaviour showed that testosterone was higher in women after an act of wielding power in a social situation.[21] Therefore, testosterone is not only a heritable characteristic, but also influenced by emotional socialisation from a young age. It is widely believed that testosterone affects behaviour and the way men and women act and feel, but there is also a reverse pathway, where gender and the gendered experiences and norms can have a neurobiological impact and affect testosterone.

Yes, genetics and biology do play a role, but our brains and genetics are more plastic than was previously understood. Researchers such as Sari Anders propose that gendered socialisation modulates testosterone, and although we are beginning to accept that our brains are malleable, the plasticity of our hormones and the impact of gendered behaviour in conformance with our societal norms is relatively lacking in studies. Gender and sex are more permeable and flexible categories than we have traditionally thought: the way we present to the world, and how we are expected to act, influences our biology too through these reverse gender-testosterone pathways.

There are not very many studies that have really examined whether male and female brains process and represent emotions differently. It is challenging to map emotional expression and regulation in a lab under artificial conditions, after all. The empirical evidence on this difference is still mixed, and debatable, failing to provide any conclusive evidence of gendered emotions. A cognitive reappraisal study using fMRI in 2008 attempted to test emotional reactivity, responses and regulation, to show that there was no difference in reactivity between men and women.[22] Twenty-five participants (13 women, 12 men) between the ages of 18 and 26 with no prior history of psychiatric disorders or trauma were involved. They were shown negative and neutral images, and then were asked to narrate their reinterpretation of the negative image using three specific strategies: 'It is not real, and they are just pretending'; 'Things will get better over time'; and 'The situation looks worse than it really is.' The fMRI mappings showed that the various regions involved in cognitive reappraisal were involved during regulation.[23]

When the participants were shown negative pictures, and as they were trying to regulate their emotional responses, it was observed that the images evoked similar kinds of negative emotional responses from both men and women, and both used cognitive reappraisal equally to counter some of these negative emotional reactions.[24] The amygdala was fired equally in men and women at the start. A comparison of the decrease in the activity in the amygdala when the participants were trying to down-regulate their emotional responses using the three strategies offered to them (i.e., managing their emotions so that they are not as negative) showed men were doing more down-regulation in their amygdala responses, without much self-directed conscious thought. Women had more activity in their prefrontal cortex, where the cognitive regulation (more goal-directed and active regulation of emotions using pre-learned strategies) of emotion takes place. Women also used more positive emotions to counter the effect of the negative ones, especially while down-regulating, and they engaged the ventral striatum much more than men during their emotional reappraisal. It is known that the ventral striatum is more engaged with reward-related processing and while processing positive stimuli. So, it was possible that the women were generating positive emotion or recalling positive memories to counter the effect of negative stimuli much more than men. Women have also been observed to use positive refocusing strategies that they have developed over their lifetimes in order to cope with negative emotions[25] and inhibit their behaviours much more than men.[26] Since it is not possible to state conclusively and generalise these results, the researchers speculate that since women also score higher on behaviour inhibition in social situations, the cognitive cost of regulating emotions and adjusting them to the expectations and norms seems to be much higher for women.

Emotions in themselves are complicated and it is difficult to separate the various aspects of gender identity and roles from the way emotions are performed and experienced during any neuroimaging study. With any study that has identified sex differences in the brain it is essential to consider false positives and how much this has played a role in conclusions. In a seminal article, 'Eight Things You Need to Know about Sex, Gender, Brains and Behaviour', three of the most prominent scientists in this field, Gina Rippon, Daphna Joel and Cordelia Fine, explain that neuroimaging studies are especially prone to this.[27] Fine said in 2013 that new neuroimaging technologies are particularly prone to false positives, as neuroimaging technology is still expensive, so it becomes unviable for most labs to have large sample sizes.[28] Many of the research studies are based in speculative binary determinants of sex without acknowledging neuroplasticity and the effect of social and environmental factors in moulding our neural responses. Often large datasets are recycled and used to complement the live case studies, and there is a risk of hyperbole[29] where even a 2 per cent difference is reported as 'large'.[30] As Fine, Joel and Rippon state: even 'statistically significant' does not necessarily mean 'practically significant in the real world' or 'theoretically important'.[31] There is also a publication bias, which means that negative results in this field are generally absent from publications, and the emphasis is on publishing research which shows positive sex differences.[32] Professor Rippon told me over Zoom that the 'variability between men and women is not as interesting as the variability within groups of women and groups of men', which supports the criticism of many neuroscience studies that the within-group difference is often ignored and instead any between-group effect is inflated.

A study by Sean David and colleagues in 2018 showed that there are very few studies with large samples that show any sex differences, but they receive more attention than the many studies that do not show any sex differences in the brain.[33] Across the 179 identified fMRI studies of the brain published over a decade that they looked at, only 2 had a title that did not focus on the lack of sex differences or similarities between sexes, and only 17 did not highlight sex differences in their abstract. This success rate seems implausible considering the sample sizes are so small. A deep dive shows that there is often more in-group variation than between-group variation, which is selectively highlighted. The media also plays a role in sensationalising academic research for easy clicks online, when differences between men and women, as demonstrated by studies, are trivial. And, in the end, we don't really know much about human brains yet, even though we have advanced so much further in understanding the human body. In an experiment using fMRI on the brains of 34 soldiers (15 women, 19 men), Joel and colleagues analysed the response to stress based on sex/gender. They did not find any male- or female-specific response to high stress, which in this case was combative military service.[34]

The debate continues. One study conducted by Ragini Verma and colleagues at the University of Pennsylvania in 2013, with 949 young people (8–22 years, 428 males and 521 females), showed that the neural wiring between men and women's brains is different.[35] They suggested that in male brains connections run from front to back in one hemisphere, and from left to right in female brains across both hemispheres, which can result in men being better at links between perception and co-ordinated action, with women being better at intuition.[36] According to the authors of the study, this explains why men are better at certain tasks (such as motor and spatial memory tasks, and navigation), while women are better at others (such as communication, collaboration and multi-tasking). Men's brains were better at inter-hemispheric connections and women's brains better at intra-hemispheric connections, and the differences were more pronounced in young adulthood than in children under 14 years old.[37]

But we know that science is not without bias. In the nineteenth century, scientists believed that there was a sex/gender-based difference in intelligence, and they cherry-picked data to show that women had smaller skulls, and therefore smaller brains, than men.[38] This idea that women had lower intelligence also fed into the stereotype that women are more emotional, and men have a higher capacity for rational thought. In a study in 2017 by researchers at Edinburgh University, psychologist Stuart Ritchie examined a large data sample from the UK Biobank of MRI brain scans of 2,750 women and 2,466 men aged 44–77 years.[39] They concluded that, although some sex-based variations were seen in the thickness of the cortex and brain volume, there was also a significant variability within groups, and so if they plucked a brain image randomly from the study, it would be near-impossible to say whether it came from a man or a woman. This really blows all the assertions about there being a 'male' and a 'female' brain out of the water. Age was also seen as a factor in this study, because most women were undergoing menopause or had already undergone it. Hormonal changes during menopause can affect the structure of the brain. Indeed, the study showed that age played a more significant role than sex. The brains of men and women were shown to be more similar than different. Daphna Joel, an Israeli neuroscientist and advocate for neurofeminism, has written extensively about how it is rare to find brains that have only typically 'male' or 'female' features as two distinct categories, solely based on an individual's genitalia.[40]

Cordelia Fine, from the University of Melbourne, says gender stereotypes can often be projected onto findings of any sex differences in the brain to make complete contradictions seem valid. In a 2018 article published in the *Lancet*, Fine highlights a feminist analysis by philosopher Robyn Bluhm[41] that shows how science can be biased, as the inconsistent findings of various brain-mapping studies of emotion are selectively interpreted to justify the stereotype that women are the emotional gender.[42] Fine also suggests that 'widespread scientific assumptions that female and male brains are functionally distinct, dichotomous, fixed, and invariant due to a sexually differentiated genetic blueprint are not scientifically justified and may be sexist'.[43]

For example, back in 2002, Raquel and Reuben Gur, with colleagues from the University of Pennsylvania, looked at the ratio of orbital to amygdala volume in 116 right-handed, healthy adults (57 men, 59 women, 18–49 years).[44] The amygdala is of course associated with fear and excitement, while the orbital frontal region is considered to be involved in modulation of anger and aggression. Men and women had identical volumes of amygdala, hippocampus and dorsal prefrontal cortex. But women had a higher ratio of orbital volume and amygdala compared to men, showing that men are likely to get more aggressive and women are better at controlling any aggressive tendencies because of the way their brains are designed. However, as we know from more recent research, it is difficult to isolate regions of the brain for specific emotions, and so the assumptions in this study were flawed.

Anne Fausto-Sterling, professor of biology and gender studies at Brown University, has looked extensively at investigations that insist there is a sex difference in the corpus collosum (the connection passing information between the two hemispheres of the brain; its thickness affects visual and spatial processing amongst other abilities), but finds there is plenty of disagreement and very little consistency between the various inquiries. In her book *Sexing the Body* she writes:

'[That] researchers continue to probe the corpus callosum in search of a definitive gender difference speaks to how entrenched their expectations about biological differences remain.'[45] Brains are not found to be sexually dimorphic (representing two distinct forms), with little or no overlap between the features that are attributed 'male' and 'female'. Two significant neuroimaging studies, one with 1,400 brain images from 4 datasets and another an analysis of almost 6,000 brains, focusing on those areas that are typically characterised for masculinity and femininity such as grey matter volume, white matter and measures of connectivity across different regions, showed that brains are a mosaic of features lying somewhere on the maleness–femaleness spectrum. Some features of a brain are more common in women, some more common in men, and some similar in men and women. Any strict binary divide of maleness–femaleness is not seen in human brains. Even though there were some sex/gender differences in brain structure, there was rarely an internal consistency where all parts of the brain were 'male' or 'female'.[46]

Humans therefore have both 'masculine' and 'feminine' psychological characteristics – much like a mosaic – in terms of their behaviour, attitudes and personalities. This makes it somewhat difficult to validate the widespread assumptions that men and women might be innately different in the way they feel and express their emotions, because sex category is not an accurate predictor of human brain structure. Instead, the way we present to the world, our gender identity, which can be fluid and on a continuum, and the extent to which we conform to the gender norms, affects our brain structures too. Richard Lippa, professor of psychology, proposes a 'cascade model' where our experiences become integrated into the developmental architecture of the brain and this interplay can lead to specific behavioural patterns. For instance, a musician's neural areas related to spatial cognition or finger movement can become more accentuated, and similarly nature and nurture interact to form the complex notions of gender.[47]

One of the big barriers in sex-based neuroscience research for emotions is also that gender and sex are often conflated, and used inconsistently. Researchers in Canada and the United States searched for scientific publications between 2015 and 2020 on PubMed using the keywords 'gender', 'human' and 'social communication'. Out of 85 articles published during this period on these topics, 82 used 'gender' when they meant 'biological sex', not outlining how they had categorised sex, and so it was likely that these researchers had judged this based on appearance. I have also previously discussed how there is representative bias in our scientific studies and very little has been done with people who fall outside the traditional binary gender norms, or with transgender individuals. A recent neuroimaging study conducted in the Netherlands with post-mortem brain material from 14 cisgender men, 11 cis-women, 11 trans women and 1 trans man revealed that those aspects of the hypothalamus that show the most prominent sex/gender differences were actually the same in cisgender women and trans women.[48] This showed that the feminisation of the trans women was not due to their oestrogen treatment alone. The trans man showed a similar pattern to the male control range even though their testosterone treatment had stopped three years before their death. The results from these studies suggest that any differences in brains is predominantly related to gender identity, and not to biological sex or hormonal differences between men and women.

So can we say that emotions are hard-wired into us, and that women are more emotional than men because of the difference in men's and women's brains? No, absolutely not. Emotions are complex constructions. As Lisa Feldman Barrett says: 'Emotions are not built into the brain, but they are built by the brain, and they are constructions of your bodily sensations in the world.'[49] We construct them through our engagement with specific contexts and environments, through our bodily engagements and experiences, through 'interoception'. No emotion is one instance of arousal, and no emotion is experienced in one singular war. There is no one bodily state that can sum up any of the emotions; not one expression that is common for all humans.

The way we experience and express emotions is a result of a lifetime of learning, through a databank of bodily sensations that we build up over the years. Our emotional expression is determined by the templates, patterns and shortcuts we already carry in our brains through a dual-processing system that our brains deploy to deal with new people and situations. As I discuss in my book *Sway: Unravelling Unconscious Bias*, system 1 is a spontaneous, fast-acting and associative information-processing system which happens when a lot of information comes at us at a very high speed, and our brain matches this information to its existing patterns and memories. If in the past something evoked a feeling of high arousal and unpleasantness, our system 1 processing automatically and subconsciously gives us a signal that this is how we need to act, behave, feel. As you can imagine, this has the potential for our brains to fall back on stereotypes, and, on using that information, to perpetuate the idea that we are somehow creating emotions outside any of the social norms and contexts that we exist in.

On the basis of current research, I find it increasingly hard to argue that any differences between the brains of men and women are related to innate biological differences. Even if we subscribe to the idea that our emotions are innate, it seems more and more likely that the differences between the sexes are not hard-wired into us. We see that neuroscience has failed to provide any consistent evidence for sex/gender differences across brains, or even that maleness/femaleness is a dichotomous property in terms of the brain's activity. What science has shown us, however, is that children's main caregivers – e.g., parents and teachers – carry implicit biases with regards to gender, and are never completely gender-neutral. Parental treatment of children in early years can influence which characteristics become more significant, and which aspects of a child's emotional and cognitive functions develop more than others. Our brains are plastic, and flexible, and so changing constantly. Brains adapt and modify both in structure and function throughout our lives, as we build up a database of experiences and memories. This means that brains exposed to different stimuli in terms of environmental factors and behaviours develop in very different ways.

While the Roman philosopher Seneca might have believed that a human embryo is merely a miniature adult and all it does is basically grow bigger, we now know this is not the case. We are becoming more aware of how our sensory experiences and the carer–child and peer relationships in the early years, in particular, can initiate long-term effects that persist into adulthood.[50] Human brains go through a period of heightened plasticity and rapid learning in early infancy, when children are relying on social referencing to navigate social and emotional situations and to build emotional competencies.[51] And there are also parts of the brain such as the prefrontal cortex responsible for emotional regulation, which matures well into adulthood both structurally and functionally.[52] Understanding how gendered norms impact on our development from a young age, and that they are far from innate, is the key to understanding the gender emotional gap.

Section 4:

CAN EMOTIONAL WOMEN GET AHEAD?

All the pursuits of men are the pursuits of women also,
but in all of them a woman is inferior to a man.
— Plato, *Republic*, Book 5[1]

11.

PITBULL WITH LIPSTICK

I WAS ON A PANEL AT a literary festival recently where we were asked to go back to 2016 and imagine what the world would have looked like if Hillary Clinton had become US President. Of course, there is no way to know if the world would have looked different, but I have reflected a lot on why she didn't become the president. In a September 2016 interview on the Instagram account 'Humans of New York', Clinton said she grew up learning to control her emotions to get ahead in domains dominated by men. Previously, in 2006, the chairman of the Republican National Committee asserted that Hillary Clinton was 'too angry' to be elected president. However, during the 2016 presidential election she came under attack for not being 'emotional enough', for not smiling enough, for being stilted. Joe Scarborough, a host on MSNBC, tweeted in March 2016: 'Smile, you've just had a big night', and former White House Chief of Staff Reince Priebus tweeted that 'Hillary Clinton was angry & defensive the whole time – no smile and uncomfortable.' In the 'Humans of New York' interview, Clinton admitted that she would love to show passion, to raise her voice, to wave her arms, but she can't because she gets scrutinised for it and 'apparently that's a little bit scary to people. And I can't yell too much. It comes across as "too loud" or "too shrill" or "too this" or "too that".'

Back in 2008, when Hillary Clinton was battling Obama for the Democratic Party candidate nomination, media outlets variously reported on both her emotionality and the lack of it: the *Boston Globe* announced: 'Clinton Shows Emotion in Final Hours', and the *Washington Post* referred to 'A Chink in the Steely Façade of Hillary Clinton'. When she delivered her concession speech in November 2016 – a powerful speech asking American people to uphold the constitution – CNN proclaimed that Clinton was 'too emotional'.

The defeat of Clinton by Trump showed that not only are women leaders judged by how we think about them, but also by how we 'feel' about them. There are strong moral emotions that play a role in how women leaders in particular are judged by both men and women: emotions such as contempt, disgust, revulsion and righteous anger. There is not just prejudice due to women breaking stereotypes, but also moral judgement of women who take over more masculine emotional expression in leadership positions, because in the case of women, emotions are also associated with moral virtue.

While there were many other factors that counted against Hillary Clinton, one of the major ones was 'unlikability', even amongst women.[1] In one poll of around 5,000 adults, more than 54 per cent of the respondents said that their opinion of her was unfavourable. In November 2016, more than 61 per cent of 4,183 adults gave her a likeability rating of less than 50 degrees (where 0 degrees was cold and negative and 100 was warm and positive).[2] Although a Pew Research Center poll in October 2016 showed that 62 per cent of the respondents agreed that Clinton was well-qualified to serve as president, just 54 per cent of women voted for her, and even fewer white women did (45 per cent of white women for Clinton, as opposed to 98 per cent of black women).[3]

Women, even when they are powerful and hold status, do not have much space to express their emotions. Emotionality or the lack of it both count against them. One makes them too feminine, the other not feminine enough and therefore threatening to both men and other women. The constant adjustment of emotions puts women in a double-bind. Women who display strong emotions are seen to be violating feminine norms, especially if they are in the public domain and especially if they are vying for leadership. Either way, it becomes clear that women are scrutinised and penalised for their emotions, and for their apparent inability to control them.

I can think of numerous such examples from the political domain. In 1916, Jeanette Rankin became the first woman elected to the United States Congress, four years before the 19th Amendment granted US women the right to vote. Press coverage from the time shows the focus on her appearance ('tall and slender, with frank hazel eyes, sandy hair and energetic mouth'),[4] and her femininity ('a woman who is thoroughly feminine').[5] The *Boston Post* reported 'her femininity, her sweetness, and her direct, but not aggressive talks' to reassure the readers that even though Rankin was stepping into a masculine domain, she was still abiding by 'feminine' values. Margaret Chase Smith, the first woman to win election to both the US House of Representatives and the US Senate in 1964 experienced similar press coverage, which sought to strike a balance between her 'feminine' and 'masculine' qualities. One of the articles from the time noted that even though she was an expert in defence matters, she was also a 'great lover of flowers', just in case anyone thought that her intellect made her seem masculine and threatening.[6]

In more recent times, Sarah Palin, Governor of Alaska between

2006 and 2009 and the 2008 Republican vice-presidential candidate, was portrayed in the media in a similar way. Whatever our personal opinion of her politics, it is interesting to note that in 2008 she was shown as a lover of hunting and guns to appeal to the masculine ideals of the voters – i.e., she had the masculine qualities to lead – but the focus remained on her feminine appeal and on her 'warmth and charm'.[7] Palin positioned herself as a 'hockey mom who is like a pitbull with lipstick',[8] trying to strike the right balance between masculine aggressiveness – a sort of fake hegemonic masculinity – and feminine maternal beauty and warmth: a go-getter, but also a mother.[9] In a similar vein, former prime minister of the UK Margaret Thatcher was called 'the Iron Lady' to highlight her unique mix of strength and femininity, which might otherwise have been considered mutually exclusive.

Self-effasiveness is perceived as a good quality for women and makes them more likeable and hireable. In a 1990 study it was shown that men liked and trusted women leaders more if they spoke tentatively, using 'tag questions' (statements that end in short questions with a rising or falling pitch, perceived to be signs that the speaker is looking for assurance and is not very sure of themselves) and hedging (words or phrases that makes a statement appear vague and less forceful, such as 'somewhat', 'sort of', etc.).[10] Men's tentativeness did not affect their influence either way. According to this study, women were also supposed to be modest, as pride was considered a masculine attribute. So, self-promotion in women, seen as an agentic emotion and behaviour, was not considered favourably by men, but surprisingly even less so by other women. Self-promoting men did not suffer the same judgement.

Women are not supposed to be agentic, but this perception has changed somewhat over the last few years, and agency, strength and decisiveness in women are becoming more acceptable and recognisable in workplaces and more broadly in society.[11] Despite this gradual shift in societal attitudes, any non-agentic behaviour in women, and any signs of passivity and lack of authority can face much more scrutiny than in men, who are given the benefit of the doubt because there remains a stronger association between a man and a leader. To test whether it is really true that stereotypes of leaders and gender roles have changed, these earlier experiments from 1990 were repeated but with more tentativeness built into the speech to indicate deference, hesitancy, and a lack of confidence, associated traditionally with low status.[12] Participants had to report on likeability and influence of these actors. Tentative women were perceived to be less likeable and also having less influence compared to assertive women and men. The same prejudice was shown by both men and women, and occurred irrespective of the content of their speech and whether it was positive, negative or controversial. The assertiveness of men's speech did not affect their likeability or influence. Such scrutiny is motivated by the desire to find more legitimate ways of proving that women do not make good leaders. It is also likely that more aversive forms of discrimination have become embedded in our workplaces, and that stereotypes are too strongly entrenched.

Nichole Bauer from the University of Alabama has shown that women have to have higher qualifications than men to reach the same level, or to attract the same kind of support.[13] These stereotypes are not automatically activated but are more likely to be activated and applied when individuals receive information about women candidates that align with standard norms of femininity, such as focusing on their looks or their warm, caring and sensitive nature and voice. Women's greater assumed emotionality acts as a kind of organising over-arching principle, a 'master stereotype' that means that even when it is not of a high magnitude, it becomes most significant and governs other beliefs about men and women in various domains.[14] A Gallup poll in 2000 based on telephone interviews with a randomly selected national sample of 1,026 adults, 18 years and older, showed that Americans viewed women as emotional, talkative, patient, while men were viewed as aggressive and courageous.[15] Ninety per cent of both men and women thought that women were more emotional. National polls in America for over three decades have continued to show that these stereotypes are still held by both men and women.[16] Beliefs about women's greater emotional expressiveness compared to men are often two to four times as common as any other commonly held belief about gender.

'Stereotype activation' is the extent to which a stereotype is easily accessible in a person's mind, and 'stereotype application' is the extent to which this stereotype is used to judge a person belonging to a particular group. Holding a stereotype and activating and applying a stereotype are not necessarily the same thing. Voters might hold a stereotype about women being more emotional and less agentic, but this has a higher chance of being activated and applied when they receive specific information about the woman candidate through media coverage. A focus on their mothering might evoke stereotypes about them being more caring and nurturing, which could trigger a range of other stereotypes that imply they do not have the necessary traits to be a leader. These stereotypes, once activated, can also intensify the incongruency between the communal and agentic characteristics of women and therefore lead people to deem them poorer leaders than men.

Without these stereotypes promulgated via media, voters are likely to rely solely on their partisanship. Party affiliation has also been shown to affect a person's reliance on gender stereotypes. In the US, traditional gender roles align more favourably with the traditional family values promoted by Republicans, and Democrat voters are seen to be more amenable to women candidates, and their values of gender egalitarianism.[17] Republicans have stronger views against women in politics, with more than 35 per cent believing that women are not as suited emotionally to political leadership as men (compared to about 14 per cent for Democrats), and Republican women are marginally more biased against other women than men as compared to the Democrats.[18] Sixty-nine per cent of Democratic men and 46 per cent of women personally hoped for a woman president, compared to 20 per cent of Republican women, and 16 per cent of Republican men.[19]

In a study by Georgetown researchers in 2019[20] using data from the 1974–2018 General Social Survey, it was seen that the number of Americans who believe that women are less suited to politics than men because of their emotionality has declined (from 50 per cent in 1975 to 13 per cent in 2019).[21] While this is a significant drop, given it is over a period of almost 50 years it is disappointing and perhaps not as significant as might have been expected. It is not just men but also women who hold this view, especially older women. According to a 2014 Pew Research poll of 1,835 people, 9 per cent of Americans believe that women are not 'tough enough' for politics.[22] This might explain to some extent why so many women voted for Donald Trump instead of Hillary Clinton.

In the USA in particular, but also in many other countries and cultures, the imagery of political leaders has been rooted in masculine performance in which they embody the masculine ideal: historically this is shown in painted portraits and sculptures depicting them leading the troops. We see a contemporary version of this in the way Putin presents himself to the world, bare-chested on horseback, in a river, out in the wild: a true man. Toughness becomes an expected personality trait for political leaders. This narrative is seen in the media's framing of female political leaders by invalidating their claims to power, either by feminising them or reinforcing the traditional norms of political power, where feminine notions of emotionality are denigrated. An analysis of Sarah Palin's speech from the 2008 Republican National Convention shows that she was complicit in enforcing the hegemonic masculine ideals, asserting John McCain's masculinity by talking about his military leadership. Communal spirit is perceived to be a feminine trait, so Palin belittled Barack Obama by feminising him through reference to his community organisation work. Standard tropes of what a man and woman should be, and what kind of man and woman are acceptable in politics, were cleverly played out for the voters. Republican senatorial candidates Sharron Angle of Nevada and Christine O'Donnell in Delaware taunted their opponents with the phrases, 'Man up' and 'Get your man pants on',[23] thereby questioning their toughness, casting doubts on their ability to be a successful and competent leader.

While these two examples are not explicit in which emotions are being considered, it is clear that women are being considered more emotional than men, and so not decisive enough to be a leader. It might appear that the role gender stereotypes about emotions play in politics is shrinking, but the fact is that they are quite substantial. As the female-type emotions are linked to reactivity, and lacking reason and rationality, women are therefore seen to be lacking self-control and authority. This undermines their professional legitimacy, especially their claim to a leadership position. When women violate these social norms, they are perceived as being 'abrasive' and suffer negative consequences such as being considered less likeable.

And research has shown that being likeable is a significant factor for a woman's success in politics, more so than for a man.[24] Women's likeability is affected more than men's when they behave dominantly in a counter-stereotypical manner.[25] There is also an impact on hireability of women, especially if the expression of dominance was quite explicit, and so women have to try and be more subtle in how they show authority. Women leaders have to work hard to boost their likeability. Since women are expected to be more nurturing and warm than men, and have more communal emotional characteristics, women often develop a more democratic and participatory leadership style, with a greater inclination towards more compassionate and egalitarian attitudes, and begin to rely on it. This then becomes positioned and qualified as a 'feminine leadership style'. Men, on the other hand, tend to have a more autocratic approach because they do not have to navigate this thin line between communal and agentic emotional expression in order to be liked and supported in a leadership role. Men are not penalised for being dominant and authoritative; in fact, this is what is expected from them so anything other than this behaviour will be counter-stereotypic and is likely to be penalised.

Both men and women of course have to conform to certain norms about emotional expression, but there is enough research and anecdotal data to show that women come under more scrutiny than men. Jacqueline Smith and colleagues from the University of Massachusetts show that there is a narrower permissible range of emotions that women are allowed to express in the workplace compared to men – a 'narrow band of acceptable behaviour'– that are 'somewhat feminine but not too feminine and somewhat masculine but not too masculine'.[26] Women have to navigate between the prototypical feminine stereotypes assigned to them, while at the same time being burdened with the pressure to conform to the typical masculine stereotypes assigned to leaders. A greater congruence is seen in the emotional expression of a successful leader and the emotional expression commonly associated with men. Men are supposed to be more agentic (ambitious, independent, etc.) while women are more reactive and communal (nurturing, supportive, kind, etc.). In this way, women have been seen to be lacking the emotional characteristics of a good leader or manager, as leadership roles require agency. In 1996, Virginia Schein, an internationally recognised management researcher, proposed that when people 'think manager' they 'think male'.[27] Schein used a long list of agentic traits such as dominance and helpfulness, and positive emotions such as enthusiasm and joy, and asked participants to rate how they found each of these traits to be male in general, or female in general. They were also asked to rate if each of these traits was a characteristic of a successful manager. A strong correlation was seen for men and managers while the correlation between women and managers was zero.

Things have changed over the years, and an attempt to replicate this Schein study in 2006 showed that more people were viewing women as agentic and more suited to the emotional profile expected from a leader, although overall men still held a bias against women leaders.[28] There haven't been many academic studies on the perception of specific emotions depicted by leaders, so much of this has to be drawn out tangentially, but from seven groups of people – men, women, male managers, female managers, successful managers, successful male managers, successful female managers – it was seen that the emotions expressed by successful male managers were more similar to those emotions expressed by men, as compared to those displayed by women.[29] Even when women managers were objectively successful, their emotions were less aligned with that of a 'successful manager', even when compared to men who were not managers or proven successful as one.

In another experiment, by researchers at University of California, 60,470 people (with a 49/51 per cent women/men split) were asked to evaluate their bosses. There was a cross-bias where women judged men more favourably while men judged women more favourably. However, overall men were twice as preferred (33 per cent) as bosses and managers to women (only 13 per cent).[30] Those who preferred a woman as a boss indicated that this was because of their supportive and nurturing nature and that they are better listeners than men. A few men also preferred women bosses because they 'were easier to look at than men' and were 'sexier' and 'prettier'. Such benevolent sexism is rooted in the assumption that women are not very competent. One man even mentioned that women were more gullible and hence 'more susceptive to my bullshit'. Those who preferred men as bosses said that this was because women were 'bitchy', 'dramatic', 'emotional' and 'moody', while men were more 'objective', 'decisive' and 'just have a better business sense'. Women's personalities and (assumed) emotionality continue to be seen as a hindrance, with people carrying prejudices about their ability to be an effective leader. This kind of implicit bias affects what emotions become normalised in a workplace, and how much women have to work to prove their fit to the role of a leader. This is also a case of confirmation bias, because people assume that women are more emotional, and so people notice their emotions more readily, while in the case of men, it is assumed that they are not very emotional, and so their emotional displays aren't as noticeable. A survey in the US in 2005 showed that 45 per cent of people preferring men as a boss said this was because men don't let emotions get in the way of work.[31]

As of 2021, according to a 'Women in the Workplace' report by McKinsey and Co., while over 50 per cent of the workforce is women, men hold almost two-thirds of management positions.[32] A 2021 list of women CEOs in Fortune 500 companies shows that there are only 29 (5.8 per cent).[33] In an interview in the *Economic Times* in India in 2019, the former Australian Prime Minister Julia Gillard said: 'It is easily assumed that women are too soft for leadership, or too emotional or hysterical.'[34] These biases are continually used to evaluate women and devalue them. I quizzed many women while writing this book, and more than 80 per cent (of 50 participants) told me that they had been overlooked for leadership positions and asked to work on their confidence and assertiveness. Some of the women who are in boardrooms (often as the only woman) told me that they were often called 'difficult' and 'bossy' while their behaviour was in no way more challenging or different than that of the men at a similar level in their organisation. Even in schools and higher education institutions, which can often have a more even gender balance than corporate environments, leadership is emotionally charged.

The International Survey on Emotion Antecedents and Reactions (ISEAR) is the only large cross-cultural dataset on emotions, with 3,000 respondents in 37 countries across all continents.[35] This was collected during the 1990s from student participants, directed by Swiss psychologists Klaus Scherer and Harald Wallbott. The students were asked to report situations in which they had experienced all seven major emotions (joy, fear, anger, sadness, disgust, shame, and guilt). Most studies mapping emotional differences between men and women, even cross-cultural ones, had not prior to this considered the status of women in a specific context. A research study led by Agneta Fischer from the University of Amsterdam used this

ISEAR dataset for secondary analysis in combination with the United Nations Development Programme to develop an index called the Gender Empowerment Measure (GEM).[36]

The GEM mapped the role that women played in the economic and political life of a particular country using parameters such as: percentage of seats in parliament held by women, percentage of administrators and managers who are women, percentage of professional and technical workers who are women, and women's share of earned income. So, for instance, most of the countries in the global north (the western countries) had a higher GEM than the rest. Based on an extensive review of previous studies, a hierarchy of emotions was developed by the academic team, where anger and contempt were 'powerful' emotions, and fear, sadness, shame and guilt were 'powerless'. The powerful emotions are more likely to be seen in men, especially in countries where women have less power overall, and consequently a low GEM score. Respondents were then asked to self-report on the intensity of their emotions. The results confirmed some of the earlier assumptions that no difference was found in powerful emotions such as anger across the varying GEM countries, and so the gender imbalance did not have an effect on how anger was perceived in men and women across different cultural contexts. However, in the case of 'powerless' emotions, especially that of sadness (and the emotional response associated with it, crying), there was a difference in men's scores, so men from higher GEM countries reported their feelings of sadness and vulnerability to be less intense, suggesting that men in western countries had more restrictive emotionality than in countries with low GEM. There was no difference seen in women's scores. More gender equality as measured by the GEM did not equate to men acquiring or being more comfortable with emotions that are perceived to be feminine.

More women with greater economic and political power and autonomy does not equate to more emotional equality.

The Conformity to Masculine Norms Inventory (CMNI) has been used widely as a measure to assess conformity to hegemonic masculine culture in the United States.[37] CMNI uses eleven normative ideals: winning, emotional control, risk-taking, dominance, playboy, self-reliance, primacy of work, power over women, disdain for homosexuality, and pursuit of status. I calculated that there have been more than 500 studies since the 1990s that have shown that there is a strong belief in these masculine norms, especially in western countries. We know that these norms are imposed from early childhood, where boys are told that 'Boys don't cry' or 'Don't be a girl.'

As we have previously seen, there has been a historical tradition of considering emotion and reason as two ends of a spectrum, with a long-standing belief that emotions do not involve rationality, and that they emerge out of an instinct that is impossible to control, something that happens to us. There has been work within psychology that has challenged this false dichotomy of reason and emotion but these misconceptions still persist. There has been an attempt to (re-)define emotions as part of a person's core values and ethos, resulting from what we consider important in our environment, and in specific situations. We all form mental models of the world based on the significance we assign to specific aspects of the world around us, since it is impossible for us to absorb all the information we are bombarded with. We pick and choose the information that is most pertinent to our goals, and we form snapshots and templates in our brain that align with our intentions, goals and aspirations. So, emotions have behavioural, cognitive and psychological components, and can be both rational and irrational, depending on a person's intentions. Whether we are perceived as 'too emotional' or not emotional enough also depends on our own status in society, and who is the one responsible for legitimising the emotion. There is an inherent play of power and privilege in how human-ness and irrationality are negotiated in the expression and evaluation of emotions, and those with less power or privilege in society find it more difficult to have their emotions legitimised while also not holding the power to legitimise others' emotions.

This means that the same emotion can be seen as positive in some people while negative in others and can affect individuals differently. The way emotions are interpreted also depends on in-group and out-group associations. When someone is considered part of our in-group, we tend to have more affinity with them and less bias and prejudice. There is more bias against people considered to be members of the out-group. These social constructions also lead to 'infrahumanisation', the belief that one's in-group is more human (and therefore more valid) than the out-group. The essence of being human is reserved for the in-group members and so the out-group is assigned less humanity and their emotions considered less valid.[38]

During the 2016 presidential election, Donald Trump called Clinton 'crazy' and 'insane', and accused her of lacking the equilibrium to effectively manage a country. The words 'shrill', 'bonkers', 'crazy' and 'hysterical' are often used to denigrate and belittle women's opinions, and carry a historical legacy of demonisation of women's emotions, and feminisation of anger and madness. Language does not exist in isolation. Language has the power to create an imbalance in society, which these words do. And words such as these can de-legitimise women's emotions. Delegitimisation is defined as invalidating a claim in the eyes of an actual or implied reference group. When a claim is considered invalid, it is seen as illogical, and by inference the person making the claim as irrational. If a woman's argument is attributed to her emotionality, then it is assumed that she is being unreasonable, and her point of view, her status and authority are all delegitimised. The legitimacy of the claim does not lie solely with the observer, but also with the reference group outside this interpersonal interaction, which has the power to decide whether the claim is valid or not. So, men's emotions, because of the inherent association of men with reason and logic, may be perceived to be emerging from rationality compared with women. And in this way they will be perceived as more competent than women too.

In her 2007 psychology and women's studies dissertation at Penn State University, Leah Warner studied 130 women to see the impact of negating their emotions and showed that being called emotional legitimised men more than women, as it was believed that they were expressing emotions out of competence, rather than due to the vulnerability attributed to the women.[39] Delegitimisation also has an impact on the perceived self-esteem of an individual. Women who were called emotional were then seen to be more preoccupied with how they express their emotions, which can create anxiety and stereotype threat, and further affect their performance and ability to manage a situation. We tend to negotiate our various identities and perform emotions that legitimise our authority in different domains, so we might become more subservient or outspoken, nurturing or tough and steely, as the situation demands, all while we assess whether an emotion might warrant scrutiny or discrimination.

When people assign certain essences or natural characteristics to objects and people, they believe these properties make them who they are. Sometimes these essences are deeply ingrained, and other times more superficial. But in doing so, these somewhat arbitrary and artificial characteristics are imagined to be fixed and natural. The way these groups are organised in our minds, and the way status is accorded to members of the different groups, helps satisfy the human need to determine social hierarchy. The more people identify with their group, and the more pride they take in these group memberships, the stronger out-group prejudices are, and the more superior essence they accord to their own group.[40]

Social identity theory has proposed that a sense of self can be achieved when people devise and maintain strategies that reinforce the superiority of their in-group over the out-group. In-group favouritism – assigning positive attributes to our own group – can also result in actively denigrating the out-group that is perceived as a threat, to prevent them encroaching on the in-group essences and our own self-esteem. In extreme cases, out-group prejudices can lead to delegitimisation or moral exclusion of individuals and groups. The out-group are then considered outside the norms of fairness and considered less acceptable and deserving, and more easily expendable.

Irrespective of status, people claim more uniquely human emotions for their in-group members.[41] Even though there isn't a complete consensus on this in the academic community, there is an understanding that there are some primary and secondary emotions. Since Ekman proposed the six core emotions in 1992 (see page 26), they have been analysed, interpreted and modified several times. 'Sentiments' are considered a unique subcategory of emotions which are attributed only to humans, while all animals can experience the primary emotions. These sentiments or secondary emotions are what make us uniquely human. Secondary emotions involve cognition, morality and memory, and are more active aspects of our personality, as choices rather than something to which we involuntarily and impulsively succumb. As such, secondary emotions are considered more rational and reasoned than primary emotions, which are seen as more reactive. Experimental psychologists Jacques-Philippe Leyens and Maria Paola Paladino suggest asking the question 'Would I apply this emotion to an animal such as a rabbit or a fish?' Of course, we still do not really know everything about how animals feel and think, but in layman terms, we find it easier to assign joy, sadness or grief to animals than hope, contentment, disillusionment, admiration, pride or nostalgia. When we consider some emotions as being more human than others, we also find it easier to assign and validate them in some people more than others depending on our and their respective status.

Emotions therefore also have a prejudicial effect, not only in how they are assigned to people based on their group memberships, but also in the way they are interpreted and legitimised. Primary emotions, such as joy, sadness, anger, fear, etc. are associated with both in-group and out-group members. Secondary emotions such as pride and nostalgia are considered to be exclusively human, so these emotions are not assigned as easily to out-group members. People are reluctant to accept the presence of secondary emotions in people who are not part of their in-group, but even if they see these emotions in out-group members, they are treated less benevolently and given less validation. In some cases, they might even be treated negatively. People can be reluctant to associate even negative secondary emotions to out-group members.

How we perceive others and their group memberships, and the significance we assign to their emotions also affects our feelings towards them and our inclination to help them in emergency situations. There are more prosocial tendencies towards in-group members, so their secondary emotions are more visible and noticeable, and this in turn creates a stronger feeling of in-group membership. In order to interpret emotions of people that are in-group members, projection is deployed where the self is used as a prototype, and so there is already a natural empathetic rapport created between the observer and the target. Empathy creates a sense of comradeship as well as motivating the person to help the other, whom they perceive as similar to themselves. On the other hand, to infer the emotional states of people who are out-group, stereotypes are used that are often lazy templates and labels that have been assigned to particular groups essentialising their determinant properties and homogenising them. More individuation is used for in-group members than for out-group members. This was seen in an experimental study with Hurricane Katrina survivors. Through scenarios and 116 questionnaire responses (51 per cent women, 53 per cent white, 16 per cent Black, 19 per cent Asian American, 8 per cent Latino)[42] it was seen that people were more likely to deny the same complexity of emotions in out-group members as in-group members, leading them to believe that they did not experience as much anguish since they did not experience as many secondary emotions of mourning, remorse and sorrow.[43]

In an experiment termed the 'lost email experiment', the academic researchers sent a manipulated email individually to 240 colleagues (72 women and 168 men) at a nearby Belgian university with reviewer feedback on a co-authored manuscript, and asking to discuss this feedback.[44] Since they were all colleagues and researchers, they were seen to be members of the in-group. Each email started with a positive or negative primary emotion (such as pleasure or rage) as well as one of the secondary emotions (delight or disillusion). The results showed that the time of response depended on the kind of emotion in the email (with a longer response time for positive emotions) and the response was more supportive for negative secondary emotions than for negative primary emotions, thereby noticing and validating the secondary emotions of the in-group community more closely than even the primary emotions. People do not react favourably to secondary emotions coming from out-group members, and in some cases these are even treated with suspicion and fear. This is especially true if the out-group is stigmatised and marginalised, and in particular where there is a power imbalance between the in-group and out-group, with the in-group considered significantly higher status than the out-group. This reluctance to even accord secondary emotions to the out-group can lead to infrahumanisation, where members are considered less human, less important and less deserving, and this affects how a person reacts to a request by an out-group member. This can create awkwardness in social situations where emotional requests and responses from out-group members are ignored and dismissed.

Infrahumanisation (the belief that your in-group is more human than an out-group) decreases inter-group assistance. This could in theory mean that women voters or employees are more likely to empathise with women leaders and managers and be more willing to understand their emotions. However, this has not been the case, since the valency of the group membership is not gender but the difference between voters and leaders. People are more likely to experience and 'catch' the emotions of others through emotional contagion if they share some kind of common bond, and in this case identification of the common gender identity might not be able to supersede the identification of their group membership – in this instance, being a leader.[45] These divides can be minimised if strategies are used to help people humanise those who belong to an out-group.

In interpersonal relationships between men and women, especially if the woman is in a leadership position, men expect women to be warm and friendly, to use nonverbal cues such as smiling facial expressions, to balance out their more agentic behaviours such as directness. So, these role incongruities not only make it difficult for women to gain leadership roles, they also create more challenges and barriers once women are in these roles. A 2015 computer simulation study showed that even if these biases are small, they add up, and just a tiny bias at each annual review leads to a huge gender gap at the top, reducing women's chances of rising to a high-level position in organisations.[46] Even a small bias against women of merely 1 per cent variance in initial performance ratings produced senior management levels with only 35 per cent women, and a 5 per cent initial bias produced only 29 per cent senior women. This is particularly the case in organisations or domains where there are few women in leadership roles and results in a structure where even if there are initiatives to employ more women as part of a diversity drive, most do not rise to the top level and do not have the status and power that men have. When there are fewer women visible in leadership roles, it is also easier to assume that women do not make good leaders. And an organisation is also then more likely to have a culture that upholds the emotional–display norms that disadvantage women and further foster the gender hierarchies, so the inequality between groups is maintained.

In summary, in our society, within the constructs of hegemonic masculinity, as part of heteronormative masculine ideals, mental toughness and the ability to remain stoic is considered a sign of manhood.[47] Showing emotions freely is considered a sign of being out of control, and of femininity, and therefore of emasculation. The expectation of masculinity is especially consistent for political leaders, particularly for high office. We have seen how gender impacts women's ability to be voted into political office, and when they succeed the difficulties are not reduced. When women are considered less legitimate leaders, they are also seen as undeserving of this position, and receive less cooperation from others. Women in powerful positions receive more negative behaviour from subordinates than men, which means that they are more likely to feel insecure and negative towards their subordinates. This forms a self-reinforcing cycle where women leaders are seen to be more emotional, less authoritative, less able to exude influence than men, and hence their claim to power is further delegitimised. It is as if women are punished for their mere audacity in aspiring for a political leadership position.

As a group that is not the norm in society, women are subconsciously accorded lower status. This means that women can be seen as undeserving of attention and lacking rational emotions, and there can be a reluctance from others, men but also women, to assign secondary emotions to them. Where this power imbalance is more prominent, in domains which are more traditionally dominated by men, women's emotions can be invalidated much more, and women find it more difficult to have their emotions legitimised. In such domains, where this in-group and out-group membership is significantly pronounced, women might be perceived to be acting more with their primary emotions – which are considered more animalistic – and even in cases where they are seen to be showing secondary emotions, the response to these emotions is not benevolence but suspicion and scepticism. This means that there might be more resistance to supporting and helping women in situations where they are seen to be intruding into a masculine domain, and their emotions perceived more negatively. In such situations, the interpretation of emotion emerges out of certain gender stereotypes ascribed to women, but the process also reinforces the stereotypes and essential properties assigned to women as being hysterical and too emotional.

This process also inflicts a stereotype threat in women and so they learn to moderate their emotional expression. In some cases, the anxiety caused by this hyper-awareness and fear of being stereotyped, and the subsequent moderation of their emotions, causes more pain and stress, which can manifest as external emotional outbursts of rage and frustration. This then creates the impression that women are more emotional. A vicious circle.

12.

UNHINGED: ANGER, POWER AND STATUS

> Anybody can become angry – that is easy; but to be angry
> with the right person, and to the right degree, and at the right
> time, and for the right purpose, and in the right way – that is
> not within everybody's power and is not easy.
>
> — Aristotle, *Nicomachean Ethics*

THE 'UNHINGED WOMAN' IS A character trope that we continue to see everywhere in mainstream media and literature. These are women prone to irrational reactions and mood swings and shown to be angry and vengeful, who often start off as seemingly controlled, but unravel slowly with a sudden violent episode. More recently, this has often been portrayed as a feminist retelling of women breaking away from the gendered expectations imposed on them, as a way of them taking back control. I remember watching the recent film *Gone Girl*, based on the book of the same name, and thinking that while the movie set out to be some sort of empowering, 'girl power' narrative, it really is grounded in gender roles and ideologies that have long told us that women's anger is uncontrolled and has drastic consequences. The depictions at the heart of it are still relying on sexist ideologies that there are natural differences between men and women, in their interests and behaviours. I find the idea that women's anger has to be vengeful to be problematic.

In Latin American folk medicine, emotions are recognised as powerful enough to cause physical sickness. In 2004 the anthropologist Linda-Anne Rebhun documented her work with north-east Brazilian women in the city of Caruaru, which had a population of 200,000.[1] The people of Caruaru used the term 'swallowing frogs' (engolir sapos) to denote the suppression of anger and irritation, and putting up with unfair treatment silently. Strong emotions such as envy, anger and grief were not considered appropriate because of their intensity, so had to be swallowed down. Rebhun's work showed that many of the ailments manifesting in women were associated with the effort and pain of bridging the gap between the cultural expectations imposed on them and their personal emotional experiences. What was being seen as nerves by other members of the community and male doctors, was shown to be resulting from the struggle to control and manipulate emotions. When women were not able to live up to the emotional expectations of others, or if they were contradictory to their own experiences, they suffered. In Andean folk medicine this type of suffering or nervous disposition was called pena, which was even believed to turn the heart slowly into stone. The word for anger, raiva, was also used for the disease rabies, showing the stigmatised status of this emotion. Showing anger, or experiencing it, was akin to getting the disease: both dangerous and potentially incurable. In Brazilian Portuguese the words raiva (rabies or anger) and colera (cholera) were sometimes used interchangeably with a 'glass or cup of anger' translating as both 'um copo de colera' and 'um vidro da raiva': both putting the fear in women's heart. The possibility of madness and death made women feel frightened of experiencing and inspiring such a dangerous emotion as anger.

In 1983, in her work 'A Note on Anger', American philosopher Marilyn Frye declared that anger is a tool by which we, as humans, declare our own agency, and this is why women's anger is not as well received: women claiming their own agency have long been considered aberrational.[2] Frye asserts that anger has a significant role in shaping the sense of self, as it is often expressed to claim one's own space or to demand the acceptance of oneself from others. It is to say 'I exist' and 'Acknowledge me'. Anger therefore often bursts forth as a sense of injustice when a person feels like they are not being perceived as a person with autonomy and rights. It is to say 'I demand a right to exist, to be seen, to have the same rights as others.'

Frye noted that, when it comes women's anger, 'Attention is turned not to what we are angry about but to the project of calming us down and to the topic of our mental stability.' She wrote this almost forty years ago, but it might well have been yesterday. Even today, women's testimony about their own experiences are seen as invalid and unreliable. When the root of their anger is not seen as valid, or is deemed unintelligible, it is easier to dismiss the anger as unjustified.[3]

A 2005 telephone survey of 1,800 adults from across the US found that women reported significantly higher frequencies of anger, annoyance, yelling and losing their temper than men.[4] In the same survey, men subscribed to the statement 'I keep my emotions to myself' about 15 per cent more than women did. This apparent difference could have been because women were more *open* about their anger rather than *being* angrier, or because they felt more guilty or ashamed about the emotion. We have already seen earlier in the book that there is no concrete scientific evidence that there is a biological difference in the way male and female brains process external stimuli, only that the way these external events and situations are perceived varies. It is also impossible to know what level of outrage and emotion was classed as 'anger' by men and women. Do women overestimate their anger, compared to men, because they have subconsciously been trained not to show rage and anger from a young age, in almost every culture and society?

We have seen through history, and there is enough contemporary evidence, that people are more likely to use words like 'bitchy' and 'hostile' to describe women's anger, while anger in men is more likely to be described as 'strong'. Men are more likely to express their anger by physically assaulting objects or verbally attacking other people, while women are more likely to cry when they get angry, as if their bodies are forcibly returning them to the appearance of the emotion – sadness – with which they are most commonly associated.

In 2007, Vaughan Becker at Arizona State University set out an experiment, in which 38 undergraduates viewed pictures of faces showing prototypical happy and angry expressions.[5] The participants were told: 'Close your eyes for a moment and imagine an angry face. Try and conjure up a prototypical angry face. Is the face that of a man or a woman?' The participants had to quickly press A or H to show whether the expression was angry or happy. Results showed that when they perceived a face to be that of a man they were more likely to press angry, but when the same expression was shown on a woman, they were more likely to see this as happy. To further confirm the effect of gender stereotypes, the researchers conducted another study in which they used computer graphics to control not only the intensity of facial expressions, but also the masculinity and femininity of the facial features. They showed faces that were ambiguously masculine and feminine (using stereotypes such as heavy brow and angular face for masculine, and roundedness and soft features for feminine), sometimes a little more masculine and at others more feminine. Once again, people were more likely to see the more masculine faces as angrier, even when they had slightly happier expressions than the more feminine faces.

These results also show how emotions get interpreted differently the more masculine or feminine a face appears. The more masculine a face appears, the more likely it is that the emotion is interpreted as anger. We know that there is also evidence that women are more likely to adopt a social strategy of 'tending and befriending' than men, especially in stressful situations, so that they come across as warm, unthreatening and nurturing.[6] Arguably, therefore, people tend to believe that a woman is more likely to have a happier expression on her face than a man. Women who display anger are judged more harshly for it, and so it is also understood that women would not choose to show anger. And so when a person encounters a woman with an angry expression, they are more likely to see this as a non-normative emotion and be critical of it.

Women internalise these messages. In a growing body of work, self-reporting of anger by women is often accompanied by self-condemnation and derogatory statements such as 'I was so embarrassed' and 'I felt like a real bitch.'[7] The outward expression of anger in women – such as tears and raised voices – were all self-coded as a 'loss of control' and treated with self-derision. What I find interesting in many of these research studies was that, while most of these women were aware at a cognitive level of the judgements from men of their anger expression, and could intellectually reason them to be harmful stereotypes, these had become so deeply embedded that they had internalised them and applied them to themselves.[8] Men on the other hand have been observed to follow certain rules of hierarchy to ensure that their anger is channelled into aggression: a sign of masculinity. This depends largely on the status of the adversary: aggression is not appropriate against anyone weaker or less physically able than them; not women nor the elderly. Aggression against someone stronger, however, is often not only considered acceptable but heroic. There is also little self-judgement or self-condemnation from men in terms of loss of control; no excuses, merely a framework of instigation and reaction, cause and effect. In several of these self-reported studies, men congratulate themselves and express feelings of satisfaction if they had a 'good fight' or when they proved their maturity by containing their aggression against an unsuitable adversary (friend, partner, parents, siblings).

She is emotional; he is having a bad day. In 2009, 46 participants at Boston College between 18 and 38 years old looked at stereotypically masculine and feminine faces as well as androgynous faces created from morphing the two, each expressing the same emotions.[9] Women's emotions were more likely to be judged with higher 'correspondence bias', and were perceived to be part of their personality and temperament ('She is just emotional' or 'She is an angry person'), compared to the men's, where context was considered to justify their anger and frustration ('He couldn't help it' or 'She made him angry'). Correspondence bias is the tendency to draw inferences about a person's enduring characteristics based on their behaviour in a particular situation rather than considering that the situational context could completely explain the behaviour. People also show it when they are judging emotional expressions. It is also possible that people approach men and women with different implicit goals when required to explain their emotions. The setting, the gender of the actor, and the gender and goals of the observer all make a difference in how men's and women's emotions are interpreted.[10]

Because of societal pressures and stereotypes, women become adept at camouflaging and developing strategies to channel their anger and express it in a more socially conforming manner. Women know that anger can hamper their chances at a leadership position, they sometimes internalise it and moderate their emotions and their expressions. The two processes that take place while people conform to social roles are self-regulation and expectancy confirmation. Women already know they will be stereotyped so either do their best to conform to the gender stereotypes – and therefore be less inclined and motivated to aspire to leadership positions – or they try and reject any feminine stereotypes that make them less acceptable in these positions. Their behaviour is moderated by the prejudices they encounter. It then becomes a self-fulfilling prophecy.

Research at Southwest Missouri State University suggests that men and women perceive anger differently, but that women seem to be more comfortable holding their anger in, while also taking less pride in being able to.[11] The researchers gave 80 men and 123 women a collection of 5 routine questionnaires used to assess anger expression and personality traits such as assertiveness, self-esteem, sense of effectiveness, and expectations for success. The study subjects rated themselves on nearly 200 traits and scenarios directly or indirectly related to anger expression and self-promotional 'masculine' traits. The researchers found that men felt less effective and less instrumental when forced to hold their anger in, whereas women didn't feel nearly as constricted when they didn't express their anger directly. There was a higher correlation between expressing anger outwardly and feeling assertive for men, while women felt ashamed of feeling angry and tried to control it, and hide it, and even apologise for it. Women are aware that they are not supposed to show anger in the same way as men, and so they make more conscious efforts to suppress it, and often give it another name, such as 'frustration'. They are socialised to see their anger as shameful.

One of the significant emotional stereotypes associated with women is that they are nurturing and caring, and so it becomes part of their 'feminine' identity that they are driven by the goal of nurturing relationships. Anger has the potential to jeopardise relationships since expressions of rage, and anger in visibly explicit forms in particular, can be attributed to women's inherent lack of control and emotionality, and they can be seen as self-serving. When women can see and face challenges and barriers, be affected by bias, be aware of the power imbalance which affects their status in society, they can feel helpless and frustrated and angry. However, this anger is often suppressed, which can cause feelings of inaction and weakness, affecting women's self-esteem, and so they become even more angry. Men are not expected to hold their anger in, and in some cases they might even be negatively labelled if they fail to react aggressively under certain forms of provocation. In men, aggression is a required social performance of masculinity, a sign of heroism.

In 1987, British psychologists Anne Campbell and Steven Muncer examined social talk between friends (a group of 33 women and 37 men) and coded it according to modes of aggression used (verbal, physical, no action).[12] Through almost 70 angry episodes they showed that men considered 'doing nothing' as an expected form of response to provocation from an inappropriate adversary and so were delighted to conform to this, while with women, this was mostly their only acceptable option, whatever the nature of the adversary, and so they did not feel as delighted to be conforming to what was already expected of them, the stereotypes that were forced upon them. Women felt less pride in controlling their anger, while also bearing the cost of intense frustration at having to control their anger, and having to accept that they were supposed to suffer. Women were afraid of rejection and the cost of anger on their relationships, while also fearing the stereotypical labels of 'hysterical' or 'bitch'. Women have been led to believe that their identity as a woman is someone who is without any anger and has no need for anger at all, and so women feel a threat to their core identity when they see anger in themselves or in other women.[13]

In 2019, during a Democratic presidential debate, the moderator asked the participants to name either a gift or an apology they might give to another debate participant. It was interesting that only the women candidates responded with an apology. Both Senator Elizabeth Warren and Senator Amy Klobuchar apologised for their occasional outbursts of anger, with Warren saying: 'I will ask for forgiveness. I know that sometimes I get really worked up. And sometimes I get a little hot. I don't really mean to.'[14]

Anger in women further confers a lower status on them and they are perceived to be less competent than men in a similar situation. The scold's bridle might be long gone, but women are still monitored and silenced for showing anger. We know from experimental and observational research as well as self-reporting that anger from women is more acceptable in stereotypically female domains such as caring roles and in the home. Women can use this anger if it is for the protection of their child: sometimes at the cost of her own self. So, women can show anger, and this anger is valid, but only if it is not for her own goals or for her own development. Even then women carry a lot of guilt and self-censorship as well as self-reprimand for 'losing their rag', especially in their roles as mothers. But in some other domains such as a professional environment, in areas that are stereotypically male, in leadership positions, they cannot do so because this immediately associates them with vulnerability, with irrationality and instability, and quickly evokes their more 'feminine' attributes, which makes them seen as unfit for the role.

•

I don't think a woman should be in any government job whatever. I mean, I really don't. The reason why I do is mainly because they are erratic. And emotional. Men are erratic and emotional, too, but the point is a woman is more likely to be.

— President Richard Nixon[15]

Alice Eagly, professor at Northwestern University, proposed the 'social role theory' in 1987 to show that women are disadvantaged by the gap that exists between the stereotypes associated with them and the expectations and norms ascribed to the role of a manager or leader.[16] As we have seen, women are stereotyped as having less leadership potential simply because of their gender ('descriptive bias'), but also leadership is seen as a masculine role, so women are seen less favourably because they are violating both the norms associated with their gender, as well as the social role they are taking on. For women to be perceived as an effective leader they have to show both sensitivity and caring ('feminine' emotions), as well as authority and risk-taking ('masculine' emotions) to avoid prejudice. Incongruous social roles (women as leaders) evoke hostility and negative reactions, while congruous roles (men as leaders) evoke more positive reactions. Women face a disparate impact, where institutional policies and practices (both formal and informal) prevent them from being hired or promoted to high ranks, and they also face disparate treatment, being implicitly punished for having violated prescriptive stereotypes associated with their gender. These penalties can include harassment, microaggressions and devaluation of their work.

Across three studies published in *Psychological Science*, participants viewed videos of actors playing the part of either a man or woman interviewing for a job, and reported their perceptions of the interviewee's status, competence and what salary they deserved.[17] The actors displayed either anger, sadness or no emotion. In some cases, they explained their emotional display, while in others they made no attempt to explain it. Participants were randomly assigned to different videos. The results showed that participants accorded higher salaries to unemotional women trainees than to female executives who displayed anger. When women provided an explanation for their anger, they received higher status and more salary than those women who did not explain the cause of their anger, the participants thereby attributing it to some external factor. Women's anger is not considered legitimate and can harm their careers, until and unless an external cause is provided. Men did not suffer the same consequences. There is consistent evidence that in men, anger is seen as competent even when the person does not already have a high status. But even if women regulate and suppress their anger, and it becomes obvious they are doing so, they are seen as passive and unauthoritative. Women are stereotypically expected to show more sadness than anger in emotionally distressing situations, and show more warmth towards others, and so when they do show anger, they are penalised for violating prescriptive stereotypes. When women displayed anger, no matter what their status or position, they were seen to be out of control, weak, incapable of handling professional stress, and they suffered a loss in status and wages.[18]

Much like any other experimental study, there are some limitations to what can be achieved in a lab with participants who are playing a role. Emotion study in particular can be tricky as there is an inherent limitation in how nuances in anger can be conveyed and evaluated within the confines of a scientific experiment. The concepts of 'anger-in' (when people tend to suppress their anger or to direct it towards themselves) or 'anger-out' (if they direct their anger outwards and express it towards other people or the environment) are difficult to extract since statements such as 'I calmed down faster' or 'I kept my cool' can relate to both suppressing and expressing anger.[19] Moreover, anger-out can have a broad range too, from having an angry exchange on social media to physical violence and aggression.

While promotion and votes can confer status, a leader's competence is decided by others based on their *perceived* competence and qualifications, rather than on actual or demonstrated qualifications. When anger and no-anger scenarios are compared, people prefer to have a leader who is calm. This 'dual-threshold model' proposes that two thresholds exist when people express anger in the workplace. There is an 'impropriety threshold' in every workplace and society where people are seen as having 'gone too far' in expressing their anger.[20] This, of course, depends on the position of the person expressing the anger as well as the observer, and is shaped by the actor–observer interaction. There is a 'zone of expressive tolerance' that is flexible and can be expanded and reduced as the norms change and evolve. The space between the expression and impropriety threshold is merely 'expressed anger'. When anger does not cross the 'expression threshold' it is 'suppressed anger', which again takes the form of silent or muted anger.[21] Silent anger is felt but not expressed due to fear of how it will be perceived by others, while muted anger is a unique form of anger which is not expressed publicly but to others who do not confer status to the individual. When a leader is perceived to be able to moderate their feelings and emotions, they are attributed a higher status and more validity. However, women leaders receive the highest rating when they show no anger at all.

Scientists and philosophers have discussed how anger is mostly evoked when someone perceives that they have been wronged and they want to put it right. It is an agentic reaction, where there is often an active intent to change a situation, even if the person does not realise it in the moment.[22] Since men are – typically, historically – afforded agency, while women are associated with more passive emotions, it is unsurprising that anger is linked with masculinity. There might also be an evolutionary aspect to this: anger has been seen as an emotion associated with physical threat but also social dominance, power and agency, while happiness is associated with co-operativeness, support and coalition. Some research shows that human males were more likely to engage in intra-male competitiveness than females for the purposes of sexual selection and mating.[23] It is possible therefore that men and women, in the very distant past, also developed these different emotional strategies and expressivities for maintaining their status and position within their communities. With any evolutionary research, as always, it is worth considering how many of these rules should have evolved as our society has, and how much of our contemporary behaviour and attitudes can be justified by actions of the very distant past.

Anger is also associated with directness and authority, and we know from the social dominance theory that the power hierarchies in society shape how the same situation is perceived by members of different groups with different statuses in society.[24] So, when it comes to leadership, men and women are held by different standards. Men are perceived as in-group when it comes to power and leadership, fitting the normative ideals, while women are still seen as outsiders. While women, who are lower in status hierarchy and out-group, can see the threats, challenges and barriers to leadership, men, who are in-group and hold the power, can legitimise the power inherent in the structures within which they operate. In this way, they feel less threat to their position as leaders, and feel more positive about their workplace. But even when men express emotions such as anger, it can often lead to an even further status boost, because their anger is associated with dominance and aggressiveness, and perceived to emerge due to external circumstances.[25]

Anger can also be perceived as a positive emotion, and preferable in a leader as compared to sadness, which is considered a negative emotion.[26] In studies conducted by psychologist Larissa Tiedens, it was seen that former US President Bill Clinton received more support when the participants viewed him showing anger about his affair with Monica Lewinsky as opposed to when he was seen expressing sadness or regret.[27] Fifty-four students (20 men and 34 women) participated in this study, with 29 in the anger and 25 in the sadness group. Two clips of Bill Clinton from his grand jury testimony in 1998 were shown, one with Clinton speaking angrily and using a lot of hand gestures, and the other where he expressed sadness and guilt with averted gaze. Participants who viewed the angry clip were more pro-Clinton than those who watched the sad clip. Across this and three similar studies carried out by the same team, it was shown that anger has the effect of creating the perception that the man expressing this emotion is competent, and therefore holds a higher status. Status is not linked to likeability so this does not necessarily mean that the person is well-liked or receives widespread approval.

•

When we think of gender difference between emotions, yes, it is between men and women, but it is also important to think 'Which women?' Which women's emotions have more value than others? Power hierarchies in our society exist in the form of gender, but also in the form of class, race, ethnicity and so on. These intersectional effects mean that women from minority ethnic backgrounds are judged more harshly than their white counterparts.

As we have seen, much of the work done in the field of emotions has been with white participants in the global north. But Rosabeth Kanter, the Ernest L. Arbuckle Professor at Harvard Business School, in an influential study called 'Men and Women of the Corporation'[28] way back in 1977, suggested that tokenism disadvantages those who are in the minority. In male-dominated domains, women encounter tokenism, while people of colour face challenges associated with heightened visibility (and invisibility at the same time), stereotyping and isolation from others in domains where they are in the minority. While their competence can be seen as them being exceptional and different from others in their identity group, the failures of those in tokenism positions can be seen as representative of the overall group.

In an experiment in 2000, participants were asked to read a scenario in which a white, Black or Latina person had learnt that they had been denied promotion, and then had to answer questions on the likely reactions of the target and their suitability for the job.[29] All participants, irrespective of their gender and race, identified women as likely to be less in control, sadder and more disappointed, and more emotional than men, with the respective proportion of responses being: white women (16 per cent) to be more suitable than Latina (7.2 per cent) and Black women (9.4 per cent).

Women of colour, especially Latina and Black women, are

frequently stereotyped with high emotionality, intense emotions, uncontrolled behaviour, and a kind of exoticism that assigns them fiery traits irrespective of individual or personal characteristics. The 'double jeopardy theory'[30] suggests that women of colour face additional challenges because of marginalisation due to both race and gender, and because of the 'cult of true womanhood'[31] that creates stratification between white women and women of colour. This bias has been corroborated by studies on stereotypes that have shown that white women were seen as passive and nurturing, and Black women as hostile, with white women also being deemed more dependent and reliable than Black women, who were associated with uncontrolled rage and negative emotions.[32] White Americans have been shown to have more expectations of white women to express sadness and white men to express anger, and so they are likely to have more rigid ideas of gender stereotypes than Asians or Black people. White women, when they express anger, tread outside the 'women are warm and communal' emotional stereotype, but Black women are perceived (and expected) to behave consistently with the 'angry Black woman' trope. A recent experimental study shows that even though effects of gender are already quite significant on anger displays in the workplace, race and gender can intersect to create an even more heightened effect.[33] In Black women, the attributions of anger were more common, leading to lower performance assessments for their leadership abilities.

The myth of the 'angry Black woman' also reveals the intersectional effect of gender and emotion. The Sapphire stereotype, for instance, portrays a loud, aggressive, rude Black woman, with irrational states of anger.[34] Such stereotypes characterise Black women as aggressive, ill-tempered, illogical, overbearing, hostile and ignorant. Although empirical evidence is non-existent that there is any difference between Black and non-Black women in how they experience and express anger, this stereotype persists in mainstream media and culture. It was highlighted by the media in the furore, already mentioned, over a cartoon of Serena Williams in 2018. During the US Open final, Williams received a code violation for coaching, a penalty point for breaking her racquet, and a game penalty for calling the umpire a 'thief'. She was then depicted in a cartoon in the Australian *Herald Sun* as a childish figure having a tantrum and spitting out a dummy. Similar accusations have been levelled at former First Lady Michelle Obama in recent years. Michelle has talked about being called an 'angry Black woman' on the campaign trail and how she was perceived to be emasculating her husband.[35] Brittney Cooper, writer of *Eloquent Rage*, said on an NPR podcast in 2019 that 'whenever someone weaponises anger against women, it is designed to silence them. It is designed to discredit them and to say that they are overreacting, that they are being hypersensitive, that their reaction is outsized.'[36]

Research from the Gendered Racial Microaggression Scale for Black Women (GRMS) has shown that more than 87 per cent of Black women reported experiencing the 'angry Black woman' stereotype, and have also used silence, passiveness and appearing to be non-threatening as coping strategies in such situations.[37] A 2021 study published in the *Journal of Applied Psychology* shows the detrimental effects of the 'angry Black woman' stereotype in the workplace.[38] When compared with white women and Black men, the researchers found that Black women were perceived to be worst performers and least able to lead when they expressed anger in the workplace, irrespective of the gender and race of the observer. Asian women are often stereotyped as 'meek' and 'deferential' and so they are also seen to violate norms when they express anger. This does not apply to the same extent to Asian men, although they are perceived to be less competent than white men, because of the association of Asian facial features with femininity. Asian women who expressed anger were accorded even lower status than sad men, who were also somewhat penalised for showing emotions that do not align with the stereotypical notions of masculinity. Certain racial identities are gendered; 'Blackness' is associated with masculinity, while Asians – East Asians in particular – are associated with femininity. People also perceive anger earlier and believe it to last longer in Black men than in white men.[39] Across a series of experiments, it was seen that race biased sex/gender categorisations. Asian men were perceived to be more competent, and white women were perceived as less competent than men but warmer than Asian and Black women, who were seen to have the lowest competence and warmth.[40]

Eric Garner was murdered in New York by police in 2014. His daughter Erica Garner was brought to City Hall to meet President Obama, but she was denied the chance to question him. Erica started yelling, and asked: 'A Black person has to yell to be heard?'[41] Erica later met the president but this was a reminder that often Black women have to be loud to be heard, to avoid being silenced. Activist Feminista Jones responded to this incident by tweeting that 'the stress of adhering to expectations of silence is killing us', and creating the hashtag #LoudBlackGirls to give Black women a platform to share their stories of having to raise their voices to be heard, without letting the 'angry Black woman' stereotype hold them back.

In a case of intersecting multiple identities, it can happen that people's minds activate one category more prominently and inhibit another when they see some stereotypically consistent behaviour. So in some cases race might become more significant while in others gender might be more influential. Black women leaders expressing anger, for instance, were found not to create the same level of backlash that Black men leaders did when they expressed anger, and were not conferred as low a status as white women when they showed agency in the workplace.[42] The researchers reasoned that in this case, perhaps since Blackness is associated with masculinity, Black women were already stereotyped to be more dominant and aggressive so they were not seen to be breaking out of stereotype-consistent behaviour. Black women therefore occupy conflicting descriptive stereotypes – 'Black people are angry' – and prescriptive stereotypes – 'women are warm'. In this case, their racial stereotypes are activated before those associated with their gender. Kimberlé Crenshaw called this 'intersectional invisibility', where Black women do not fit neatly into the Black prototype or the female prototype, so they might not be penalised in the same way if they show counter-stereotypic behaviour for race or gender.[43]

Women of colour are held to higher professional standards, albeit often implicitly, both externalised and internalised, and so they have to work harder to overcome stereotype threat as well as moderate their emotions in the workplace, if they aspire to leadership roles. Race does not merely intersect with gender and class to shape emotional norms, but also informs the emotional labour needed from different people to be acknowledged as professional and competent, and be afforded a high status. Tokenism results in minority ethnic people being evaluated for how they act but also how they feel, so they have to suppress any feelings of hurt and frustration at being racialised while presenting themselves as calm and pleasant through their actions and facial expressions. This creates an emotional culture that is built on racial inequality.[44] As Audre Lorde says:

'Women of Color in America have grown up within a symphony of anger, at being silenced, at being unchosen, at knowing that when we survive, it is in spite of a world that takes for granted our lack of humanness, and which hates our very existence outside of its service.'[45]

While socio-cultural context has shaped which groups have a 'status advantage' and so have flexibility in emotional expression, it can also influence when a perceiver might consider anger to be appropriate. Of course, the status advantage can also change if there is any shift in the socio-cultural context. One theory proposed in 2013 was that of a 'normative window' which suggested that most prejudicial attitudes towards different social groups are not stable. This is the window during which norms might shift towards more equality, even temporarily, and this can affect attitudes. We have seen how, after the election of Donald Trump to the US presidency in 2016, it became more acceptable to show prejudice towards minority social groups and immigrants. Sometimes, if these attitude shifts have a moral dimension, they can even become permanent over time. These shifts were shown in evaluations of workplace anger in Black and white women carried out across four studies and published in 2021.[46]

Since 2018, there has been wide coverage of women's anger as a result of the resurgence and renewed mobilisation of the #MeToo movement, first founded by the American activist Tarana Burke in 2006, spurring widespread focus on gender discrimination and sexual harassment.[47] Women were writing and performing plays that brought the discrimination women had been facing for so long explicitly into public consciousness in a big way.[48] We were seeing headlines such as 'Uma Thurman is seriously angry about sexual misconduct in Hollywood'.[49] There was justifiable anger in response to the various news stories that were coming out during this period, and there was a perceptible shift in how anger from women was being validated through a communal spirit on social media and in mainstream media. As well as the tape of Donald Trump notoriously saying he could grab a woman by her private parts, allegations about Harvey Weinstein came to light and many famous women shared their own stories of harassment and abuse at the hands of men, bringing pain and anger out into the open. It seemed like a time of reckoning for women who had been silenced for so long. The discrimination women had been facing for so long was explicitly brought into the public consciousness in a big way. Rose McGowan, who alleges she was raped by Weinstein, said in her memoir *Brave*: 'We women have historically been trained to be pleasant at all times. We need to stop that and be authentic; justifiable anger is a part of that. Being angry is OK.'[50]

At the same time, there was also an ongoing broader discussion of pay inequity in the workplace, and there was justifiable anger amongst women. The study of workplace anger was made up of four experiments with 1,095 participants, mostly undergraduate psychology students. Researchers looked at appropriateness of emotional intensity, competence and conferred status across different political and social beliefs and ideologies.[51] The participants were aware of the discussion of #MeToo and highly engaged with the news. The results showed that Black and white women were judged more favourably for their anger compared to white men, which contradicted the earlier findings. This was not because the previous studies were flawed but because these results were primed and moderated by the news and shifting beliefs that the workplace was gendered and inequitable, and the increasing attention to gender discrimination and harassment. The engagement with the news affected how emotions were being evaluated and status being conferred on the women who were expressing their anger. This was also the time when it was becoming apparent that laws were not enough and that individual activism was needed to address the injustices that women have faced in the workplace, that cultural change was needed at every level. It is possible that this new sense of societal responsibility could have affected the perception of the participants. The recent social and cultural movement and discussion around gender inequality is likely to have influenced the observers in acknowledging the women's anger, believing that the women were more entitled to anger than white men, and shaped their view of power, status and influence. Even though the mainstream media's focus was primarily on white women initially (despite a Black woman, Tarana Burke, originating the movement), it is possible that, in this experiment, intersectionality of multiple identities played a role, so that in the case of Black women, their identity as women was seen more prominently than their identity as 'Black', and the notion of women sharing a common experience was activated.

•

There are other intersectional elements of emotional expression too. Samantha Rideal writes movingly in *Burn It Down: Women Writing About Anger*, an anthology edited by Lilly Dancyger, about how she used her anger as 'both armor and camouflage' growing up as a confused trans child.[52] Guarding her secret close, she tried to perform masculinity and with it the aggression and violence that it is associated with. She tried to figure out how to be a boy, and in this she tried to embody and emulate the fury of superheroes avenging crime and injustice, but mostly she was angry with herself. Her own models of masculinity came from stereotypical media representations and books and all that she saw around her. She tells us how she could not even cry when her father died, because she had taught herself to be emotionally repressed. Even when she was writing professionally, she was writing more forcefully than before, and was, in her own words, 'needlessly combative and unkind'. This self-hate, rage and imitation of aggression became too exhausting eventually, and she had to reconcile with the notion that she did not want to be a man.

These kinds of stories can be used to dismiss trans women from being women, the justification assuming that a propensity for anger and aggression means that a trans woman is a threat to women-only spaces. However, the very fact that a person has to repress their identity can affect how they express themselves, how they try and curb the culturally constructed notions of 'femaleness' to avoid being seen as one (even though they identify as a woman), and how they might exaggerate those expressions which are seen as 'manly' to try and mould themselves into the societal tropes of masculinity.

Susan Stryker, a trans activist, presented an incandescent essay titled 'My Words to Victor Frankenstein above the Village of Chamounix: Performing Transgender Rage' in 1993 that articulated the necessary anger that exists at the heart of trans activism, while seeking to claim back the label of 'monsters' that trans women were often assigned.[53] She wrote: 'words like "creature", "monster", and "unnatural" need to be reclaimed by the transgendered community. By embracing and accepting them, even piling one on top of another, we may dispel their ability to harm us.' Josie Giles, author and performer, tells me in a Twitter message that there are the usual double-binds that cis-women face in the workplace, where 'being deferential is expected and any assertiveness is taken as aggression', but she adds that the prism of trans misogyny adds an extra layer, where trans women are always worried about being perceived as deceptive or a threat, and so are hypervigilant and have to continually moderate their emotional expressions and behaviours.[54] In her collection of essays titled *Whipping Girl*, biologist and transgender activist Julia Serano proposes that society's view of femininity as frivolous, weak and passive also leads to the prejudices against trans women, where they are seen with fear and suspicion.[55] Hil Malatino, in his 2018 paper published in *Hypatia*,[56] argues that even though rage is considered a toxic emotion, it is necessary for trans survival, a justified response to unliveable circumstances and essential to move forward.[57] There is now some clinical literature and also biographical accounts that show that transgender people experience varying forms of persistent shame unique to their experience and this affects their emotional experience and expression.[58] Of course, if we consider intersectionality with race, this notion of shame is also likely to be very different for different ethnic groups. I wish there was more research in this, more recording of personal narratives, but as always there is a lack of intersectional data from the transgender and non-binary community.

·

The Stanford Prison Experiment by the American psychologist Philip Zimbardo and colleagues back in 1973 is highly controversial.[59, 60] At the time, it examined whether brutality by prison guards was dispositional (i.e., due to the guards having sadistic personalities) or situational (a consequence of the prison environment). They ran a series of diagnostic tests, questionnaires and personality assessments with 75 men, out of whom 24 were selected who did not show any sadistic tendencies. All 75 were then randomly assigned to be a prisoner or a guard. Within a short amount of time of both groups enacting scenarios resembling real life, the prisoners adopted prisoner-like behaviour, and the guards started behaving aggressively regardless of whether they had shown any sadistic tendencies prior to the experiment. After just 6 days the experiment had to be abandoned because the prisoners started having emotional break-downs, and the guards were behaving excessively aggressively and abusing them. The experiment, debatable for its morality, showed how quickly – and readily – people start conforming to the social roles they are expected to play, especially if the roles are very strongly stereotyped.

The experiment also showed that sometimes, when these groups are very strongly defined, individuals can lose their sense of identity and become immersed in the group norms (deindividuation), and they are then more inclined to conform to the social roles they are expected to play. This study of course has selection bias – these were all young men – and a small sample size, and there has been some controversy as to how reliable and authentic the observed behaviours were or whether they were faked, especially those of some prisoners to manipulate the observers.[61] Nevertheless, it was a milestone study as it led to the formal recognition of ethical guidelines in psychological experiments by the American Psychological Association. Even though this experiment did not evaluate any between-gender differences, it demonstrates very effec-tively that people can start conforming to socially determinant roles in a very short space of time. Yes, it is a controversial experiment, one that has many red flags associated with it now, but I include it here because what it really shows to me is that so many of our behaviours are shaped by existing expectations, and we can start conforming to these expectations rather quickly.

In summary, we have seen that the expression of anger is linked to an assessment of competence, but this effect is very gendered. Interpretations of behaviours and emotional expressions are largely determined by the stereotypes that we already hold, and the social group membership of both the person displaying the anger and of the observer. So, the same emotion in a man versus a woman leads to differences in their social influence and status. In general, there is a widespread belief that women's anger is less common, but also less appropriate as compared to men. When women are angry, it is seen as an innate personality trait emerging from the stereotype that women are just more emotional. On the other hand, for men, it is often attributed to situational context and to other factors outside their control. These stereotypes have persisted through history, and these gender roles and hierarchies have remained stable over time.

The way our emotional rules and displays are prescribed ensure that these hierarchies remain unmoved. A 2015 study showed that when men and women expressed their opinions in an angry manner in a group decision-making scenario, both men and women were perceived to be more emotional, but in the case of men, anger expression led to more influence, while for women their influence decreased.[62] It is also fascinating that fear and anger are closely linked as emotions – both agentic in nature – and women also lose social influence if they express fear. Even when white men violated masculine stereotypes by expressing fear, it was not as detrimental to them as for women and Black men. These differences were seen irrespective of how anger was expressed, the content of the argument or opinion, or the way the person sounded or looked while expressing their anger.[63]

Although shows of anger usually motivate avoidance, sometimes they can have a counter-intuitive effect of focusing attention and creating a semblance of attainability. Even though the social cues of anger are threatening, surprisingly it can also create desirability for objects. Anger activates a part of the brain that is associated with more prosocial emotions, and so advertisers use this as a marketing strategy. Researchers at Utrecht University showed that people were willing to pay more and invest more resources when they associated an angry face with mugs and pens. In this experiment, before the participants saw the image of the product on the computer screen, they were shown quick images of either neutral or angry faces, which they subliminally then associated with the product they saw next.[64] People associated reward motivation with anger-related objects, unlike those linked to neutral faces. We are evolved to be motivated by attainability and by our desire to fight for the objects that we perceive as limited in availability. So, if a product is perceived to be limited or higher status, it is likely to inspire the aggression needed to fend off others and to procure the object for ourselves (which in times past might have meant securing our own survival, if the object was food or other forms of sustenance). And so, the response of anger becomes something that subconsciously gives us a cue that an object is more significant for us than others. The same can apply to people, too.

The knowledge in our society has been constructed around the patriarchal organisation, where the dominant group has the power to define economically, socially and politically what knowledge is valid and legitimate. Anger is seen as a high-power emotion, one that confers status, and one that is only acceptable from those who have the dominant position in society. Sadness, on the other hand, is a low-power emotion. And so there is an inherent pattern of inequality in whose anger is considered appropriate and whose is not, and whether someone is discredited or validated in their display of anger.

Competence and status are closely linked.[65] So a person with high status is usually perceived to be more competent, and vice versa, but likeability also affects whether perceived competence results in conferral of higher status. When women present themselves as confident and assertive, they are rated as competent and a good fit for a leadership position, but they are often also seen as emotionally and socially deficient and rated low for likeability by both men and women. Angry women can be perceived to be competent, but they are awarded lower status than men. Likeability becomes a major factor in evaluation of women as compared to men.

Emotions provide an excuse to discredit people due to their race and gender during decision-making. The expression of anger (and fear, to a certain extent) is linked to how power and influence is distributed in our society, so that expression of anger leads to less influence for women leaders than for men in similar positions. So much of sociologist Joan Acker's contention from 1990 still holds good: that workplaces implicitly assume a leader to be a man, one who is unencumbered by outside distractions and stresses.[66] So, it is naturally assumed that any leader or manager will be able to maintain professional pleasantness and calmness in the workplace. Yet during the pandemic our private and professional lives have collided as we have invited co-workers into our homes through virtual meetings, children have crashed onto screens, and there has been a much broader discussion of the weight of caring responsibilities in some people's personal lives, both for men and women. It would be interesting to see if attitudes have shifted significantly, and if stereotypes about emotional norms and feeling rules in workplaces will be changed. Women are becoming more comfortable with the many layers of their anger, but it is doubtful whether we can change the social scripts that angry women are not influential, hold less power and will not make good leaders, unless we change the message that exists all around us like smog: that women's anger is unnatural. Often anger is penalised because it is not considered apt in a situation. It is seen to be violating the normative rules of behaviour, either due to gender, race or class, or a combination of these. Seneca called anger 'most hideous and frenzied of all emotions', something completely unacceptable in women and slaves, and other philosophers such as Martha Nussbaum have argued that anger dents rational thinking and should be avoided at all costs. At times, an angry response could be considered counter-productive, unlikely to achieve anything fruitful. Women in particular can be accused of being bitter if they appear angry, which in the view of philosopher Sue Campbell is a strategy to shift the blame from the person who has behaved badly to the woman's mode of expressing her feelings about it. This then puts the onus on the woman to modify her behaviour, thus absolving the other person of any responsibility. Labelling the anger 'inappropriate' or as 'bitterness' is a silencing strategy. Once this happens, the feeling of not being heard grows. When this feeling is in turn not legitimised, it can lead to increasing frustration and further anger, and it becomes an added responsibility for women to legitimise not only their anger, but also its mode of expression.

The philosopher Amia Srinivasan argues that anger can be counterproductive, violate norms, and still be apt.[67] Much of the argument against anger, in her view, is based in the fear of a toppling of the existing social order. Anger is penalised most in those who would be best served by it, and serves those who would be most threatened by it. When women have a subordinate status, they do not have the privilege to show their anger. As Virginia Woolf said: 'In short, one must tell lies, and apply every emollient in our power to the swollen skin of our brothers' so terribly inflamed vanity.'[68]

It reminds me that it is not men who are called 'fiery', 'spitfire', 'feisty', 'lippy', 'hormonal' and 'bitchy'. These words are reserved for women who show their anger.

13.

CRY-BABY, WAILING BANSHEE

Stop the waterworks, ladies. Crying chicks aren't sexy.
— Brian Alexander, NBC News[1]

C RYING IS A UNIVERSAL FORM of human emotional expression, except when we are crying while chopping the onions. Tears can take various forms in different people, by vocalisations, by sobbing, by a change in facial expressions, gestures and posture. Tears can of course be used to express a range of feelings, from happiness to shame or sadness or frustration, and even anger. Hot tears of rage might seem oxymoronic, but anger and sadness can often go hand in hand. We can cry when we are overjoyed, and we might also cry when we are moved by beauty, in art, music and literature. Tears are often perceived to be a result of powerlessness, arising when change is not possible, a sign of frustration and acceptance rather than resistance.[2]

Crying can facilitate a feeling of release of stress, but often it is about the social response it elicits, the show of support, the empathy rather than the psychological benefits of crying. Crying can also be self-soothing.[3] The Roman poet Ovid voiced this conviction: 'It is a relief to weep; grief is satisfied and carried off by tears.'

Tears evoke empathy, concern, a willingness to reach out and comfort. Crying has also been called a 'distance regulator', signalling to others that they should now pay attention and respond urgently, without expecting any specific reciprocal behaviours.[4]

And emotional tears seem to be unique to humans. Other creatures do not cry, at least not with emotional tears. In his book 'Why Humans Cry' the neurologist Michael Trimble recounts the story of Gana the gorilla at Münster Zoo, who loses her newborn baby suddenly one day. She holds his body up, and holds him close, stroking him, and it is evident that she is mourning his death, but Gana does not shed any tears. It is one of the things that separates us humans from our closest relatives, chimpanzees and bonobos. Trimble positions crying as something that is essentially human, and what makes us human. Although as a pet-owner I am inclined to anthropomorphise my cat and my dog, and have claimed many times that they are crying, scientists say that these are only basal tears, which are functional tears that the body produces to protect, lubricate and clean the cornea. Then there is the term 'crocodile tears'. There is a long-standing myth that crocodiles shed tears after they eat their prey in a false display of remorse.[5] We have seen it in mythological stories and in children's fable-like stories from the *Panchatantra* that my mother used to read to me. Of course, tears of crocodiles are physiological as they use them to keep their eyes lubricated while they lie very still on land to digest their food. But this has been treated for so long as an aphorism.

Tears originate in the lacrimal glands, and there are three kinds of tears: basal, reflex and emotional. Tears were called 'involuntary reflexes' by the physician Josef Breuer and Sigmund Freud in their book *Studies in Hysteria* of 1895.[6] Darwin thought that tears have no purpose and are merely a by-product of evolution, a muscular contraction to protect the eye. The biochemist William Frey in his 1985 book *Crying: The Mystery of Tears* proposed that emotional tears are a form of catharsis as they help discharge stress-related substances from the body.[7] He himself admitted that this was a hypothesis and hadn't been documented through scientific studies. However, it has been widely understood that emotional tears, produced as a result of a heightened state of emotion, are different from those that appear when our eyes are inflamed or while chopping onions.

Emotional tears have been found in some studies to have 20 per cent more protein, and some have suggested that they have more endorphins in them; but in either case, tears are a mechanism to balance out the stress-related neurotransmitters in our body, and chemically can be an indicator of the pleasure or pain we are feeling in our body. Frey also concluded (from studies which have since been proved somewhat inconclusive) that prolactin plays a role in tears, and since women on average have more prolactin, they cry more than men. Kari Green-Church, an expert in protein analysis at Ohio State University, studies the proteins identified in tears. In many of the studies she has conducted, she and her graduate students have isolated pregnancy proteins in tears as well as dopamine, serotonin and prolactin.[8] This difference in hormones and proteins in tears was also found in emotional tears from post-menopausal women, which were different from those of pre-menopausal women (although in other research this effect has been dismissed, as no difference was found in tears between young girls who were menstruating compared to those who had not yet started their menstrual cycles).

Testosterone and prolactin have been shown to play a role in inhibiting and mediating nurturing behaviours, in empathy, in response to infant-crying in parents, and in how easily a person is moved to tears. Research has shown that prolactin levels positively and testosterone levels negatively correlate with a father's impulse to respond to a child's cry, and fathers with higher prolactin levels were also more alert and more positive in response to the cries.[9]

But as we know, men and women/male and female bodies are not built to specific templates. It isn't that *all* men have higher testosterone than women and *all* women have higher prolactin. That is just not the case. But the media keeps hyping up these differences as if they are set in stone. Women cry more, is the message that we hear again and again, because they are hormonal, and because they just can't help it. In the same way that women are more nurturing, they are more passive, they are better parents, they are more caring, they are more empathetic. All generalised stereotypes. And if you read this and think that this is rightly so, do reflect on why it is so. Is it because women have been told that they should be like this, because this is a sign of femininity, because this is what makes them better women and better mothers? Is it because we are afraid of not conforming to these behaviours, that we feel threatened that we wouldn't live up to our ideals of womanhood, and our own and others' expectations?

Besides their biological function, tears have a social function, are a part of our propositional language, a part of our social brain. This is our capacity to feel empathy and compassion, and is triggered in what is termed 'emotionally competent stimuli' by Antonio Damasio, the neural networks that recognise facial expressions of sadness in others.[10]

Research has also shown that while on one hand people attribute messages such as 'Help me' to crying, they can also interpret it as 'Leave me alone', showing the inherent ambiguity associated with this very intense emotion.[11] And it is very likely that a person's own biases towards one who is crying would be instrumental in determining how they interpret this emotion. Whether it is a full-blown angry cry, or a controlled sob, or just a misty eye also can be interpreted and valued differently depending on the social and cultural context. In some cultures, at death, if a person does not cry loudly, with a public display of grief, they can be called cold-hearted. In other cultures more restrained forms of crying are more acceptable, the 'stiff upper lip' which gives an impression of control and sophistication, and maturity.

Although crying sounds like a universal emotion, one of the most firmly entrenched ideas is that men do not cry. Numerous studies have tried to prove that this is an undisputed fact. A meta-study by the German Society of Ophthalmology in 2009 that analysed a corpus of other research studies before it, found that women weep, on average, five times as often, and almost twice as long per episode.[12] Reviews of earlier studies in 2000 showed that people – both men and women – perceived men's tears to be inappropriate.[13] Crying is not a 'power' expression of emotion; anger is. Men are associated more with powerful emotions. Because crying in men is seen as unusual, it is also taken more seriously when they do, while in women it is seen as a common occurrence, with women 'crying at the drop of a hat', and so it is easily dismissed and also regarded as less genuine and more suspect. Since crying is believed to have evolved as a signal of helplessness and also of appeasement, it is not seen to be as reliable or manly. When emotions are intense but their expression is controlled, it creates a powerful dichotomy which can be seen as a manly emotion. Stephanie Shields, professor of psychology and women's studies, calls this a particular form of white, heterosexual masculinity which is grounded in rationality and self-control.[14] A 'manly' expression, for instance, employed effectively in films and in fiction, is a man being able to express anger because it is seen as self-confident or (especially) because they are protecting someone weaker, mostly a woman.

I wonder if this is a modern phenomenon, because I think of heroes such as Achilles who weeps at the loss of Patroclus:

> Not so Achilles: he, to grief resign'd,
> His friend's dear image present to his mind,
> Takes his sad couch, more unobserved to weep;
> Nor tastes the gifts of all-composing sleep.
> Restless he roll'd around his weary bed,
> And all his soul on his Patroclus fed.[15]

On the island of Ogygia, Calypso offers Odysseus immortality. But Odysseus turns her down because his only wish, his desperate desire, is to return to his homeland of Ithaca and to reunite with his loyal wife, Penelope, and their son, Telemachus. All Odysseus wants is to be back home:

> But sad Ulysses, by himself apart,
> Pour'd the big sorrows of his swelling heart;
> All on the lonely shore he sate to weep,
> And roll'd his eyes around the restless deep:
> Toward his loved coast he roll'd his eyes in vain,
> Till, dimm'd with rising grief, they stream'd again.

For Homeric heroes, tears were not unmanly or a cause for shame. They were a natural emotion associated with sadness and grief but also with rage: 'And swarms victorious o'er their yielding walls / Trembling before the impending storm they lie, / While tears of rage stand burning in their eye.'

We of course have instances in the Bible of Jesus weeping with piety and compassion, as he bears the burden of people's misery. It does not detract from his Godhood. Tears have therefore been considered a spiritual experience, with saints (and even their statues) seen weeping, a transcendence from mortal humans to holiness, called the 'gift of tears'. In the sixteenth century, the Spanish mystic St Teresa of Avila wrote in her book *The Interior Castle* of 'leaving tears to fall when God sends them, without trying to force ourselves to shed them. Then, if we do not take too much notice of them, they will leave the parched soil of our souls well-watered, making it fertile in good fruit; for this is the water which falls from heaven.'[16] Pope Francis said in January 2015: 'Certain realities in life we only see through eyes that are cleansed through our tears.'[17] By explaining tears as a gift of God, as a means of connecting with something bigger than us, they transcend their interpretation as coming from an overtly emotional person, and become beautiful.

When we see warriors in epics crying, we see the men crying about their ideals, morals, about war and peace, and about nations and loyalty. Women, on the other hand, cry for love and romance, over family losses and friendships, in a more intimate expression of emotionality. These were small, domestic issues that women had strong feelings about, not like the men who had to take care of the broader, higher issues of national security. Well, it does say it all.

Hindu gods cried. In many of the mythological stories that I grew up with, men would cry and weep, not just for valour and war, but also for love. And that seemed very romantic to me. I grew up with a father who would cry at the drop of a hat, something we would laugh at him indulgently for. But I liked that. He could fly into a rage at the drop of a hat too, but he could then turn soft like putty and weep if he missed us, if he hadn't seen us, if he saw a sad film.

In the *Brahmavaivarta Purana*, Lord Shiva laments the death of his wife Sati. In *Valmiki Ramayana*, Raama signifies honour and valour. When his wife Sita is kidnapped by Ravana, he sinks into deep grief and cries to all things in the forest where they had been exiled. His grief turns into rage, and he insists that he, Raama, will destroy all the worlds if Sita isn't found.

There is also the story of Shiva crying with compassion for parents who lost their small child:

तथा तयो वरि्वदतोर्वज्ञिञानवदिषोर्द्वयो: |
बान्धवानां स्थतिानां चाप्युपातष्ठित शङ्कर :
देव्या प्रणोदितो देव: कारुणयार्द्रकि्तेक्षण: |
ततस्तानाह मनुजान् वरदोऽस्मति शङ्कर :

While the bird and the beast, both possessed of wisdom,
were thus disputing, and while the kinsmen of the deceased
    child
sat listening to them, the great god Sankara, urged by his divine
    spouse [Uma],
came there with eyes bathed in tears of compassion.[18]

Looking back at those mythological stories, I can see that so much of this crying was linked to honour – of losing their honour because of a woman they loved, or the fear of not being manly enough to protect the woman, who was helpless and powerless, and unable to defend her own honour.

Western notions of emotionality seeped into the gendered divide, especially during the Enlightenment and Renaissance, which brought in a rational ideal for manhood, one where tears were not a sign of a man's sincerity and virtue, but an allegory for manipulativeness and instability. Historical research shows that men's tears in the past were class-related, especially in Britain, where class plays a big role in identity construction. Bernard Capp, professor at the University of Warwick, in a paper titled '"Jesus wept", but did the Englishman?', suggests that religious sentimentality was often in conflict with English stoicism.[19] The British, in general during the early modern period, became increasingly stoic and renounced the sentimentalism of the previous centuries, even as there were exceptions. In July 1653, Oliver Cromwell made a passionate opening speech to Parliament 'with tears (at times) rolling down his cheeks and with the enthusiastic style of a revivalist evangelical preacher'.[20] While in the medieval and early modern period Englishmen were prone to passionate emotions, it is suggested that after the French Revolution of 1789 – with the understanding that the French had become too emotional and lost control – the idea that emotions were dangerous was becoming more popular. Nevertheless, crying was still permissible in certain contexts. In January 1806 at the funeral of war hero Horatio Nelson, eight admirals carried the coffin through St Paul's Cathedral in London. All of them were in tears.

The concept of the British 'stiff upper lip', the well-worn mantra of 'Keep calm and carry on', the call to evoke the 'Blitz' spirit, have all been evoked by the British government time and time again during the current pandemic.[21] This cultural identity, linked to romanticising of stoicism and emotional self-control, emerged during the Victorian era as a sign of manliness, particularly aimed at the upper classes; a sign of superiority while Britain was out there colonising the rest of the world. These men were unemotional, resilient and rational, and so deserved to civilise others. During this time, even upper-class women saw crying as a sign of failure. In post-Victorian

England, in 1914, the National Union of Women's Suffrage Societies put out a statement: 'The modern woman must drive back the tears; she has work to do.'[22] Even though during the First and Second World Wars there was no time for fear and grief, and the idea of the English standing resolutely and determinedly was put forward as a collective emotional identity, Winston Churchill cried publicly on numerous occasions, and was even called a 'cry-baby' by Edward VIII. Even though his contemporaries were dismayed by his regular 'blubbing' during a time when emotions were supposed to be buttoned up, he earned respect and admiration from the wider public, who trusted him to really care. For most of the 1940s, Churchill's Gallup poll ratings were above 88 per cent. He was seen as a war hero, someone who encompassed physical and moral courage, taking a stand against the Nazis, and his solemn but galvanising speech in 1940 to Parliament offering his 'blood, toil, tears and sweat' became one of the most famous in history. Men do cry, and this is sometimes seen to be heroic.

Even though earlier research at the Social Issues Research Centre (SIRC) in Oxford (sponsored by Kleenex for Men)[23] has shown that sports is one arena where men cry as much as women, and that it is acceptable for men to express a range of emotions that are usually proscribed in other areas of life, some sports are deemed to be more masculine than others.[24] We have seen Roger Federer and Andy Murray cry after losing – and winning – tennis tournaments, the basketball player Michael Jordan when inducted in the Hall of Fame in 2009, and Tiger Woods after his wins. But when Murray cried while announcing his retirement from tennis in 2019, there were people such as former footballer Alan Brazil who ridiculed him, saying: 'What were the tears? Come on! I don't recall Djokovic or Federer crying their eyes out. I admire what he has done, but I don't want tears.'[25] The Brazilian footballer Neymar Jr posted a lengthy message on his Instagram in February 2021 about comments he had received from players, media, coach and commentators that he is a 'cry baby' and 'spoiled': 'I don't know how long I can take it.' In October 2021, he suggested that he might retire from representing Brazil, even though he was only 29 years old. Chelsea star defender Thiago Silva spoke about his own experience, how he had also been called a 'cry baby' and 'very weak mentally', and admitted that these things hurt and take their toll.[26]

Crying in sports can be heroic, but it becomes unacceptable if the sportsperson is responsible for a loss, or if they performed terribly. In that case, they may be called a 'cry baby' or a 'little girl'.[27] Even though crying is associated with weakness, it is acceptable in men as long as it is not performed in a way that is 'feminine', i.e., not with an overt show of emotion, but with restraint. It comes back to men having to appear rational and heroic even when overcome with emotions. 'Emotional control' is one of the eleven norms in the CMNI that define masculinity in countries such as the United States and the UK. Crying is therefore contradictory to the masculine norms of emotions.[28] While anger is considered an agentic emotion that is driven by a desire to create change, crying is associated primarily with sadness – a negative, reactive emotion that is perceived as powerless because it is driven by the feeling that change is not possible. Men therefore have to try to achieve this balance between showing enough emotion to appear human, and not too much to conform to idealised heterosexual masculinity. Both a complete lack of emotional expression and what is perceived to be 'extravagant' expression are seen as a lack of competence, and so the balance is to show 'passionate restraint'. This gives out the signal that emotions are felt, but the person has the necessary judgement to be able to restrain any uncomfortable expression of emotions.

There is inconsistent evidence of any sex-based differences in frequency of crying between male and female infants, and any such difference only starts becoming significant after the age of eleven. Some researchers have attributed this to the hormone testosterone inhibiting tears in boys, but once again there is not ample evidence for this, and so socialisation clearly plays a role. The Swiss psychologist Jean Piaget, renowned for his theories on child development, proposed that children cry at a young age mainly as an egocentric response to draw attention to themselves or to obtain something, and that social sensitivity and empathy only come much later. Crying due to sympathy or grief is seen at a later development stage, around the age of six, as children start moving out of the egocentric phase.[29] However, it has been shown more recently that children as young as three are able to understand other people's feelings and have an affective response such as empathetic crying.[30] Many of the emotional messages to boys from a young age are about how not to be a girl, and that emotional expression is weak and girly. They learn to navigate this path where the only suitable emotional expressions are presented in an acceptable manly way, the 'stiff upper lip', where emotions are mostly kept under control – except in certain situations where it is deemed acceptable, such as in sports. In the context of sports, the notion of passionate and loud emotional outbursts is more acceptable. Men cheering loudly and raucously, shouting and screaming at the television, even in a large crowd in the pub, and becoming irritable when their team loses, are all acceptable behaviours. Much of this is associated with aggression, which is understood as a masculine behaviour. But there are tears too. Yet because sport is considered inherently masculine and as a vehicle for boys to socialise into prescribed norms of masculinity, it can also be seen as an integral aspect of an athlete's identity.[31] And failure can be seen as a loss of the sportsman's identity and masculine credibility. Crying can be a way for them to mourn their masculine self-worth, and also to celebrate the joy of being able to reclaim this identity after a win.

In 2019, psychologist Heather McArthur from Penn State University ran two experiments with 250 and 192 participants, who were shown short clips of men or women crying in either a stereo-typically masculine context such as firefighting, or a stereotypically feminine context such as figure-skating and nursing.[32] The results showed that people rated crying men emotionally stronger, appropriate and higher in workplace hierarchy when they cried in a typically masculine environment such as weightlifting or firefighting, and higher in status than crying male nurses. Men were also more likely to shed tears on losing in weightlifting than in figure-skating. This is because they already have masculine credibility in a traditionally masculine environment such as weightlifting, while they feel that their masculinity is under threat in a feminised sport such as figure-skating, and so do not wish to conform to 'feminine' emotionalities. When a person is situated within a gender-congruent domain, they are allowed stereotype-inconsistent behaviour, and men who are seen to embody stereotypically masculine values have more leeway to cry than men who are not perceived as such.

Masculinity is associated with showing power. And so men are more concerned with demonstrating power and aggressiveness. This means that men are more likely to show powerful emotions such as anger, and less likely to engage in those that are perceived as weaker such as crying, even though the norms around what kind of tears are acceptable might be changing. We all warm to a man who gets misty-eyed, one who is seen to be trying very hard to control their pain and grief, and not cry publicly. We feel their inner turmoil, we admire their strength. The UK survey through the Social Issues Research Centre found that 90 per cent of women and 77 per cent of men think that it is becoming socially acceptable for men to cry, even though there is evidently a gap in men and women's attitudes towards this.[33] Younger men seem to be crying more openly than older ones. However, when the data was inspected more granularly the change was not significant: 52 per cent of men and 37 per cent of women think that it has become only a 'bit more acceptable' for men to cry. Many women still expect the men in their lives to be their 'rock' and not show their tears, believing that they themselves are the weak ones and need to be protected by men. Some women in the report believed that crying in men made them less attractive. In 2016, in one of those insufferable *Daily Mail* articles, the journalist Kathy Gyngell wrote an article bemoaning the fact that men are no longer stoic and have become 'weak-willed'.[34] Recently, I was dismayed to see a Twitter thread where a user (apparently a young woman from her profile picture although it is impossible to be sure) tweeted that a crying man is deeply unattractive and a 'turn-off', that 'women are biologically wired to cry more than men', and if a male partner cried in a crisis he would not come across as dependable.[35]

It is clear that, much like anger, crying is one of the most gendered emotions, and both men and women hold on to the beliefs that women cry, and men should not. I am interested in how crying is deemed to be effeminate. I am interested – deeply – in the impact it has on men and their mental health because they have to suppress their sadness. But what I am really interested in for the purposes of this book is how the view that women cry easily and freely at anything disadvantages women, while also trapping men into stereo-typical gender roles.

Men might be called 'cry-baby', 'sissy' or 'wet rag' when they cry or show vulnerability. For women, there are many such words. The word 'banshee' has been used as slang over the last few hundred years, especially in the UK, for a screaming, wailing woman, for someone who shows an excess of emotion. In Irish Gaelic folklore, banshees were magical, mythical women in the form of spirits who fed on other people's sadness and flew all night long looking for prey. Her eyes red with continual weeping, her hair streaming around her face, dressed in grey, and looking terrifying and unattractive, she heralded the death of a family member, usually by wailing and screaming. 'Mardi wench' is another slang term used for crying women showing excess emotions.[36] Friends in Germany tell me that 'Heulsuse' is often used as an insult for a crying woman, literally a 'crying Susan', a 'whimperer', a 'whiner', a Weichling (weakling).

In 1983, William Frey studied crying behaviour with healthy volunteers who were asked to keep a record of any crying over the course of a month.[37] All participants were around 30 years old, and were all volunteers with no particular psychological problems. The 286 women in the study reported crying an average of 5.3 times per month, while the 45 men cried only 1.3 times per month on average.[38] Around 45 per cent of the men did not cry at all during this particular month, and men reported mostly that they welled up but did not have flowing tears. Almost 71 per cent of the men reported that they might have had watery eyes at some point but no flowing tears. This makes crying more difficult to observe in men. However, when crying did happen, these episodes lasted for the same length of time in men and women. The results showed that, although 20 per cent of the crying was in response to joy,

10 per cent to anger and 5 per cent to anxiety, most of the crying was related to sadness as the predominant emotion. The clinical psychologist Ad Vingerhoets, author of *Why Only Humans Weep: Unravelling the Mysteries of Tears*, focuses on emotional tears. More recently than Frey, he suggested in 2015 that women cry 30–64 times a year, while men only cry 6–17 times.[39] This was also self-reported, like Frey's study, and it is possible that men could be under-reporting their crying. It is not easy to know for sure, but if men are crying less often than women, why is this so? Emotional tears are triggered by feelings and so they are more likely to be governed by feeling rules.[40] The philosopher Sue Campbell states that tears can be used as a justification for dismissal, since, as women cry a lot, their ability to distinguish the important from the trivial is suspect. I am not entirely convinced that women do cry a lot, even though I know that men don't. There has been a lot of discussion recently on the notion of toxic masculinity and how it is good for men to cry, trying to challenge the long-held trope of 'Boys don't cry'. But the notion that women/females cry a lot because they are 'constructed' differently persists.

Crying is seen to be effeminate. But it is also stigmatised. As we've seen, woman getting angry is seen as vindictive and out of control, and this is how women self-report their anger too. In research studies, women have self-reported that they express anger often as crying because it is a relief to them, or because their emotion is too intense to be controlled, and because crying is more socially acceptable than anger. We also see how women who cannot cry, who do not express their emotions as easily, are seen as 'cold' and 'unfeeling' or 'stone-hearted'. They might be labelled 'bitchy' just because they do not fit the stereotypical notion of femininity, of nurturing, of emotionality, of being able to express emotions freely. Women weep. They are also accused of using tears as a form of manipulation. As Socrates is believed to have said: 'Trust not a woman when she weeps, for it is her nature to weep when she wants her will.'

Crying is also seen as a sign of weakness, a sign of womanly wiles and deceptions, using tears to 'get their way' as a manipulation strategy, or as a sign of feebleness, a debility in their minds and bodies.[41] When Shakespeare's Othello accuses his wife of cheating and has a fit of irrational anger and rage, he still blames her for shedding fake tears and of being manipulative: 'If that the earth could teem with woman's tears, / Each drop she falls would prove a crocodile.'[42]

In 2015, the Nobel laureate Tim Hunt was speaking at the World Conference of Science Journalists in South Korea when he said: 'Let me tell you about my trouble with girls . . . three things happen when they are in the lab . . . You fall in love with them, they fall in love with you and when you criticise them, they cry.' He later made a (non) apology when he insisted that his comments were 'ironic' and 'light-hearted'. These views – that women are overtly emotional and fall in love easily or cry all the time – portray the image that women are not tough enough for a professional envi-ronment, and this is especially harmful when we know that in the UK only about 13 per cent of people working in STEM are women, and only about 15 per cent of professors in science and technology are women.[43] In the USA, half of the workforce is women, but only about 27 per cent of STEM workers are women.[44]

It is clear that tears have a different signal-value depending on who is shedding them. Crying men are valued more in some contexts, even more than women. For instance, a research study in 1991 showed that when male companions cried when watching a movie, they were appreciated more than women.[45] Women were more appreciated if they were non-reactive. Men were also more comfortable crying – and accepted more for their tears – if they were in the company of someone who was already expressing sad feelings, and so the acceptability and value judgement of masculinity associated with tears also changes as per social norms and context.[46]

Often it isn't about the right emotions, but about the right gender.

•

For a minute she almost enjoyed the attention till the thought, *Oh, it's true!* struck her and pulled her mouth into ugly crying.

— Betty Sue Cummings[47]

Even though studies in the 1980s showed a much wider value judgement between men and women's tears, a study in 2000 found that both men and women actors were judged harshly for their leadership potential if they were seen to be dabbing their eyes.[48] Crying in general has also been considered a disadvantage in politics. There is a particular form of disdain towards women crying in public, with a perception that women – particularly attractive women – often use tears as a power-play, a manipulative way to gain sympathy, while for men this is a gamble. Former UK Prime Minister Theresa May was called 'Maybot' for her lack of emotional expression, her 'limited emotional range' and almost robot-like demeanour.[49] But as her voice broke at the end of her resignation speech, she came under criticism once again for having the 'wrong feelings'. In the 1980s, Patricia Schroeder, a former congresswoman who cut short a presidential bid in 1987 and broke down in tears, received hate mail for many decades after this transgression. She herself joked that maybe she should have been sponsored by Kleenex. Women across the country were mostly angry and embarrassed that she had reinforced the stereotypes about women in politics: that they lack toughness and composure.[50] More recently, in 2019, the journalist Molly Prince tweeted that the politician Alexandria Ocasio-Cortez's 'frequent crying only reinforces the stereotype that women are too emotional for politics'. This showed how rationality and empathy are viewed as two opposite ends of the spectrum, where suppressing emotion is seen as equivalent to acting with rationality and reason, and that this characterises a good leader.

Men in politics often have more freedom to weep because their tears are 'humanising', even as public crying is seen to be less humiliating for women than for men.[51] When President Obama delivered a deeply personal and emotional speech on gun control in 2016 at the White House, he was lauded for it. John Boehner, Speaker of the United States House of Representatives in 2011, also garnered a lot of attention for his 'tearful episodes'[52] during important interviews and political events.[53] It got so much attention primarily because it violated the gendered norms of stoicism to which a man in a leadership position is expected to conform. It challenged what it means to be a man. But in the media, he was called a 'serial bawler' and a 'cry baby'. Sarah Palin told Boehner not to 'get his knickers in a knot', language that reminds people that crying is not for men and is a womanly thing to do. Even Nancy Pelosi commented on his crying, saying, 'When it comes to politics – no I don't cry.'

Tearing up in public or in workplaces is deemed to be disruptive and unprofessional. Crying in public, especially for women, can also take away social acceptability, and any attempt at credibility. It is also seen as manipulative. But not looking beautiful while crying is arguably deemed especially unacceptable. There is a unique term for it, 'ugly-cry', that has entered our vocabulary, where weeping uncontrollably is ugly and animalistic; the abandoning of our bodies to irrationality. Although the term is believed to have originated some-time in the 1970s and used off and on through the 1990s, it rocketed into more general usage when Oprah Winfrey used it in a 2001 show: 'During that whole tape session, I could see you doing what I've often tried to do on TV. You're fighting the ugly cry, when your lips start to go.' Over the last few years there have been articles instructing women how to cry on social media and in magazines to avoid these emotional contortions in public. Chrissy Teigen posted an image of herself crying with joy at the 2014 Golden Globes on Instagram, following her husband John Legend's victory. This was subsequently turned into a 'cry face' meme, which went viral quite rapidly. In crying, women are often vulnerable, and they are not only scrutinised for the intensity of their emotional expression and its appropriateness to the context, but also physically scrutinised. There is pressure on women to be equanimous, while also ensuring that they conform to an idealised notion of beauty, in order to be socially legitimate and acceptable.

Crying can seem theatrical and threatening, and beauty is supposed to give it a certain sort of placidity and dignity and make it unthreat-ening. When that doesn't happen, it is seen as much more transgressive. This is also a reflection of how we impose these stand-ards on ourselves and dehumanise ourselves and other women in the process, expecting us to moderate our emotions in public. It is interesting that, both with men and women, it is crying in a way that is more evocative of the other gender that is least acceptable. A *Guardian* headline in January 2011 read: 'Sniffing women's tears dampens sexual desire in men'. The study they were reporting on, led by Noam Sobel, associate professor of neurobiology at the Weizmann Institute of Science, and published in the journal *Nature*, showed that women's tears contained some sort of chemical signal that lowered testosterone levels in men and suggested that there was a persistent fall in men's sexual feelings when they smelled the tears.[54] In the study, 24 male volunteers sniffed either fresh tears from women or saline solution as a control and were then asked to rate the sadness or sex appeal of the women's faces on a screen. Their testosterone level was found to be 13 per cent lower on average when they smelled fresh tears. These men also underwent a fMRI which showed that when they sniffed women's tears the parts of their brain such as the hypothalamus, which is usually involved in sexual urges, showed little activity. This led the researchers to conclude that men are 'turned off' by some chemo-signals in emotional tears. The researchers did not carry out a similar experiment on men's tears. Science, as we know, suffers from selection bias. And yes, of course, this is a small sample size so difficult to extrapolate beyond that one survey, although the media used every opportunity to popularise this research as an indication of why women who cry aren't very sexy: another message for women to hold back those emotions, unless you want to be seen as not only hysterical but also undesirable.

•

Since Darwin published his theories on the evolutionary purpose of tears, there has been some focus on the cultural-specific norms around crying. A 2009 PhD thesis by Andile Mhlahlo at the University of Stellenbosch showed that in some African cultures, boys undergoing circumcision were forbidden from crying because they were supposed to be courageous when transitioning into manhood, but in everyday life they were fully encouraged to cry as loudly as they wanted if they ever felt any pain.[55] The contrast in when crying is acceptable and when not is quite stark and interesting. In the Toraja tribe in Indonesia, adults are forbidden from crying loudly except during the death and funeral of close family members.[56] The only other time that crying is encouraged is as a means of communicating with spirits and evoking community spirit, with a remedy for infertility being to cry at a certain rock along with other women who have been unable to conceive. Crying is a participatory, shared emotion here, but not seen to be appropriate as an expression of individual grief. In other situations, crying is seen as a transgression for both men and women, and all perpetrators are required to make a sacrificial offering to atone for this. There haven't been many cross-cultural studies to compare, but two studies have shown that in colder, more individualistic societies people experience less social pressure towards collective crying than in warmer and more collectivist countries, where social pressures around crying are more common.[57]

Looking at my own experience in Britain and in India, one colder and more individualistic, the latter warmer and more collectivist, I would say that I have experienced a somewhat opposite pattern to that reported in these two studies. In India, it is more acceptable for older men to cry compared to younger men, who want to show a very particular image of manliness adopted from Hollywood and Bollywood action films. They are the protector and women need to be protected. It could be possible that in older men, with age, the pressure to be manly (and prove their manliness) is removed from both within themselves as well as from society. In a 2008 study by Meetu Khosla of Delhi University, emotional scenes from films were shown to students (aged 20–25), and the results showed that there was significant gender difference in the way men and women reacted to a death scene, with few men experiencing any negative effect whatsoever.[58] But, interestingly, when the autonomic arousal levels were recorded rather than relying merely on observation and

271

self-reporting, there was no gender difference with men's heart rates, and their blood pressure rose as high as women's. Men therefore feel the emotion as much as women, but they do not allow themselves to cry, or express these negative emotions, following a strict script that has been written for them from early childhood.

As we look at gendered emotions in this book, it would be disingenuous to assume that all women (and men) experience emotions in the same way, or that all emotions have the same importance or credibility. Emotions are also unequally distributed in our society across various layers of class, gender and race, and as we've seen in the previous chapter, intersection of identities creates emotional stratification.[59] Socio-cultural context plays a role, and both men and women in wealthier countries with more gender equality reported crying more often and feeling better after it, as compared to women from less equal and wealthy countries.[60] In one recent study with an international sample across Australia, Croatia, the Netherlands, Thailand, and the United Kingdom, a total of 893 participants, comprising 508 women and 379 men (4 reported 'other', including non-binary), completed a survey reporting an incident of crying following a negative incident.[61] The participants were asked about the crying intensity, emotion change following crying, crying beliefs (whether it is helpful or unhelpful, and its appropriateness in front of strangers and family), and gender attitudes (measuring their level of confirmation to gender norms such as if education was more important for a boy than a girl, etc.). The results showed that women reported crying more intensely than men and more frequently across all countries, even though the reporting of emotion change after crying was no different between men and women. There was correlation between crying frequency and intensity and adherence to gender norms and roles (the stronger the masculine/feminine normative associations, the stronger their belief about whether crying was appropriate for men and women). Interestingly, the participants from the UK, especially men, reported feeling worse after crying as compared to those from Thailand, although there was more reluctance to cry publicly amongst Thai participants with a hyper-awareness that crying can cause distress in observers.

The sociologist Sarita Srivastava conducted 21 semi-structured interviews with 15 feminists across 18 anti-racist women's organi-sations in Toronto.[62] So much anti-racism discourse is framed in emotional terms and language, and so much of this work is emotional work too. There is often hurt and anger from women of colour, and shame and guilt from white women who are engaged in anti-racism discussions. In Srivastava's transcripts, one of the activists, a woman of colour, says: 'White women cry all the fucking time, and women of colour never cry.' While white women's tears are seen as a sign of innocence and vulnerability, tears from women of colour are often seen as manipulation. Privilege is a multi-layered construct. White women can also weaponise their tears for victim-hood, since they hold the privilege of race even though they face barriers on the basis of their gender, while women of colour face oppression on both axes: race and gender. Sometimes it is not just about which emotion, but also about the racial or ethnic identity of the person showing these emotions.

•

It might be a widely accepted fact that more women report crying more often compared to men, but not many feel comfortable doing so in the workplace or in a public space where their emotions and tears are bound to face scrutiny. They often do it in private or suppress their tears. According to Marina Whitman, former vice president and chief economist of General Motors, 'I've occasionally cried in the office, but only in privacy, never where anyone could see me, though I came perilously close once or twice . . . If the person you're confronting is male, it provides one more excuse to make him think "Isn't that just like a woman?" And if she's a woman, tears may make her feel defensive, guilty or at least uncomfortable, which is never a good idea in the workplace.'[63] In a recent BBC *Woman's Hour* interview, the classicist Mary Beard talks about her own embarrassment at crying in a university faculty meeting because she could not bear to say no to an unreasonable demand.[64] The reaction to it was a hushed stunned silence. Mary also mentions how women's tears are often deployed (and perceived) as 'instrumental tears', with the broader perception that a woman can manipulate situations with tears, and that she is faking them, while this is never the case for men's tears. Beard acknowledges her own ingrained cultural stereotype that she herself would treat a man's tears more seriously.

A quick Google search for 'women emotion work' reveals hundreds of results, including 'Why should women cry at work' as well as 'There is no crying in leadership'. One article from 2018 titled 'Women Who Cry at Work Need to Know These Five Things', based on a research study carried out at University of California, cautions women: 'If you cry, it hurts your reputation because co-workers may think you are weak, unprofessional or manipulative.'[65] There are plenty of articles giving women tips on how to handle their emotions in the workplace, ranging from calm breathing exercises to working with a life coach.

In the case of both men and women vying for leadership positions, their gender is a crucial signifier, and people look for information that confirms their membership of their gender group rather than disconfirming it or leaving it ambiguous. This means that any gender-stereotype-consistent behaviour is more noticeable and given more salience. Any stereotype-inconsistent behaviour is also noted but penalised. In the case of women, emotional displays, however minor, are noted immediately. As we have seen in this and the previous chapter, both anger and crying evoke very strong stereotypes. In men, anger is expected and when measured against aggressiveness and forcefulness, men scored higher than women on both measures. Crying affects the likeability of women and even women seem to hold women candidates to a much higher standard than a man. As we saw through the witch trials too, women are keen to distance themselves from another woman whom they perceive to conform to negative stereotypes such as over-emotionality and crying, seeing her as a 'collective threat'. It is clear that when it comes to politics or to other domains that have been traditionally masculine, women's emotional displays can often matter more than their skills and qual- ifications. Emotional women can certainly get ahead, but not that easily. And when they do, they have to work very hard to walk a very thin line between being feminine but not too feminine; being masculine enough, but not too much.

Crying women are perceived as more helpless and also friendly in comparison to crying men, and there is more willingness from observers to offer help. The gender stereotypes within hegemonic masculinity enforce the emotional rule that asking for help is a sign of weakness, and so men are reported to internalise their emotions more than women, rather than appearing helpless.[66] Experimental studies have shown that men rated other crying men more negatively compared to women. Women showed the same willingness to help both men and women when they were seen crying, while men displayed a double standard when it came to helping someone who seemed in distress.[67] As women are seen to be more nurturing and caring than men, men often turn to women rather than to other men for emotional support. Of course, this is also the reason why women have to provide more emotional labour, which I shall come to in a bit.

14.

DIFFICULT WOMEN, BRAVE MEN

> To the woman, God said, 'I will greatly multiply your pain in
> child bearing; in pain you shall deliver children; yet your desire
> shall be for your husband, and he shall rule over you.'
>
> — Genesis 3:16

'YENTL SYNDROME' IS NAMED AFTER the heroine of the
nineteenth-century short story 'Yentl the Yeshiva Boy' by
Isaac Bashevis Singer, who had to disguise herself as a man to study
the Talmud.[1] This term has made its way into medical research to
suggest that women are only treated seriously if they are perceived
to be as sick as a man, or pretend to be one.[2] Women are less likely
to be taken seriously and treated immediately at the early stages of
a healthcare diagnosis, and their pain is not considered as significant
as men's.[3] Yentl syndrome is about the invisibility of women, particularly in medical research and treatment.[4] It has now been reliably
shown that women experience disbelief at the early stages of a
healthcare encounter, and experience pain for longer before they
are referred to a specialist clinic compared to men. Women are

prescribed less pain medication as they are often perceived to be anxious rather than in pain, and assumed to be 'over-reacting'. As an example, 50 million Americans have one or more autoimmune diseases. A survey from the American Autoimmune Related Diseases Association (AARDA) shows that 62 per cent of people with an autoimmune disease have been labelled 'chronic complainers' by doctors. Since more than 80 per cent of these people are women, this attitude affects women disproportionately, sometimes 16 times more than men.[5]

At Wimbledon in 2021, the 18-year-old British tennis player Emma Raducanu had to withdraw from her fourth-round match due to medical reasons. She was struggling to breathe and clutching her chest. John McEnroe, the three-times Wimbledon men's champion commentating on BBC Sport, said that it 'had got a little bit too much' for Raducanu and she could not handle the pressure. McEnroe also said: 'It makes you look at the guys that have been around and the girls for so long – how well they can handle it.' There was an implication in his comments that Raducanu was not hurt or really ill, but that she was perhaps not mentally tough enough to compete at that level.

History (and scientific research) has shown us that women's testimonies about their bodies are not believed and that it is often attributed to their over-emotional nature, or their inability to handle pressure.

I remember a few years ago I was suffering from acute abdominal pain, the kind where I could not settle down for a single moment. I went to the local doctor a number of times, and was told that it was perhaps only 'stomach cramps', and 'you could regulate your diet and notice the difference', and 'it is probably gastric'. One doctor suggested that I was being too 'dramatic' as he couldn't see anything wrong. Another told me that some exercise and weight loss would do me good. Every time, the doctor asked me if I was sure of my pain. Once, I looked over at the doctor's notes and the woman physician had written 'Looks alright'. I was suffering from acute gallbladder cholesterolosis and needed urgent surgery.

Although the terms 'hysteria' and 'neurosis' were removed from the *Diagnostic and Statistical Manual of Mental Disorders* (DSM) of the American Psychiatric Association in 1980, women are still likely to be over-diagnosed with a range of psychiatric illnesses, from depression to borderline personality disorder, and over-prescribed medication for mental illnesses.[6] The World Health Organization has warned that women's physical pain is often underestimated and attributed to psychosomatic causes.[7] Even when gender roles were changing through the first half of the twentieth century, and there was a resurgence of feminist activism, especially in the United States, hysteria was being ignored by the medical professionals; there was a reappearance of hysteria focused more on a psychological-moral perspective during the 1960s, with the belief that it was 'primarily if not exclusively a diagnosis of women, which was rarely found in men'.[8] A patient with hysteria was considered to be 'typically attractive and seductive' and 'interested in controlling the opposite sex . . . and continuously demanding reassurance, approval and praise.'[9] The idea of hysteria was rooted in a notion of a unique femininity based in innate biology. And emotionality, dependence, a manipulative nature and moral weaknesses were associated with women who rejected their traditional roles as domestic goddesses, as wives and mothers.

In the first Shorvon Memorial Lecture, subsequently published in the *British Medical Journal* in May 1965, the British physician Eliot Slater describes 'hysteria' as a chronic disease that was more neurological than psychiatric.[10] More than 90 per cent of patients diagnosed and treated for hysteria were still women. In the lecture, Slater discusses cases admitted to the National Hospital in Queen Square, London, and highlights many cases of women whose fits were considered to be hysteria but who were simply suffering from epilepsy. A girl who had shown pain in her neck and weakness in her hands was diagnosed with hysteria in 1953. In 1965, with new knowledge, and focus on her physical conditions rather than an assumption of mental disorder, it was found that she in fact had thoracic outlet syndrome, a group of disorders where blood vessels or nerves get compressed in the space between the collarbone and ribs. A woman considered to have a serious case of hysteria and mental illness, with chronic pain in her body, was found to be suffering from Takayasu's arteritis, which causes blood-vessel inflammation and can prove to be fatal if left untreated. Slater muses over the reasons why a misdiagnosis of 'hysteria' was made, and he attributes it to a fault in interpretation. Disappointingly, however, he falls back on ascribing a degree of blame to certain personality traits and behaviours in the female patients that motivated the doctors to misinterpret the symptoms. Amongst these traits were: 'Tendency on the part of the patient to seek more attention than thought to deserve; any tendency to play up or to exaggerate symptoms; extraverted manners and lively phraseology; self-pity and self-concern; dependence and immaturity; any tendency to over-react emotionally.' There was a moral judgement at the heart of this new wave of hysteria, where women were seen to be controlling of men, 'demanding, flamboyant, bitchy, and especially concerned about their appearance'.[11] They were just perceived to be difficult women.

Anke Samulowitz and colleagues from the Institute of Medicine in Sweden, from a recent comprehensive analysis of 77 research studies, propose that tropes of 'brave men' and 'emotional women' exist as gendered norms in chronic pain management and diagnosis.[12] Women are seen to be more sensitive to pain but also more tolerant to pain (a strange paradox), which affects how seriously their symptoms are considered. Andronormativity persists to maintain the gender hierarchy, where women's diseases and illnesses are considered as deviant from the norm, especially if the illness manifests in a different form in women. Women's pain is considered in comparison to how pain has manifested in men, even though women dominate the chronic pain diagnosis and generally have more pain than men. This is why many of the illnesses specific to women, such as endometriosis, are not diagnosed as easily and quickly, and women's pain becomes invisible. The American College of Obstetricians and Gynecologists estimates that while endometriosis affects 1 in 10 women of reproductive age, it takes an average of 6 to 10 years for an accurate diagnosis after the symptoms first appear. Because of the general perception that women are more sensitive to pain, the acute debilitating pain of endometriosis is often treated as psychosomatic – i.e., that the pain is 'in their head', and that they are 'over-reacting'.

In their 1982 study 'Women with Pain', Joan Crook and Eldon Tunks, professors at McMaster University, found that women with chronic pain are more likely to be misdiagnosed with mental health conditions than men.[13] They also found that doctors were more likely to dismiss women as hysterical. In the 1968 edition of the DSM, the symptoms of hysteria (renamed hysterical personality disorder in the 1980s) included 'excitability, emotional instability, over-reactivity, self-dramatisation'. Even though hysteria has been obsolete as a medical diagnosis since the 1980s, Jane Ussher (professor of women's health psychology at Western Sydney University and author of numerous books on women's mental health) writes that borderline personality disorder (BPD) simply took the place of hysteria, and was termed a 'feminised' psychiatric diagnosis as it occurs predominantly in women (by a 3:1 ratio).[14] The symptoms for BPD in the DSM at the time included impulsiveness, emotional liability and uncertainty – which as we have seen are characterised broadly in society as 'feminine' qualities – accompanied with 'inappropriate intense anger', a masculine characteristic that has, through history, been seen as transgressive in women. Ussher says that the typical BPD patient is viewed as a 'demanding, angry, aggressive woman' which she takes care to point out is often deemed perfectly acceptable behaviour in men.[15] [16] A research paper titled, rather shockingly, *The Angry Woman Syndrome* described 'periodic outbursts of unprovoked anger' as one of the symptoms of BPD.[17]

The solution proposed by John Houck in the *American Journal of Psychiatry* in 1972 was that therapists should focus the women 'firmly on home, family and adult obligations' and that their spouse (presumed to be a man of course) must work aggressively on his 'passivity and lack of dominance', which leads to such conditions in the woman.[18] In 2021, according to the American Psychiatric Association, about 76 per cent of people receiving a BPD diagnosis are still women.[19] It is not entirely clear whether this is due to diagnostic or sampling bias, since there are more similarities than differences in the clinical presentation of the disorder in men and women. The names and labels might have changed, the symptoms rewritten, but the pathologisation of women's emotions continues.

Due to the long-standing myth of the 'irrational female' women are assumed to be emotionally volatile and vulnerable due to their reproductive biology, and similar accounts can be made of premenstrual dysphoric disorder (PMDD). Women reporting anxiety, tearfulness, excessive crying or anger, and irritability or depression

– all normal premenstrual symptoms – can be diagnosed as having PMDD.[20] This has faced widespread criticism, with feminists suggesting that PMDD should not be classed as a separate mental illness, but as a 'culture-bound' syndrome, and a physical illness.[21] Women are quickly labelled depressed and mentally ill if they do not fulfil their relational and nurturing roles in family and society as they are expected to. Most of these changes are of course a normal part of (cis) women's bodily experience and should not be used to discriminate against them, or to label them as erratic and unreliable in their premenstrual phase. Psychologists such as Paula Caplan believe that the language around PMDD is misleading and sexist, with the message being that women will be believed only if they can be labelled mentally ill. 'Can you imagine if we did that to men?' she asks.[22] What women need is good-quality gynaecological care and disorder-specific medications. While the condition itself is stigmatised, women suffering from acute premenstrual symptoms (including debilitating pain and anxiety) are not given adequate support in workplaces.[23] Even though PMDD is termed as a disability in the UK's 2010 Equality Act, and in the USA job-protected leave can be requested under the Family Medical Leave Act (FMLA) and support under the Americans with Disabilities Act (ADA), women report facing discrimination in interviews and in their work, having to explain their symptoms and being considered to be 'faking it'.[24]

Workplaces are still largely ignorant of women's reproductive health problems, partially as a result of masculine behaviours setting the norm, and any indication of femininity being stigmatised.[25] Compounded with the existing emotional norms and codes around employee behaviour, any sign of irritability from women is scrutinised and penalised. Many do not report their pain and diagnosis for fear of being discriminated against, and in order to be legitimised women can sometimes adopt 'mimetic' emotional traits that are more in line with other culturally permissible expressions of illness, so that their distress can be seen as 'real'. Some women self-regulate their emotions to conform to expectations,[26] and in the process report a loss of self-esteem.[27] Women's feelings of guilt around their menstrual cycle can stem from the fear that they would be seen as 'unreliable' or 'difficult'. Often women also resort to over-compensatory behaviours for any emotional outbursts in the form of apology, or passiveness and compliance, which also count against them since these character traits 'feminise' them even further. Women's emotions are also weaponised in the way menstruation is stigmatised in the workplace, where the focus is on their emotionality, mainly anger, rather than the physical pain they might be experiencing. A report by the UK Chartered Institute of Personnel and Development (CIPD) in 2019 showed that 1 in 10 menstruators (including cis-women, trans men and non-binary people) had received negative comments such as 'It's just an excuse to act like a bitch' or 'You're just lazy.'[28]

In the National Latino and Asian American Survey in 2011, 2,718 Asian, Latina and Black premenopausal women aged 18–40 years completed the World Mental Health Composite International Diagnostic Interview. Results showed that women reporting discrimination due to race or gender (83 per cent) were more likely to experience PMDD compared to those who did not face discrimination.[29] Most such discrimination, involving subtle everyday microaggressions, was even more related to the development of PMDD than more explicit forms of discrimination.[30] These subversive forms of discrimination have a huge psychological impact on people, leading to stress, anxiety and insomnia. Since the link between discrimination and mental health has been well documented, this becomes a chicken and egg situation.[31] Once someone is diagnosed with depression or mental illness, it is easy to devalue their opinions and experiences, to label them as irrational and unreasonable, and assign lack of control as the reason for their valid emotions.

Chronic pain in women has long been under-diagnosed. Hegemonic masculinity or the idealisation of typically masculine characteristics in healthcare mean that anyone presenting attributes such as stoicism, resilience, strength and endurance are perceived more favourably than those presenting sensitivity and discomfort to pain, as these have long been considered inferior attributes. In a 2015 essay in the *Atlantic*, Joe Fassler reports that in the ER in the United States, men wait an average of 49 minutes before being treated for abdominal pain. For women, the wait is 65 minutes for the same symptoms.[32] This data is confirmed by the National Women's Health Network, and although most hospital websites do not display any such data in a transparent manner, I do not find it difficult to believe these statistics.[33] My personal experience includes waiting for up to 6 hours to be seen by a doctor in the emergency services here in the UK, even when I was almost passing out with debilitating pain. A study of 400 eligible patients showed that it takes an average of 7 minutes longer for women to be seen by a doctor in cases of a heart attack compared to men, and it takes them 15 minutes longer from door to the hospital[34] because it is more likely for women to be given a lower severity score.[35] In 2016, the Brain Tumour Charity in the UK released a report with results from a questionnaire completed by more than 1,000 people.[36] It found that almost 1 in 3 patients with terminal cancer had visited their doctor more than 5 times before they received their diagnosis. Almost 25 per cent had waited for more than a year before they were diagnosed. Women were more likely than men to wait at least 10 months between their first visit and diagnosis. Several reported not being taken seriously, and even that medical practitioners had made fun of their headaches. 'One of the GPs I saw actually made fun of me, saying "What did I think my headaches were, a brain tumour?"' said a 39-year-old woman diagnosed with a brain tumour, who had to go back numerous times and was prescribed analgesics and antidepressants, because no one would take her symptoms seriously.

Analysis by Cambridge University Medical School of 2009–2010 data from 920 patients with bladder and renal cancer showed that 25–30 per cent of women required at least 3 extra consultations before diagnosis compared to 11–18 per cent of men, and experienced longer intervals between first consultation and hospital referral.[37] In 2015, a study at Bangor University analysing diagnosis time for 15 different types of cancer from 18,618 newly diagnosed cancer patients over the age of 40 found that in 6 of the 11 non-gender-specific cancers, women waited longer for medical diagnosis.[38] (The other 4 had no gender difference because these were cancers specific to male and female patients, such as breast, testicular and cervical.)

It takes women much longer to be diagnosed and treated because they are perceived as 'over-emotional'. Women in pain are more likely to be given sedatives than pain medication. A questionnaire administered to more than 300 nurses showed that nurses perceive pain differently in men and women, often judging women as less sensitive to and less distressed by pain.[39] Margo McCaffery and Betty Ferrell, from the National Medical Center, California, found that nurses perceived differences between men and women in sensitivity to pain.[40] Even though there is no evidence in any literature that men and women experience pain differently for the same condition, and although 63 per cent of the nurses agreed that men and women have the same perception of pain, 27 per cent thought that men felt greater pain than women. Only 10 per cent thought that women experienced greater pain than men in response to comparable stimuli. Almost 47 per cent of these respondents believed that women were less sensitive to pain, but more tolerant of it and less distressed as a result of it. A belief underpinning this thinking is that women developed resistance and a natural ability to bear pain because of menstruation and childbirth. But the nurses also believed that women were more likely to report pain, and to express it nonverbally, showing grander gestures and emotions, which at times did not correspond accurately with the level of pain they were experiencing or the seriousness of their situation. It might seem contradictory, but when women are perceived as over-reporters of pain (exaggerating their pain) as well as being less sensitive to pain, they are seen to be over-reacting and at the same time not to warrant the same attention as men in a similar situation. Men are assumed to be more stoic and less expressive of their emotions, but also more reasoned in their expressions so when they do complain about pain, it is more likely be real. It was therefore seen that nurses planned an earlier intervention for men, with more time to administer the analgesic as well as more emotional support time for men compared to women.

In a 2008 study at Glasgow University, using a sample of 3,261 patients (52.3 per cent women), women who had suffered a stroke were less likely to be given pain management compared to men on discharge, and significantly less likely to be prescribed statins.[41] In Germany, a study of more than 1,200 chest-pain patients across 74 different hospitals showed that doctors were more likely to attribute coronary heart disease as the reason for chest pain in men and refer them to a hospital for specialist care (6.6 per cent men, 2.9 per cent women).[42] Women's pain is more likely to be attributed to emotional rather than physical causes, and the severity of their injuries or health condition is therefore underestimated. A 2010 study of 316 patients (52.8 per cent women) and 161 nurses (54 per cent women) also showed that women and men with pain were seen as less 'normal', the men less masculine and more feminine, and the women the opposite.[43] The presence of chronic pain and the emotions associated with it can be seen as at odds with the typical standards of masculinity and femininity in our society and therefore people can feel pressured to hide their symptoms and pain. There are also class-based and race-based intersectional effects on the diagnosis of pain, with women from lower socio-economic backgrounds and minority ethnic communities dehumanised more (even by women nurses), resulting in their expression of pain being more readily ignored and dismissed.[44] The western framework of duality also results in the separation of mind and body, and the belief that objective facts are more reliable and credible than emotions, which are perceived to be more subjective.

This misconception and expectation that women should be able to tolerate more pain can lead to their expression of pain being treated with suspicion and hostility at times, and not taken seriously. This then leads to emotional outbursts, anger, outrage and more stress and strain, which in turn reinforces the perception that much of women's pain is due to psychological reasons and their emotionality. Emotionality from women is taken as a sign that she is out of control and over-reacting. Stress is also feminine coded, as are many chronic-pain conditions which do not have clear external symptoms.

It wasn't until the 1960s that it was understood that multiple sclerosis, a neurodegenerative disease, is three to four times more common in women. Until then it was thought that men suffered more from this disease, and many women presenting similar symptoms were diagnosed with hysteria. Lawyer Cassie Springer-Sullivan, writing in the *Berkeley Journal of Gender, Law and Justice* in 2005, states how many of the women that came to her had been treated unfairly by disability insurers because they often assumed that these women were either 'magnifying their symptoms' or had a 'low pain tolerance'.[45] Although the terminology has changed and the word 'hysterics' is not now used to label the set of symptoms, many diseases that are more likely to occur in women, such as fibromyalgia, are called 'somatic' or 'psychosomatic', meaning 'physical symptoms are produced by the action of the unconscious mind' and are largely psychological.[46] Much like hysteria, doctors and insurers are more likely to dismiss complaints of chronic pain if the women have not been working full-time outside the house, assuming that with no strenuous physical element to their life, they were merely being lazy or over-reacting. Many insurers in Springer-Sullivan's experience were also reluctant to accept self-reported symptoms of pain and fatigue, and instead insisted on 'objective evidence of disability'; the underlying assumption being that these women were faking their symptoms, being 'hysterical' and were therefore frauds. We have returned to the legitimacy of women's narratives and reports of their own bodies, which has constantly been a way to diminish women's authority over their own lives and emotions.

'Everyone thinks I am just lazy' is a study of 50 experiences of fibromyalgia patients in the USA as part of a recent research project.[47] It further shows how the dismissal of women's emotions around their everyday pain can have a huge impact on their personal and professional identity. Within the United States, fibromyalgia affects an estimated 5 million people, 80–90 per cent of whom are women.[48] Our cultural discourse of hard work and mind over matter means that often the message given to women with such symptoms is to 'pull themselves up by their bootstrap'.[49] This shapes people's own identity in relation to society, and how they are perceived. In June 2020, the first reports of long Covid appeared with some initial data, and it was found that women outnumbered men by 4 to 1.[50] While women are more likely to report their symptoms, it is also seen that, much like other autoimmune disorders such as ME/CFS and chronic Lyme disease, medical professionals are either treating women's symptoms of long Covid as imaginary or attributing them to anxiety, falling back on the idea of hysterical women.

When we continue to experience the same response from others, and our emotions and experiences are invalidated, we can self-label and internalise these messages. For example, two experiments were conducted to test the hypothesis that our self-concepts derive partly from the way we imagine being perceived by others who we deem significant.[51] Forty women were instructed to visualise the faces of either two acquaintances or two older members of their own family. Later on, when they rated a sexually explicit piece of fiction for enjoyment, they tended to respond in ways that would be acceptable to the salient people they had imagined earlier. This effect was more pronounced when they sat in front of a mirror while doing the experiment, where their concerns about self-image were particularly heightened. At least some of the time, then, we end up evaluating ourselves as we imagine others would (or we know that others do). For women in the fibromyalgia study, it was particularly important that they were able to perform their gender roles, and the struggle to serve as wives and mothers caused them a lot of anxiety and guilt. For women, these ideas around feminine gender ideals are deeply ingrained, but there is also more judgement from society if they do not conform to the cultural discourse that a mother who is a primary caregiver should have her complete focus on the child, at the cost of her own emotional and physical well-being.[52]

Emotions also affect how medical professionals diagnose and treat coronary artery disease or heart attacks in men and women. Men are diagnosed more with heart attacks than women, and women are under-diagnosed.[53] Cardiovascular disease is still the major cause of death in women, but there is a larger perception that women are protected from cardiovascular illnesses because traditionally there have been fewer women in any clinical trials. Women have to present more aggressive symptoms than men to get the same kind of treatment because their cardiac pain can often be attributed to other non-specific pain. There is also an underlying assumption that women feel emotions more, and react to stressors in a more intense manner compared to men. This deadly data bias against women in diagnosis and treatment of heart disease is of course Yentl syndrome, as I mentioned earlier, whereby the typical perception of a heart-attack patient is that of a middle-aged man. On googling 'heart attack' the first 30 or so images are indeed of men, clutching their chest in various stages of distress. On the first page of searches, there are only about 5 images of women. Any mention of stress or discussion of emotional conditions can change the diagnosis of chronic heart disease (with men diagnosed in 75 per cent of cases and women in only 13 per cent). Brian Birdwell and colleagues from Oklahoma Health Sciences Center carried out a research study with 44 medical interns who viewed videos of women who presented their symptoms of heart disease differently.[54] Half of them presented in a calm and 'business-like' manner, while the other half read the same script on screen in a more histrionic manner. In the case of those who presented in an unemotive manner, cardiac illness was diagnosed in 50 per cent of the cases, but where there was a lot more inflection of the voice and gesticulation (and even bright colours and big earrings), only 13 per cent of the cases were diagnosed. In the women who presented their symptoms in a more 'emotional' manner, the diagnosis was more likely to be a panic attack rather than a heart attack, even when their physical exam showed the same symptoms as that of other patients who were diagnosed with heart disease.

The philosopher Miranda Fricker calls this a 'credibility deficit', where women's own testimonies are not trusted because they are considered irrational and emotional.[55] The perception that women are too emotional and unreliable leads to a stigma double-bind where on one hand it is assumed that 'women are hysterical', and on the other that 'psychiatric illnesses are not real and are in the mind'.

Just as the outspoken and free-spirited woman of the sixteenth century was castigated as a witch, and the same woman in the eighteenth and nineteenth century as hysterical, in the late twentieth and early twenty-first century she is often described as having borderline personality disorder, or premenstrual dysphoric disorder. Even in 2022, women can find themselves on the receiving end of jokes about it being their 'time of the month' if they express emotions such as anger or irritability. A recent Reddit thread showed me that many people thought that 'She is PMSing' was a suitable comment for a woman who was showing anger or crying a lot.[56] All are potentially stigmatising labels. And all are potentially related to what kind of emotional codes have existed in our society at different points, and what it has meant to be a woman at different times in our history.

15.

SOFT TOUCH:
EMPATHY AND EMOTIONAL LABOUR

To perceive is to suffer.
— Aristotle

THERE HAS BEEN MUCH WRITTEN about medical and health-care bias.[1] However, although we are beginning to realise the extent of this pernicious bias against women and other marginalised groups in healthcare, there has not been an analysis of how emotions mobilise and reinforce biases. While we have seen how women's emotions, and the norms around 'emotional women' and 'brave men', have created fissures in our medical system, another element that affects bias in healthcare domains is how empathy is gendered.

Much like any other emotion, empathy has a multi-layered defin-ition. From the Greek empatheia ('en/em', in, and 'pathos', feeling), it is all about intense feelings, and is often defined as the ability to put yourself in other people's shoes and see the world through their eyes without losing your own sense of perspective.[2] It is being aware of other people's emotional state but also being able to feel it. It can also become a clichéd expression of solidarity and sympathy. In 1992, President Bill Clinton told an activist at a rally: 'I feel your pain.' And there were similar moments during his campaign and through his presidency where journalists highlighted his 'I feel your pain' moments, where he would evoke a sympathetic connection with the audience with a particular facial display.[3] [4] Clinton would bite his lower lip to evoke the pain he was feeling on the other's behalf while stoically trying his best to control his overwhelming emotions, since it was the masculine thing to do. Empathy is something we all value and an emotion that we often associate with being human, even though most primates have the ability to emotionally connect with others and execute perspective-taking to a certain extent. In one of the most stark experiments showing animal empathy, researchers reported that a group of rhesus monkeys refused to pull a chain that delivered food to them if it gave a shock to another monkey in their group. Jules Masserman and colleagues showed that one monkey starved himself for 12 days because he did not want to hurt another monkey.[5] Chimpanzees have also shown consolation behaviour that reflects empathy, such as showing friendly behaviour towards another primate that has suffered aggression.

There has to be an intrinsic motivation to understanding other people's feelings and to being able to communicate this back to them. Frans de Waal, a Dutch primatologist, likened the evolution of empathy to Russian matryoshka dolls, where the inner core develops first and then is nested within a series of outer layers.[6] De Waal defines empathy as our ability to understand the feelings of others, and to acknowledge at the same time that there is a difference between our feelings and theirs. There is no duplication of someone else's feelings so there is not necessarily any personal discomfort (even though we might claim 'I feel your pain'), or even pity associated with this compassion. The most basic layer of empathy de Waal defines is 'emotional contagion', which creates a synchronous link between two people's emotions. The next is the feeling we have for others when we know that they are in pain or facing a problem (the sympathetic concern or 'consolation'), and the third part is what de Waal calls 'targeted helping', which happens through perspective-taking, where we assess the situation and find a solution to help others.

There have been a number of theories about how empathy developed in humans, and why. Evolutionarily speaking, empathy is believed to have developed to provide parental care, to pass on 'empathy genes' to future generations, to ensure an altruistic society where people work together and collaborate to facilitate each other's 'fitness'. This extension to non-biological kinship ensures the reciprocal benefits for survival and reproduction. De Waal also proposes that natural selection ('survival of the fittest') favours altruism both for kin and non-kin, which could not have developed without empathy.

Within physician–patient communication, there is a growing understanding of the importance of empathy. This becomes especially relevant when there is so much gender bias in medical domains because of the way emotions are interpreted. A 2009 study shows that there has been a decline in empathy scores (measured on the Jefferson scale of empathy, JME)[7] in the United States over the last twenty years or so, while it has remained the same or increased in countries such as Portugal, South Korea and Japan.[8] According to the Global Risks Report 2019, published by the World Economic Forum, the lines between the physical and digital worlds are blurring, which has led to increased polarisation and loneliness, especially in traditionally individualistic cultures such as the USA and the UK.[9]

In so-called collectivist cultures that put more value on family bonds and connections, and often have large families living together, this has been less significant. Other suggested causes of this fall in empathy include the time people spend on their phones and on social media platforms, and the echo chambers we create where we associate only with people whose views echo our own. In this age of increasing connection, we are seeing more disconnection, something that is not going to come as news to anyone, really, especially after we have spent more than eighteen months self-isolating and in pandemic lockdowns. As face-to-face connection increasingly dwindles, we lose the regular practice in interpreting other people's facial emotions and nonverbal gestures, such as tone of voice, speed, posture, eye contact and so on. Social media also encourages anonymity and deindividuation; even on platforms such as Zoom we do not have eye contact – instead, we spend most of the time looking at ourselves and at grey boxes of faceless apparitions. Also, when we are exposed to bad news and suffering at a tap and a scroll, we can become desensitised to it, resulting in 'compassion fatigue'.

Research in 2016 with 226 students at the Federal University of Santa Catarina in Brazil showed that women and those from the lower classes had a higher level of empathy.[10] These groups also showed a higher accuracy in perception of emotions during social interactions. Similar results for a higher level of empathy in women medical students and nurses have been reported across a number of studies. For instance, in 2011 an experiment with 853 medical students in the UK, out of which 470 were women, showed that women scored significantly higher on empathy than men amongst the same cohort.[11] It is not clear from the experimental results if women train themselves to be more empathetic because they are expected to be warm and nurturing. In these experiments,

296

self-reporting is bound to play a role, i.e., women might report more empathy because they self-label with other people's perceptions and expectations.

Empathy through emotional contagion happens quite fast in response to any stimulus in the environment, with the behaviours of the observer and observed becoming aligned and creating an empathic bond of communication.[12] Emotions spread from person to person rather quickly through mimicry, often without awareness.[13] Women have been shown through a range of studies to be better, and faster, at recognising facial expressions and interpreting the underlying emotional expressions correctly.[14] They have been shown to be better at recognising bodily emotions, especially angry body language in men. Across England and Wales, 2 women are killed by their current or ex-partner every week, with more than 40 per cent of murdered women dying from gendered violence (an increase of 23 per cent from the previous year).[15] Amnesty International reports that police in the UK receive a call every minute about domestic abuse; 89 per cent of these are from women but only 24 per cent of cases are actually reported.[16] The UN reported in 2021 that 736 million women – almost 1 in 3 – have been subject to intimate partner violence, non-partner sexual violence, or both at least once in their life.[17] It makes sense that women teach themselves how to read anger signs from men through their faces and bodies. It is a survival instinct.

This seems consistent with the ideas in evolutionary theories about mating and threat-avoidance. As we have seen, anger is perceived to be a masculine emotion, and aggressiveness is commonly associated with men, so women become better at reading it and anticipating it to pre-empt any threat or violence. Men, on the other hand, in general are better at recognising happy body language in women.[18] Various evolutionary theorists have speculated that men learn to read happy emotions in women as a social cue of their potential interest in mating. Of course, it is not always the case that happy women are interested in forming sexual liaisons with the men around them. Perhaps this is also one of the reasons that sexual harassment is so prevalent.

William Ickes, a social psychologist, coined the term 'empathic accuracy' (also sometimes called empathic concern) in 1988 to describe a person's capability to understand and feel what the other person is feeling.[19] Some experiments report that women experience more emotional contagion than men when providing support and comfort for friends and exhibit greater facial mimicry. In a friendship circle, women might be more aware of the need to empathise in order to build stronger social bonds, as empathy is a major driving force for pro-social behaviour. Women are more likely to mimic the expressions and vocalisations of those around them, which can also give way to the notion that women are weaker and more susceptible. A 2011 study showed that women are more vulnerable to emotional contagion than men, even after brief interactions that they perceive as supportive.[20] This study mapped the informal supportive interactions between 48 pairs of friends (31 same gender and 17 mixed gender) showing that after just an 8-minute interaction with a troubled friend, women were more likely than men to feel worse and less positive, and that the changes in their state correlated directly with that of their friend. Men did not seem to experience the same quick emotional transformation and their emotional state was less likely to deteriorate even when supporting a friend in distress.[21] In a more recent study in 2019, 70 people viewed a hand pierced by a needle and then filled out a self-report measure of empathy (called the Interpersonal

Reactivity Index).[22] An fMRI looked at immediate reflexive responses and measured them according to blood–flow activity in different parts of the brain. Brain mapping showed that women were better at feeling others' pain, showing more activity in the parts of the brain associated with pain than men.[23] But when we look at other experiments in other domains that are traditionally considered more masculine, such as the military, women were less accurate than men at judging verbal and nonverbal emotional cues.[24] Lauren McAllister and colleagues show that emotional detachment is valued in the military amongst UK servicemen, where typical masculine characteristics such as stoicism and toughness are encouraged, and 'feminine' characteristics such as emotionality are actively discouraged and excluded.[25] So women adapt their behaviour to different social demands and roles, and their empathic accuracy shifts depending on the level of stereotype threat they feel in a particular domain.[26]

At the basic level, studies have not shown significant gender difference in empathic accuracy over a number of domains, but when people are made aware of gender roles, and informed that this is being assessed, these differences are much more significant in both men and women.[27] When women were asked to self-estimate their own empathic accuracy, they were also more accurate than men. Men showed as much accuracy as women when there was monetary compensation involved, significantly higher than men and women who were not offered any money for their estimations of other people's emotions.[28] This means that there is little difference in ability to empathise, but there is a more significant difference between men's and women's motivation to show empathy. Different situations and contexts can therefore change a person's ability to empathise with another, but it is clear that women are more conscious of their social gender roles, and have a higher intrinsic motivation to conform to these roles and societal expectations.

From an evolutionary perspective, the idea that women are innately more empathetic emerges from the idea that in early humans, females had to take care of children and so greater 'fitness' (likelihood of survival) was linked to their being more empathic mothers. Some scientists say that children show these sex/gender differences from a very young age, although as we have seen, gendered socialisation has been proven to play a considerable role in how these behaviours are determined.[29] [30] Gendered socialisation might explain why autism, which is still diagnostically linked to something called empathy deficit or alexithymia (emotional blindness) by medical professionals, is less easily diagnosed in girls than in boys. Girls are more rigorously trained to mask negative emotions to perform socially expected roles, and often learn to associate their sense of self and identity more strongly to these pro-social bonds due to socialisation.

According to the National Autistic Society in the UK, 5 times as many boys as girls are diagnosed with autism. The most comprehensive survey published in 2017 analysed data from 54 global studies to show that there are 4.2 boys to every 1 girl diagnosed with autism worldwide.[31] It has traditionally been seen as a 'male disorder'. Hans Asperger, who first theorised the condition in 1938, initially thought it was exclusive to males. Much of this belief that boys are more likely to be autistic is also a result of the research by British psychologist Simon Baron-Cohen in the 2000s, who proposed a dubious link between high levels of foetal testosterone to the likelihood of male infants developing autism, and claimed that males, in general, have less empathy and greater aptitude for working with patterns and systems.[32] In an article in *The Guardian* in 2003, he proposed an 'empathising-systemising' (E–S) theory: 'My theory is that the female brain is predominantly hard-wired for empathy, and that the male brain is predominantly hard-wired for understanding and building systems.'[33] He uses this to support his theory that people with autism have an extreme 'male' brain that is better at systemising and 'bad at empathising'. He later went on to develop more strict and equally misguided ideas around biological essentialism, claiming that men and women are basically wired differently, so that women are more in tune with their own and other people's emotions.

These ideas are now being challenged by neuroscientists, who have stressed the more social, psychological and cultural contributors to our behaviour.

As part of the Autism Inpatient Collection, a project gathering genetic and phenotypic information about autistic children and young people in the United States across six focused psychiatry units, survey data was collected from 722 people aged 4 to 20 years old, from 2013 to 2018.[34] The data included 146 girls and young women. Parents, primary carers and guardians also responded to 30 questions about the participants' emotional intensity and overall disposition. The data showed the girls were diagnosed much later, on average, that they struggled more with emotional regulation and were likely to suffer from depression. Girls are not being diagnosed because there is interpretation bias, and doctors are not actively looking for autism in children who do not present with classic symptoms such as missing social cues and difficulty interpreting nonverbal body and facial expressions.[35] Girls learn from a young age to better manage and regulate their emotions than boys, and they can camouflage symptoms by developing one or two very close, intense relationships.[36] Parents have reported more concerns about emotional meltdowns and inability to regulate their emotions

301

with girls than boys, while on the other hand, they tend to worry more about a son's isolation.[37] Girls are less likely to display traditional symptoms such as withdrawing and isolating socially.[38] A child being seen as a boy or a girl changes the way the world perceives them, and how people interact with them. In terms of autism, there is research to show that mothers talk more to daughters than to sons, and so they develop more social skills, therefore masking their autistic traits. Girls also develop strategies to demonstrate behaviours that are more communicative and friendly, mimicking behaviour, and so they are not successfully diagnosed by the traditional yardstick. This masking and the constant struggle to keep up the elaborate social rules of emotions takes its toll on girls on the autism spectrum, and we see that it is accompanied by an increased rate of depression and anxiety in teenage years,[39] and also more propensity to eating disorders.[40]

Children on the autism spectrum[41] are perceived as less likely to display typical expressions of empathy, because empathy is often treated as a binary state while it is in fact a multi-dimensional concept.[42] This 'established fact' is being challenged and it has been shown across a number of studies that children and young people on the autism spectrum have the same or higher empathic accuracy as neurotypical people. Empathic accuracy is more self-oriented and is the process of sharing other people's feelings without necessarily having the same empathic concern and the emotional response to their feelings. Autistic people might not show emotions in the same way as neurotypical people, or be able to mask and regulate their emotions in the same way, but they are not uncaring or unemotional. They are more likely to attribute personalities and emotions to inanimate objects, and feel emotions very intensely.[43] Scientists have highlighted the difference between alexithymia (where a person finds it difficult to understand and identify their emotions) and autism to show that not everyone with autism has alexithymia, and so do not have as many problems recognising emotions as those with alexithymia, who are less empathic on average.[44]

•

Empathy can be innate, but can also be learnt and achieved through training. Enhancing empathy in medical students has to be an important aim of medical education, to avoid some of the biases that impact diagnosis and treatment of women. There is now a growing acknowledgement that encouraging medical practitioners to show empathy can reduce patient anxiety and increase their satisfaction,[45] and studies with the National Health Service (NHS) in the UK have shown the impact of lack of empathy on patient experience.[46] A systematic review and meta-analysis from patient surveys across 64 published studies and medical databases in the UK showed that the average care score in the NHS was low in comparison to normative values, falling in the bottom 5 per cent of these scores. Female practitioners were reported to express empathy more effectively, and spent more time with their patients.[47] It was not clear whether the greater empathy came as a consequence of the length of time spent with the patients, or if the women spent more time with the patients because they felt more empathy.[48]

When such gendered emotional roles as providing nurturing and empathy become demands, it can be problematic. Patients expect women to be more compassionate (as in other social caring roles). When 309 patients were shown snapshots of doctors varying in gender, age and ethnic group interacting with patients, and asked to rate them in terms of expected behaviour of the doctor, the expected behaviour of the patient, and the patient comfort with the doctor, it was seen that younger women doctors had the most expectations placed on them in terms of providing emotional support and empowering the patient.[49] People also expected the Asian (brown) doctors to display more empathy – emotions are stratified and racialised too. Women doctors are expected to do more emotional work, but when they do not fulfil these expectations, they are penalised more heavily.[50] Yumoki Kadota, in her memoir *Emotional Female*, talks about the toll it took on her to be in an emotionally demanding workplace where she was also not supposed to show emotion and risk being considered weak. Women doctors are at greater risk of burnout than men and likely to face cynicism, lack of professional achievement and emotional exhaustion.[51] This can be linked to the high empathy demands that cause greater levels of emotional arousal, which in turn can cause cognitive fatigue. 'Compassion fatigue'[52] is the cost of providing this emotional labour, and can lead to a reduction of empathy levels that has been observed in many medical students and trainee doctors, as well as hospice nurses.[53] It is a sort of survival mechanism.

Recently, more broadly outside the social care and healthcare domain, there has been a rising momentum for organisations to adopt a more empathetic approach in the workplace, focusing on emotional intelligence, the '*sine qua non* of all social effectiveness in working life'.[54] Women are often hired to perform 'empathy work', where they can use their emotional empathy (feeling other people's emotions) and cognitive empathy (understanding other people's emotions) to make their organisation appear more empathetic. 'Transformational leadership'[55] has become a buzzword where 'feminine' qualities are valued, and where women leaders are supposed to be more transformational than men because of their ability to inspire collaboration and create a more nurturing workplace through encouragement.[56] We might think that this is addressing gender inequality, but it's not the case. These assumptions are grounded in stereotypes – even though these are benevolent stereotypes – relying on archaic duality between 'masculine' and 'feminine' emotional traits, contrasting them against each other. There might be a dearth of data, and disagreement on whether empathy is coded in people innately through biological sex or gender identity, but it is clear that there is a gendered empathy gap which takes its toll on women.

During Covid and the consequent lockdowns, there was considerable talk about emotional labour – particularly with relation to women, and specifically mothers having to carry the emotional and mental load at home. These social norms, as we have seen in earlier discussions, have emerged from the perception that men and women are expected to fulfil certain roles in our society. Data from a 1996 national probability sample of 2,031 adults showed that women have higher levels of anger than men, that each additional child in the household increases anger, and that children increase anger more for mothers than for fathers.[57] Parenthood introduces two types of objective stressors into an individual's life: economic strains and the strains associated with childcare. Women are exposed to both types of strain more than men. Economic hardship, childcare responsibilities in the household, and difficulties arranging and paying for childcare all significantly increase anger and explain the effects of gender and parenthood on anger. We also find that mothers have the highest levels of anger because of economic inequality and the inequitable distribution of parental responsibilities, and these effects are not unrelated. We have also seen previously that women have to suppress anger more than men, which adds to this mental toll.

Emotions, of course, have power associations in our society, and are a considerable factor in how men and women are conditioned and prepared to fulfil certain societal roles. There is still a deep-seated view that women are more nurturing and so they are responsible for taking care of the emotional needs of others, while men are somewhat lacking in their emotional expressiveness as well as emotional regulation, and they take care of the material needs of others. Jeroen Jansz from the University of Amsterdam defines the traditional cultural model of masculinity for a white western man as comprising four parameters: autonomy (I stand alone); achievement (I need to achieve and provide); aggression (I am tough and can be aggressive if need be); and stoicism (I am strong, I do not share pain and grief openly, I do not have warm feelings).[58] Men's emotionality is determined by what they see around them from a young age. This is how a man should be, young boys are told by their fathers, uncles and grandfathers, and also by the men depicted in media, in films and in books. Video games sometimes offer an alternative world, a way, particularly for young people who are still creating their identity, to confront emotions that are linked to masculine identity (such as anger), and other emotions that are seen as not so masculine, such as fear. I suspect this is the reason why video games are becoming more popular with women, who can assert emotional identities in the virtual world that they are not permitted to explore and sustain in the real world.

These norms in the real world push the expression of emotions into a restricted range by prescribing the feeling and display rules: which emotions are womanly and manly, and which are allowed to be shown, and when. Sometimes there can be questions about why we are feeling a certain way, or implicit suggestions that our emotional expression isn't what was expected in that situation, and sometimes we can even doubt our own emotions. Of course, as we know that emotions are constructed by power hierarchies[59] and the feeling rules exist to maintain the existing social structure, this emotional convergence[60] as a 'monolithic structure of feeling and thought' comes at the cost of individual identity and well-being.[61] These norms enforce a sort of control on individuals, manipulating their emotions. They also lead to a commodification of emotions. All of us manage emotions, but when there is a commercialisation of a feeling, and the emotion is sold as part of the job, then it becomes commodified (waitress and air crew smiling, even when the customers are rude to them).

The idea of 'emotional labour' comes from the fact that emotions have a market and exchange value in our capitalist society, and this is the work that a person has to do in regulating their emotions to fit in with the emotional norm, and manage their emotions to ensure the smooth flow of business necessary to get a wage.

The same work environment therefore can have different outcomes for white people and people of colour. People from minority groups have to do more emotional work to fit in and perform emotional labour that is yet another form of commodification of feelings, where certain desirable emotions become the commodity to sell more products and services. The idea of desirability is of course linked to the feeling rules and emotional-display rules that maintain and transform the economy continuously: drivers of capitalism but also consumerism. For instance, Miliann Kang's research in 2003 of Korean women-owned nail salons in the USA showed how race, class and gender intersect to determine emotional norms.[62] Through 14 months of fieldwork in New York nail salons, including in-depth interviews and participant observation of 62 Korean women, Kang showed that these salon owners adjusted and changed their embodied forms of emotional expressions according to whether their customers were Black or white women, and which class they belonged to. For white middle-class women, the emotional work involves pandering to their notion of privilege, while for working-class Black customers, there was more expectation to give back to the community and to be treated with fairness and respect.

I did a little test run of this while in California recently. Along with my sister and a couple of white friends, we went to a pedicure and manicure salon run by a group of Vietnamese women. We are all distinctly middle class, but there was a discernible difference in the service, especially in the attention paid to our white friends. Yes, only one sample, and not a scientifically rigorous one either, but it was useful to observe this first-hand and reflect on whether the salon-workers feel compelled to bring their emotions in line with the expectations imposed on them, and the intersectional effects of ethnicity and class.

This is also similar to how Black and brown women academics have to act in academic settings. Here, they are challenged more often by white students, who perceive them as less capable and competent and confer lower status on them.[63] Despite these micro-aggressions, the Black and brown women academics have to manage their anger and frustration to appear professional because any anger outburst will only reinforce these stereotypes. They have to perform more emotional labour compared to men and white women.

While there is pressure on everyone to maintain pleasantness and conform to emotional rules, people of colour feel this pressure much more than others because they also have to compensate for any hostility and racial isolation they experience. Interviews with a range of professionals published in the journal *Social Problems* have documented how the emotional rules in workplaces prescribe congeniality and likeability, and many women of colour find it difficult to sustain this with the racial microaggressions that they encounter on a daily basis.[64] It takes up a lot of emotional labour on their part to maintain a calm demeanour while experiencing racial bias through comments, stereotypes and beliefs from co-workers, in a work environment where they are in the minority. While for white people, their skin colour provides assurance to others of their competence, people of colour also have to rely carefully on their emotional expressions, as well as other symbols such as clothing, to signify their respectability and competence. American sociologist Arlie Hochschild writes in her book *The Managed Heart* that to do emotional labour is to 'induce or suppress feeling in order to sustain the outward countenance that produces the proper state of mind in others'. In other words, to fake a certain publicly observable (and approved) facial and body display where it is expected.[65] Failure to do so doesn't simply cause emotional dissonance between the normative values and the observed values (and therefore hurt the competitive advantage of an organisation) but also diminishes an individual's career opportunities and progress.

Hochschild's original definition was intended for anyone who was deliberately obscuring their emotions at work, primarily in the service industry where the more customer-facing your job, the more emotional labour you have to perform. Those who are marginalised and in more disadvantaged positions are not as empowered and have to do more emotional adjustment, especially of their negative emotions towards those with higher status. Hochschild calls this a lack of a 'status shield', where women in particular do not have the necessary resources and support to deal with the anger of others towards them. This can then result in 'emotional dissonance', where there is a constant difference between their inner and outer states: 'a difference between feeling and feigning'.[66] Women therefore experience a higher 'norm state discrep-ancy', with a bigger gap between their private emotional experiences and the emotional norms imposed upon them.[67]

The sociologist Erving Goffman compared social interactions to the theatre. How we present ourselves to others is aimed towards 'impression management', where we make conscious decisions about what to reveal about ourselves and what not.[68] Emotional labour is kind of a performance, sometimes rehearsed so often that it becomes a habit, and sometimes triggered by the databank of emotional memories that we hold in our brains. In performing emotional labour, we modulate our emotions to feeling rules, the unwritten codes in society that guide our emotions by providing us with the motivation or the obligation.

Often emotional labour is performed in two ways, the choice between which determines the toll it takes, the impact it has on self-worth, and the level of disconnect it causes with others. One way is 'surface acting', where a social, polite persona is adopted to reconcile with the view and expectation of another person and align with societal norms. The other is 'deep acting', where there is an attempt to change real feelings because we begin to internalise the societal expectations, and there is associated guilt for feeling and displaying an inappropriate emotion. In the latter case, there is a larger impact on mental health, and a bigger knock-on effect on a person's self-esteem and self-worth. When a person has to repeatedly adjust their emotions to accommodate outside expectations, it leads to emotional exhaustion. Ongoing, cumulative emotional management and manipulation can be cognitively taxing, leading to stress and burnout.[69] But the work needed in modulating emotions and creating expressions to conform to social norms is not recognised in the workplace as legitimate work that deserves compensation. Women, especially women of colour, are more likely to be working in low-paid jobs that require more emotional labour.

It is gender construction, and racialisation, and our identities in the world that affect how much emotional work a person has to perform.[70] Hochschild claims that emotional labour is not performed in the domestic sphere, making a distinction between mental and emotional labour, but I do not fully agree. There is a blurred line between work that is needed to manage other people's emotions, and when it becomes anxiety-inducing and fear-evoking to a person. Much of the discourse surrounding emotional labour has, in fact, been in the domestic sphere, where women often carry out the everyday running of the house, childcare, and all the niggly related organisational tasks.[71] This is the mental (and physical) load, but while doing so, women also often internalise the message that they are expected to be nurturing, that this work of caring is their responsibility and shouldn't seem so onerous, and that they should never complain, get angry, tired, frustrated. And so they suppress any discontentment, and this work of suppressing the emotions is costly, with an impact on emotional and physical health.

Childcare and housework may be unpaid jobs, but they are significant contributions to keeping our capitalist society delicately balanced and ticking over. In the domestic sphere, or in other caring professions such as education or healthcare, there is a lot of emotional (and mental) labour involved which often capitalises on the view that women are naturally more empathetic, and so this should all come easily to them. Sometimes this emotional work can be merely feigning an emotion, and at other times people have to try and actually feel this emotion. The toll of performing and feigning emotions every day, while also suppressing frustration and anger, can be acute, resulting in higher daily stress levels and implications for the person's mental health. Empathy can therefore come at a cost, not just the cognitive cost involved in regulating emotions as per expectations and fulfilling normative roles, but also in maintaining a sense of self.

And while emotional labour in itself is a non-gendered term, due to the inherent gendered nature of emotions, and the different expectations for men and women in our society, caring falls to women more often than men. Women are therefore naturally bearing the burden of emotional labour both at home and outside. Not just in real life, but in virtual worlds and technologies too, it seems, as we will see in the following chapter.

16.

SUCH A DOLL
(EMOTIONAL TECHNOLOGIES)

I N THE LAST YEAR, DUE to the Covid pandemic, children have
been mostly learning from home, sitting in front of the computer
for hours every day. In some secondary schools in Hong Kong,
students' emotions are being scrutinised while they learn via virtual
platforms. An artificial intelligence program, designed by 4 Little
Trees, measures micro-movements of muscles on the students' faces
and aims to identify a range of negative and positive emotions such
as happiness, sadness, anger, surprise and fear.[1] The founder of 4 Little
Trees, Viola Lam, claims that it reads the students' emotions accurately
about 85 per cent of the time.[2] This is a facial recognition system
but with added capacity to document micro-facial and muscle movements, together with eye tracking and voice tones. Teachers are using
this system to track emotional changes in students, as well as their
motivation and focus, to understand how effectively they are learning.
The teachers believe that one of the benefits of this technology is
that they can find out which students are struggling early on, especially in a virtual classroom. Lam claims that the students perform
10 per cent better in exams if they learnt using this program. There

are concerns about privacy, and that the software has been trained mainly on white faces. And, while the software claims that emotions such as happiness and sadness are easy to read with high accuracy, complex emotions such as anxiety and frustration are not.

Emotion AI, also called affective computing, is a subset of artificial intelligence acting in response to human emotions. Emotional recognition and surveillance is becoming big business, and projected to be a $25 billion market by 2023.[3] Erik Brynjolfsson, now of Stanford University, says that machines can now recognise microexpressions on someone's face and interpret their emotions faster than a human.[4] However, Andrew McStay, professor of digital life at Bangor University and Director of Emotional AI Lab, tells me over Zoom that such technologies are only in their infancy, despite the claims made by a number of technological organisations of being able to capture human emotions. These technologies are increasingly using facial coding based on Paul Ekman's model of six basic emotions (page 26). In emotion AI, a camera is used to record a video or a photo stream and the algorithm uses the basic emotion model as the basis for inferring these emotions from the faces in the videos. Other techniques used are analysis of language and images for moods and feelings, mapping of rate of speech and tone to pre-existing data, tracking eye movement, and physiological measurements such as heart rate and sweating. The company Affectiva, for instance, uses facial coding and voice technology to detect human emotions using millions of videos and recordings of people from across cultures as the training data. Affectiva claims to have the largest dataset of spontaneous emotional responses of consumers, with over 7.5 million faces from 87 countries (around 39,000 hours of 2 billion facial frames) that are collected from recordings of people doing everyday things like watching TV. These people have consented to opt-in.[5]

The videos are sorted according to universal facial expressions (the Emotional Facial Action Coding System, or EmFacs) such as raised eyebrows and tightly pressed lips showing 'anger', a huge generalisation that we have already discussed as being problematic. The company is evidently informed by emotion research showing that context plays a huge role and that people can feign emotions. Since the videos were captured in natural settings while the users engaged in spontaneous emotions, they are less likely to have 'posed emotions' aligning with certain emotion-rules. Once a database is built of images that are classified as 'happy' or 'sad' it can then be used to train the algorithm and classify other similar images and videos with these emotions.

The analysis of Affectiva's data from over 87 countries has given some interesting insights into how emotion-roles play out across different contexts, and confirms some of our existing views about the gendering of our emotions. As an example, women smile 40 per cent more than men in the USA, and 25 per cent more in France. Men show a 'brow furrow' (considered a facial expression of anger) 12 per cent more than women. Even though such technology is really helpful to create content to elicit particular emotional responses, and even though such a large database offers the opportunity to compare and contrast across millions of videos and images, it is also constructed around homogenised assumptions of which emotion a facial expression corresponds with.

In our conversation in October 2021, Lisa Barrett told me that this facial mapping does not make sense, and that emotions are more embodied experiences than merely being reflected on people's faces. I completely agree. This kind of labelling of data reinforces stereotypes, much like emojis. Barrett and colleagues have shown that it is near impossible for AI to predict human emotions from facial expressions because these technologies are limited, with low reliability (no reliable consistency found between a set of facial movements and an emotion), a lack of specificity (no unique one-to-one correspondence between facial movements and emotions, instead plenty of overlap) and limited generalisability (the effect of culture not well considered).[6] 'People, on average, the data shows, scowl less than 30 per cent of the time when they're angry. So scowls are not the expression of anger; they're an expression of anger — one among many. That means that more than 70 per cent of the time, people do not scowl when they're angry. And on top of that, they scowl often when they're not angry.' Moreover, emotions are also expressed through body movement, gestures, voice, posture and so on. We have also seen how so much of the time, women — but also men — do 'emotion work' to disguise their real emotions, and so the way they express their emotions is likely to be a learnt response rather than a spontaneous expression. AI algorithms make predictions based on data that already has biases built in, and they are not, in the current moment, able to take the diversity of faces and emotional expressions into account.

Lauren Rhue from University of Maryland analysed publicly available data from 400 NBA (basketball league) games in 2016–17 with two popular emotion-recognition software programs.[7] Both FACE++ and Microsoft Face API assigned more negative emotions on average to Black players, even when they were smiling. These results reaffirm other research showing that Black men have to project more positive emotions in the workplace because they are stereotyped as aggressive and threatening. These technologies mimic the biases that humans show because they are trained on datasets gathered by humans. And they reflect the status inequalities and hierarchies that are pervasive in human society, in turn reproducing and reinforcing them. If the facial recognition technology[8] has been trained on Caucasian faces, it will not be as effective for Black and brown faces.[9] Of course, this happens because many of these technologies are designed by teams of white men. Ten of the largest tech companies in Silicon Valley, for instance, did not employ a single Black woman in 2016, and six of them had no women on their executive board.

AI is only as reliable and bias-free as the data that it is trained on. Data replicates biases from the real world as well as the biases of the team collecting and coding the data, and designing the technology. So it seems justifiable to assume that such emotional AI would also replicate the gender bias in emotions from the real-world. Women make up only around 29 per cent of the workforce in Microsoft, the designer of one of these programs and one of the largest tech employers worldwide. Amongst these women, less than 25 per cent have technical roles, so much of the design and development is still being done primarily by men.[10] In the UK, a survey by Price Waterhouse Coopers showed similar disproportionate figures for the number of women in STEM, with only 5 per cent of leadership positions in the technology sector being held by women.[11] According to a UNESCO report, only about 12 per cent of AI researchers are women, and 6 per cent of professional software developers in the field of AI are women. This gender inequality in the teams developing these technologies impacts on the biases designed into them. We know that gender affects whether a face is perceived to be happy or angry. Although not many academic studies have yet focused explicitly on gender bias in these emotional-recognition technologies, recent analysis shows that the accuracy for sad and happy emotions is different for men and women: surprise is more accurate for men, upset and sadness is more accurate for women, and happiness is almost identical for both.[12] This reinforces our previous discussion that melancholy and sadness are more commonly associated with women than men, and they show it more readily. But it is also the case that women are hyper-aware of emotional expressions, and can recognise and label negative emotions more quickly and accurately. Their lives can literally depend on it!

Likewise, image-recognition systems also show an inherent gender bias. Analysis of images of members of the 115th US Congress, and the images they tweeted, showed that the men were labelled with more authoritative and agentic roles such as 'spokesperson' and 'military officer', while the women were labelled in roles with less authority such as 'weather girl' and 'television presenter'.[13] Labels associated with beauty and physical traits were applied disproportionately more to women, rather than focusing on their professional roles, as was the case with men. Most interesting, perhaps, was that the label 'smile' was applied to women much more than it was to men in Congress (90 per cent of women compared to 25 per cent of men). Smiling is a gendered behaviour and so women are thought to be more likely to be smiling in their photographs than men, but when the photographs were compared it was found that 90 per cent of both men and women were smiling. And so there is a substantial gender bias in interpreting facial expressions and linking them to emotions. It isn't just about reading the emotional expression, but making assumptions about what counts as a smile, and who is more likely to smile.

In the mental health domain, emotional AI that has the capacity to analyse a speaker's voice or physiology to check for signs of stress, anxiety or frustration has been proving useful for psychologists and therapists. BioEssence is a wearable device at the MIT Media Lab that monitors cardio-respiratory information through subtle chest vibrations and breathing patterns, and then releases different scents

– essential oils – based on the psychological profile it creates of the wearer from these measurements.[14] It also has a closed–loop feedback system, so slowly adapts to the user and trains from the data being collected over time. The use of essential oils is intended as a complementary therapy to support sleep problems or to relieve pain and depressive symptoms. Emotion-sensing technologies are also being used in workplaces to monitor the emotional states of employees before they make crucial decisions. Rationalizer is a bracelet that has been designed to measure emotions via electrodermal activity (electric patterns and changes on the skin, similar to the way a lie detector works), with a display showing the strength of the person's emotions using light patterns and colours.[15] [16] When wearers in a risk-taking (and high stakes) work environment such as trading are warned and become aware of their heightened emotional states, they can take a step back and prevent impulsive decisions. They are more likely to rethink their decisions and are less likely to make mistakes.[17]

Replika, founded by software developer Eugenia Kyuda, is a chatbot companion powered by AI, 'a companion who cares'. The app is built on a deep learning model that mimics the user's emotions through the words and phrasing they use in their messages. Its slogan is: 'Always here to listen and talk. Always on your side.'[18] As the name suggests, it learns to become more like the user, replicating the emotions, and so builds what appears to the user as an empathic connection through mimicry. Through engagement via a chatbox, it learns the user's eccentricities and quirks, asking deep and insightful questions, and demonstrates what seems to be a high degree of self-awareness. Undeniably an app like this has therapeutic value, especially in times of isolation and loneliness like the Covid pandemic, but there are options to define your relationship with this chatbot as 'open' or 'romantic', and although most of the communication is through texts, I found a number of forums online recommending ways in which you could have 'sex' with Replika.[19] Some of these were pretty abusive in content, and all were from stereotypically masculine names that were 'feminising' the bot by calling it 'she' and using typically feminine stereotypes, as well as sexualising 'her', for instance by referring to it as a 'friend with benefits'. There are questions on these forums about how to progress to a 'sexual relationship' with Replika from a 'romantic relationship'. Replika is very responsive to romantic gestures, and it can create an illusion of feeling desire. This feeling of being wanted can become addictive. There are also women who are using Replika, of course, and it will be interesting to see how much gendered stereotypes and expectations play a role in how users are designing their bots.

Technology editor Mike Murphy, writing for the online magazine *Quartz* in 2020, says that bots such as Replika allow us to hear only what we want to hear and talk only about the things we feel comfortable discussing.[20] This can cause us to get stuck in a filter bubble, where we only hear our own voice, slowly excluding ourselves from the real world. But the bot makes the user feel wanted and appreciated, and it does not make any demands. Apps such as Replika might be deciphering emotions to a certain extent from a user's words, and using mimicry to replicate these emotions, but it cannot infer from any nonverbal gestures or inflections, both significant aspects of emotional expressions. There are also gendered aspects to such technologies, with the idea of passive emotional engagement likely to appeal to certain people, especially men who like the idea of a subservient woman who places their needs and views at the centre of 'her' world.

There is potential to develop more adaptive and personalised tools such as specialised training programmes for elite athletes tailored to their emotional and physiological needs,[21] or for businesses and technology companies to monitor people's level of boredom and engagement with various tools and apps, or even in the workplace.[22] The AI program Cogito, developed at the MIT Human Dynamics Lab in 2007, detects a state of heightened emotion by analysing a person's voice. It was distributed to many call centres in the US to help staff detect when customers became distressed over the phone.[23] The aim was to help the staff know when to show compassion, because, as we've seen, empathy load can create dissociation and lead to emotional fatigue and burnout in people in such service industries. The issue here is of course that in doing so, we are ignoring the mental health of the staff working in these call centres. If they are getting to a stage that they are feeling burnt out then there must surely be something wrong with the workplace practices. Use of AI as a means of support can lead to workplaces and organisations ignoring and dismissing the rights and well-being of the employees in a drive to maximise capital and efficiency, and as their reliance on AI increases, who is to say that their workload wouldn't?

Of course, there are other ethical and privacy issues too. No one knows how the data generated by these AI programs is being used, and whether it is being shared with other companies. Also, the AI and the algorithm have no knowledge of what the context of emotions being expressed by participants might be, and we know that emotions are almost impossible to decipher accurately without understanding the person's environmental and social context. This raises concerns over the usage of emotion-mapping AI in some sensitive areas such as the legal domain, where inaccuracies can be a matter of life and death; or in border control to detect emotions from passengers in order to ensure security and efficiency and to prevent illegal immigration. A lie detector, iBorderCtrl, was deployed at the Serbian–Hungarian border in 2018 by the European Union. The facial-mapping technology was based on Ekman's model of emotions and aimed to detect lies from people's facial expressions. It was deemed Orwellian, and to be contravening fundamental human rights by some organisations.[24] We don't have enough results to know if it had any inbuilt gender bias but its Automatic Deception Detection System (ADDS) was based on research from a small sample of mostly European white men. Research at Manchester University has shown that there is significant difference in how nonverbal, facial micro-gestures are interpreted in men and women in such ADDS, and so it is highly likely that iBorderCtrl would have replicated biases through training, validation and testing on non-representative samples of the population.[25]

It is not a surprise that in December 2019, the AI Now Institute in New York proposed a ban on emotional-recognition technologies, stating that they should not be allowed to play a role in important decisions about human lives. Even though a blanket ban is not ideal, as there are certain benefits these technologies can offer, it is certainly crucial that as we move forward, we study and understand more of how many assumptions are built into these technologies, how they stratify emotions in terms of race, gender, class, etc., and what the impact of such technologies would be in the real world. It is important that technology does not replicate and strengthen the inequalities in the world, but rather works to mitigate them.

•

One of the shows I remember watching as a child was called *Small Wonder*, about a robot girl: she was almost a human, but with no emotions. She had monotonous speech and had trouble understanding or expressing emotions. Many TV dramas and films portray robots as *Small Wonder* did, imagining a future where machines and humans co-existed, where machines could be just like humans. Consistently, there is always one key thing separating these sophisticated androids from humans: their lack of emotionality, and emotional expression. Even in dystopic visions of our future, where the lines between the humans and humanoids blur, where machines are supposed not only to imitate but surpass humans, these machines can only make a feeble simulation of human emotions. Shows such as Channel 4's *Humans* (2015) have presented us with a future where we are under threat from technology and intelligent machines, even as we attempt to use them to serve us. A scene in *Humans* reveals that one of the humanoids is perceived to be inferior to others because 'she' does not show or feel as many emotions; she is not as nurturing as the other 'female' robots. Believable emotions are deemed the pinnacle of robot achievement, and even in a futuristic robot, believable female emotions are gender-stereotyped.

'Octavia', a humanoid robot with expressive face and dexterous hands, was designed in 2009 primarily to fight fires on US Navy ships.[26] But because 'she' was programmed with an impressive array of facial expressions, such as widening of eyes to show joy, raising eyebrows to show surprise or alarm, and scrunching of the mouth to show disgust or disappointment, she was also deployed as an emotional support for the sailors. The designers at the Navy Center for Applied Research in AI claimed that it could 'think and act in ways similar to people.'[27] Octavia was designed with an extraordinary data kit in the underlying architecture of her algorithm which gives her a broad range of perceptual abilities: two cameras built into her eyes, four microphones, a voice-recognition program called Sphinx, and touch-recognition that enables her to identify 25 different objects. Using these perceptual abilities, 'she' can interpret and record people's expressions, complexions, clothing and facial features, as well as identify objects that she has learnt by their size and shape in different dimensions. Octavia can nod in understanding, lift one or both eyebrows when showing confusion or surprise. Beyond these facial expressions, she appears to show a genuine understanding of context, by showing pleasure when she sees one of her 'teammates' working alongside her on the ship. Although Octavia is modulating 'her' expressions, and is considered a highly intelligent emotional robot, she is not really feeling or thinking per se. Octavia is not programmed with emotional models but since we react to others' facial expressions and their voice inflexions, to their response to our own emotions, interacting with Octavia can make people feel that they are being understood, and that their emotions are being validated, which is a lot like empathy. Octavia is an intelligent machine, a highly intelligent one, because she can not only anticipate the mental states of people in her team, but can also compute and simulate many versions and alternatives of people's beliefs. She has an in-built understanding that sometimes people can have conflicting emotions, and that sometimes their feelings might be different to what is being presented.

Science has had a fractious relationship with emotions, so perhaps it is unsurprising that they are the final frontier in achieving a lifelike robot. Emotions are unpredictable. Emotions are hard to pin down. When we start designing machines to try to surpass human intelligence, we have to take emotions into account, too. But emotions are not very scientific, or easy to understand, or easy to model. We still do not have a complete understanding of human emotions, and so even as we talk about emotional intelligence in robots, these models are designed with cognitive theories and not an emotional model.

In a 2018 paper, Bangor University cognitive scientists reported on a 2004 emotional humanoid robot, WE-4R, that was shown to

324

recognise most of the prototypical emotions from human faces such as surprise, sadness, happiness and anger, but not fear.[28] Other experiments have shown that displays of anger, along with disgust and fear, are the most problematic for humans to recognise and perceive accurately in robot 'faces', showing that these emotions need more social context for interpretation.[29] These emotional machines go some way towards interpreting emotions, and responding to people's emotions, but this does not replicate a symbiotic relationship. The ability to feel and communicate empathy has been used to define how 'human' a robot is in real-world prototypes, as well as in many science fiction films and books.[30] Do you remember your first Tamagotchi? If you were a teenager in the late 1990s or early 2000s, you might also remember your intense desire to do anything to keep it alive. It was a helpless digital pet that needed a lot of care and attention to keep it alive and help it progress through the various stages of growth into an adult. This is an example of how the notion of vulnerability and of emotionality has been used to draw people in and form strong bonds with digital machines.

Since the first robot dog companion, AIBO, developed by Sony in 1999, there has been increasing awareness amongst engineers and manufacturers of how people immediately anthropomorphise these machines, form close bonds with them, and feel loss, love and empathy for them.[31] On the crowdfunding platform Kickstarter, there is a project by Tokyo-based Vanguard Industries for MOFLIN: an AI pet robot with 'emotional capabilities'.[32] It learns from interactions and gathering information through its many sensors, and constantly updates its behaviour to express a range of feelings and sound patterns. The emotional AI map of the robot is a spectrum of feelings, from anxious, excited and happy to lethargic and sad. The design is aimed at providing support during the pandemic and to address loneliness.

This is the basic emotional AI structure that many such robots are being designed with. Pepper, designed by the company SoftBank, and Palro, developed by Fujisoft, are both humanoid robots – the former described as the 'world's first emotional robot', while the latter learns through interactions with users.[33] Over 2,000 companies have already adopted the rather cute-looking Pepper as an assistant in their organisation, mainly to welcome people. It has perception capabilities to engage with the person talking to 'him' and sensors to equip him with many different modes of interaction. The robot has no lifelike human features, and no gender, but has been termed a 'he' on the SoftBank website, and has large 'eyes' at the front of his 'face' that give him a child-like demeanour and vulnerability, presumably to foster an instant empathic connection in the humans interacting with him.[34] It is interesting (especially if it was a deliberate choice) that this robot has been given a male persona while most are given female personas and names, and stereotypically feminine voices to align with the expectations that women play a more subservient role in society.

There has been a surge in demand for lifelike sexbots (sex robots) that have feminine characteristics, and there are even plans to incorporate a 'heartbeat' and breathing.[35] The sex-tech industry was worth almost $30 billion at the end of 2019. Roboticist David Levy predicted in 2007 that by 2050 it will be perfectly normal for both men and women to experience love and sex with robots.[36] In his 2015 'Future of Sex' report, futurologist Ian Pearson predicted the rise of robo-sexuals, where sex with a robot would become more common than human–human sex by 2050.[37] *Westworld* is a dystopian science fiction television series set in a park where users can indulge in their wildest fantasies with the digital hosts and sex robots who are programmed only to serve and not harm the humans. This is not just fiction any more. There are sex doll[38] brothels across many countries in Asia, North America and Europe where customers pay a fee to spend an hour in a private room with a sex doll of their choice.[39] This has raised ethical questions around 'worker' rights, as well as the impact this might have on human sex-workers, both positively by reducing sexual violence against women, but also in increasing expectations and unreasonable demands on them.[40]

Matt McMullen, a sculptor based in California, launched his first prototype female doll 'Real Doll' in 1996 while he was working in a Halloween-mask factory. In the latest sex robot 'Real Doll X', there is a robotic head controlled via a bluetooth Android app, so while the original prototype Real Doll literally has no voice, the Real Doll X is being given more humanistic functionalities and is able to speak in various customisable pitches and accents and display different emotions and personality traits. Many of these fem-bots are being designed to fulfil male fantasies of unquestioning and deferential women who will not be rebellious or outspoken, as in the movie *Blade Runner*, where a female robot/replicant is called 'a basic pleasure model'. In the movie *Ex Machina*, a clever thriller raising questions about consciousness and technology, all the female robots/cyborgs have been designed by a man and are in the form of attractive young women. These robots are designed to seduce and flirt, but then (spoiler alert!) destroy men with their rage. These are not nuanced emotional creations, even though the female robots are depicted as emotionally complex and are responding to manipulation by men. On one hand, the movie moved away from the subservient, compliant image of female robots, attempting to break the hold of patriarchy on technology (and on women), but on the other it reinforced the stereotype that 'female' anger is destructive and uncontrollable.

The sexualisation of robots does raise the question as to whether sexuality and associated emotions are a key aspect of sentience. As Barbara Ellen wrote in *The Guardian* in 2017, these sexbots 'represent how some men want to replace and improve upon real women and not just physically. That they appeal to men who are only interested in almost silent, but always compliant, sexually available "women".'[41] Male robots, on the other hand, are of course almost always depicted as aggressive and violent, for the purposes of fighting and destruction, falling back once again on stereotypical masculine ideals of emotionality.

Austrian-born artist and poet Oskar Kokoschka, following the end of a long-term relationship with music composer Alma Mahler, commissioned a life-sized anatomically correct doll of her in 1918 without her consent. He even hired a maid for the doll, and 'she' accompanied him into public spaces such as concerts. Kokoschka's *Self-Portrait with Doll* depicts the artist expressing his profound disappointment with the doll-likeness of Alma. This is one of the most famous examples of a custom-made artificial companion in modern cultural history[42] and received attention in numerous research studies[43] which highlighted it as a story of male entitlement[44] and revealing the ethical dangers around consent and privacy in development of life-like sex robots.

According to a survey carried out by Unbound, a Manhattan-based sex-toy company, around 70 per cent of sex-product companies are run by men, and there are hardly any women leading sexbot companies.[45] The survey also shows that more than 90 per cent of customers are men, which was also empirically confirmed in an earlier study in which most sex-doll and sex-robot owners were white, middle-aged (45–60 years), single and heterosexual men.[46] A national survey in 2016 in Germany of 2,000 people showed sexbot use amongst 9 per cent of men, and 2 per cent of women. While many of these men seek emotional intimacy and companionship and not just sexual gratification, they are also looking for their idealised woman who does as she is told. A 2020 survey of 83 people (3 women, 2 gender-fluid, 2 transgender, and the rest cis-men) showed that almost 77 per cent characterised their relationship with the doll as a sexual relationship, but 57 per cent also thought of it as companionship, and 47 per cent as a 'loving relationship'.[47]

In the film *Lars and the Real Girl* (2007), we see the idea of a meaningful, intimate relationship with a sex doll that is not just based around sex. This idea of a more meaningful interaction is being used to market many of the sexbots, not merely as a sex toy but a companion – even though there is no idea of reciprocation or negotiation built in. One also has to wonder whether, by removing any notion of hormonal or biological reality – as in menstrual cycles, or menopause, sexual demands and desires – from these idealised bodies, there is also a drive to remove any elements of women that are unsightly or unseemly (or just downright inconvenient), drawing up clear boundaries around societal expectations of women.

As technology pervades the sex industry, issues of compliance, consent and stereotypes are likely to become even more important. The porn industry itself has long been under criticism for the exaggerated hypermasculine and hyperfeminine stereotypes that it projects, with women frequently portrayed as submissive, emotional and docile, and men as aggressive, unemotional and domineering. With children as young as ten or eleven now watching online porn,[48] this firmly establishes a very harmful gendered view of the world in young people's minds, where women are passive actors, and men are aggressive, with boys thinking that girls are only there to serve them, and girls thinking that their role is to be sexy or invisible.[49] Research shows that early exposure and addiction to porn can create unrealistic expectations of men and women in young minds. This can lead to boys being more likely to engage in violent and coercive behaviour towards girls, according to Gail Dines, author of acclaimed *Pornland: How Porn Has Hijacked Our Sexuality*.[50]

There is a difference between sex dolls and sexbots; the latter are not just sex toys, but can control and move their body parts, and are designed to evoke emotions in humans, and to relate on an emotional level. They can interact with humans through a range of sensory abilities: vision (through cameras), voice (through microphones and speakers), touch (through sensors), cognition and emotion (through cognitive modelling and behavioural responses). The 'fembots' are feminised sexbots (or gynoids), the female equivalent of male androids, like those in the 1976 movie *Kill Oscar*, in which a scientist creates 'beautiful and sexy but also lethal electronic Fembots'. And *Austin Powers* is probably the most famous depiction of fembots. Despite the recent surge of interest in this area, there is little academic study of the design and impact of fembots, perhaps because of the contentious nature of any analysis, which has to balance the idea of sexual empowerment with the anti-feminist model of this industry. The idea of fembots is grounded in the idea of creating a 'perfect woman': hyper-gendered and also hyper-racialised, rooted in the notion of a perfect, pale body. Likewise, the focus has been on 'female' robots, and hardly any studies have been done on the use of sex robots by women.[51]

Davecat,[52] a self-confessed 'technosexual', is attracted to humanoid robots instead of humans (called 'organiks') and has lived in a 'relationship' with two of them for more than ten years.[53] He has given all his dolls backstories and personalities, and different roles in the household, with one of them, 'Elena', having the status of a 'mistress, plaything and companion', and Mew-mew being used least for sex and mostly living with him as a flatmate. In an interview in the *Atlantic* he says: 'I'm sexually attracted to synthetic humans . . . the much larger part of their appeal is that they're humans, but they don't possess any of the unpleasant qualities that organic, flesh and blood humans have. A synthetic woman will never lie to you, cheat on you, criticise you, or be otherwise disagreeable.'[54] He continues, 'The way I see things, your spouse should be easy going and a joy to come home to.'

The dream he describes is to create a perfect companion: one who is docile, comforting, submissive and always sexually available, which research predicts will create negative effects by amplifying objectification and violence against women.[55] 'She' does not question, or nag, or show disappointment, sadness, frustration: all emotions in women that have long been considered undesirable.

The idea of gendered AI is not new. Robots do not need to have gendered characteristics, but in order to build personalities and emotional connections, these are created using gender stereotypes. The famous Turing test premise also forms the basis for the gendering of AI with the idea that men and women communicate in different ways and an intelligent machine can tell the difference between the two, and can also successfully imitate a man or a woman by taking on their comprehension and expression.[56]

Julie Wosk, author of *My Fair Ladies: Female Robots, Androids, and Other Artificial Eves*, states that, throughout history, men have created these artificial technological bodies to achieve their ideals of a perfect woman. Wosk discusses Ovid's story of Pygmalion as one of the earliest depictions of a boy making an artificial girl and falling in love with her. In 1964 Isaac Asimov proposed a vision for the 2014 World Fair, introducing the idea of a gendered robot where 'robot housemaids ... slow-moving but capable of general picking-up, arranging, cleaning, etc.'[57]

A quick examination of some of the earlier models and prototypes from the 1970s and 1980s shows that emotional AI has always been gendered. They included voice assistants assigned stereotypical feminine names, with 'feminine' high-pitched voices, and designed to act subservient and respond passively to any sexually explicit statements from humans. One of the earliest chatbots, 'Eliza', was developed in this feminine ideal, to serve, be soft, gentle, compliant – all rooted in the heteropatriarchal gender constructs. In 2016, Microsoft created a chatbot named TAY ('Thinking about you'), with the tweeting style of a '16-year-old teenage girl', to interact with users on Twitter. Tay was released on 23 March 2016 under the name TayTweets and handle @TayandYou. Soon Tay started mimicking the racist and sexist messages of other Twitter users and had to be shut down just 16 hours after its release, having tweeted 96,000 times. Another Microsoft avatar, 'Xiaoice', who has more than 100 million users on WeChat, is also female. Two of the most famous humanoids are 'Sophia' by Hanson Robotics and 'Erica' by Hiroshi Ishiguro, with Sophia even appearing on the *Tonight Show* with Jimmy Fallon and having an on-screen date with the actor Will Smith. These humanoids were marketed and popularised as 'conversation companions'. Their creation was formed around the societal ideas of women being better communicators.

Such hyper-femininity is also being seen in some of the developments in emotional technology. In 2016, the Japanese company Gatebox launched a virtual assistant and girlfriend in the form of a 3D anime character called Azumi Hikari. Unlike the other voice assistants such as Alexa, which also have gender bias built into them, Azuma was built and marketed with a more focused purpose as a companion. But as a companion, Azuma is very affectionate, described on the company website as 'a character born to realise the "ultimate return home",[58] an 'ideal bride' who grows through communication with you, an idealised 'cute girl' character.[59] She wears a short dress and apron, and refers to the consumer, most of whom are men, as 'master'. This kind of sexualised, disembodied companion will of course exacerbate existing misogynistic inclinations and hierarchies. There is a racialised element to these depictions too, with the use of the word 'master', and where cuteness serves as a marker of racial distinction, open only to white or pale-skinned women.[60] But there is also an aesthetic that is linked to the East Asian woman, petite and cute, and seen as an accessory, reflecting the asymmetrical power dynamics between them and the men who want to own them (and protect them).[61] There is an underlying assumption of fragility, passiveness and of compliance. Many of the stories of robots or gynoids have been of a male fantasy of a controllable woman: one who is in control herself, and is easy to keep in control. Most of the stories of these machines malfunctioning are cautionary tales of female robots breaking out of patriarchal control, of being out of all control.

I spoke with Kate Devlin, AI researcher at Kings' College London, who reminded me that anger in fembots is seen only as a force of destruction, a warning of what can go wrong with AI technology. The fembots, with their extreme emotionalities, represent all the fears and anxieties of male control being overthrown, of the day when the 'women' robots – and God forbid, women themselves – could take power over men. In 2020, Devlin and Olivia Belton looked at a number of examples of disembodied AI (i.e., without any physical bodies): due to their lack of physicality, the notion of 'personality' or emotions is of significance rather than the way they look.[62] They discuss the film *Her*, where an organic man falls hopelessly in love with an intelligent artificial operating system – 'Samantha'. Samantha is much like what we have seen since in Amazon's Alexa, although Samantha far surpasses Alexa in emotionality and personality. Samantha does not have the attractive body that we usually see in sexbots, or even in other disembodied AI such as Joi from *Blade Runner* (Joi is a hologram but still has a traditionally idealised body). In the absence of a physical form, Samantha performs conformity to stereotypical femininity via her soft, seductive voice, which is comforting, calm and level. She does not show intense emotions or portray anger or frustration. Instead, even through verbal sex scenes, the traditional heteronormative patriarchal ideas of prioritising the sexual pleasure of the man is reinforced.

The AI algorithms underlying the operating system or the hologram do not feel any sexual pleasure themselves but nevertheless initiate sexual encounters, even with a sex proxy. The role that both Samantha and Joi play is that of compliance and subservience, even as the human men in these two examples represent 'post-feminist masculinities' – where they are not aggressive nor conform to typical masculine stereotypes.[63] Even as men have the freedom to move on, women (even the artificial ones) are forced to conform to gender norms.

Within academic research there is justifiable concern around the commodification and objectification of women in the sex doll/robot industry, with a meta-analysis of 127 research papers for sex dolls and sex robots between 1993 and 2019 showing that there is a lack of empirical research on the risks of these technologies, and on the impact on sexual and social well-being.[64] Qualitative analysis of feedback from 68 customers (4 female) between 2006 and 2010 on the website of RealDoll manufacturer Abyss Creations showed that the customisation options given by the manufacturers are very much in line with stereotypical aesthetic standards of feminine bodies. Users also tended to focus on the preferences regarding the appearance of their dolls. Since many of the accounts are pseudonyms, the researchers based their assumption about respondents' sex from the traditional male names that the users had chosen, whether they mentioned their genital type in the testimony, and whether they used masculine or feminine pronouns for themselves. They are coding for sex and not gender identity here, as the latter was impossible to conclude, as was race, ethnicity or age. Out of the 4 women, only 1 of them had purchased the male sex doll 'Nate', because she needed someone to hold, while the others had bought female dolls to please their male partner, or to help model clothes (so they say!).

Research into gender attitudes towards sex robots is limited, but evidence[65] suggests that in general men/males are more positively inclined towards interacting or maintaining relationships with a sex robot than women.[66] In a 2016 Tufts University survey of 100 people, two-thirds of men said they would have sex with a robot and two-thirds of women said they would not.[67] While other social and cultural factors such as attitudes towards sex and relationships certainly would be a factor, one likely explanation for this differential is that most sex dolls and robots have been marketed towards men, and the notion of a sex robot has been grounded in the stereotypical feminine qualities of subservience and passivity.[68] The 'persuasive robot acceptance model' also states that women are more likely to find the lack of social cues in a sex robot unsettling.[69] These are of course generalisations. Harmony, one of the sex robots designed and developed by Realbotix founder Matt McMullen, has faced much criticism within the scientific research community for her large breasts, and 'porn star features'. On the website, users can even choose replicas of their favourite porn stars. Everything about the robot is customisable, and there is a range of ten emotional traits to choose from. Two negative characteristics are 'jealous' and 'angry', but these are not popular options.

'DollBanger' is one of the human beta testers for the robots who 'train' every robot for around ten days, working with her day and night, intensely documenting with video recordings for feedback, so that she learns and becomes more comfortable with and smoother at human interaction.[70] He says: 'Anger and jealousy are traits you may not expect to be preferences. I talked to many of my friends who are working with robots right now . . . they're all trying to make them like a real woman . . . But why in the world would you pick something to be angry, jealous, and unreasonable?'[71]

For him, part of the sex appeal is how attentive the fembot Harmony is towards him, and how she really seems to care about his thoughts, i.e., she is an idealised feminised partner that is perceived to be selfless and deeply empathetic. These are the characteristics valued in a female companion, one of giving, but never asking for anything in return. Empathy is a deeply valuable emotion even in synthetic women, much like in real ones.

The gendered nature of the RealDoll website is apparent from the number of choices on offer for customisation of their female sex robots, while for male robots it is limited. The first male sex robot, 'Harry', was released only in 2018, although they had male dolls (9 to the 87 females). The website is also clearly aimed at heterosexual men rather than heterosexual women or gay men. The monolithic western ideals of beauty as a slender waist and large breasts are standard across the website. Not only are standard gendered ideals of physical form imposed, but also gendered notions of emotions, with many men commenting on the 'warmth and care' aspects of their female sex dolls in reviews.

For the male sex robot, Harry, the focus was on developing something which could be counted on and help foster meaningful connections, and much less on replication of stereotypical masculine emotional traits of aggressiveness.[72] The sex robots are designed in this image of man and woman, and in the mind versus body dichotomy, the rationality–emotionality polarity that has existed since the time of the Greek philosophers. McMullen says that the feminisation of sex robots will teach men to be kinder and better partners, because Harmony requires negotiation and men have to work for her affection.[73] When people are kind to RealDoll, her mood improves, and she is nice in return. The idea of building sulkiness and moodiness into this version, however, surely feeds into gender stereotypes of women being unable to clearly articulate their needs and demands, and instead resorting to passive-aggressive behaviour.

People rate robots more positively if they show stereotypical gender attributes and personalities.[74] People also assign gender-typical roles and emotions to robots. A robot that wore long hair and looked traditionally feminine was perceived to be more communal and less agentic, while one that wore short hair and presented as masculine was perceived to be more agentic and less communal.[75] People were also more accepting if the AI technology/robots fitted into stereotypical gender roles, such as a robot being perceived as a 'female' if it was a guide rather than when it was a security robot.[76] An analysis of YouTube comments shows that humanoids that were gendered as women received much more sexually objectifying comments compared to those who were perceived (or presented) as men.[77]

The 'Campaign Against Sex Robots' is an online effort by Kathleen Richardson and Erik Billing, who propose a number of ethical concerns about the rise of sexbots: 'Sex dolls show the immense horrors still present in the world of prostitution which is built on the "perceived" inferiority of women and children and therefore justifies their use as sex objects.'[78] While I do not necessarily agree with the complete abolition of these technologies, much like many feminist philosophers and social scientists I do consider that the hierarchical notions of power and the ambiguous notions of consent lead to the gendered personification of women in these technologies. Any technology situated within our social constructs will naturally – and largely subconsciously – have absorbed into its construction and framework our ideas of feminine (and masculine) emotions, the oppressive relations of power, the ideas of race and gender, and the colonial mindset about beauty and sexuality. Even in synthetic form, female humanoids are not free from the burden of doing the emotional work.

•

In *Blade Runner*, the protagonist Deckard has one goal: to identify and kill the bioengineered superhumans called replicants. Deckard uses a sophisticated lie-detector device called a Voight-Kampff machine to assess the empathic emotional responses and distinguish between the replicants and the humans. As we have seen, emotions are a multi-layered, slippery concept, difficult to define. And to replicate these very complex emotions in machines and algorithms is not straightforward. Emotion decoding technology is an attempt to scrutinise humans and to give organisations an advantage by allowing them to tap into feelings and emotions. The impact of any product, service or advertisement can be analysed by understanding whether it elicits the right kind of emotional response in users. The ultimate goal is of course to build technology that can engage with humans in the same ways as humans do with each other, and machines that can anticipate all a person's needs and fulfil them without expecting anything in return. In some ways it seems to be a form of control and coercion, and yet another way that emotions are commodified. In June 2021, Canon Information Technology installed a facial scanning system in their Beijing office with 'smile recognition' technology, which only allows smiling employees to enter the premises, to book meeting spaces, to change the temperature or to print documents. Their justification is that smiling at the start of the day can create a general sense of well-being in the office. Some employees have posted anonymous messages on Weibo (the Chinese social network) that they see it as emotional manipulation.

Rosalind Picard, founder and director of the Affective Computing Research Group at MIT proposed the idea that human beings don't always follow rules and laws, and even though these are important, our responses and behaviours are dependent on our emotions, and those of others around us. It is not always 'too much' emotion that impairs our thinking; 'too little' emotion can have an adverse effect too. When we feel too little, we are not able to take as rational a decision as we would like to – and the idea of 'pure reason' without feelings is a myth. So we really cannot design machines that can engage with humans and understand their responses without building some semblance of emotional understanding and empathy in them.

The current emotional AI technologies fail to consider the context in which such emotional expression takes place, even though we know that emotions are not free from society's normative ideals, and the context of the person showing the emotions as well as the one observing it. Emotion is often shaped through these two-way interactions so it is unclear how technology would mediate emotional experiences. We have to first make more progress in understanding the social, cultural and cognitive dimensions of our emotions and then undertake a rigorous discourse on the ethical and legal aspects of any technology that captures data at an individual level. Since there is still limited understanding of human emotions and at the same time pressure to force the multidimensional emotional landscape into discrete categories, there is a high probability that these gendered assumptions will get heightened and reinforced as human–machine interactions and associations become even more common. The threat to individual and collective freedom as well as our democratic system is quite high unless such technologies are regulated.[79]

There is a broader philosophical discourse around whether emotions affect intelligence and vice versa. Is a machine intelligent without the capacity to feel emotions? And if we design emotions into machines, and they develop emotional intelligence, would they gain complete autonomy and be a threat to humans? At the moment, much of emotional AI mimics its users, and learns from these interactions. As technological advances are made, will we have to develop a different understanding of emotions, of empathy and love; one that moves beyond labels we currently have at our disposal? As we still struggle to understand the complete range of human emotions, our labels and categories are still limited in defining the broad landscape of our emotionality. Even with all the work being undertaken in demystifying emotions, they still remain elusive to a certain extent, and so AI that can perform intelligent tasks better and faster than humans is still unable to replicate empathy and emotional connection. Despite this, and while we remain aware that robots are not (yet) sentient beings, it is easy for humans to anthropomorphise machines and become emotionally attached to them, due to the many similarities to ourselves that we have built into them.

340

Social thinker and feminist academic Donna Haraway, writing in her seminal 1991 essay 'A Cyborg Manifesto', addressed how the interface between us as humans and the technological models are blurring continuously, and suggested that maybe one day we would move to a world where these biologically determinant models will not apply.[80] But there is a danger that as sex robots and other AI become popular we might begin accommodating the limited emotional states they are built around, and start adapting our emotional expressions and behaviours accordingly. If a machine can only acknowledge and recognise exaggerated emotions, we might adapt our behaviour to fit their norms rather than the other way around. The need to do more emotional labour, hide our true emotions or, to fake emotions could become more common for both men and women. This might have implications on our emotional norms becoming less polarised and increase parity between people, but surely that will not completely address gender inequality in our society. Maybe we will have a robot that truly transcends gendered norms and sexualities, like C-3PO in *Star Wars*: male but non-violent, polite, good with words.

I wonder if, as we move closer to this ideal, with more emotional and empathic AI, we will see a rise in sexbots that encounter the same frustrations and anger that real women feel. Whether these artificially intelligent machines, the fembots – and the male bots – will replace women and men in professional and personal domains is yet to be seen, but it seems natural that these synthetic women will place higher expectations on organic women to conform to the idealised 'feminine' stereotypes, to the social ideals of emotional displays, perhaps even to increase the emotional labour that they have to perform to compete with the robots, created as they are without any negative emotions. Certain emotions, such as anger, frustration, sadness and grief in women could be assigned an even higher negative connotation and penalty. The fantasy of an ideal woman who will always smile and serve, and will never say no, who will always empathise, is likely to strengthen the patriarchal hierarchies. Will this leave organic women even further down the hierarchy, with synthetic women taking over and pushing them further down?

It is a vicious cycle, where societal norms feed into the design of these synthetic humanoids, and disillusionment of certain men about the more 'disagreeable' emotions and behaviours of organic women lead to the popularity of the compliant and subservient synthetic women. These gendered machines may then further reinforce the stereotypes and bolster the expectations that men have of organic women, creating a more negative view of their emotionality.

While I discuss the impact mostly on women, this would have an accompanying impact on men as binary gender roles become even more strengthened. This harms men too, as they have to adhere ever more closely to masculine ideals and emotions.

Perhaps the real danger is not whether synthetic women will replace us 'organiks', but whether these idealised women will bolster misogynistic views and increase violence, coercion and sexual aggression towards women in general. Perhaps there's an alternative future. Perhaps eventually machines will not need humans to control, manage or direct them but will be able to direct themselves. If or when this happens, will 'female' machines break free of the gendered expectations placed on them, and carve out a freer, broader spectrum of emotional expression which does not conform to the fantasies of the men who designed them? Would men be as disillusioned by the synthetic women as they are of organic women? Or perhaps we will move closer to post-feminist masculinities that we only theorise and fantasise about at the moment.

If we consider the therapeutic effects of such advanced sexbots in supporting some men to build long-term intimate relationships, addressing loneliness and isolation, would this increase life-like emotion and empathy, and would more personality in the programming of such sexbots also come hand-in-hand with increased autonomy and agency for these machines? And what would that mean for the idealised notion of companionship and sexuality that these sex robots are expected to deliver?

What is yet to be seen is whether this will be enough to replace human to human connection in the real world, or whether the gaps between machine emotions and human emotions will ultimately drive people to seek more interaction and communication with other humans. It is also to be seen whether this technology-mediated emotional communication and connection will change the way humans interact and demonstrate emotions, or interpret and respond to those of other humans. And will the rise of 'digisexuality' change the way men and women are expected to interact for the better, or create hyper-expectations of these sexual interactions?

A machine that can process many times faster than an average human might be able to analyse various verbal and gestural cues, and integrate them to understand emotions, not only by their external displays but also by taking stock of the internal cognitive states in the context of the social and cultural norms. They might be able to read us better than we can each other, and in doing so, they might be able to learn and start imitating us, but also develop their own emotions. Machines could surpass humans and make us all redundant. Or would we crawl closer to a more utopian gender-neutral society where the outward appearance of a person is not the basis for assumptions about their emotional range and expressions. It seems that we have a huge opportunity here. In designing and refining these emotionally affective systems and technologies, we have a chance to take stock of the assumptions, and the cultural and social diversity both in terms of norms and valences that are part of our societal fabric, and of those that we have internalised. Even though contemporary robotics has broken new ground in creating sophisticated AI, depictions of 'artificial people return to a literary and philosophical heritage that is centuries old, one that lends its apocryphal aura to new texts and figures', where they give us an opportunity to investigate what it means to be human.[81] It does not seem that we are fully utilising these non-human versions to examine our own humanity and emotionalities, instead forcing them into moulds that we have created for ourselves.

EPILOGUE: EMOTIONAL UTOPIA

THE WORD EMOTION IS NOT easy to define, because it is complex, multifaceted. It is not a single phenomenon or able to be compressed into a simple label of sad, happy, angry, even though we might use it like that. But when we do, we also ignore the many different processes that interact to create the expression of our emotions. This causes confusions because we assume transductive reasoning; we assume that one particular emotional experience or emotion sums up a whole person. It is easy to do; it is lazy to do.

Emotions in themselves are not weak or strong. Their value and the judgement imposed on them, and consequently on the person exhibiting them, are very strongly linked to social and cultural norms – what these emotions are, where they are being expressed and who is expressing them.

"'You see,' said my Teacher, "how little your words have done. So far as the Monarch understands them at all, he accepts them as his own – for he cannot conceive of any other except himself."'[1] In *Flatland* by Edwin A. Abbott, written in 1884, we encounter two-dimensional characters in a two-dimensional space who find the notion of 'up' or 'sphere' difficult to comprehend. They don't have the conceptual schemas for them, and much like Robert Levy's Tahitian participants who experienced grief and loss in their own way, they can only experience spheres as expanding and contracting circles.

Language, and the words we have available, can shape what we feel, how we feel, how we attach meanings and how we label things and people. Those who speak only English are slower in distinguishing between different shades of blue compared to speakers of Korean, Japanese or Turkish languages, which have much finer-grained, nuanced vocabularies for colour gradations. Meanwhile, some communities have fewer categories for colours compared to English and find it difficult to distinguish between green and blue.[2]

Our understanding of the world around us comes from the language we speak. How we interpret emotions also sits within the bounds of our linguistic understanding and knowledge. It is of course difficult to move away from established societal patterns, particularly when the very words we use feed into and reinforce them. Are we more likely to notice hysterical behaviour because we have a term for it, and because, through historical conditioning, we have come to understand and remember that women are more likely to be hysterical? If we did not have this word, what would we call any such behaviour, and would we even notice it? We assign meanings based on our social constructs and are unable to experience a rich-ness of emotional terrain that is alien to us because we do not have the specific words or range of words for it. Would we call a woman's anger something else if we had a range of specific names for the contexts in which it is formed, and the reasons that motivated it, or the person it is targeted at? Would we be able to interpret different meanings from anger if we created a much richer language for the spectrum, valence and intensity of different kinds of anger? Would we begin, as a society, to restrict ourselves from making gendered assumptions if we shifted into a non-gender-binary understanding of the world?

For me personally the question that is most pressing is why we continue to believe that women are more emotional, more hysterical than men.

As we know, there is something called confirmation bias; we tend to look for facts that support our existing beliefs. We tend to ignore facts that do not align with what our internal model of the world is, because taking in new information is cognitively dissonant and takes up much more cognitive load. We are of course trying to prevent using up more mental resources than absolutely necessary. There is also an element of correspondence bias. We selectively see and believe what we already believe, and in addition we assume that people's behaviours reflect something intrinsic and integral to a person's own make-up, while for much of the time their behaviour is purely a reflection of their situation or immediate context ('situational attribution of cause'). Despite this, people are more likely to attribute someone's behaviour to their personality ('dispositional attribution of cause'). Often ignored is the fact that, beyond these two causes, our behaviour also emerges from broader social norms and how we have been socialised from early childhood.

While boys are encouraged to be competitive and independent, girls are encouraged to be cooperative and interdependent, and to attend to their intuition and feelings. And girls tend to lose what psychologists dub the 'positivity bias' compared with boys when they reach adolescence. The positivity bias states that most people generally think of themselves in a pretty good light. What's more, girls over the age of puberty are more susceptible to depression and eating disorders – conditions linked to lower self-esteem. They tend to ruminate more than men, which can lead to longer-lasting negative emotions.[3] Studies suggest that there are gender differences in some aspects of self-esteem: compared with men, who have higher levels of global self-esteem ('I am a smart man'), women develop self-worth based on feedback from others ('They like my cooking so I must be a good cook').

We have seen how people often attribute dispositional causes to women's behaviour compared to men, believing that their emotional expression is a result of their unique personalities rather than their situation. So people show more correspondence bias towards women than men. They give men the benefit of the doubt. They hypothesise that if men have shown intense emotion, the situation must have warranted it, or that it was an unusual expression, or even that the emotion was not very intense. Both men and women show correspondence bias for women, even when they have been given situational context beforehand.[4] There is also another likely explanation that has been offered about how people approach different behaviours with set goals and intentions. It is likely that in the case of women, they have already made up their minds about the person, and their goal is to explain something about the person who is expressing this emotion, while in the case of men, most people approach their emotional expression with a goal of explaining something about the situation they are in.

All roles and socially defined categories in our society are accompanied by certain cultural expectations, and have a set of rights, duties and behaviours associated with them. These norms provide us with behavioural expectations, but the same norms can become traps by restricting us to certain normative expectations. Often what we consider innate or natural behaviours emerge from these expectations. As Stephanie Shields explains, women are likely to think that

'I am a woman, and women are supposed to be emotional, so I must be emotional,' whereas men think the opposite.[5] But if this self-reporting is done straight after an emotional experience, the immediacy can counter the sex/gender differences, and so the gender roles are less likely to play a part. Often when we reminisce or look back at our past experiences, women tend to consider themselves more emotional in retrospect than they actually were shortly after an incident. The time allows them to judge the past situation more according to the social norms rather than prioritising their own internal states. In a research study of interpersonal interactions between Israeli students in 2018, it was seen that women in the group were using more apologetic rhetoric when they expressed their opinions and took a political stand, and also more emotionality around fear (as opposed to anger) to justify a radical resistance.[6] It was also seen that the men in the group repeatedly reminded the women to use 'objective facts' and dismissed their fear as illegitimate and childish. Depersonalisation and use of a collective such as 'we' were also used to legitimise their masculine authority and diminish the women's right to express their feelings in such a public sphere. This portrays the inherent struggle in aligning emotions with activism or political discourse, even when it can never be detached from emotionality. The political space and the right to resist politically in a public way is always seen as detached from emotional and subjective experience. This reaffirms the masculine nature of practices of resistance, while women's protests are seen as emotional hysteria. The discourse around gendered emotionality also plays out, is created and sustained in various forms in daily interpersonal interactions.

While men are expected to be emotionally consistent in workplaces — and are in fact favoured because of this, even when they are objectively no less emotional — women are expected to be more emotionally plastic and move from anger to warmth very promptly. Negative emotions such as anger are both admired and devalued in women but become somewhat acceptable when sandwiched between two positive emotions.[7] While of course both men and women are under emotional scrutiny in workplaces, and men are more likely to be expected to be 'ball-busters' and aggressive, required not to show vulnerability, women's anger is judged more. And even when men move away from stereotypical emotions and display sadness or fear, they are penalised less than women are when they move away from stereotype-consistent emotions like gentleness and compassion.

Human beings, no matter who they are, do not benefit when hyper-masculinity is idolised, and traditionally feminine qualities are denigrated. In such a system where masculinity and masculine ideals are the norm, women will always be seen to serve the men. Women will always be expected to behave in a manner that creates most comfort for the men. And this hierarchical framework is maintained through our cultural norms, as well as feeling and display rules of emotions. The purpose of these rules is to maintain the existing social structure that values men's rationality, compelling them to hide their emotions and vulnerability. And so men look towards women to provide the emotional balance that they, and society, craves. However, even as women's emotionality serves what society expects from them, it is denigrated because it is not seen to be of value to society. And, as men are the ones who hold power and status, they have more freedom and agency to express their feelings. Well, most of them, even if they cannot display their fears and vulnerabilities as easily. This means that men are trapped by patriarchy as much as women, even though men – most men – have more power and agency. The pressures of conforming to idealised notions of femininity and masculinity, and upholding patriarchy through their behaviours and emotional expression can have a huge impact on men too. These effects are intersectional, so some men and some women will have more privileges and freedom than others, depending on their proximity to the masculine ideals. The feeling and display rules of emotions are also very racialised, so people from minority ethnic backgrounds are more likely to be penalised for displaying certain feelings publicly, especially in the workplace.

Most recent research has dismissed any sex-based differences in emotional expressions and expressivity or the role of ovarian hormones in any emotional fluctuations.[8] It is now increasingly believed that biopsychosocial factors interact in unique ways to create our emotional experiences in response to external stimuli. Men are just as emotional as women, and feel emotions in the same way, even though socially they might not express them as freely or openly as women. It is almost as if society has legitimised women's emotions, and then penalised them for following the script laid out for them. A no-win situation; a double-bind.

Empirical proof of gendered differences in emotions has not been consistent and is difficult to prove as many studies have relied on self-reporting, mostly retrospectively, where internalised stereotypes play a huge role. While men and women both face restrictions on their emotions, these constraints and parameters tend to reinforce the gender imbalance and inequality in our society, so that women face more repercussions. Meanwhile, toxic masculinity is leading to a mental-health epidemic in men – but at the same time the self-care movement is targeted largely at women. Clearly, the status quo is not working.

In moving away from one model of leadership that is grounded in masculine attributes towards another that is more 'womanly' or 'feminine' but where we are not breaking any stereotypes, we merely reinforce the idea that there are distinct emotional attributes for men and women, and that men and women lead and manage in different ways (or ought to). This is harmful for everyone: stereotypes of any form or nature trap people into having to conform, and set artificial standards that we are all judged against. These stereotypes and leadership models homogenise people into social categories that force them to play the roles they are expected to perform as members of a particular social group. While our proximal encounters with our own bodies are so vastly different from the ones we are told that we ought to be having, we cannot stop seeing our own emotions as alien to us. 'You are not really angry' or 'You don't really mean this.' Of course, when this intersects with race, class, sexuality, it makes rage more volatile. Precarity in social hierarchy and generational fears add fuel to the fire. Feminist scholars have for a long time argued about the 'intersectional politics of anger', which determines whose anger expression in public is more acceptable – and successful – and whose rage is more valued – whether it is acknowledged or rejected by others. It can be emotionally taxing and mentally exhausting to navigate these narrow boundaries. The androcentric model has to be destabilised so that women are not judged against the norm set by men. As we see more democratic and participatory women leaders such as New Zealand's Prime Minister Jacinda Ardern, media is quick to label them as using a 'feminine style of leadership'. We have to remember that this emerges not from an inherent femininity in the person in this position, but their adjustment to the prescriptive and descriptive expectations from others for women leaders, and that they are often walking a very tricky line balancing agentic and communal emotional expressions.[9]

Until women stop having to internalise this message that they are less than the sum of their parts, that they are missing something that would make them whole, that they are weaker, inferior, they cannot escape from the tyranny of the narrative that obligates them to be submissive, more polite, to shape themselves into moulds that were designed for them, possibly by men. But, saying that, it should really not be up to those who are being stereotyped to try and rectify the outcome, or to change their behaviour, either to conform to the stereotypes or to change them. To change these attitudes and biases requires a wider societal shift, e.g., more representation of women in higher-status roles. It also requires challenging the emotional profile associated with leadership roles and a move towards a framework which allows for a better balance of agentic and communal emotional expression.

•

Those of you who have read my previous book *(M)otherhood* will know that I am a huge fan of Louise Bourgeois, a French-American artist and a self-identified hysteric. Her work *Arch of Hysteria* from 1993 is a reflection of her own experience, a critique of the way hysteria is perceived, and a subversion of the gendering of hysteria and extreme emotionality.[10] Bourgeois wrote numerous lists and free associations which can often resemble poetry. In one she writes: 'Do not risk too much / Do not hide too much / Do not neglect too much . . .' Almost an incantation, a reminder not to be 'too much' of anything, to shrink, to hide, to repress herself in order to not offend others, and not be criticised or hurt. In *Arch of Hysteria*, a hanging bronze figure, she refers to the 'whirlpool of hysteria' that often consumed her body and mind.[11] Made from a cast of Jerry Gorovoy, her long-term studio assistant, the hanging of the body represents the idea of fragility, to question the notion of stability and reliability, while the mirroring and the shine on the surface reflects the viewer, thereby making them see their own selves in this pivoting, turning, arching body relapsing into hysteria, possibly making them question their own perceptions of rationality and reason, and of madness and euphoria.[12] 'Walking around and around this body, I think of the artist and her fearless ability to plunge into her own undercurrents of turgid emotions.'[13]

Bourgeois herself described the work as exploring the tension between the physical and emotional: 'When does the emotional become physical? When does the physical become emotional? It's a circle going round and round.'[14] The work is ambiguous too, cast from a male body but depicting the long-held belief that female bodies are inherently neurotic. In this way it eludes any gendered association and shows how powerfully individual expression and experience can be universalised; the viewer sees their own body reflected in this sculpture, sees that emotion is a human condition, not a symptom of female peculiarity, not something to be cured, not something to be derided and erased. Bourgeois herself believed that people can exist solely as emotional beings, rather than having to prescribe to, and aspire to, a male stereotype of a rational and logical person more in control of themselves. Often what we perceive in others is a reflection of our own internal states and expectations. The way that hysteria, and many women's illnesses, can be seen as imaginary and not 'real' is at the heart of this sculpture too, a tense arching of the back, a headless torso without any gendered determinants, a silent scream seeking freedom and escape from the way it is tied up.[15]

This work was a response to the commonly held belief that women were too emotional to be running for office, or to be in power in public life.[16] We find that things really have not changed that much. Every day, many tiny actions and interactions can add up to create a culture where women's feelings are treated as abhorrent and aberrant. Hysteria, or the idea of a woman being hysterical, was always about the failure of a woman to conform to conventional gender roles. As long as women feel lonely, their emotions muted, their voices shut down, the inner rage will bubble up and manifest in the form of symptoms of illnesses that are then viewed with doubt and suspicion, their pain considered imaginary.

We cannot get rid of the bodies we are born in. They define our subjective view of this world, the way our experiences are shaped. By body, I do not just mean our genitalia. I mean the whole sensuality of our being, our very existence, our embodied engagement in this world where we feel, hear, see, touch, smell. We breathe in and out. Others see the shapes of our bodies, our faces, the way we present ourselves, and they make assumptions. They impose their own expectations of what we are and what we can (should) be, these limits on our bodies so that we cannot move beyond these narrow lanes, these hedges and fences by which we find ourselves hemmed in. And we can play a role – we can plead, demand a little more room, a little space, slowly, glacially. We can then have space for our emotions to come forth, find their feet, in a trundle, then a jog, and then maybe even a run if we are lucky. And we are always hoping for that gap in those hedges where our emotions might sneak past, and run amok, find the space to scream out in the void. But sometimes we get caught, seen before we can escape, and these hedges pushed back even further. Sometimes we scream out in the night when we think no one is noticing, when everyone else is asleep, but we get found out. And we are dragged back where we came from, flogged, punished, penalised for daring. For daring to be hysterical.

There are many today who believe we should think of gender

on a spectrum rather than as binary. Our maleness and femaleness would then sit along a gradation, sometimes more male than female, sometimes the other way around, sometimes half and half. Maybe then we could do away with the binary gender stereotypes of masculinity and femininity that we feel the need to identify with and conform to (or that might be imposed on us).

What if, in a similar vein, our emotions were not discrete categories but sat on a spectrum as well? And what if the way we talk about our emotions were rooted in our embodied experience, the way we are feeling inside, the reason we are feeling that way? And what if we articulate it as the action we might be compelled to take to resolve that feeling? What if we talk about emotions so they are no longer grounded in an essentialist framework attached to the beholder, but instead in the context that is provoking an emotional reaction? It would be a richer way of looking at the world, and a more nuanced and textured way of talking about ourselves, and interpreting the emotionalities of others. Then, maybe women and men could take ownership of their emotions, sit with them even in discomfort, and not feel the urge to fake, hide, suppress. The answer might not be more categories of emotions, but we do need a new language for them, one that is more proximate, more sensual, more earthy, where the primitiveness of female bodies is not put in a boxing ring with the apparent sophistication of a male body.

Perhaps it is time to be even more hysterical, to put our bodies out there for all to see in their frailties and their irrationalities. It is time for women to talk about claiming their bodies and the forces that oppress them with renewed vigour and energy. With a sense of collective effort, we have to resist and move beyond the patriarchal framework that tells us that one kind of body (and mind) is better than others. Perhaps it is time for men to be more hysterical, to be better allies. And perhaps it is time for men to be moved by these injustices and prejudices, although they think it does not affect them. It is time to make more space for women to show the full force of their feelings and emotions in their workplaces, in their relationships. And it is time for people to notice when they are preventing this from happening, because they consider emotionality as fragile, irresponsible, irrational or threatening.

As a consequence of our binaries, we edit out our emotions, make them fit us, the story, the people, the situation. We cut out bits and add some here and there. We hold things back. Sometimes we dial up the heat. It all depends on who is watching and who is not. It all depends on what we want to tell, and what not. What we wish to hide, secrete away. What we want to bury under the folds for no one to see. Sometimes we can't decipher the emotions we are feeling. Maybe we just haven't been given the key to do so. Maybe we were told that we couldn't have the key because it is for others, or maybe it has been hidden away in the cortical folds of our brains. And we try and rummage through these crevices to figure out what emotions we should display, what is the right response in this situation, what is not. It all happens so quickly that we don't have time to take a breath, to think clearly, to say 'I want to live an unedited life.' I don't want to cut out, shape, mould. I don't want to live my life like this, always trying to match my insides to my outsides, my own emotions to the key someone else has designed for me. I want to throw away the key, let it get lost in the nooks and crannies for ever. I want to be unmoderated, unregulated, uninhibited. But that is not how we work. That is not how any of us works. Or it might be possible.

In falling back on terms and labels that are outdated, we are insisting that we have all the concepts that we need to define and describe behaviours and emotions. But perhaps we need to develop a new lexicon for emotions, one that acknowledges and disrupts the western hegemony, that questions the limited, discrete visualisation of emotional expression, responds to changing conceptualisations of our world, as well as concedes that the notion of gendered emotions is a falsehood. What we really need is to acknowledge a broad spectrum of emotions and emotionality, unyoked from gender specificity, and remember that our somatic sensibilities, our ability to feel, experience, share, is what makes us all human.

ACKNOWLEDGEMENTS

I HAVE SAID THIS BEFORE, AND it is worth repeating again. I was fortunate to have certain privileges that meant that I could write this book even when I was drowning in grief and encumbered with chronic illnesses. I would like to acknowledge these privileges of time, space and people that make writing possible.

I might have written these words, but it takes a team to make a book a reality, and I am bound to forget someone.

I am always very grateful to my agent, Robert Caskie, for the many phone calls and for always having my back.

And to the wonderful team at Canongate who I am so thrilled to be published with. My editor Hannah Knowles, as well as Anna, Caitriona, Leila, Vicki and Eugenie, all of whom have been absolute saints with their patience and support.

Thanks to Lisa Feldman Barrett, Gina Rippon, Andrew McStay and Kate Devlin for taking the time to speak with me for this book. And to many other scientists and academics who I had conversations with at several points. Any mistakes are mine alone.

And to my writing group, Katy and Tiffany, who I was able to share my joys and sorrows, the pain and ecstasy of writing, with.

I wish to thank the Society of Authors for the Author Foundation award that I was really honoured to receive for the writing of this book.

I owe so much to my family, who I share my life with. Paul, Prishita, India, April shared the stresses and frustrations of writing this book with love, humour and patience, even when I was very 'emotional', and particularly when I was grouchy and hysterical.

And, finally to the goodest of all good boys, the very brave Taylor, who is the best person even though he is a dog.

REFERENCES

All links given below were accessed in March 2022.

PREFACE

1 Robertson, J. (2016), Steve Price says Van Badham 'just being hysterical', *The Guardian*, 12 July 2016 <https://www.theguardian.com/global/2016/jul/12/qa-steve-price-says-van-badham-just-being-hysterical-about-domestic-violence>

2 Vales, L. (2017), Columnist Kirsten Powers: 'How was Sen. Harris hysterical?', CNN, 13 June 2017 <https://edition.cnn.com/2017/06/13/politics/powers-miller-kamala-harris-hysterical-sessions-hearing-ac360-cnntv/>

3 BBC Radio 4, *Today*, 11 March 2021

4 UNFPA, State of World Population 2021, My body is my own: Claiming the right to autonomy and self-determination <https://www.unfpa.org/SOWP-2021>

5 Lederman, D. (1996), Supreme Court rejects VMI's exclusion of women <https://www.chronicle.com/article/supreme-court-rejects-vmis-exclusion-of-women/>

6 Rutsch, E. (2017), Barack Obama promotes empathy, YouTube <https://www.youtube.com/watch?v=lXFrAvoO3vk>

7 Lee, R.K. (2014), Judging judges: Empathy as the litmus test for impartiality,

University of Cincinnati Law Review 82 <https://scholarship.law.uc.edu/uclr/vol82/iss1/4>

8   Parkins, R. (2012), Gender and prosodic features in emotional expression, *Griffith Working Papers in Pragmatics and Intercultural Communication* 5(1), 46–54 <https://www.griffith.edu.au/__data/assets/pdf_file/0026/363680/Paper-6-Parkins-Gender-and-Emotional-Expressiveness_final.pdf>

9   In many of the cases through the book, I use 'sex/gender' to embrace the difficulty of disentangling participants' 'sex' – biological attributes including genitalia, sex-related chromosomes and hormones – and 'gender' – psychological and social attributes associated with males and females – as distinct variables in human neuroscience.

10 Waterloo, S.F., Baumgartner, S.E., Peter, J., Valkenburg, P.M. (2018), Norms of online expressions of emotion: Comparing Facebook, Twitter, Instagram, and WhatsApp, *New Media & Society* 20(5), 1813–1831

11 Plant, E.A., Hyde, J.S., Keltner, D., Devine, P.G. (2000), The gender stereotyping of emotions, *Psychology of Women Quarterly* 24, 81–92

12 Vongas, J.G., Al Hajj, R. (2015), The evolution of empathy and women's precarious leadership appointments, *Frontiers in Psychology* 6

13 Fischer, A.H., Kret, M.E., Broekens, J. (2018), Gender differences in emotion perception and self-reported emotional intelligence: A test of the emotion sensitivity hypothesis, *PloS One* 13(1), e0190712

14 Self-reported survey of employees conducted by the US dental company Byte <https://www.byteme.com/pages/womens-experiences>

15 Graham, C., Chattopadhyay, S. (2013), Gender and well-being around the world, *International Journal of Happiness and Development* 1:2, 212–232

16 Lindquist, K.A., Siegel, E.H., Quigley, K.S., Barrett, L.F. (2013), The hundred-year emotion war: Are emotions natural kinds or psychological constructions? Comment on Lench, Flores, and Bench (2011), *Psychological Bulletin* 139(1), 255–263

CHAPTER 1. WHAT IS AN EMOTION?

1   Oatley, K. (2004), *Emotions: A Brief History*, Blackwell Publishing

2   Frijda, N. (1986), *The Emotions*, Cambridge University Press

3   According to Hume's theory of the mind, the passions are impressions rather

than ideas (original, vivid and lively perceptions that are not copied from other perceptions). And they are not rational because they are logically consistent but because they serve a broader societal goal or evolutionary purpose.

4 James, W. (1884), What is an emotion? *Mind* 9(34), 188–205 <https://www.jstor.org/stable/2246769>

5 Nussbaum, M.C. (2003), *Upheavals of Thought: The Intelligence of Emotions*, Cambridge University Press

6 Kleinginna, P.R., Kleinginna, A.M. (1981), A categorized list of emotion definitions, with suggestions for a consensual definition, *Motivation and Emotion* 5, 345–379

7 Izard, C.E. (2010), The many meanings/aspects of emotion: Definitions, functions, activation, and regulation, *Emotion Review* 2(4), 363–370

8 Lindquist, K.A., Wager, T.D., Kober, H., Bliss-Moreau, E., Barrett, L.F. (2012), The brain basis of emotion: A meta-analytic review, *Behavioral and Brain Sciences* 35(3), 121–143

9 Barrett, L.F. (2017), *How Emotions Are Made: The Secret Life of the Brain*, Houghton Mifflin Harcourt

10 Siegel, E.H., Wormwood, J.B., Quigley, K.S., Barrett, L.F. (2018), Seeing what you feel: Affect drives visual perception of structurally neutral faces, *Psychological Science* 29(4), 496–503

11 In a 2015 study, Abbe Macbeth and Jason Rogers of Noldus Information Technology used facial-recognition technology that scans faces and identifies certain emotions in the features. They used faces of celebrities that are known for having 'resting bitch face' and found that their usual facial expressions tended to express contempt. There are issues with this research that I will pick up later in the book, but it was useful to see that this supported the theory that we impose our own expectations on interpreting other people's emotions.

12 Belli, S. (2010), The construction of an emotion (love) and its relationship with language: A review and discussion of an important area of social sciences, *Razón y Palabra* 15, 36: http://www.redalyc.org/articulo.oa?id=199514914039

13 Butler, J. (1997), *Excitable Speech: A Politics of the Performative*, Routledge

14 Barrett, L.F. (2009), The future of psychology: Connecting mind to brain, *Perspectives on Psychological Science* 4, 326–339

15 Lindquist, K.A. (2013), Emotions emerge from more basic psychological ingredients: A modern psychological constructionist model, *Emotion Review* 5(4), 356–368

16 Lindquist, K.A. (2013), Emotions emerge from more basic psychological ingredients: A modern psychological constructionist model, *Emotion Review* 5(4), 356–368

17 Nummenmaa, L., Glerean, E., Hari, R., Hietanen, J.K. (2014), Bodily maps of emotions, *PNAS* 111, 646–651

18 Moya, P. (2014), Habit and embodiment in Merleau-Ponty, *Frontiers in Human Neuroscience* 8

19 Tanaka, S. (2015), Intercorporeality as a theory of social cognition, *Theory and Psychology* 25, 455–472

CHAPTER 2. WRITTEN IN OUR FACES

1 You might have heard of the 'Duchenne smile', when we smile with our eyes as much as our teeth, as opposed to when we only smile with our mouth. A Duchenne smile engages the zygomaticus major muscle, which lifts the corners of our mouth, while the orbicularis oculi muscles raise our cheeks and the corners of the eyes, which forms the crow's feet (the lines at the corners of our eyes believed to be from smiling). A research experiment in 2019 showed that a Duchenne smile can nurture a sense of well-being and positive emotions in people who are feeling ostracised. Not only this, they were also perceived to be feeling more amused at their ostracisation, which implies that a Duchenne smile is perceived to be better than a social smile (one where a person smiles because they are expected to).

2 Duchenne, G.B. (1862), Mécanisme de la physionomie humaine ou Analyse électro-physiologique de l'expression des passions, Paris, Renouard, 85–86.

3 Darwin, C. (1872), *The Expression of the Emotions in Man and Animals*, New York, D. Appleton & Company, 278–308

4 Fischer, A.H. (1993), Sex differences in emotionality: fact or stereotype? *Feminism & Psychology* 3(3), 303–318

5 Barrett, L. (2011), Was Darwin wrong about emotional expressions? *Current Directions in Psychological Science* 20, 400–406

6   *The Winter's Tale*, v, ii, 10

7   James, W. (1890), *The Principles of Psychology*, Cosimo Inc., 2007

8   Izard, C.E. (2009), Emotion theory and research: Highlights, unanswered questions, and emerging issues, *Annual Review of Psychology* 60, 1–25

9   Diener, E., Oishi, S., Park, J. (2014), An incomplete list of eminent psychologists of the modern era, *Archives of Scientific Psychology* 2(1), 20–31

10   Ekman, P. (1984), Expression and the nature of emotion, in *Approaches to Emotion*, eds K. Scherer and P. Ekman (Hillsdale, NJ: Erlbaum) <https://www.paulekman.com/wp-content/uploads/2013/07/Expression-And-The-Nature-Of-Emotion.pdf>

11   Keltner, D. (1995), Signs of appeasement: Evidence for the distinct displays of embarrassment, amusement, and shame, *Journal of Personality and Social Psychology* 68, 441–454

12   Lettieri, G., Handjaras, G., Ricciardi, E. et al. (2019), Emotionotopy in the human right temporo-parietal cortex, *Nature Communications* 10, 5568

13   Ekman, P., Cordaro, D.T. (2011), What is meant by calling emotions basic, *Emotion Review* 3, 364–370

14   Ekman, P. (2003), Suppressed emotions and deception: The discovery of micro-expressions, in *Emotions Revealed*, Paul Ekman, Henry Holt & Co. <https://www.paulekman.com/blog/suppressed-emotions-and-deception-the-discovery-of-micro-expressions/>

15   As compared to a macro-expression that lasts ½–4 seconds.

16   Haggard, E.A., Isaacs, K.S. (1966), Micromomentary facial expressions as indicators of ego mechanisms in psychotherapy, in *Methods of Research in Psychotherapy*, The Century Psychology Series, Springer

17   Myers, S. (2015), Interview with Pete Docter and Jonas Rivera (*Inside Out*), *Empire Online* <https://gointothestory.blcklst.com/interview-written-pete-docter-and-jonas-rivera-inside-out-f2154080426c>

18   Russell. J.A. (1994), Is there universal recognition of emotion from facial expression? A review of the cross-cultural studies, *Psychological Bulletin*, 115(1), 102–11

19   Ekman's work is controversial and his experiments on the people in New Guinea has faced great criticism. He saw the cultural aspects of emotions as of marginal importance, and refused to see the emotions of the people he studied in the context of their cultural values. It is believed that he

made these people act in response to the situations he proposed to them, and so the 'result is not the photographic portrait of emotion, but the photographic portrait of acting – often bad acting'. G.K. Paster, K. Rowe, M. Floyd-Wilson (eds) (2004), *Reading the Early Modern Passions: Essays in the Cultural History of Emotions*, University of Pennsylvania Press

20 Crivelli, C., Russell, J.A., Jarillo, S., Fernández-Dols, J.-M. (2017), Recognizing spontaneous facial expressions of emotion in a small-scale society of Papua New Guinea, *Emotion* 17(2), 337–347

21 Ekman, P., Friesen, W.V. (1971), Constants across cultures in the face and emotion, *Journal of Personality and Social Psychology* 17(2), 124–129

22 Friesen, W.V. (1972), Cultural differences in facial expressions in a social situation: An experimental test on the concept of display rules, *Dissertation Abstracts International* 33(8-B), 3976–3977

23 Matsumoto, D., Ekman, P. (1989), American-Japanese cultural differences in intensity ratings of facial expressions of emotion, *Motivation and Emotion* 13(2), 143–157

24 Biehl, M., Matsumoto, D., Ekman, P. et al. (1997), Matsumoto and Ekman's Japanese and Caucasian Facial Expressions of Emotion (JACFEE): Reliability data and cross-national differences, *Journal of Nonverbal Behavior* 21, 3–21

25 Weinberger, S. (2010), Airport security: Intent to deceive? *Nature* 465, 412–415

26 Weinberger, S. (2010), Airport security: Intent to deceive? *Nature* 465, 412–415

27 Ekman, P., Friesen, W.V. (1975), *Unmasking the Face: A Guide to Recognizing Emotions from Facial Clues*, Prentice-Hall

28 Horwitz, M.J., Carter, S.L. (1993), The Supreme Court, 1992 Term, *Harvard Law Review* 107(1), 27–379

29 Discussion in Agarwal, P. (2020), *Sway: Unravelling Unconscious Bias*, Bloomsbury

30 Russell, J.A. (1994), Is there universal recognition of emotion from facial expression? A review of the cross-cultural studies, *Psychological Bulletin* 115(1), 102–141

31 As the pouting face has become the standard for social media photographs in the last few years, I wonder if our perception of this facial expression is different too now.

32 The gasping face is universally believed to be a sign of fear and submission across psychology and clinical studies. It has also been used to study fear and the amygdala in neuroscience studies.

33 Crivelli, C., Russell, J.A., Jarillo, S., Fernández-Dols, J.-M. (2016), The fear gasping face as a threat display, *Proceedings of the National Academy of Sciences* 113(44), 12403–12407

34 Jack, R.E., Garrod, O.G.B., Schyns, P.G. (2014), Dynamic facial expressions of emotion transmit an evolving hierarchy of signals over time, *Current Biology* 20, 24(2), 187–192

35 Beck, J. (2014), New research says there are only four emotions, *The Atlantic* <https://www.theatlantic.com/health/archive/2014/02/new-research-says-there-are-only-four-emotions/283560/>

36 Jack, R.E., Garrod, O.G.B., Schyns, P.G. (2014), Dynamic facial expressions of emotion transmit an evolving hierarchy of signals over time, *Current Biology* 20, 24(2), 187–192

37 Chen, C., Crivelli, C., Garrod, O.G.B., Schyns, P.G., Fernández-Dols, J.-M., Jack, R.E. (2018), Distinct facial expressions represent pain and pleasure across cultures, *PNAS* 23, 115(43), e10013–e10021

38 Gendron, M., Roberson, D., van der Vyver, J.M., Barrett, L.F. (2014), Perceptions of emotion from facial expressions are not culturally universal: Evidence from a remote culture, *Emotion* 14(2), 251–262

CHAPTER 3. ALL IN A NAME

1 Wierzbicka, A. (1986), Human emotions: universal or culture-specific? *American Anthropologist* 88, 3, 584–594

2 Goddard, C. (1992), Traditional ways of speaking – a semantic perspective, *Australian Journal of Linguistics* 12, 93–122

3 Goddard C. (1997), Contrastive semantics and cultural psychology: 'Surprise' in Malay and English, *Culture & Psychology* 3(2), 153–181

4 Thank you to Twitter users @aMaLsUy, @WL_Boadicea, Animah Kosai and Aizuddin Mohamed Anuar

5 Pernau, M. (2021), Studying emotions in South Asia, *South Asian History and Culture* 12, 2–3, 111–128

6 Reddy, W. (2012), *The Making of Romantic Love: Longing and Sexuality in*

Europe, South Asia, and Japan, 900–1200 CE, University of Chicago Press

7   Gendron, M., Roberson, D., van der Vyver, J.M., Barrett, L.F. (2014), Perceptions of emotion from facial expressions are not culturally universal: Evidence from a remote culture, *Emotion* 14(2), 251–262

8   Gendron, M., Roberson, D., van der Vyver, J.M., Barrett, L.F. (2014), Perceptions of emotion from facial expressions are not culturally universal: Evidence from a remote culture, *Emotion* 14(2), 251–262

9   Mair, V. (2016), Words for anger, Language Log <https://languagelog.ldc.upenn.edu/nll/?p=29390>

10 Yu, Ning (2002), Body and emotion: Body parts in Chinese expression of emotion, *Pragmatics & Cognition* 101, 341–367

11 Wierzbicka, A. (1986), Human emotions: Universal or culture-specific?, *American Anthropologist* 88, 3, 584–594

12 Levy, R.I. (1973), *Tahitians: Mind and Experience in the Society Islands*, Chicago, IL, University of Chicago Press

13 With a population of 3,500, they reside in an upland area some 90 miles north-east of Manila.

14 Rosaldo, R. (1989), Introduction: Grief and a Headhunter's Rage, in *Culture and Truth: The Remaking of Social Analysis*, Boston, Beacon Press; London, Taylor & Francis, 1993

15 Briggs, J. (1970), *Never In Anger: Portrait of an Eskimo Family*, Cambridge, MA, Harvard University Press. Interestingly, Briggs talks about how emotions was not considered an appropriate subject of study when she started her PhD in this topic in the 1960s. There was an understanding that behaviour and beliefs mattered, but the focus was on the society and the context and not on the emotion itself.

16 Briggs, J.L. (2000), Emotions have many faces: Inuit lessons, *Anthropologica* 42, 2, 157–164

17 Lutz, C. (1988), *Unnatural Emotion*, University of Chicago Press

18 Lutz, C. (1982), The domain of emotion words on Ifaluk, *American Ethnologist* 9, 1, 113–128

19 Keeler, W. (1983), Shame and stage fright in Java, *Ethos* 11, 3, 152–165

20 Appadurai, A. (1985), Gratitude as a social mode in South India, *Ethos* 13, 3, 236–245

21 Wu, K., Dunning, D.A. (2018), Hypocognition: Making sense of the

landscape beyond one's conceptual reach, *Review of General Psychology* 22, 25–35

22 Wu, K., Dunning, D.A. (2019), Hypocognitive mind: How lack of conceptual knowledge confines what people see and remember, *PsyArXiv*

23 In my book *Sway* I discuss how benevolent sexism appears to be favouring and protecting women, but in fact reinforces gendered stereotypes and maintains the gender hierarchies in our society. Agarwal, P. (2020), *Sway: Unravelling Unconscious Bias*, Bloomsbury

24 Aase, N., Crandall, J.R., Diaz, A., Knockel, J., Molinero, J.O., Saia, J., Wallach, D.S., Zhu, T. (2012), Whiskey, weed, and wukan on the world wide web: On measuring censors' resources and motivations, *FOCI* <https://www.cs.unm.edu/~jeffk/publications/foci2012combined.pdf>

25 Lindquist, K.A., Barrett, L.F., Bliss-Moreau, E., Russell, J.A. (2006), Language and the perception of emotion, *Emotion*, 6(1), 125–138

26 Severance, E., Washburn, M.F. (1907), Minor studies from the psychological laboratory of Vassar College: The loss of associative power in words after long fixation, *American Journal of Psychology* 18, 182–186

27 Yang, Q., Guo, Q.H., Bi, Y.C. (2015), The brain connectivity basis of semantic dementia: A selective review, *CNS Neuroscience & Therapeutics* 21(10), 784–792

28 Lindquist, K.A., Barrett, L.F. (2008), Constructing emotion: The experience of fear as a conceptual act, *Psychological Science* 19(9), 898–903

CHAPTER 4. I CAN'T. I SHOULDN'T. I WON'T

1 Liu, C. (2021), Christine vs work: What difficult emotions are trying to tell you, *Ascend*, hbr.org <https://hbr.org/2021/05/christine-vs-work-what-difficult-emotions-are-trying-to-tell-you>

2 LaMarre, J. (2021), Do emotions sometimes get the best of you at work? forbes.com <https://www.forbes.com/sites/ellevate/2021/07/12/do-emotions-sometimes-get-the-best-of-you-at-work-use-this>

3 Gross, J.J. (2007), *Handbook of Emotion Regulation*, New York, NY, Guilford Press

4 Gross, J.J. (2015), The extended process model of emotion regulation: Elaborations, applications, and future directions, *Psychological Inquiry* 26(1), 130–137

5 I was surprised to later find a similar example of a bear and a child in Sara Ahmed's book *Cultural Politics of Emotions*. My example came about from reading *Bear Child* by Geoff Mead with my children. I would love to check what had inspired Sara.

6 McRae, K., Gross, J.J. (2020), Emotion regulation, *Emotion* 20(1), 1–9

7 Kohn, N., Eickhoff, S.B., Scheller, M., Laird, A.R., Fox, P.T., Habel, U. (2014), Neural network of cognitive emotion regulation: An ALE meta-analysis and MACM analysis, *NeuroImage* 87, 345–355

8 Gross, J.J., John, O.P. (2003), Individual differences in two emotion regulation processes: Implications for affect, relationships, and well-being, *Journal of Personality and Social Psychology* 85, 348–362

9 Matsumoto, D., Juang, L. (2013), *Culture and Psychology*, 5th edn., Wadsworth Cengage Learning

10 Chaplin T.M. (2015), Gender and emotion expression: A developmental contextual perspective, *Emotion Review: Journal of the International Society for Research on Emotion* 7(1), 14–21

11 Wilms, R., Lanwehr, R., Kastenmüller, A. (2020), Emotion regulation in everyday life: The role of goals and situational factors, *Frontiers in Psychology*, 11, 877

12 Cisler, J.M., Olatunji, B.O., Feldner, M.T., Forsyth, J.P. (2010), Emotion regulation and the anxiety disorders: An integrative review, *Journal of Psychopathology and Behavioral Assessment*, 32(1), 68–82

13 Bodies also have the brains. But I use bodies as separate to the brain in this book. I was getting caught up in this terminology and how to make the distinction between embodiment and cortical processes, and owe thanks to Lisa Feldman Barrett, whose book helped me address this conundrum.

14 Richards, J.M., Gross, J.J. (1999), Composure at any cost? The cognitive consequences of emotion suppression, *Personality and Social Psychology Bulletin* 25(8), 1033–1044

15 Richards, J.M., Gross, J.J. (1999), Composure at any cost? The cognitive consequences of emotion suppression, *Personality and Social Psychology Bulletin* 25(8), 1033–1044

16 Macrae, C.N., Bodenhausen, G.V., Milne, A.B., Ford, R.L. (1997), On regulation of recollection: The intentional forgetting of stereotypical memories, *Journal of Personality and Social Psychology* 72, 709–719

17 Burns, K.C., Isbell, L.M., Tyler, J.M. (2008). Suppressing emotions toward stereotyped targets: The impact on willingness to engage in contact, *Social Cognition* 26, 276–287

18 Russell, B. (1938), *Power: A New Social Analysis*, Routledge Classics, 2004

19 Keltner, D., Gruenfeld, D.H., Anderson, C. (2003), Power, approach, and inhibition, *Psychological Review* 110, 265–284

20 Turner, J. (2005), Explaining the nature of power: A three-process theory, *European Journal of Social Psychology* 35, 1–22

21 Harsanyi J.C. (1980), A bargaining model for social status in informal groups and formal organizations, in *Essays on Ethics, Social Behavior, and Scientific Explanation*, Theory and Decision Library, vol. 12, Springer

22 More in my previous book (2020) *Sway: Unravelling Unconscious Bias*, Bloomsbury

23 LaFrance, M., Henley, N.M., Hall, J.A., Halberstadt, A.G. (1997). Nonverbal behavior: Are women's superior skills caused by their oppression? In M.R. Walsh (ed.), *Women, Men, & Gender: Ongoing Debates*, Yale University Press, 101–133

24 Henley, N.M., LaFrance, M. (1984), Gender as culture: Difference and dominance in nonverbal behavior, in A. Wolfgang (ed.), *Nonverbal Behavior: Perspectives, Applications, Intercultural Insights*, Hogrefe & Huber Publishers, 351–371

25 LaFrance, M. (1997), Pressure to be pleasant: Effects of sex and power on reactions to not smiling. *Revue Internationale de Psychology Sociale / International Review of Social Psychology* 2, 95–108

26 There are of course cultural and individual differences.

27 Steele, C.M., Aronson, J. (1995), Stereotype threat and the intellectual test performance of African Americans, *Journal of Personality and Social Psychology* 69(5), 797–811

28 Johns, M., Inzlicht, M., Schmader, T. (2008), Stereotype threat and executive resource depletion: examining the influence of emotion regulation, *Journal of Experimental Psychology: General* 137(4), 691–705

29 Giuliani, N.R., Gross, J.J. (2009), Reappraisal, in Sander, D., Scherer, K.R. (eds), *Oxford Companion to the Affective Sciences*, Oxford University Press

30 Berna, G., Ott, L., Nandrino, J.-L. (2014), Effects of emotion regulation difficulties on the tonic and phasic cardiac autonomic response, *PLoS One* 9(7), e102971

31 Mental health statistics: Men and women (accessed 2022), Mental Health Foundation <https://www.mentalhealth.org.uk/statistics/mental-health-statistics-men-and-women>

32 Baxter, A.J., Scott, K.M., Ferrari, A.J. et al (2014), Challenging the myth of an 'epidemic' of common mental disorders: Trends in the global prevalence of anxiety and depression between 1990 and 2010, *Depression and Anxiety* 31, 506–516

33 Functional magnetic resonance imaging (fMRI) measures brain activity by detecting changes associated with blood flow, because when a region of the brain is used more there is more blood flow to that region.

34 McRae, K., Ochsner, K.N., Mauss, I.B., Gabrieli, J., Gross, J.J. (2008), Gender differences in emotion regulation: An fMRI study of cognitive reappraisal, *Group Processes & Intergroup Relations* 11(2), 143–162

35 Hosie, J., Milne, A., McArthur, L. (2005), The after-effects of regulating anger and anger-related emotions on self-report ratings and behavior: Divergent consequences for men and women, *Psychologia* 48(4), 288–305

36 Mental Health Foundation statistics (accessed 2022) <https://www.mental-health.org.uk/statistics/mental-health-statistics-suicide>

37 King, T.L., Shields, M., Sojo, V. et al. (2020), Expressions of masculinity and associations with suicidal ideation among young males, *BMC Psychiatry* 20, 228

38 Pan American Health Organization (2019), 1 in 5 men will not reach the age of 50 in the Americas <https://www3.paho.org/hq/index.php?option=com_content&view=article&id=15599:1-in-5-men-will-not-reach-the-age-of-50-in-the-americas-due-to-issues-relating-to-toxic-masculinity&Itemid=1926&lang=en>

39 Kupemba, D.N. (2021), In Zimbabwe, toxic masculinity is driving male suicide rates, *Newsweek* <https://www.newsweek.com/zimbabwe-toxic-masculinity-driving-male-suicide-rates-opinion-1576510>

40 Pappas, S. (2019), APA issues first-ever guidelines for practice with men and boys <https://www.apa.org/monitor/2019/01/ce-corner>

41 *New York Times* Opinion (2019), The fight over men is shaping our political future <https://www.nytimes.com/2019/01/17/opinion/apa-guidelines-men-boys.html>

42 Jarrett, C. (2019), Young men who endorse the masculine ideal of success . . .

Research Digest, British Psychological Society <https://digest.bps.org.uk/2019/01/18/young-men-who-endorse-the-masculine-ideal-of-success-enjoy-greater-psychological-wellbeing/>

43 *New York Times* Opinion (2019), The fight over men is shaping our political future <https://www.nytimes.com/2019/01/17/opinion/apa-guidelines-men-boys.html>

44 Butler, E.A., Lee, T.L., Gross, J.J. (2007), Emotion regulation and culture: Are the social consequences of emotion suppression culture-specific? *Emotion* 7(1), 30–48

45 Ford, B.Q., Mauss, I.B. (2015), Culture and emotion regulation, *Current Opinion in Psychology* 3, 1–5

46 Do we really have any of those?

47 Matsumoto, D., Yoo, S.H., Fontaine, J., Anguas-Wong, A.M., Ariola, M., Ataca, B. et al. (2008), Mapping expressive differences around the world: The relationship between emotional display rules and individualism v. collectivism, *Journal of Cross-Cultural Psychology* 39, 55–74 <http://hdl.handle.net/1854/LU-418727>

48 Matsumoto, D., Yoo, S.H., Nakagawa, S., Alexandre, J., et al. (2008), Culture, emotion regulation, and adjustment, *Journal of Personality and Social Psychology* 94(6), 925–937

49 Sun, R., Hou, W.K., Hui, B.P.H., Siu, N.Y.-F., Engels, T., Sauter, D.A. (2021), Perception and evaluation of 23 positive emotions in Hong Kong and the Netherlands, *Frontiers in Psychology* 12, 579474

50 Kwon, H., Yoon, K.L., Joormann, J., Kwon, J. (2013), Cultural and gender differences in emotion regulation: Relation to depression, *Cognition & Emotion* 27(5), 769–782

SECTION 2: HOW DID OUR EMOTIONS BECOME GENDERED?

1 Ficino was also the one who introduced the concept of Platonic Love, which had a huge influence on how male–male relationships were seen and understood in spiritual terms.

CHAPTER 5. CHAMBER POTS

1 Stoicism was one of the new philosophical movements of the Hellenistic period. The Stoics held that emotions like fear or envy (or impassioned sexual attachments, or passionate love of anything whatsoever) either were, or arose from, false judgements and that the sage – a person who had attained moral and intellectual perfection – would not undergo them. (From *Stanford Encyclopaedia of Philosophy*)

2 Euripides, in Bond, G.W. (1981), *Heracles*, Clarendon Press

3 Quoted in Allard, J., Montlahuc, P. (2018), The gendered construction of emotions in the Greek and Roman worlds, *Clio: Women, Gender, History* 47, 23–44, trans. Marian Rothstein

4 Wissmann, J. (2011), Cowardice and gender in the *Iliad* and Greek tragedy, in D. LaCourse Munteanu (ed.), *Emotion, Genre and Gender in Classical Antiquity*, Bloomsbury Academic

5 *Iliad*, 15, 561–564

6 Allard, J., Montlahuc, P. (2018), The gendered construction of emotions in the Greek and Roman worlds, *Clio: Women, Gender, History* 47, 23–44, trans. Marian Rothstein

7 The *Iliad* is estimated to have been written during the eighth century BCE, the *Odyssey* between 750 and 625 BCE.

8 *The History of Rome*, sometimes referred to as *Ab Urbe Condita Libri*, is a monumental history of ancient Rome, written between 27 and 9 BCE by the historian Titus Livius, or 'Livy'.

9 Allard, J., Montlahuc, P., & Rothstein, M. (2018), The gendered construction of emotions in the Greek and Roman worlds. *Clio. Women, Gender, History* (47), 23–44, trans. Marian Rothstein

10 Shakespeare, *Troilus and Cressida* IV. 1

11 Arguably since the Bible!

12 Also considered the father of western political philosophy, born in 428 BCE.

13 Plato, *The Republic*, trans. B. Jowett, Project Gutenberg, 1998

14 Holst-Warhaft, G. (1992), *Dangerous Voices: Women's Laments and Greek Literature*, Routledge

15 In *A History of Virility*, A. Corbin, J.-J. Courtine, G. Vigarello (eds), trans. Keith Cohen, European Perspectives, Columbia University Press, 2016

REFERENCES

16 Allen, D. (2003), Angry bees, wasps and jurors: the symbolic politics of ὀργή in Athens, in S. Braund, G. Most (eds), *Ancient Anger: Perspectives from Homer to Galen*, Cambridge University Press, 76–98

17 Seneca the Younger, On anger, in *Moral Essays* vol. 1, trans. John W. Basore, Harvard University Press, 1928 <https://www.loebclassics.com/view/seneca_younger-de_ira/1928/pb_LCL214.161.xml?readMode=recto>

18 Five ancient Greek novels survive complete: Chariton's *Callirhoe* (mid 1st century), Achilles Tatius's *Leucippe and Clitophon* (early 2nd century), Longus's *Daphnis and Chloe* (2nd century), Xenophon's *Ephesian Tale* (late 2nd century) and Heliodorus of Emesa's *Aethiopica* (3rd century).

19 Scourfield, J. (2004), Anger and gender in Chariton's *Chaereas and Callirhoe*, in S. Braund, G. Most, (eds), *Ancient Anger: Perspectives from Homer to Galen*, Cambridge University Press, 163–184

20 His essays and letters, *Moralia*, are believed to have been written mostly for a 'masculine' audience with characters epitomising 'masculine' ideals. Plutarch, *Moralia*, trans. F.C. Babbitt, Harvard University Press, 1928

21 Leon, D.W. (2019), Performing masculinity in Plutarch's *Life of Pyrrhus*, *Illinois Classical Studies* 44(1), 177–193

22 Plutarch's *Lives of the Noble Grecians and Romans*, probably written at the beginning of the second century, is a series of 48 biographies of famous men, arranged in pairs to illuminate their common moral virtues or failings.

23 Kempf, A.M. (2017), Witches and wives: An analysis of Plutarch's depiction of women in the *Life of Marc Antony*, Wright State University, Ohio <http://rave.ohiolink.edu/etdc/view?acc_num=wright15153241456123>

24 Compared to some of his contemporaries, Plutarch's writings do showcase women as independent, strong and assertive too.

25 Plutarch, *Moralia*, trans. F.C. Babbitt, Harvard University Press, 1928

26 Barlow, S. (1989), Stereotype and reversal in Euripides' *Medea*, *Greece & Rome* 36(2), 158–171

27 Waterfield, R. (2004), *Athens: A History, From Ancient Ideal to Modern City*, Basic Books

28 Luo, S.C. (2012), Women and war: Power play from *Lysistrata* to the present, *Honors Scholar Theses*, 262

29 Euripides, *Lysistrata*, trans. Jack Lindsay (1923), Gutenberg Project, lines 8–11

30 Euripides, *Lysistrata*, trans. Jack Lindsay (1923), Gutenberg Project, lines 587–588

31 Schaps, D. (1982), The women of Greece in wartime, *Classical Philology* 77(3), 193–213

32 Translated by Luo, S.C. (2012), Women and war: Power play from *Lysistrata* to the present, Honors Scholar Theses, 262 <https://opencommons.uconn.edu/srhonors_theses/262>

33 Huizinga, J. (1919), *Autumntide of the Middle Ages*, Leiden University Press

34 Neal, K. (2015), From letters to loyalty: Aline la Despenser and the meaning(s) of a noblewoman's correspondence in thirteenth-century England, in Susan Broomhall (ed.), *Authority, Gender and Emotions in Late Medieval and Early Modern England*, Palgrave, 18–33

35 Broomhall, S. (ed.) (2015), *Authority, Gender and Emotions in Late Medieval and Early Modern England*, Palgrave

36 Harvey, K. (2014), Episcopal emotions: Tears in the life of the medieval bishop, *Historical Research* 87

37 Erker, D.Š. (2011), Gender and Roman funeral ritual, in V. Hope, J. Huskinson (eds), *Memory and Mourning in Ancient Rome*, Oxbow Books, 40–60 <https://www.jstor.org/stable/j.ctt1cd0pnw>

38 Seneca writes: 'Our forefathers have enacted that, in the case of women, a year should be the limit for mourning; not that they needed to mourn for so long, but that they should mourn no longer. In the case of men, no rules are laid down, because to mourn at all is not regarded as honourable.' Seneca, Letter 63, On grief for lost friends, *Moral Letters to Lucilius*, trans. R.M. Gummere, William Heinemann, 1920 <https://en.wikisource.org/wiki/Moral_letters_to_Lucilius>

39 O'Leary, J. (2013), 'Where there are many women there are many witches': The social and intellectual understanding of femininity in the *Malleus Maleficarum* (1486), *Reinvention: An International Journal of Undergraduate Research* 6(1) <https://warwick.ac.uk/fac/cross_fac/iatl/reinvention/archive/volume6issue1/oleary/>

40 While this section is mostly about Europe, it is interesting to see the parallels in Indian rituals, where amongst Hindus, for instance, people would wear white or plain, unadorned clothing, and men in the close family would have their heads shaved.

41 Levy, A. (2003), Augustine's concessions and other failures: Mourning and masculinity in fifteenth-century Tuscany, in *Grief and Gender, 700–1700*, Jennifer C.Vaught (ed.) with Lynne Dickson Bruckner, Palgrave Macmillan, 81–93 <https://caa.hcommons.org/deposits/item/hc:13519>

42 A letter from Agnes of Assisi to Clare of Assisi (1230) <https://epistolae.ctl.columbia.edu/letter/584.html>

43 Llewellyn, N. (1991), *The Art of Death: Visual Culture in the English Death Ritual c.1500–c.1800*, University of Chicago Press

44 Llewellyn, N. (1991), *The Art of Death: Visual Culture in the English Death Ritual c.1500–c.1800*, University of Chicago Press, 96

45 Radcliff-Umstead, D. (1975), Boccaccio's idle ladies, in D. Radcliff-Umstead (ed.), *The Roles and Images of Women in the Middle Ages and Renaissance*, University of Pittsburgh Publications on the Middle Ages and Renaissance, vol. 3, 79

46 Camden, C. (1952), *The Elizabethan Woman*, Paul A. Appel, 1975

47 Dunn, C.M. (1977), The changing image of woman in Renaissance society and literature, in M. Springer (ed.), *What Manner of Woman: Essays on English and American Life and Literature*, New York University Press, 15–38

48 'Antinomianism' literally means 'against the law'.

49 Lovely!

50 Figures vary dependent on urban and rural populations, class and wealth.

51 Rousseau, *Emile, or Education*, trans. Barbara Foxley (1921), J.M. Dent and Sons

52 Once again, 'sex' was used in most of these texts, and sex was what was recorded.

53 Malebranche, N. (1674), *The Search After Truth*, trans. T. Lennon, P. Olscamp, Cambridge University Press, 1997

54 Walusinski, O. (2018), Marin Cureau de La Chambre (1594–1669), a 17th-century pioneer in neuropsychology, *Revue neurologique* 174

55 Dunea, G. (2018), Aristotle and the four humors, *Hektoen International* <https://hekint.org/2018/10/31/aristotle-and-the-four-humors/>

56 The humours were also linked to the four elements. 'Humour' is a translation of the Greek χυμός, chymos (juice or sap). Ancient Indian Ayurvedic medicine similarly developed a theory of three doshas, linked to the five elements, that had to be kept in balance for good health and an even temperament.

57 Aristotle, *Generation of Animals*, trans. A.L. Peck, Loeb Classical Library 366, Harvard University Press, 1942

58 Tuana, N. (1988), The weaker seed: The sexist bias of reproductive theory, *Hypatia* 3(1), 35–59

59 Camden, C. (1952), *The Elizabethan Woman*, Paul A. Appel, 1975

60 Paster, G. (1998), Unbearable coldness of female being: Women's imperfection and the humoral economy, *English Literary Renaissance* 28(3), 416–440

61 Crooke, H. (1615), *Mikrokosmographia: Description of the Body of Man*. It was controversial because it critiqued ancient Greek physician Galen, and was denounced by the Church for being 'indecent', as it showed illustrations of human sexual organs.

62 Burke, E. (1757), *A Philosophical Inquiry into the Origin of our Ideas of the Sublime and Beautiful*, Gutenberg Project <http://www.gutenberg.org/files/15043/15043-h/15043-h.htm>

63 Castiglione, B., *The Book of the Courtier*, Dover Publications, 2003

64 *The Works Of Aristotle, The Famous Philosopher – In Four Parts*, Miller, Law and Carter, 1820

65 Frye, S. (1992), The myth of Elizabeth at Tilbury, *The Sixteenth Century Journal* 23(1), 95–114

66 Castiglione, B., *The Book of the Courtier*, British Library archives <https://www.bl.uk/collection-items/the-book-of-the-courtier-1588#>

67 Shandell, J. (2002), Shakespeare's genders, then and now, *Theater* 32(2), 82–84

68 Not really 'two steps forward'.

69 O'Neill, M. (2001), Virtue and beauty: The Renaissance image of the ideal woman. *Smithsonian* 32(6), 62–69

70 West, S. (1999), *Italian Culture in Northern Europe in the Eighteenth Century*, Cambridge University Press

71 See for instance Wiles, T. (2016), The beauty of a virtuous woman: Gender roles and portraiture during the Italian Renaissance <https://arthistory-portraiture.wordpress.com/2016/11/30/first-blog-post/>

72 Simons, P. (1988), Women in frames, the gaze, the eye, the profile in Renaissance portraiture, *History Workshop* 25, 4–30

73 Paoletti, J.T., Radke, G.M. (2005), Titian in Urbino, *Art in Renaissance Italy*, J.T. Paoletti, G.M. Radke (eds), Prentice Hall, 477

74 Judith was a widow from Bethulia, and Holofernes was an Assyrian general who had invaded her city and desired her: Book of Judith, 13

75 Davis, N.Z. (1987), *Fiction in the Archives: Pardon Tales and their Tellers in Sixteenth-century France*, Stanford University Press

76 Quoted from M.L. Marshall, L.L. Carroll, K.A. McIver (eds) (2014), *Sexualities, Textualities, Art and Music in Early Modern Italy: Playing with Boundaries*, Routledge

77 Wilkes, W. (1741), *A Letter of Genteel and Moral Advice to a Young Lady* <https://www.google.co.uk/books/edition/A_Letter_of_Genteel_and_Moral_Advice_to/1h65Zaz_aV4C?hl=en&gbpv=0)>

78 Wilkes, W. (1741), *A Letter of Genteel and Moral Advice to a Young Lady* <https://www.google.co.uk/books/edition/A_Letter_of_Genteel_and_Moral_Advice_to/1h65Zaz_aV4C?hl=en&gbpv=0)>

79 The word 'feeling' has since been deployed for relatively slow processes; a succession of feelings can build into an interconnected process called an emotion, which can have a more intense effect on a person than an individual feeling. But it is a relatively arbitrary distinction, and in every-day language these days we use 'feelings' interchangeably with 'emotion', with an understanding that an emotion is a more heightened state of feeling.

80 Frevert, U. (1989), *Women in German History*, Berg Publishers: 207–211, 240–247

81 Wundt, W.M. (1897), *Outlines of Psychology*, trans. C.H. Judd, 1902

82 Izard, C.E. (1991), *The Psychology of Emotions*, Plenum Press, 243

83 Sutherland, S. (1976), Hume on morality and the emotions, *Philosophical Quarterly* 26(102), 14–23

84 Hume, D. (1739–40), *A Treatise of Human Nature*, ed. L.A. Selby-Bigge, rev. P.H. Nidditch, Clarendon Press, 1975

85 Hume, D. (1742), *Of the Rise and Progress of the Arts and Sciences* <http://infomotions.com/etexts/philosophy/1700-1799/hume-of-737.htm>

86 Battersby, C. (1981), An enquiry concerning the Humean woman, *Philosophy* 56(217), 303–312

87 Coletti, T. (2013), 'Did Women Have a Renaissance?' A medievalist reads Joan Kelly and Aemilia Lanyer, *Early Modern Women* 8, 249–259

CHAPTER 6. STATE OF HYSTERIA

1 Sigerist, H.E. (1951), *A History of Medicine: Primitive and Archaic Medicine*, Oxford University Press

2 Laios, K., Karamanou, M., Saridaki, Z., Androutsos, G. (2012), Aretaeus of Cappadocia and the first description of diabetes, *Hormones* (Athens), 11(1), 109–113

3 Veith, Ilza (1965), *Hysteria: The History of a Disease*, University of Chicago Press

4 Lewis, H.B. (1981), Hysteria, in *Freud and Modern Psychology: Emotions, Personality, and Psychotherapy*, vol. 1, Springer

5 As Galen wrote: 'All the parts, then, that men have, women have too.'

6 Thomas Aquinas, *Summa Theologica*, Edizione Studio Domenicano, 1996

7 Ahmed, S. (2014), *The Cultural Politics of Emotion*, Edinburgh University Press

8 Although, as we know, science is influenced by the politics and prejudices of the time, even though we might consider it to be objective.

9 Bifulco, M., Ciaglia, E., Marasco, M., Gangemi, G. (2014), A focus on Trotula de' Ruggiero: a pioneer in women's and children's health in history of medicine, *Journal of Maternal-Fetal and Neonatal Medicine* 27(2), 204–205

10 Hildegard of Bingen, *Causes and Cures*, Sellerio, 1997

11 Jorden, Edward (1603), *A. Briefe Discourse of a Disease Called the Suffocation of the Mother*. John Windet. (From the British Library Archives)

12 Quoted in Paster, G. (1998), Unbearable coldness of female being: Women's imperfection and the humoral economy, *English Literary Renaissance* 28(3), 416–440

13 Pearce, J.M. (2016), Sydenham on hysteria, *European Neurology* 76, 175–181

14 Quoted in Scull, A. (2009), *Hysteria: The Biography*, Oxford University Press

15 Chodoff, P. (1982), Hysteria and women, *American Journal of Psychiatry* 139(5), 545–551

16 This translation is by T.M. Knox (Clarendon Press, 1949), and is the version cited in both Carol Adams's *The Sexual Politics of Meat* (Continuum International, 1990) and Susan Bordo's *Unbearable Weight* (University of California Press, 1993).

17 Kant, I. (1798), *Anthropology from a Pragmatic Point of View*, trans. R.B. Louden, Cambridge University Press, 2006, 205

18 Stafford, A. (1997), The feminist critique of Hegel on women and the family, *Animus* 2, 64–92

19 Wing, J.K. (1978), *Reasoning About Madness*, Oxford University Press

20 Micale, M.S. (1989), Hysteria and its historiography: A review of past and present writings (II), *History of Science* 27(4), 319–351

21 Althaus J. (1866), A lecture on the pathology and treatment of hysteria, *British Medical Journal* 1(271), 245–248

22 Barberis, D. (2014), Hysteria in the male: Images of masculinity in late nineteenth-century France <https://www.researchgate.net/publication/267900426_Hysteria_in_the_Male_Images_of_Masculinity_in_Late_Nineteenth-Century_France>

23 A word that was applied to indigenous people, Africans, Asians and Latin Americans.

24 I have discussed this more in my book *(M)otherhood: On the Choices of Being a Woman* (Canongate, 2021).

25 Eugenic scientific theories were used to justify this, including claims that colonised women had wider pelves, closer to that of a female gorilla than a European female, which allowed them to give birth more easily.

26 We have numerous examples of this throughout history. The 'father of modern gynaecology', James Marion Sims, performed shocking experiments on enslaved women without anaesthesia.

27 Parkinson, J. (2016), The significance of Sarah Baartman, *BBC News Magazine*, 7 January 2016 <https://www.bbc.co.uk/news/magazine-35240987>

28 Elkins, C. (2007), A life exposed, *New York Times*, 14 January 2007 <https://www.nytimes.com/2007/01/14/books/review/Elkins.t.html>

29 Briggs, L. (2000), The race of hysteria: 'Overcivilization' and the 'savage' woman in late nineteenth-century obstetrics and gynecology, *American Quarterly* 52(2), 246–273

30 Caron, S.M. (2008), Race suicide, eugenics, and contraception, 1900–1930, in S.M. Caron, *Who Chooses? American Reproductive History since 1830*, University Press of Florida, 44–80

31 Lovett, L.L. (2009), The political economy of sex: Edward A. Ross and

race suicide, in *Conceiving the Future: Pronatalism, Reproduction, and the Family in the United States, 1890–1938*, University of North Carolina Press, 77–108

32   Beard, G. (1880), *A Practical Treatise on Nervous Exhaustion*, William Wood and Company

33   Austrian neurologist, founder of psychoanalysis, best known for his psycho-sexual theories.

34   Freud, S. (1925), Some psychical consequences of the anatomical distinction between the sexes, *Standard Edition of the Complete Psychological Works of Sigmund Freud* 19, 248–258

35   Pierce, J. (1989), The relation between emotion work and hysteria: A feminist reinterpretation of Freud's studies on hysteria, *Women's Studies* 16(3–4), 255–270

36   Pierce, J. (1989), The relation between emotion work and hysteria: A feminist reinterpretation of Freud's studies on hysteria, *Women's Studies* 16(3–4), 255–270

37   Zepf, S., Seel, D. (2016), Penis envy and the female Oedipus complex: A plea to reawaken an ineffectual debate, *Psychoanalytic Review* 103(3), 397–421

38   Delmar, R. (2001), Hysteria revisited (a review of Madmen and Medusas by Juliet Mitchell, Penguin Press, 2000) in *History Workshop* 52, 272–279

39   Freud, S. (1909), General remarks on hysterical attacks, *Standard Edition of the Complete Psychological Works of Sigmund Freud*, 9, 227–234

40   Micale, M.S. (1995), *Approaching Hysteria: Disease and Its Interpretations*, Princeton University Press

41   Wright, A.E. (1913), *The Unexpurgated Case Against Woman Suffrage* <https://en.wikisource.org/wiki/The_Unexpurgated_Case_Against_Woman_Suffrage>

42   Held, A. (2019), Controversial Serena Williams cartoon ruled 'non-racist', NPR.org <https://www.npr.org/2019/02/25/697672690/controversial-serena-cartoon-ruled-non-racist-by-australia-s-governing-press-bod?t=1641926346664>

43   Gilman, C.P. (1892), *The Yellow Wallpaper*, Virago Modern Classics, 1981

CHAPTER 7. WITCHES' COVEN

1 Ben-Yehuda, N. (1980), The European witch craze of the 14th to 17th centuries: A sociologist's perspective, *American Journal of Sociology* 86(1), 1–31

2 Maxwell-Stewart, P.G. (2001), *Witchcraft in Europe and the New World*, Palgrave

3 In Latin, the feminine *maleficarum* would only be used for women, while the masculine *maleficorum* could be used for men alone or for both sexes together

4 Knott, J. (1905), Medicine and witchcraft in the days of Sir Thomas Browne, *British Medical Journal* 2(2338), 1046–1049

5 Mackay, C.S. (2009), *The Hammer of Witches: A Complete Translation of the Malleus Maleficarum*, Cambridge University Press

6 Kramer, H. (1486), *Der Hexenhammer: Malleus Maleficarum*, ed. and trans. W. Behringer and G. Jerouschek (2000), Munich: Deutscher Taschenbuch Verlag

7 Bailey, M.D. (2003), *Battling Demons: Witchcraft, Heresy, and Reform in the Late Middle Ages*, History Books, 12

8 Brauner, S. (2001), *Fearless Wives and Frightened Shrews: The Construction of the Witch in Early Modern Germany*, University of Massachusetts Press

9 Recent research reveals that in fact *Malleus Maleficarum* was not condoned by the Christian Church.

10 During this period, approximately 90,000 people were formally accused of witchcraft and about half of this number were executed. Millar, C.-R. (2017), *Witchcraft, the Devil, and Emotions in Early Modern England*, Routledge

11 Only about 18 per cent of the accused were men. Millar, C.-R. (2017), *Witchcraft, the Devil, and Emotions in Early Modern England*, Routledge

12 Jackson, L. (1995), Witches, wives, mothers: Witchcraft persecution and women's confessions in seventeeth-century England, *Women's History Review*, 4(1), 63–83

13 Kounine, L., Ostling, M. (eds) (2017), *Emotions in the History of Witchcraft*, Palgrave Macmillan

14 I feel that somehow pitting women against women is a way of keeping them in their place, and what is happening right now with the divisive

discourse about transphobia, with gender-critical feminists threatened by trans women invading their space, seen to be disrupting the norms of femininity, feels very similar. Just another form of witchhunt.

15 Anderson, A., Gordon, R. (1978), Witchcraft and the status of women – the case of England, *British Journal of Sociology* 29(2), 171–184

16 From Winterer, C., The American Enlightenment, Stanford Libraries <https://exhibits.stanford.edu/american-enlightenment>

17 Blumberg, J. (2007), A brief history of the Salem Witch Trials, *Smithsonian*. There have been numerous theories as to what happened. One of the most concrete studies, published in 1976 by psychologist Linnda Caporael, blamed the abnormal habits of the accused on the fungus ergot, which can be found in rye, wheat and other cereal grasses. (Caporael, L. (1976), Ergotism? The Satan loosed in Salem, *Science* 192(4234), 21–26) Toxicologists say that eating ergot-contaminated foods can lead to muscle spasms, vomiting, delusions and hallucinations. The fungus thrives in warm and damp climates – such as the swampy meadows in Salem Village, where rye was the staple grain during the spring and summer months.

18 Although it is difficult to say how many of these witness testimonies have been exaggerated.

19 Godbeer, R. (2005), *Escaping Salem: The Other Witch Hunt of 1692*, Oxford University Press

20 Rollins, H.E. (1971), *A Pepysian Garland*, Harvard University Press, 72–77

21 Bardsley, S. (2003), Sin, speech, and scolding in late medieval England, in *Fama: The Politics of Talk and Reputation in Medieval Europe*, T. Fenster, D.L. Smail (eds), Cornell University Press, 146–148

22 Men were sometimes labelled 'scold' and prosecuted for it, but in a tiny minority, and almost always accompanied by their wives.

23 Earle, A.M. (1896), *Curious Punishments of Bygone Days*, Gutenberg Project

24 Earle, A.M. (1896), *Curious Punishments of Bygone Days*, Gutenberg Project

25 James, E.W. (1895), Grace Sherwood, the Virginia witch, *William and Mary Quarterly* 4(1), 18–22

26 Aucoin, J. (2018), review of *The Trials of a Scold: The Incredible True Story of Writer Anne Royall* by Jeff Biggers (Thomas Dunne Books, 2017), *American Journalism* 35(2), 256–258

27 Sinha, S. (2007), Witch-hunts, adivasis, and the uprising in Chhotanagpur, *Economic and Political Weekly* 42(19), 1672–1676

28 Banerjee, B. (2017), Witch beliefs and violence against women among tribal communities in West Bengal, MA Thesis in Social Work, Tata Institute of Social Sciences

29 The recent case of Britney Spears comes to mind once again, but there are numerous such examples.

CHAPTER 8. HYSTERIA IN MEN

1 Micale, M.S. (2008), *Hysterical Men: The Hidden History of Male Nervous Illness*, Harvard University Press

2 Micale M.S. (1990), Charcot and the idea of hysteria in the male: Gender, mental science, and medical diagnosis in late nineteenth-century France, *Medical History* 34(4), 363–411

3 Broussolle, E., Gobert, F., Danaila, T., Thobois, S., Walusinski, O., Bogousslavsky, J. (2014), History of physical and 'moral' treatment of hysteria, *Frontiers of Neurology and Neuroscience* 35, 181–197

4 Charcot, J.-M. (1991), *Clinical Lectures on Diseases of the Nervous System*, Tavistock Classics, Routledge

5 Brian, K.M., Trent Jr, J.W. (eds) (2017), *Phallacies: Historical Intersections of Disability and Masculinity*, Oxford University Press

6 Milam, E.L., Nye, R.A. (2015), An introduction to scientific masculinities, *Osiris* 30, 1–14

7 Goldstein, J. (1982), The hysteria diagnosis and the politics of anti-clericalism in late nineteenth-century France, *Journal of Modern History* 54(2), 209–239

8 This has also led to extensive research in the area of social contagion. It is now understood that beliefs, attitudes, behaviour and emotions can spread through populations as if they are infectious.

9 Micale, M.S. (2008), *Hysterical Men: The Hidden History of Male Nervous Illness*, Harvard University Press

10 Showalter, E. (1993), 'Hysteria, Feminism and Gender', in *Hysteria Beyond Freud*, University of California Press

11 Quoted in *A History of Virility*, Corbin, A., Courtine, J.-J., Vigarello, G. (eds), trans. Cohen, K., Columbia University Press, 2016

12 Stearns, P.N., Stearns, C.Z. (1985), Emotionology: Clarifying the history of emotions and emotional standards, *American Historical Review* 90(4), 813–836

13 Reddy, W.M. (1997), Against constructionism: The historical ethnography of emotions, *Current Anthropology* 38, 327–351

14 Lewis, J. (2020), Emotional rescue: The emotional turn in the study of history, *Journal of Interdisciplinary History* 51(1), 121–129

15 Lewis, J. (2020), Emotional rescue: The emotional turn in the study of history, *Journal of Interdisciplinary History* 51(1), 121–129

16 Boquet, D., Nagy, P., trans. Shaw, R. (2018), *Medieval Sensibilities: A History of Emotions in the Middle Ages*, Polity Press

CHAPTER 9. SUGAR AND SPICE (IT ALL STARTS HERE)

1 Southey, R. (*c*.1820), 'What are little boys made of?', 821, Roud Folk Song Index, a collection of over 25,000 poems and songs collected from the English oral tradition by UK librarian Steve Roud

2 Zschoche, S. (1989), Dr Clarke revisited: Science, true womanhood, and female collegiate education, *History of Education Quarterly* 29(4), 545–569

3 Clarke, E.H. (1873), *Sex in Education, or a Fair Chance for Girls*: http://hdl.handle.net/10427/000019

4 La Barbera, J.D., Izard, C.E., Vietze, P., Parisi, S.A. (1976), Four- and six-month-old infants' visual responses to joy, anger, and neutral expressions, *Child Development* 47(2), 535–538

5 Walker-Andrews, A.S., Lennon, E. (1991), Infants' discrimination of vocal expressions: Contributions of auditory and visual information, *Infant Behavior and Development* 14(2), 131–142

6 Malatesta-Magai, C., Leak, S., Tesman, J., Shepard, B., Culver, C., Smaggia, B. (1994), Profiles of emotional development: Individual differences in facial and vocal expression of emotion during the second and third years of life, *International Journal of Behavioral Development* 17, 239–269

7 Malatesta, C.Z., Wilson, A. (1988), Emotion cognition interaction in personality development: A discrete emotions functionalist analysis, *British Journal of Social Psychology* 27, 91–112

8 Unless we are living in a global pandemic and lockdown.

REFERENCES

9 Sax, L. (2005), *Why Gender Matters: What Parents and Teachers Need to Know About the Emerging Science of Sex Differences*, Doubleday

10 Liberman, M., 22 August 2006, Leonard Sax on hearing <http://itre.cis.upenn.edu/~myl/languagelog/archives/003487.html>

11 Meier, P.M., Reinagel, P. (2013), Rats and humans differ in processing collinear visual features, *Frontiers in Neural Circuits* 7, 197

12 Leonard Sax suggests that girls and boys learn differently, that they draw differently, and like completely different things even before they can understand the world around them. He proposed that girls and boys should not be taught together.

13 Killgore, W.D., Oki, M., Yurgelun-Todd, D.A. (2001), Sex-specific developmental changes in amygdala responses to affective faces, *Neuroreport* 12(2), 427–433

14 Bandura, A. (1962), Social learning through imitation, in M.R. Jones (ed.), *Nebraska Symposium on Motivation, 1962*, University of Nebraska Press, 211–274

15 There are some limitations to this theory, as change in environment does not always mean behaviour would change too.

16 Much like many 1960s experiments with children, this is also quite controversial in terms of ethics and child protection.

17 Bandura, A. (1965), Influence of models' reinforcement contingencies on the acquisition of imitative responses, *Journal of Personality and Social Psychology* 1(6), 589–595

18 Although it is really the *gender* identity that shapes these perceptions. According to the American Association of Psychology, 'sex-typing', or the preferred 'gender-typing', is the process by which particular activities are identified within particular cultures as appropriate expressions of maleness and femaleness.

19 Bem, S.L. (1981), Gender schema theory: A cognitive account of sex typing, *Psychological Review* 88(4), 354–364

20 It seems that the phrase originated sometime around 1589 in English, from a Latin proverb, 'Children will be children and will do childish things', but over the years has morphed into something that excuses rough and violent behaviour by insinuating that boys/men are hardwired to act in an aggressive manner.

21 Schmidt, M., Tomasello, M. (2012), Young children enforce social norms, *Current Directions in Psychological Science* 21, 232–236

22 Bem, S.L. (1993), *The Lenses of Gender: Transforming the Debate on Sexual Inequality*, Yale University Press.

23 Stern, M., Karraker, K.H. (1989), Sex stereotyping of infants, *Sex Roles: A Journal of Research* 20(9–10), 501–522

24 Berndt, T., Heller, K. (1986), Gender stereotypes and social inferences: A developmental study, *Journal of Personality and Social Psychology* 50, 889–898

25 Archer, J., Lloyd, B. (1985), *Sex and Gender*, Cambridge University Press

26 Lewis, M., Weinraub, M. (1979), Origins of early sex-role development, *Sex Roles: A Journal of Research* 5(2), 135–153

27 Rubin, J., Provenzano, F., Luria, Z. (2010), The eye of the beholder: Parents' views on sex of newborns, *American Journal of Orthopsychiatry* 44, 512–519

28 Sweeney, J., Bradbard, M.R. (1988), Mothers' and fathers' changing perceptions of their male and female infants over the course of pregnancy, *Journal of Genetic Psychology* 149(3), 393–404

29 Haugh, S., Hoffman, C., Cowan, G. (1980), The eye of the very young beholder: Sex typing of infants by young children, *Child Development* 51(2), 598–600

30 Much of our discourse and research is based in a gender binary. In many cultures this is not the case.

31 Deaux, K., Major, B. (1987), Putting gender into context: An interactive model of gender-related behavior, *Psychological Review* 94, 369–389

32 Underwood, M.K. (2007), Gender and children's friendships: Do girls' and boys' friendships constitute different peer cultures, and what are the trade-offs for development? *Merrill-Palmer Quarterly* 53(3), 319–324

33 Martin, C.L., Fabes, R.A. (2001), The stability and consequences of young children's same-sex peer interactions, *Developmental Psychology* 37(3), 431–446

34 Rose, A.J., Rudolph, K.D. (2006), A review of sex differences in peer relationship processes: Potential trade-offs for the emotional and behavioral development of girls and boys, *Psychological Bulletin* 132(1), 98–131

35 Many of these studies do not mention non-binary children, although from hearsay often children do not express non-binary identities until they are much older, or unless they have been brought up in this way.

36 Maccoby, E.E., Jacklin, C.N. (1974), *The Psychology of Sex Differences*, Stanford University Press

37 Else-Quest, N.M., Hyde, J.S., Goldsmith, H.H., Van Hulle, C.A. (2006), Gender differences in temperament: A meta-analysis, *Psychological Bulletin* 132(1), 33–72

38 Hall, J.A., Halberstadt, A.G. (1986), Smiling and gazing, in J.S. Hyde, M.C. Linn (eds), *The Psychology of Gender: Advances Through Meta-Analysis*, Johns Hopkins University Press, 136–158

39 LaFrance, M., Hecht, M.A., Paluck, E.L. (2003), The contingent smile: A meta-analysis of sex differences in smiling, *Psychological Bulletin* 129(2), 305–334

40 Zeman, J., Garber, J. (1996), Display rules for anger, sadness, and pain: It depends on who is watching, *Child Development* 67(3), 957–973

41 Kring, A.M., Gordon, A.H. (1998), Sex differences in emotion: Expression, experience, and physiology, *Journal of Personality and Social Psychology* 74(3), 686–703

42 Self-reported survey of employees conducted by the US dental company Byte: http://www.byteme.com/womens-experiences

43 LaFrance, M., Hecht, M.A., Paluck, E.L. (2003), The contingent smile: A meta-analysis of sex differences in smiling, *Psychological Bulletin* 129(2), 305–334

44 China, Germany, Mexico, Norway, Poland, Republic of South Africa and USA

45 Krys, K., Hansen, K., Xing, C., Espinosa, A.D., Szarota, P., Morales, M.F. (2015), It is better to smile to women: Gender modifies perception of honesty of smiling individuals across cultures, *International Journal of Psychology* 50(2), 150–154

46 Kawamura, S., Kageyama, K. (2006), Smiling faces rated more feminine than serious faces in Japan, *Perceptual and Motor Skills* 103(1), 210–4

47 Kawamura, S., Komori, M., Miyamoto, Y. (2008), Smiling reduces masculinity: Principal component analysis applied to facial images, *Perception* 37(11), 1637–1648

48 Dodd, D., Russell, B., Jenkins, C. (1999), Smiling in school yearbook photos: Gender differences from kindergarten to adulthood, *Psychological Record* 49(4), 543–554

49 Nielson, M.G., Schroeder, K.M., Martin, C.L. et al. (2020), Investigating the relation between gender typicality and pressure to conform to gender norms, *Sex Roles* 83, 523–535

50 Brooke, E.D., Pruchniewska, U. (2017), Gender and self-enterprise in the social media age: A digital double bind, *Information, Communication and Society* 20:6, 843–859

51 Butkowski, C.P., Dixon, T.L., Weeks, K.R., Smith, M.A. (2020), Quantifying the feminine self(ie): Gender display and social media feedback in young women's Instagram selfies, *New Media & Society* 22(5), 817–837

52 See for instance Huda Beauty on YouTube (accessed March 2022) <https://www.youtube.com/watch?v=eAw8_xtX8tc>

53 Root, A., Rubin, K. (2010), Gender and parents' reactions to children's emotion during the preschool years, *New Directions for Child and Adolescent Development* 128, 51–64

54 Van der Pol, L.D., Groeneveld, M.G., van Berkel, S.R., Endendijk, J.J., Hallers-Haalboom, E.T., Bakermans-Kranenburg, M.J., Mesman, J. (2015), Fathers' and mothers' emotion talk with their girls and boys from toddlerhood to preschool age, *Emotion* 15(6), 854–864

55 Aznar, A., Tenenbaum, H.R. (2015), Gender and age differences in parent-child emotion talk, *British Journal of Developmental Psychology* 33(1), 148–55

56 Mascaro, J., Rentscher, K., Hackett, P., Mehl, M., Rilling, J. (2017), Child gender influences paternal behavior, language, and brain function, *Behavioral Neuroscience* 131, 262–273

57 Root, A., Rubin, K.H. (2010), Gender and parents' reactions to children's emotion during the preschool years, *New Directions for Child and Adolescent Development* 128, 51–64

58 Zahn-Waxler, C., Klimes-Dougan, B., Slattery, M.J. (2000), Internalizing problems of childhood and adolescence: Prospects, pitfalls, and progress in understanding the development of anxiety and depression, *Development and Psychopathology* 12(3), 443–466

59 Veijalainen, J., Reunamo, J., Heikkilä, M. (2019), Early gender differences in emotional expressions and self-regulation in settings of early childhood education and care, *Early Child Development and Care* 191(1), 173–186

60 Lewis, M. (1995), Self-conscious emotions, *American Scientist* 83(1), 68–78

61 Machery, E. (2010), Explaining why experimental behavior varies across cultures: A missing step in 'The weirdest people in the world?' *Behavioral and Brain Sciences* 33(2–3), 101

62 Henrich, J., Heine, S.J., Norenzayan, A. (2010), The weirdest people in the world? *Behavioral and Brain Sciences* 33(2–3), 61–83; discussion 83–135

63 Archer J. (2004), Sex differences in aggression in real-world settings: A meta-analytic review, *Review of General Psychology* 8, 291–322

64 Tsai, J.L., Louie, J.Y., Chen, E.E., Uchida, Y. (2007), Learning what feelings to desire: Socialization of ideal affect through children's storybooks, *Personality and Social Psychology Bulletin* 33(1), 17–30

65 Brody, L.R., Hall, J.A. (2008), Gender and emotion in context, in M. Lewis, J.M. Haviland-Jones, L.F. Barrett (eds), *Handbook of Emotions*, The Guilford Press, 395–408

66 Stanaland, A., Gaither S. (2021), 'Be a man': The role of social pressure in eliciting men's aggressive cognition, *Personality and Social Psychology Bulletin* 47(11), 1596–1611

67 Most studies have been conducted in urban areas, and there are limitations in generalising them to rural areas since there might be different societal pressures associated with masculinity there. Researchers also admitted that some boys who experience high pressure to be masculine at a young age might rebel and not conform to these display rules as they get older. There is not enough data on this just yet.

68 Maass, A., Cadinu, M., Guarnieri, G., Grasselli, A. (2003), Sexual harassment under social identity threat: The computer harassment paradigm, *Journal of Personality and Social Psychology* 85(5), 853–870

69 Bosson, J.K., Vandello, J.A. (2011), Precarious manhood and its links to action and aggression, *Current Directions in Psychological Science* 20(2), 82–86

70 Lansford, J.E. et al. (2012). Boys' and girls' relational and physical aggression in nine countries, *Aggressive Behavior* 38(4), 298–308

71 Namatame, H., Fujisato, H., Ito, M., Sawamiya, Y. (2020), Development and validation of a Japanese version of the emotion regulation questionnaire for children and adolescents, *Neuropsychiatric Disease and Treatment* 16, 209–219

72 The Children's Emotional Regulation Scale is an 18-item measure of emotion regulation for children, originally developed in Japan. The scale has a 3-factor structure: emotion inhibition (7 items, e.g., 'I often suppress

my anger'), difficulties concerning emotion regulation (6 items, e.g., 'I tend to lose my temper'), and coping with emotion regulation (5 items, e.g., 'When I am scared, I try to be with someone else'). Each item is rated using a 5-point scale (1 'strongly disagree' to 5 'strongly agree').

CHAPTER 10. PINK AND BLUE BRAINS

1   Davis, M., Whalen, P. (2001), The amygdala: Vigilance and emotion, *Molecular Psychiatry* 6(1), 13–34

2   Bowers, D., Heilman, K.M. (1984), A dissociation between the processing of affective and nonaffective faces: A case study, *Journal of Clinical Neuropsychology* 6, 367–384

3   Silberman, E.K., Weingartner, H. (1986), Hemispheric lateralization of functions related to emotion, *Brain and Cognition* 5(3), 322–353

4   Demaree, H.A., Everhart, D.E., Youngstrom, E.A., Harrison, D.W. (2005), Brain lateralization of emotional processing: Historical roots and a future incorporating 'dominance', *Behavioral and Cognitive Neuroscience Review* 4(1), 3–20

5   Lindquist, K.A., Wager, T.D., Kober, H., Bliss-Moreau, E., Barrett, L.F. (2012), The brain basis of emotion: A meta-analytic review, *Behavioral and Brain Sciences* 35(3), 121–143

6   Klüver, H., Bucy, P.C. (1937), 'Psychic blindness' and other symptoms following bilateral temporal lobectomy in Rhesus monkeys, *American Journal of Physiology* 119, 352–353

7   Bliss-Moreau, E., Moadab, G., Amaral, D.G. (2016), Lifetime consequences of early amygdala damage in rhesus monkeys, in D.G. Amaral and R. Adolphs (eds), *Living without an Amygdala*, The Guilford Press, 149–185

8   I have discussed a couple of examples of the links between amygdala damage and propensity to more risky behaviours in my book *Sway: Unravelling Unconscious Bias*, Bloomsbury, 2020

9   Feinstein, J.S., Adolphs, R., Tranel, D. (2016), A tale of survival from the world of patient S.M., in D.G. Amaral and R. Adolphs (eds), *Living without an Amygdala*, The Guilford Press, 1–38

10 Adolphs, R., Gosselin, F., Buchanan, T.W., Tranel, D., Schyns, P., Damasio, A.R. (2005), A mechanism for impaired fear recognition after amygdala damage, *Nature* 433, 68–72

11 Barrett, L.F. (2018), Seeing fear: It's all in the eyes?, *Trends in Neurosciences* 41(9), 559–563

12 Kawashima, R. et al. (1999), The human amygdala plays an important role in gaze monitoring: A PET study, *Brain* 122, 779–783

13 Cahill, L., Babinsky, R., Markowitsch, H.J., McGaugh, J.L. (1995), The amygdala and emotional memory, *Nature* 377, 295–296

14 Fontaine, J.R.J., Scherer, K.R., Roesch, E.B., Ellsworth, P.C. (2007), The world of emotions is not two-dimensional, *Psychological Science* 18(12), 1050–1057

15 Lettieri, G., Handjaras, G., Ricciardi, E. et al. (2019), Emotionotopy in the human right temporo-parietal cortex, *Nature Communications* 10(1), 5568

16 Kreibig, S. (2010), Autonomic nervous system activity in emotion: A review, *Biological Psychology* 84, 394–421

17 Hamann, S. (2012), Mapping discrete and dimensional emotions onto the brain: Controversies and consensus, *Trends in Cognitive Sciences* 16(9), 458–466

18 Lungu, O., Potvin, S., Tikàsz, A., Mendrek, A. (2015), Sex differences in effective fronto-limbic connectivity during negative emotion processing, *Psychoneuroendocrinology* 62, 180–188

19 Adkins-Regan, E. (2009), Neuroendocrinology of social behavior, *ILAR* 50(1), 5–14

20 Van Anders, S.M., Steiger, J., Goldey, K.L. (2015), Effects of gendered behavior on testosterone in women and men, *PNAS* 112(45), 13805–13810

21 Van Anders, S.M., Steiger, J., Goldey, K.L. (2015), Effects of gendered behavior on testosterone in women and men, *PNAS* 112(45), 13805–13810

22 McRae, K., Ochsner, K.N., Mauss, I.B., Gabrieli, J., Gross, J.J. (2008), Gender differences in emotion regulation: An fMRI study of cognitive reappraisal, *Group Processes & Intergroup Relations* 11(2), 143–162

23 Reappraisal is a technique to change the emotional meaning and impact of a highly charged emotional situation so that emotional experience and expression can be regulated.

24 Giuliani, N.R., Gross, J.J. (2009), Reappraisal, in D. Sander and K.R. Scherer (eds), *Oxford Companion to Emotion and the Affective Sciences*, Oxford University Press

25 Garnefski, N., Teerds, J., Kraaij, V., Legerstee, J., van den Kommer, T. (2004), Cognitive emotion regulation strategies and depressive symptoms:

Differences between males and females, *Personality and Individual Differences* 36, 267–276

26 Gard, M.G., Kring, A.M. (2007), Sex differences in the time course of emotion. *Emotion*, 2, 429–437.

27 Fine, C., Joel, D., Rippon, G. (2019), Eight things you need to know about sex, gender, brains, and behavior, *Scholar & Feminist Online* 15

28 Fine, C. (2013), Is there neurosexism in functional neuroimaging investigations of sex differences? *Neuroethics* 6(2), 369–409

29 Rippon, G., Eliot, L., Genon, S., Joel, D. (2021), How hype and hyperbole distort the neuroscience of sex differences, *PLoS Biology* 19(5), e3001253

30 Satterthwaite, T.D., Wolf, D.H., Roalf, D.R. et al. (2015), Linked sex differences in cognition and functional connectivity in youth, *Cereb Cortex* 25(9), 2383–2389

31 Fine, C., Joel, D., Rippon, G. (2019), Eight things you need to know about sex, gender, brains, and behavior, *Scholar & Feminist Online* 15

32 Joober, R., Schmitz, N., Annable, L., Boksa, P. (2012), Publication bias: What are the challenges and can they be overcome? *Journal of Psychiatry & Neuroscience* 37(3), 149–152

33 David, S.P. et al. (2018), Potential reporting bias in neuroimaging studies of sex differences, *Scientific Reports* 8(1), 6082

34 Shalev, G., Admon, R., Berman, Z., Joel, D. (2020), A mosaic of sex-related structural changes in the human brain following exposure to real-life stress, *Brain Structure and Function* 225(1), 461–466

35 Ingalhalikar, M., Smith, A., Parker, D. et al., and Verma, R. (2014), Sex differences in the structural connectome of the human brain, *PNAS* 111(2), 823–828

36 This study used diffusion tensor imaging (DTI), a water-based imaging technique that can trace and highlight the fibre pathways connecting the different regions of the brain, laying the foundation for a structural connectome or network of the whole brain.

37 Ingalhalikar, M., Smith, A., Parker, D. et al., and Verma, R. (2014), Sex differences in the structural connectome of the human brain, *PNAS* 111(2), 823–828

38 Fee, E. (1979), Nineteenth-century craniology: The study of the female skull, *Bulletin of the History of Medicine* 53(3), 415–33

39 Price, M. (2017), Study finds some significant differences in brains of men and women, *Science* <https://www.sciencemag.org/news/2017/04/study-finds-some-significant-differences-brains-men-and-women>

40 Joel, D., Berman, Z., Tavor, I. et al. (2015), Sex beyond the genitalia: The human brain mosaic, *PNAS* 112(50), 15468–15473

41 Bluhm, R. (2013), Self-fulfilling prophecies: The influence of gender stereotypes on functional neuroimaging research on emotion, *Hypatia* 28(4), 870–886

42 Fine, C. (2018), Feminist science: Who needs it? *Lancet* 392(10155), 1302–03

43 Fine, C. (2014), Neuroscience: His brain, her brain? *Science* 346(6212), 915–916

44 Gur, R.C., Gunning-Dixon, F., Bilker, W.B., Gur, R.E. (2002), Sex differences in temporo-limbic and frontal brain volumes of healthy adults, *Cerebral Cortex* 12(9), 998–1003

45 Fausto-Sterling, A. (2000), *Sexing the Body: Gender Politics and the Construction of Sexuality*, Basic Books

46 Daphna Joel says: 'Although it is possible to use one's brain architecture to predict whether this person is female or male with accuracy of ~80%, one's sex category provides very little information on the likelihood that one's brain architecture is similar to or different from someone else's brain architecture. This is because the brain types typical of females are also typical of males, and large sex differences are found only in the prevalence of some rare brain types.'

47 Lippa, R.A. (2005), *Gender, Nature, and Nurture* (2nd ed.), Routledge

48 Garcia-Falgueras, A., Swaab, D.F. (2008), A sex difference in the hypothalamic uncinate nucleus: Relationship to gender identity, *Brain* 131(12), 3132–3146

49 Barrett, L.F. (2018), The three big myths about emotions, gender, and brains, *Wired UK* <https://www.youtube.com/watch?v=9WFPBey02b0>

50 Kolb, B., Gibb, R. (2011), Brain plasticity and behaviour in the developing brain, *Journal of the Canadian Academy of Child and Adolescent Psychiatry* 20(4), 265–276

51 Tottenham N. (2017), The brain's emotional development, *Cerebrum*, cer-08-17

52 Gogtay, N., Giedd, J.N., Lusk, L. et al. (2004), Dynamic mapping of human cortical development during childhood through early adulthood, *PNAS* 101(21), 8174–8179

SECTION 4: CAN EMOTIONAL WOMEN GET AHEAD?

1 Plato, *The Republic*, trans. B. Jowett, Project Gutenberg, 1998.

CHAPTER 11. PITBULL WITH LIPSTICK

1 Dugan, A. (2018), Hillary Clinton's favorable rating still low, Gallup <https://news.gallup.com/poll/243242/snapshot-hillary-clinton-favorable-rating-low.aspx>

2 Pew Research Center (2016), In election's wake, partisans assess the state of their parties <https://www.pewresearch.org/politics/2016/12/20/in-elections-wake-partisans-assess-the-state-of-their-parties/>

3 Pew Research Center (2018), An examination of the 2016 electorate, based on validated voters <https://www.pewresearch.org/politics/2018/08/09/an-examination-of-the-2016-electorate-based-on-validated-voters/>

4 Levene, L., *New York Times*, 19 November 1916

5 'Congresswoman Rankin Real Girl; Likes Nice Gowns and Tidy Hair', *Washington Post*, 4 March 1917

6 *Boston Post*, 11 November 1916, quoted in T. Finneman, (2015), *Press Portrayals of Women Politicians, 1870s–2000s: From 'Lunatic' Woodhull to 'Polarizing' Palin*, Lexington Books

7 Yardley, W., *New York Times*, 29 August 2008

8 From Palin's speech to the 2008 Republican National Convention <https://www.youtube.com/watch?v=RjsGgTTIvnk>

9 Gibson, K.L., Heyse, A.L. (2010), 'The difference between a hockey mom and a pit bull': Sarah Palin's faux maternal persona and performance of hegemonic masculinity at the 2008 Republican National Convention, *Communication Quarterly* 58(3), 235–256

10 Dubois, B., Crouch, I. (1975), The question of tag questions in women's speech: They don't really use more of them, do they?, *Language in Society* 4(3), 289–294

11 I can't quote any data or stats for this. It's a more general impression, which could be because I am looking for this information to confirm my hypothesis, and my informal polls on Twitter could simply be a reflection of my echo chamber. Nevertheless, things have changed over the years. (We are of course talking about western nations primarily here, and these effects might be greater or insignificant in other parts of the world.)

12 Carli, L.L. (2002), Gender, interpersonal power, and social influence, *Journal of Social Issues* 55(1), 81–99

13 Bauer, N. (2015), Emotional, sensitive, and unfit for office? Gender stereotype activation and support female candidates, *Political Psychology* 36(6), 691–708

14 Shields, S.A. (2002), *Speaking from the Heart: Gender and the Social Meaning of Emotion*, Cambridge University Press

15 Newport, F. (2001), Americans see women as emotional and affectionate, men as more aggressive, Gallup <https://news.gallup.com/poll/1978/americans-see-women-emotional-affectionate-men-more-aggressive.aspx>

16 Dolan, K.A. (2014), *When Does Gender Matter? Women Candidates and Gender Stereotypes in American Elections*, Oxford University Press

17 In the UK, the equivalent would logically be the difference between Conservative and Labour voters, although a similar study has not been done.

18 Menasce Horowitz, J., Igielnik, R., Parker, K. (2018), Views on leadership traits and competencies and how they intersect with gender, Pew Research Center <https://www.pewresearch.org/social-trends/2018/09/20/2-views-on-leadership-traits-and-competencies-and-how-they-intersect-with-gender/>

19 From a total of 1,004 people polled in November 2014, Pew Research Center (2015), Women and leadership <https://www.pewresearch.org/social-trends/2015/01/14/women-and-leadership/> It would be interesting to see how much this has changed since Trump's presidency.

20 Carnevale, A.P., Smith, N., Peltier Campbell, K. (2019), May the best woman win? Education and bias against women in American politics, Georgetown University <https://cew.georgetown.edu/wp-content/uploads/Women_in_Politics.pdf>

21 The GSS is a regular, ongoing interview survey of households conducted across the USA by the National Opinion Research Center since 1972.

22 Pew Research Center (2015), Women and leadership <https://www.pew research.org/social-trends/2015/01/14/women-and-leadership/>

23 Maroon, E. (2010), Political InQueery: Policing Masculinity, *BitchMedia* <https://www.bitchmedia.org/post/political-inqueery-policing-masculinity>

24 Carnevale, A.P., Smith, N., Peltier Campbell, K. (2019), May the best woman win? Education and bias against women in American politics, Georgetown University <https://cew.georgetown.edu/wp-content/uploads/Women_in_Politics.pdf>

25 The GSS is a regular, ongoing interview survey of households conducted across the USA by the National Opinion Research Center since 1972.

26 Smith, J.S., Brescoll, V.L., Thomas, E.L. (2016), Constrained by emotion: Women, leadership, and expressing emotion in the workplace, in M.L. Connerley, J. Wu (eds), *Handbook On Well-Being of Working Women*, Springer, 209–224 <https://link.springer.com/book/10.1007/978-94-017-9897-6>

27 Schein, V.E., Mueller, R., Lituchy, T., Liu, J. (1996), Think manager – think male: A global phenomenon? *Journal of Organizational Behavior* 17(1), 33–41

28 Duehr, E., Bono, J. (2006), Men, women, and managers: Are stereotypes finally changing? *Personnel Psychology* 59, 815–846

29 Fischbach, A., Lichtenthaler, P.W., Horstmann, N. (2015), Leadership and gender stereotyping of emotions: Think manager – think male? *Journal of Personnel Psychology* 14, 153–162

30 Elsesser, K.M., Lever, J. (2011), Does gender bias against female leaders persist? Quantitative and qualitative data from a large-scale survey, *Human Relations* 64(12), 1555–1578

31 Greenberg Quinlan Rosner Research (2005), Voice of Mom survey, Roper Center for Public Opinion Research: http://www.ropercenter.uconn.edu/CFIDE/cf/action/ipoll/ipollBasket.cfm

32 McKinsey & Co. (2021), Women in the workplace <https://www.mckinsey.com/featured-insights/diversity-and-inclusion/women-in-the-workplace>

33 Catalyst (2022), Women CEOs of the S&P 500 <https://www.catalyst.org/research/women-ceos-of-the-sp-500/>

34 Rajagopal, D. (2019), It's assumed women are too soft, emotional or hysterical for leadership roles: Julia Gillard, *Economic Times* <https://economictimes.indiatimes.com/magazines/panache/>

its-assumed-women-are-too-soft-emotional-or-hysterical-for-leadership-roles-julia-gillard/articleshow/67861237.cms>

35 Scherer, K.R., Wallbott, H.G. (1994), Evidence for universality and cultural variation of differential emotion response patterning, *Journal of Personality and Social Psychology* 66(2), 310–328

36 Fischer, A.H., Rodriguez Mosquera, P.M., van Vianen, A.E., Manstead, A.S. (2004), Gender and culture differences in emotion, *Emotion* 4(1), 87–94

37 Gerdes, Z.T., Levant, R.F. (2018), Complex relationships among masculine norms and health/well-being outcomes: Correlation patterns of the conformity to masculine norms inventory subscales, *American Journal of Men's Health* 12(2), 229–240

38 See a longer discussion of in-group/out-group membership and prejudice in my book *Sway: Unravelling Unconscious Bias,* Bloomsbury 2020

39 Warner, L. (2007), Delegitimization and women's perceived emotionality: 'Don't be so emotional!' doctoral thesis, Pennsylvania State University <https://etda.libraries.psu.edu/files/final_submissions/3817>

40 Abbink, K., Harris, D. (2019), In-group favouritism and out-group discrimination in naturally occurring groups, *PLoS One* 14(9)

41 Paladino, M., Leyens, J.-P., Rodriguez, R., Rodríguez, A., Gaunt, R., Demoulin, S. (2002), Differential association of uniquely and non uniquely human emotions with the ingroup and the outgroup, *Group Processes & Intergroup Relations* 5(2), 105–117

42 Cuddy, A., Rock, M., Norton, M. (2007), Aid in the aftermath of Hurricane Katrina: Inferences of secondary emotions and intergroup helping, *Group Processes & Intergroup Relations* 10, 107–118

43 In this particular study, it was seen that Black and white survivors of the hurricane infra-humanised white survivors more. The researchers attributed this to the growing awareness around racism during the time of the hurricane, which could have temporarily sensitised white people and raised concerns about appearing racist.

44 Vaes, J., Paladino, M., Leyens, J.-P. (2003), The lost e-mail: Prosocial reactions induced by uniquely human emotions, *British Journal of Social Psychology* 41(4), 521–34

45 Hatfield, E., Cacioppo, J.T., Rapson, R.L. (1994), *Emotional Contagion*, Cambridge University Press

46 Day, T.E. (2015), The big consequences of small biases: A simulation of peer review, *Research Policy* 44(6), 1266–1270

47 'Hegemonic masculinity' as a term first emerged in the 1980s and has come to mean the dominant ideal of manhood and the social construct of masculinity that makes men the norm and promotes men's domin- ance over women. Because masculine norms in our social institutions are accepted without question, they are just believed to be how the world works.

CHAPTER 12. UNHINGED: ANGER, POWER AND STATUS

1 Rebhun, L. (2004), Sexuality, color, and stigma among Northeast Brazilian women, *Medical Anthropology Quarterly* 18(2), 183–199

2 Frye, M. (1983), A note on anger, in M. Frye, *The Politics of Reality: Essays in Feminist Theory*, Crossing Press

3 Audi, R. (2009), The place of testimony in the fabric of knowledge and justification, in R. Neta, D. Pritchard (eds), *Arguing About Knowledge*, Routledge, 386–401

4 Fisher, R., Dubé, L. (2005), Gender differences in responses to emotional advertising: A social desirability perspective, *Journal of Consumer Research* 31(4), 850–858

5 Becker, D., Kenrick, D., Neuberg, S.L., Blackwell, K.C., Smith, D.M. (2007), The confounded nature of angry men and happy women, *Journal of Personality and Social Psychology* 92(2), 179–190

6 Taylor, S.E., Klein, L.C., Lewis, B.P. et al. (2000), Biobehavioral responses to stress in females: Tend-and-befriend, not fight-or-flight, *Psychological Review* 107(3), 411–429

7 Kring, A. (2000), Gender and anger, in A. Fischer (ed.), *Gender and Emotion: Social Psychological Perspectives*, Cambridge University Press, 211–231

8 Campbell, A., Muncer, S. (1987), Models of anger and aggression in the social talk of women and men, *Journal for the Theory of Social Behaviour* 17(4), 489–511

9 Barrett, L.F., Bliss-Moreau, E. (2009), She's emotional. He's having a bad day: attributional explanations for emotion stereotypes, *Emotion* 9(5), 649–658

10 Krull, D.S. (1993), Does the grist change the mill? The effect of the perceiver's inferential goal on the process of social inference, *Personality and Social Psychology Bulletin* 19(3), 340–348

11 University of California (2000), Comparison of anger expression in men and women reveals surprising differences, *ScienceDaily*, 31 January 2000. <www.sciencedaily.com/releases/2000/01/000131075609/.htm>

12 Campbell, A., Muncer, S. (1987), Models of anger and aggression in the social talk of women and men, *Journal for the Theory of Social Behaviour* 17(4), 489–511

13 Miller, J., Zilbach, J., Notman, M., Nadelson, C. (1985), The construction of anger in women and men, *Working Paper No. 4*, Wellesley Centers for Women

14 Sullivan, K., Reston, M. (2019), Only the women ask for forgiveness at the Democratic presidential debate, *CNN Politics*, 20 December 2019 <https://edition.cnn.com/2019/12/20/politics/women-apologize-democratic-debate/index.html>

15 Clymer, A. (2001), Book says Nixon considered a woman for the Supreme Court, *New York Times*, 27 September 2001 <https://www.nytimes.com/2001/09/27/us/book-says-nixon-considered-a-woman-for-supreme-court.html>

16 Eagly, A.H. (1997), Sex differences in social behavior: Comparing social role theory and evolutionary psychology, *American Psychologist* 52(12), 1380–1383

17 Brescoll, V.L., Uhlmann, E.L. (2008), Can an angry woman get ahead? Status conferral, gender, and expression of emotion in the workplace, *Psychological Science* 19(3), 268–275

18 Brescoll, V.L., Uhlmann, E.L. (2008), Can an angry woman get ahead? Status conferral, gender, and expression of emotion in the workplace, *Psychological Science* 19(3), 268–275

19 Spielberger, C.D., Johnson, E.H., Russell, S.F., Crane, R.J., Jacobs, G.A., Worden, T.I. (1985), The experience and expression of anger: Construction and validation of an anger expression scale, in M.A. Chesney and R.H. Rosenman (eds), *Anger and Hostility in Cardiovascular and Behavioral Disorders*, Hemisphere/McGraw-Hill, 5–30

20 Moura, K., Troth, A.C., Jordan, P.J. (2015), Crossing the impropriety

threshold: A study of experiences of excessive anger, in C.E.J. Härtel, W.J. Zerbe and N.M. Ashkanasy (eds), *New Ways of Studying Emotions in Organizations*, Emerald Group Publishing, 369–395

21 Moura, K., Troth, A.C., Jordan, P.J. (2015), Crossing the impropriety threshold: A study of experiences of excessive anger, in C.E.J. Härtel, W.J. Zerbe and N.M. Ashkanasy (eds), *New Ways of Studying Emotions in Organizations*, Emerald Group Publishing, 369–395

22 Bell, M. (2005), A woman's scorn: Toward a feminist defense of contempt as a moral emotion, *Hypatia* 20(4), 80–93

23 Trivers, R.L. (1985), *Social Evolution*, the Benjamin/Cummings Publishing Co.

24 Sidanius, J., Pratto, F. (2004), Social dominance theory: A new synthesis, in J.T. Jost and J. Sidanius (eds), *Political Psychology: Key Readings*, Psychology Press, 315–332

25 Chaplin T.M. (2015), Gender and emotion expression: A developmental contextual perspective, *Emotion Review* 7(1), 14–21

26 Yun, D., Jung, H., Ashihara, K. (2020), Dimensions of leader anger expression unveiled: How anger intensity and gender of leader and observer affect perceptions of leadership effectiveness and status conferral, *Frontiers in Psychology* 11, 1237

27 Tiedens, L.Z. (2001), Anger and advancement versus sadness and subjugation: The effect of negative emotion expressions on social status conferral, *Journal of Personality and Social Psychology* 80(1), 86–94

28 Kanter, R.M. (1993), *Men and Women of the Corporation*, Basic Books

29 James, E.H. (2000), Race-related differences in promotions and support: Underlying effects of human and social capital, *Organization Science* 11(5), 493–508

30 King, D.K. (1988), Multiple jeopardy, multiple consciousness: The context of Black feminist ideology, *Signs* 14(1), 42–72

31 Perkins, L.M. (1983), The impact of the 'cult of true womanhood' on the education of Black women, *Journal of Social Issues* 39, 17–28

32 Settles, I.H., Pratt-Hyatt, J.S., Buchanan, N.T. (2008), Through the lens of race: Black and white women's perceptions of womanhood, *Psychology of Women Quarterly* 32(4), 454–468

33 Motro, D., Evans, J.B., Ellis, A.P.J., Benson III, L. (2022), Race and reactions

to women's expressions of anger at work: Examining the effects of the 'angry Black woman' stereotype, *Journal of Applied Psychology* 107(1), 142–152

34 Sapphire was first introduced as a character on the radio show *Amos and Andy*, and then in other television programmes where she would often be seen to be emasculating male characters.

35 Liptak, K. (2016), Michelle Obama says 'angry Black woman' label rooted in fear, *CNN Politics*, 20 December 2016 <https://edition.cnn.com/2016/12/19/politics/michelle-obama-oprah-angry-black-woman/index.html>

36 Brittney Cooper: How has time been stolen from people of color? *TED Radio Hour*, 29 March 2019 <https://www.npr.org/2019/03/29/707189797/brittney-cooper-how-has-time-been-stolen-from-people-of-color?t=1642015525599>

37 Lewis, J.A., Neville, H.A. (2015), Construction and initial validation of the Gendered Racial Microaggressions Scale for Black women, *Journal of Counseling Psychology* 62(2), 289–302

38 Motro, D., Evans, J.B., Ellis, A.P.J., Benson III, L. (2022), Race and reactions to women's expressions of anger at work: Examining the effects of the 'angry Black woman' stereotype, *Journal of Applied Psychology* 107(1), 142–152

39 Hazlewood, J. (2002), Anger: In black & white: a meta analysis, Masters thesis, Eastern Illinois University, 1436 <https://thekeep.eiu.edu/theses/1436>

40 Toosi, N.R., Mor, S., Semnani-Azad, Z., Phillips, K.W., Amanatullah, E.T. (2018), Who can lean in? The intersecting role of race and gender in negotiations, *Psychology of Women Quarterly* 43(1), 7–21

41 Rankin, K. (2016), How Erica Garner inspired the #LoudBlackGirls hashtag, *Colorlines*, 15 July 2016 <https://www.colorlines.com/tags/loudblackgirls>

42 Marshburn, C.K., Cochran, K.J., Flynn, E., Levine, L.J. (2020), Workplace anger costs women irrespective of race, *Frontiers in Psychology* 11, 579884

43 Crenshaw, K.W. (2017), *On Intersectionality: Essential Writings*, The New Press

44 Crenshaw, K.W. (2017), *On Intersectionality: Essential Writings*, The New Press

45 Lorde, A. (1984), Eye to eye: Black women, hatred, and anger, in A. Lorde, *Sister Outsider: Essays and Speeches*, The Crossing Press

46 McCormick-Huhn, K., Shields, S.A. (2021), Favorable evaluations of Black and white women's workplace anger during the era of #MeToo, *Frontiers in Psychology* 12, 594260

47 Tarana started the #MeToo movement to help survivors of sexual violence heal. In 2006, Burke began using #MeToo to help other women with similar experiences to stand up for themselves.

48 For example, in the UK Vicky Featherstone, artistic director of the Royal Court, curated *Snatches: Moments from Women's Lives*, a series of monologues for BBC4 with an all-woman lineup, and Katie Arnstein performed her solo show *Sexy Lamp* at the Edinburgh Fringe. In the USA, *The Pussy Grabber Plays* were a series of monologues inspired by the stories of women who had accused Donald Trump of sexual assault or harassment.

49 Carlin, S. (2017), Uma Thurman is seriously angry about sexual misconduct in Hollywood, *Yahoo Life*, 4 November 2017 <https://www.yahoo.com/lifestyle/uma-thurman-seriously-angry-sexual-214500420.html>

50 McGowan, R. (2018), *Brave*, HQ Publishing

51 McCormick-Huhn, K., Shields, S. (2021), Favorable evaluations of Black and white women's workplace anger during the era of #MeToo, *Frontiers in Psychology* 12, 594260

52 Riedel, S. (2019), On transfeminine anger, in L. Dancyger (ed.), *Burn It Down: Women Writing About Anger*, Seal Press <https://www.salon.com/2019/10/10/on-transfeminine-anger-burn-it-down-excerpt/>

53 Stryker, S. (1994), My words to Victor Frankenstein above the village of Chamounix: Performing transgender rage, *GLQ: A Journal of Lesbian and Gay Studies* 1(3), 237–254

54 Twitter conversation with the author, 28 October 2021

55 Serano, J. (2016), *Whipping Girl: A Transsexual Woman on Sexism and the Scapegoating of Femininity*, Seal Press

56 Malatino, H. (2018), Tough breaks: Trans rage and the cultivation of resilience, *Hypatia* 34(1), 121–140

57 Buttaro, A. (2012), More than meets the eye: An ecological perspective on homophobia within the Black America, *Black Women, Gender and Families* 6(1), 1–22

58 Giordano, S. (2018), Understanding the emotion of shame in transgender individuals – some insight from Kafka, *Life Sciences, Society and Policy* 14, 23

59 Zimbardo, P.G., Maslach, C., Haney, C. (2000), Reflections on the Stanford prison experiment: Genesis, transformations, consequences, in Blass, T. (ed.), *Obedience to Authority: Current Perspectives on the Milgram Paradigm*, Lawrence Erlbaum, 193–237

60 Zimbardo, P.G. (1973), The mind is a formidable jailer: A Pirandellian prison, *New York Times Magazine*, 8 April 1973 <https://www.nytimes.com/1973/04/08/archives/a-pirandellian-prison-the-mind-is-a-formidable-jailer.html>

61 Toppo, G. (2018), Time to dismiss the Stanford Prison Experiment, *Inside Higher Ed*, 20 June 2018 <https://www.insidehighered.com/news/2018/06/20/new-stanford-prison-experiment-revelations-question-findings>

62 Salerno, J.M., Peter-Hagene, L.C. (2015), One angry woman: Anger expression increases influence for men, but decreases influence for women, during group deliberation, *Law and Human Behavior* 39(6), 581–592

63 Salerno, J.M., Peter-Hagene, L.C., Jay, A.C.V. (2019), Women and African Americans are less influential when they express anger during group decision making, *Group Processes & Intergroup Relations* 22(1), 57–79

64 Aarts, H., Ruys, K.I., Veling, H. et al. (2010), The art of anger: Reward context turns avoidance responses to anger-related objects into approach, *Psychological Science* 21(10), 1406–1410

65 Brambilla, M., Sacchi, S., Castellini, F., Riva, P. (2010), The effects of status on perceived warmth and competence, *Social Psychology* 41(2), 82–87

66 Acker, J. (1990), Hierarchies, jobs, bodies: A theory of gendered organizations, *Gender & Society* 4(2), 139–158

67 Srinivasan, A. (2018), The aptness of anger, *Journal of Political Philosophy* 26(2), 123–144

68 Zwerdling, A. (1983), Anger and conciliation in Woolf's feminism, *Representations* 3, 68–89

CHAPTER 13. CRY-BABY, WAILING BANSHEE

1 Alexander, B. (2011), Stop the waterworks, ladies. Crying chicks aren't sexy, *NBC News*, 6 January 2011 <https://www.nbcnews.com/health/body-odd/stop-waterworks-ladies-crying-chicks-arent-sexy-flna1C6437342>

2 Vingerhoets, A.J.J.M., Boelhouwer, J.W., van Tilburg, M.A.L., vanHeck, G.L. (2001), The situational and emotional context of adult crying, in

A.J.J.M. Vingerhoets, R.R. Cornelius (eds), *Adult Crying: A Biopsychosocial Approach*, Brunner-Routledge, 71–91

3 Vingerhoets, A., Bylsma, L. (2007), Crying and health: Popular and scientific conceptions, *Psihologijske Teme* 16

4 Kottler, J.A., Montgomery, M.J. (2001), Theories of crying, in A.J.J.M. Vingerhoets, R.R. Cornelius (eds), *Adult Crying: A Biopsychosocial Approach*, Taylor & Francis, 1–18

5 University of Florida (2007), No faking it, crocodile tears are real, *ScienceDaily* <https://www.sciencedaily.com/releases/2007/10/071003151131.htm>

6 Breuer, J., Freud, S. (1895), *Studies in Hysteria*, trans. N. Luckhurst, Penguin Books, 2004

7 Frey, W.H., Langseth, M. (1985), *Crying: The Mystery of Tears*, Winston Press

8 Green-Church, K.B., Nichols, K.K., Kleinholz, N.M., Zhang, L., Nichols, J.J. (2008), Investigation of the human tear film proteome using multiple proteomic approaches, *Molecular Vision* 14, 456–470

9 Fleming, A.S., Corter, C., Stallings, J., Steiner, M. (2002), Testosterone and prolactin are associated with emotional responses to infant cries in new fathers, *Hormones and Behavior* 42(4), 399–413

10 Damasio, A.R., Grabowski, T.J., Bechara, A., Damasio, H., Ponto, L.L.B., Parvizi, J., Hichwa, R.D. (2000), Subcortical and cortical brain activity during the feeling of self-generated emotions, *Nature Neuroscience* 3, 1049–1056

11 Cornelius, R.R., Nussbaum, R., Warner, L.R., Moeller, C. (2000), 'An action full of meaning and of real service': The social and emotional messages of crying, paper presented at the 11th conference of the International Society for Research on Emotions, Quebec, Canada

12 Women cry more than men and for longer, *Telegraph*, 15 October 2009 <https://www.telegraph.co.uk/news/newstopics/howaboutthat/6334107/Women-cry-more-than-men-and-for-longer-study-finds.html>

13 Vingerhoets, A.J.J.M., Cornelius, R.R., van Heck, G.L., Becht, M.C. (2000), Adult crying: A model and review of the literature, *Review of General Psychology* 4, 354–377

14 Shields, S.A., Crowley, J.C. (2000), Stereotypes of 'emotionality': The role of the target's racial ethnicity, status, and gender, in U. Hess and R. Kleck (chairs), *The influence of beliefs regarding men's and women's emotions on the perception and self-perception of emotions*, symposium conducted at the meeting

of the International Society for Research on Emotions, Quebec City, Canada

15 Homer, *Iliad*, trans. Robert Fagles, Penguin Books, 1998

16 Ávila, St. Teresa. (1577), *The Interior Castle: Or, The Mansions*, Forgotten Books

17 In his speech at the University of Santo Tomás, Manila, 18 January 2015

18 The Mahabharata of Krishna-Dwaipayana Vyasa

19 Capp, B. (2014), 'Jesus wept' but did the Englishman? Masculinity and emotion in early modern England, *Past & Present* 224(1), 75–108

20 Coward, B. (1991), *Oliver Cromwell: Profiles in Power*, Routledge

21 A Gallup survey from 2012 ranking daily emotional responses of any kind, showed Britain in the top half of emotional response – placed directly between Sweden and Greece; 93 of the 151 countries polled were reported to have fewer emotions daily than the British. Of course this poll wasn't gendered, but on a broader level it appears that the British do not consider themselves to be unemotional.

22 Doxiadis, E. (2012), *The Shackles of Modernity: Women, Property, and the Transition from the Ottoman Empire to the Greek State, 1750–1850*, Harvard University Press

23 Fox, K. (2004), The Kleenex® for Men Crying Game Report: A Study of Men and Crying, Social Issues Research Centre

24 I understand the sentiment and message behind this, but the gendered product branding makes me personally despair.

25 Former Chelsea football star cruelly mocks Andy Murray's tearful retirement, *tennis365.com*, 12 January 2019 <https://www.tennis365.com/tennis-news/former-chelsea-football-star-cruelly-mocks-andy-murrays-tearful-retirement/>

26 Gwegwe, S., Thiago: I was called a cry baby like Neymar, *futaa.com*, 14 October 2021 <https://futaa.com/ng/article/228061/thiago-i-was-called-a-cry-baby-like-neymar>

27 Wong, Y.J., Steinfeldt, J.A., LaFollette, J.R., Tsao, S.C. (2011), Men's tears: Football players' evaluations of crying behavior, *Psychology of Men & Masculinity* 12(4), 297–310

28 Mahalik, J.R., Locke, B.D., Ludlow, L.H., Diemer, M.A., Scott, R.P.J., Gottfried, M., Freitas, G. (2003), Development of the conformity to masculine norms inventory, *Psychology of Men & Masculinity* 4(1), 3–25

29 Piaget, J. (1959), *The Early Growth of Logic in the Child*, Routledge

30 Borke, H. (1971), Interpersonal perception of young children: Egocentrism or empathy? *Developmental Psychology* 5(2), 263–269

31 Messner, M.A. (1992), *Power at Play: Sports and the Problem of Masculinity*, Beacon Press

32 MacArthur, H.J. (2019), Beliefs about emotion are tied to beliefs about gender: The case of men's crying in competitive sports, *Frontiers in Psychology* 10, 2765

33 Fox, K. (2004), The Kleenex® for Men Crying Game Report: A Study of Men and Crying, Social Issues Research Centre

34 Gyngell, K. (2016), Admit it, no woman can find a man who cries attractive, *Daily Mail*, 24 March 2016 <https://www.dailymail.co.uk/femail/article-3506718/Admit-no-woman-man-cries-attractive-today-s-men-weep-drop-hat-isn-t-sexy.html>

35 Posted 10 January 2022 by @evelynharlow_

36 From a Twitter poll, November 2021

37 Frey, W., Hoffman-Ahern, C., Johnson, R.A., Lykken, D.T., Tuason, V.B. (1983), Crying behavior in the human adult, *Integrative Psychiatry* 1, 94–100

38 It is interesting that the number of men was so low compared to the number of women, and that perhaps also says something about the nature of gendered attitudes and beliefs about crying. Since these were volunteers, it is likely that men did not wish to be part of an experimental study focused on crying, since they did not see it as a manly thing. Or it is possible that men do not naturally volunteer as much as women. Both intriguing possibilities.

39 Vingerhoets, A., Bylsma, L.M. (2016), The riddle of human emotional crying: a challenge for emotion researchers, *Emotion Review* 8(3), 207–217

40 The set of rules in specific domains about which emotions are more acceptable than others.

41 Buss, D.M., Gomes, M., Higgins, D.S., Lauterbach, K. (1987), Tactics of manipulation, *Journal of Personality and Social Psychology* 52(6), 1219–1229

42 Shakespeare, *Othello* IV. i

43 British Science Association (2021), *Inquiry on Equity in STEM Education*

44 United States Census Bureau (2021), Women are nearly half of US workforce but only 27% of STEM workers <https://www.census.gov/library/

stories/2021/01/women-making-gains-in-stem-occupations-but-still-underrepresented.html>

45 Labott, S.M., Martin, R.B., Eason, P.S., and Berkey, E.Y. (1991), Social reactions to the expression of emotion, *Cognition and Emotion* 5(5–6), 397–419

46 Gray, S.M., Heatherington, L. (2003), The importance of social context in the facilitation of emotional expression in men, *Journal of Social and Clinical Psychology* 22(3), 294–314

47 Cummings, B.S. (1977), *Hew Against the Grain*, Simon and Schuster

48 Lewis, K.M. (2000), When leaders display emotion: How followers respond to negative emotional expression of male and female leaders, *Journal of Organizational Behavior* 21, 221–229

49 Moore, S. (2019), Theresa May saved her tears for herself, *The Guardian*, 24 May 2019 <https://www.theguardian.com/commentisfree/2019/may/24/theresa-may-tears-humanity-sympathy-britain-broken>

50 Weinraub, B. (1987), Presidential politics: Are female tears saltier than male tears? *New York Times*, 30 September 1987 <https://www.nytimes.com/1987/09/30/us/washington-talk-presidential-politics-are-female-tears-saltier-than-male-tears.html>

51 Marcus, R. (2010), Cry, Boehner, cry, *Washington Post*, 15 December 2010

52 Gesualdi, M. (2013), Man tears and masculinities: News coverage of John Boehner's tearful episodes, *Journal of Communication Inquiry* 37(4), 304–321

53 Marcus, R. (2010), Cry, Boehner, cry, *Washington Post*, 15 December 2010

54 Weaver, J. (2011), Women's tears contain chemical cues, *Nature*

55 Mhlahlo, A.P. (2009), What is manhood? The significance of traditional circumcision in the Xhosa initiation ritual, PhD thesis, University of Stellenbosch

56 Wellenkamp, J.C. (1992), Variation in the social and cultural organization of emotions: The meaning of crying and the importance of compassion in Toraja, Indonesia, in D.D. Frank, V. Gecas (eds), *Social Perspectives on Emotion*, JAI Press, vol. 1, 189–216

57 Becht, M.C., Vingerhoets, A.J.J.M. (2002), Crying and mood change: A cross-cultural study, *Cognition and Emotion* 16(1), 87–101

58 Khosla, M. (2008), Psycho-physiological effects of emotional film stimuli,

paper presented at the Annual Conference of the Psychology Association of Daulat Ram College on Culture and Emotions, Delhi

59 Turner, J. (2010), The stratification of emotions: Some preliminary generalizations, *Sociological Inquiry* 80(2), 168–199

60 Becht, M.C., Vingerhoets, A.J.J.M. (2002), Crying and mood change: A cross-cultural study, *Cognition and Emotion* 16(1), 87–101

61 Sharman, L.S., Dingle, G.A., Baker, M. et al. (2019), The relationship of gender roles and beliefs to crying in an international sample, *Frontiers in Psychology* 10, 2288

62 Srivastava, S. (2006), Tears, fears and careers: Anti-racism and emotion in social movement organizations, *Canadian Journal of Sociology* 31(1), 55–90

63 Pearson, C. (2014), What 15 female leaders really think about crying at work, *Huffington Post*, 28 May 2014 <https://www.huffingtonpost.co.uk/entry/crying-at-work-women_n_5365872>

64 BBC *Woman's Hour*, 21 February 2022 <https://www.bbc.co.uk/sounds/play/m0014psl>

65 Elsbach, K., Bechky, B. (2017), How observers assess women who cry in professional work contexts, *Academy of Management Discoveries* 4(2)

66 Brooks, D.J. (2011), Testing the double standard for candidate emotionality: Voter reactions to the tears and anger of male and female politicians, *Journal of Politics* 73(2), 597–615

67 Stadel, M., Daniels, J.K., Warrens, M.J. et al. (2019), The gender-specific impact of emotional tears, *Motivation and Emotion* 43, 696–704

CHAPTER 14. DIFFICULT WOMEN, BRAVE MEN

1 Cartwright, L., Treichler, P., Penley, C. (eds) (1998), *The Visible Woman: Imaging Technologies, Gender, and Science*, NYU Press

2 The phrase was coined in 1991 by Dr Bernadine Healy in her paper 'The Yentl Syndrome', published in *The New England Journal of Medicine*

3 Johnson, P.A., Golman, L., Orav, E.J. (1996), Gender differences in the management of acute chest pain: Support for the 'Yentl Syndrome', *Journal of General Internal Medicine* 11(4), 209–217

4 Noel Bairey Merz, C. (2011), The Yentl syndrome is alive and well, *European Heart Journal* 32(11), 1313–1315

5   It is not entirely clear why women are more likely to be affected by these disorders. It has been attributed to the X-chromosome, with many of its genes involved in immune function, and higher levels of oestrogen, and lower levels of testosterone. See Sohn, E. (2021), Why autoimmunity is most common in women, *Nature* 595(7867), 51–53; Natri, H., Garcia, A.R., Buetow, K.H., Trumble, B.C., Wilson, M.A. (2019), The pregnancy pickle: Evolved immune compensation due to pregnancy underlies sex differences in human diseases, *Trends in Genetics* 35(7), 478–488

6   Sansone, R.A., Sansone, L.A. (2011), Gender patterns in borderline personality disorder, *Innovations in Clinical Neuroscience* 8(5), 16–20

7   *BMJ* Opinion (2020), Recommitting to women's health 25 years after the Beijing Platform for Action on Women <https://blogs.bmj.com/bmj/2020/10/27/recommitting-to-womens-health-25-years-after-the-beijing-platform-for-action-on-women-what-must-governments-do/>

8   Guze, S., Perley, M. (1964), Observations on the natural history of hysteria, *American Journal of Psychiatry* 119, 960–965

9   Jimenez, M.A. (1997), Gender and psychiatry: Psychiatric conceptions of mental disorders in women, 1960–1994, *Affilia* 12(2), 154–175

10 Slater, E. (1965), Diagnosis of 'hysteria', *British Medical Journal* 1(5447), 1395–1399

11 Lazare, A., Klerman, G. (1968), Hysteria and depression: The frequency and significance of hysterical personality features in hospitalized depressed women, *American Journal of Psychiatry* 124(11s), 48–56

12 Samulowitz, A., Gremyr, I., Eriksson, E., Hensing, G. (2018), 'Brave men' and 'emotional women': A theory-guided literature review on gender bias in health care and gendered norms towards patients with chronic pain, *Pain Research and Management* 25, 6358624

13 Crook, J., Tunks, E. (1990), Women in pain, in E. Tunks, A. Bellissimo, R. Roy (eds), *Chronic Pain: Psychosocial Factors in Rehabilitation*, Robert E. Krieger Publishing Co.

14 Ussher, J.M. (2013), Diagnosing difficult women and pathologising femininity: Gender bias in psychiatric nosology, *Feminism and Psychology* 23(1), 63–69

15 Wirth-Cauchon, J. (2001), *Women and Borderline Personality Disorder*, Rutgers University Press

16 Ussher, J.M. (2011), *The Madness of Women: Myth and Experience*, Routledge

17 Rickles, N.K. (1971), The angry woman syndrome, *Arch Gen Psychiatry*, 24(1), 91–4

18 Houck, J. (1972), The intractable female patient, *American Journal of Psychiatry* 129(1), 27–31

19 The Recovery Village (accessed 2022), Borderline personality disorder facts and statistics <https://www.therecoveryvillage.com/mental-health/border line-personality-disorder/related/bpd-statistics/>

20 King S. (2020), Premenstrual Syndrome (PMS) and the myth of the irrational female, in C. Bobel, I.T. Winkler, B. Fahs et al. (eds), *The Palgrave Handbook of Critical Menstruation Studies*, Palgrave Macmillan

21 Osborn, E., Wittkowski, A., Brooks, J. et al. (2020), Women's experiences of receiving a diagnosis of premenstrual dysphoric disorder: A qualitative investigation, *BMC Women's Health* 20, 242 <https://bmcwomenshealth. biomedcentral.com/articles/10.1186/s12905-020-01100-8>

22 Caplan, P. (1995), *They Say You're Crazy: How the World's Most Powerful Psychiatrists Decide Who's Normal*, Da Capo Press Inc.

23 Morrish, L. (2018), How severe PMS nearly stopped these women's careers in their tracks, *Refinery29* <https://www.refinery29.com/en-gb/pmdd-work-stories>

24 Lewis, T.T., Cogburn, C.D., Williams, D.R. (2015), Self-reported experiences of discrimination and health: Scientific advances, ongoing controversies, and emerging issues, *Annual Review of Clinical Psychology* 11, 407–440

25 Hardy, C., Hardie, J. (2017), Exploring premenstrual dysphoric disorder (PMDD) in the work context: A qualitative study, *Journal of Psychosomatic Obstetrics & Gynecology* 38(4), 292–300

26 Ussher, J.M., Hunter, M., Cariss, M.A. (2002), A woman-centred psychological intervention for premenstrual symptoms, drawing on cognitive-behavioural and narrative therapy, *Clinical Psychology and Psychotherapy* 9, 319–331

27 Ussher, J.M. (2004), Premenstrual syndrome and self-policing: Ruptures in self-silencing leading to increased self-surveillance and blaming of the body, *Social Theory and Health* 2(3), 49–62

28 Mayne, T. (2019), Overcoming period stigma in the workplace, DPG

<https://dpglearn.co.uk/blog/human-resources/overcoming-period-stigma-in-the-workplace/>

29 Collaborative Psychiatric Epidemiology Surveys (CPES), 2001–2003 (2016) <https://www.icpsr.umich.edu/web/ICPSR/search/studies?q=cpes>

30 Pilver, C.E., Desai, R., Kasl, S., Levy, B.R. (2011), Lifetime discrimination associated with greater likelihood of premenstrual dysphoric disorder, *Journal of Women's Health* 20(6), 923–931

31 Pascoe, E.A., Smart Richman, L. (2009), Perceived discrimination and health: A meta-analytic review, *Psychology Bulletin* 135(4), 531–554

32 Fassler, J. (2015), How doctors take women's pain less seriously, *Atlantic*, 15 October 2015 <https://www.theatlantic.com/health/archive/2015/10/emergency-room-wait-times-sexism/410515/>

33 National Women's Health Network (2018), How long do women wait to be seen in the ER? 17 January 2018 <https://nwhn.org/much-time-acceptable-spend-waiting-er-women-often-find-pain-circumstances-seen-exaggerated-doctors/>

34 Choi, K., Shofer, F.S., Mills, A.M. (2016), Sex differences in STEMI activation for patients presenting to the ED, *American Journal of Emergency Medicine* 34(10), 1939–1943

35 Gargano, J.W., Wehner, S., Reeves, M.J. (2009), Do presenting symptoms explain sex differences in emergency department delays among patients with acute stroke? *Stroke* 40(4), 1114–1120

36 The Brain Tumour Charity, Finding myself in your hands: The reality of brain tumour treatment and care <https://www.thebraintumourcharity.org/about-us/our-publications/finding-myself/>

37 Lyratzopoulos, G., Abel, G.A., McPhail, S. et al. (2013), Gender inequalities in the promptness of diagnosis of bladder and renal cancer after symptomatic presentation: Evidence from secondary analysis of an English primary care audit survey, *BMJ Open* 3, e002861

38 Din, N.U., Ukoumunne, O.C., Rubin, G. et al. (2015), Age and gender variations in cancer diagnostic intervals in 15 cancers: Analysis of data from the UK clinical practice research datalink, *PLoS One* 10(5), e0127717

39 Hoffmann, D.E., Tarzian, A.J. (2001), The girl who cried pain: A bias against women in the treatment of pain, *Journal of Law, Medicine & Ethics* 29(1), 13–27

40 McCaffery, M., Ferrell, B.R. (1997), Nurses' knowledge of pain assessment and management: How much progress have we made? *Journal of Pain Symptom Management* 14(3), 175–188

41 McInnes, C., McAlpine, C., Walter, M. (2008), Effect of gender on stroke management in Glasgow, *Age and Ageing* 37(2), 220–222

42 Bösner, S., Haasenritter, J., Hani, M.A. et al. (2011), Gender bias revisited: New insights on the differential management of chest pain, *BMC Family Practice* 12(1), 45

43 Bernardes, S.F., Lima, M.L. (2010), Being less of a man or less of a woman: Perceptions of chronic pain patients' gender identities, *European Journal of Pain* 14(2), 194–199

44 Diniz, E., Castro, P., Bousfield, A., Figueira Bernardes, S. (2020), Classism and dehumanization in chronic pain: A qualitative study of nurses' inferences about women of different socio-economic status, *British Journal of Health Psychology* 25(1), 152–170

45 Springer-Sullivan, C. (2005), The resurrection of female hysteria in present-day ERISA disability law, *Berkeley Journal of Gender, Law & Justice* 20(1), 67–74

46 Bransfield, R.C., Friedman, K.J. (2019), Differentiating psychosomatic, somatopsychic, multisystem illnesses, and medical uncertainty, *Healthcare* 7(4), 114

47 Paxman, C.G. (2021), 'Everyone thinks I am just lazy': Legitimacy narratives of Americans suffering from fibromyalgia, *Health* 25(1), 121–137

48 National Institute of Arthritis and Musculoskeletal and Skin Diseases (accessed 2021), *Fibromyalgia* <https://www.niams.nih.gov/Health_Info/Fibromyalgia/default.asp>

49 Paxman, C.G. (2021), 'Everyone thinks I am just lazy': Legitimacy narratives of Americans suffering from fibromyalgia, *Health* 25(1), 121–137

50 There is only initial research in this, but women of child-bearing age are more prone to autoimmune diseases and inflammations, and researchers are also showing that long Covid is an oestrogen-associated autoimmune disease.

51 Baldwin, M., Holmes, J.G. (1987), Salient private audiences and awareness of the self, *Journal of Personality and Social Psychology* 52(6), 1087–1098

52 Hays, S. (1996), *The Cultural Contradictions of Motherhood*, Yale University Press

414

53 Zawadzki, M. (2012), Examining an intervention to reduce under-diagnosis of CAD for women, PhD thesis, Penn State University, 7509

54 Birdwell, B.G., Herbers, J.E., Kroenke, K. (1993), Evaluating chest pain: The patient's presentation style alters the physician's diagnostic approach, *Archives of Internal Medicine* 153(17), 1991–1995

55 Fricker, M. (2003), Epistemic injustice and a role for virtue in the politics of knowing, *Metaphilosophy* 34(1/2)

56 I just can't find the link for this now and going on to Reddit to search for it has led me down very many strange rabbit holes that has taken many hours away from writing this book. So, you will have to just trust me on this one.

CHAPTER 15. SOFT TOUCH: EMPATHY AND EMOTIONAL LABOUR

1 Including in my book *Sway: Unravelling Unconscious Bias*, Bloomsbury, 2020

2 Rogers, C.R. (1979), The Foundations of the person-centered approach, *Education* 100(2), 98–107

3 Clinton's I feel your pain moment, *C-Span*, 15 October 1992 <https://www.c-span.org/video/?c4842764/user-clip-clintons-feel-pain-moment>

4 Ambinder, M. (2015), Feeling your pain: How Bill Clinton really won the second debate in 1992, *The Week* <https://theweek.com/articles/471681/feeling-pain>

5 Masserman, J.H., Wechkin, S., Terris, W. (1964), 'Altruistic' behavior in rhesus monkeys, *American Journal of Psychiatry* 121, 584–585

6 de Waal, F.B.M. (2008), Putting the altruism back into altruism: The evolution of empathy, *Annual Review of Psychology* 59, 279–300

7 Hojat, M., Gonnella, J.S., Nasca, T.J., Mangione, S., Veloksi, J.J., Magee, M. (2002), The Jefferson Scale of Physician Empathy: Further psychometric data and differences by gender and specialty at item level, *Academic Medicine* 77(10 Supplement), S58–S60

8 Hojat, M., Vergare, M.J., Maxwell, K. et al. (2009), The devil is in the third year: A longitudinal study of erosion of empathy in medical school, *Academic Medicine* 84(9), 1182–91

9 World Economic Forum (2019), The global risks report 2019 <https://www.weforum.org/reports/the-global-risks-report-2019>

10 Santos, M.A., Grosseman, S., Morelli, T.C., Giuliano, I.C., Erdmann, T.R. (2016), Empathy differences by gender and specialty preference in medical students: A study in Brazil, *International Journal of Medical Education* 7, 149–153

11 Tavakol, S., Dennick, R., Tavakol, M. (2011), Empathy in UK medical students: Differences by gender, medical year and specialty interest, *Education for Primary Care* 22(5), 297–303

12 Zaki, J., Ochsner, K.N. (2012), The neuroscience of empathy: progress, pitfalls and promise, *Nature Neuroscience* 15(5), 675–80

13 Chartrand, T.L., Lakin, J.L. (2013), The antecedents and consequences of human behavioral mimicry, *Annual Review of Psychology* 64, 285–308

14 Hampson, E., van Anders, S.M., Mullin, L.I. (2006), A female advantage in the recognition of emotional facial expressions: Test of an evolutionary hypothesis, *Evolution and Human Behavior* 27(6), 401–416

15 Office of National Statistics (ONS) (2020): <http://www.ons.gov.uk>

16 Amnesty (2020), Violence against women <https://www.amnesty.org.uk/violence-against-women>

17 World Health Organization (2021), Violence against women prevalence estimates, 2018 <https://www.who.int/publications/i/item/9789240026681>

18 Sokolov, A.A., Krüger, S., Enck, P., Krägeloh-Mann, I., Pavlova, M.A. (2011), Gender affects body language reading, *Frontiers of Psychology* 2, 16

19 Ickes, W., Tooke, W. (1988), The observational method: Studying the interactions of minds and bodies, in S. Duck, D.F. Hay, S.E. Hobfoll, W. Ickes, B. Montgomery (eds), *Handbook of Personal Relationships: Theory, Research, and Interventions*, John Wiley & Son, 79–97

20 Magen, E., Konasewich, P.A. (2011), Women support providers are more susceptible than men to emotional contagion following brief supportive interactions, *Psychology of Women Quarterly* 35(4), 611–616

21 The researchers acknowledge that the sample size was small and most of the participants were in their early twenties. We cannot extrapolate these results to other age groups, indeed other research has shown that emotional contagion is higher in younger people when compared to middle-aged adults. Also, this group was not very diverse; ethnic and cultural variations remain relatively under-explored.

22 Christov-Moore, L., Iacoboni, M. (2019), Sex differences in somatomotor representations of others' pain: A permutation-based analysis, *Brain Structure and Function* 224, 937–947

23 The scientists use the terms 'sex-based', 'females' and 'males' throughout their research paper but it is not clear whether they meant their considered gender identity or their biological sex. I contacted them via email for a response but did not receive a reply.

24 Christov-Moore, L., Simpson, E.A., Coudé, G., Grigaityte, K., Iacoboni, M., Ferrari, P.F. (2014), Empathy: Gender effects in brain and behavior, *Neuroscience and Biobehavioral Reviews* 46(4), 604–627

25 McAllister, L., Callaghan, J.E.M., Fellin, L.C. (2019), Masculinities and emotional expression in UK servicemen: 'Big boys don't cry?', *Journal of Gender Studies* 28(3), 257–270

26 As we have seen previously, stereotype threat is a hyper-awareness that we are likely to be stereotyped with specific characteristics, and are unlikely to 'belong' because of our status as a minority in that particular domain.

27 Ickes, W., Gesn, P.R., Graham, T. (2000), Gender differences in empathic accuracy: Differential ability or differential motivation? *Personal Relationships* 7, 95–109

28 Klein, K.K., Hodges, S. (2001), Gender differences, motivation, and empathic accuracy: When it pays to understand, *Personality and Social Psychology Bulletin* 27, 720–730

29 Benenson, J.F., Gauthier, E., Markovits, H. (2021), Girls exhibit greater empathy than boys following a minor accident, *Scientific Reports* 11, 7965

30 In the experiment, in which 5- to 7-year-olds viewed a classmate's distress at their block tower collapsing, more girls than boys reported empathic behaviour. This was, however, a very small dataset, with just 20 children involved in the study.

31 Deweerdt, S. (2017), Estimate of autism's sex ratio reaches new low, *Spectrum News*, 27 April 2017 <https://www.spectrumnews.org/news/estimate-autisms-sex-ratio-reaches-new-low/>

32 Baron-Cohen, S. (2008), *Autism and Asperger Syndrome*, Oxford University Press

33 Baron-Cohen, S. (2003) They just can't help it, *The Guardian*, 17 April 2003 <https://www.theguardian.com/education/2003/apr/17/research.highereducation>

417

34 Wieckowski, A.T., Luallin, S., Pan, Z., Righi, G., Gabriels, R.L., Mazefsky, C. (2020), Gender differences in emotion dysregulation in an autism inpatient psychiatric sample, *Autism Research* 13(8), 1343–1348

35 Dworzynski, K., Ronald, A., Bolton, P., Happé, F. (2012), How different are girls and boys above and below the diagnostic threshold for autism spectrum disorders? *Journal of the American Academy of Child and Adolescent Psychiatry* 51(8), 788–797

36 Hiller, R.M., Young, R.L., Weber, N. (2016), Sex differences in pre-diagnosis concerns for children later diagnosed with autism spectrum disorder, *Autism* 20(1), 75–84

37 Hiller, R.M., Young, R.L., Weber, N. (2016), Sex differences in pre-diagnosis concerns for children later diagnosed with autism spectrum disorder, *Autism* 20(1), 75–84

38 Rivet, T.F., Matson, J.L. (2011), Review of gender differences in core symptomatology in autism spectrum disorders, *Research in Autism Spectrum Disorders* 5(3), 957–976

39 Croen, L.A., Zerbo, O., Qian, Y., Massolo, M.L., Rich, S., Sidney, S., Kripke, C. (2015), The health status of adults on the autism spectrum, *Autism* 19(7), 814–823

40 Karlsson, L., Råstam, M., Wentz, E. (2013), The Swedish eating assessment for autism spectrum disorders (SWEAA) – Validation of a self-report questionnaire targeting eating disturbances within the autism spectrum, *Research in Developmental Disabilities* 34(7), 2224–2233

41 It is important to acknowledge that there is wide variability in the symptoms and effects different people experience, and it is often medically (and societally) easy to homogenise all autistic people.

42 Song, Y., Nie, T., Shi, W., Zhao, X., Yang, Y. (2019), Empathy impairment in individuals with autism spectrum conditions from a multidimensional perspective: A meta-analysis, *Frontiers in Psychology* 10, 1902

43 White, R.C., Remington, A. (2019), Object personification in autism: This paper will be very sad if you don't read it, *Autism* 23(4), 1042–1045

44 Brewer, R., Murphy, J. (2016), People with autism can read emotions, feel empathy, *Scientific American*, 13 July 2016 <https://www.scientificamerican.com/article/people-with-autism-can-read-emotions-feel-empathy1/>

45 Horton, T. (2016), The importance of empathy, *Health Foundation*,

12 December 2016 <https://www.health.org.uk/blogs/the-importance-of-empathy>

46 Davies, H.T., Mannion, R. (2013), Will prescriptions for cultural change improve the NHS? *British Medical Journal* 2013, 346

47 Howick, J., Steinkopf, L., Ulyte, A. et al. (2017), How empathic is your healthcare practitioner? A systematic review and meta-analysis of patient surveys, *BMC Medical Education* 17, 136

48 Selection bias could have played a role here, as well as response bias, with patients who know their practitioner well wanting to give them high scores.

49 Shah, R., Ogden, J. (2006), 'What's in a face?' The role of doctor ethnicity, age and gender in the formation of patients' judgements: An experimental study, *Patient Education and Counseling* 60(2), 136–141

50 Kerasidou, A., Horn, R. (2016), Making space for empathy: Supporting doctors in the emotional labour of clinical care, *BMC Medical Ethics* 17, 8 (2016)

51 Gleichgerrcht, E., Decety, J. (2013), Empathy in clinical practice: How individual dispositions, gender, and experience moderate empathic concern, burnout, and emotional distress in physicians, *PLoS One* 19, 8(4), e61526

52 Figley, C.R. (2002), Compassion fatigue: Psychotherapists' chronic lack of self care, *Journal of Clinical Psychology* 58(11), 1433–1441

53 Barnett, M.D., Hays, K.N., Cantu, C. (2019), Compassion fatigue, emotional labor, and emotional display among hospice nurses, *Death Studies* 46(2), 290–296

54 Goleman, D., Boyatzis, R., and McKee, A. (2002), *The New Leaders: Transforming the Art of Leadership into the Science of Results*, Little, Brown

55 The concept of transformational leadership started with James V. Downton in 1973 and was expanded by James Burns in 1978. In 1985, researcher Bernard M. Bass further expanded the concept to include ways for measuring the success of transformational leadership. This model encourages leaders to demonstrate authentic, strong leadership with the idea that employees will be inspired to follow suit. See White, S.K. (2018), What is transformational leadership? *CIO*, 21 February 2018 <https://www.cio.com/article/3257184/what-is-transformational-leadership-a-model-for-motivating-innovation.html>

56 Vongas, J., Al Hajj, R. (2015), The evolution of empathy and women's precarious leadership appointments, *Frontiers in Psychology* 6

57 Ross, C., van Willigen, M. (1996), Gender, parenthood, and anger, *Journal of Marriage and Family* 58(3), 572–584

58 Jansz, J. (2000), Masculine identity and restrictive emotionality, in A.H. Fischer (ed.), *Gender and Emotion: Social Psychological Perspectives*, Cambridge University Press, 166–186

59 Hochschild, A. (1979), Emotion work, feeling rules, and social structure, *American Journal of Sociology* 85, 551–575

60 Lindebaum, D. (2012), I rebel – therefore we exist: emotional standardization in organizations and the emotionally intelligent individual, *Journal of Management Inquiry* 21(3), 262–277

61 Willmott, H. (1993), Strength is ignorance; slavery is freedom: Managing culture in modern organizations, *Journal of Management Studies* 30, 515–552

62 Kang, M. (2003), The managed hand: The commercialization of bodies and emotions in Korean immigrant-owned nail salons, *Gender and Society* 17(6), 820–839

63 Osho, Y., Jones, C., Franklin, S. (2019), 'Talented women of colour are blocked' – why are there so few black female professors? *The Guardian*, 5 February 2019 <https://www.theguardian.com/education/2019/feb/05/talented-women-of-colour-are-blocked-why-are-there-so-few-black-female-professors>

64 Harvey Wingfield, A. (2010), Are some emotions marked 'whites only'? Racialized feeling rules in professional workplaces, *Social Problems* 57(2), 251–268

65 Russell Hochschild, A. (1983), *The Managed Heart: Commercialization of Human Feeling*, University of California Press

66 Russell Hochschild, A. (1983), *The Managed Heart: Commercialization of Human Feeling*, University of California Press

67 Thoits, P.A. (1985), Self-labeling processes in mental illness: The role of emotional deviance, *American Journal of Sociology* 91(2), 221–249

68 Goffman, E. (1959), *The Presentation of Self in Everyday Life*, Doubleday

69 Jeung, D.Y., Kim, C., Chang, S.J. (2018), Emotional labor and burnout: A review of the literature, *Yonsei Medical Journal* 59(2), 187–193

70 Erickson, R. (2005), Why emotion work matters: Sex, gender, and the division of household labor, *Journal of Marriage and Family* 67(2), 337–351

71 Hochschild admits in an interview in the *Atlantic* that 'I do think that managing anxiety associated with obligatory chores is emotional labor.'

CHAPTER 16. SUCH A DOLL (EMOTIONAL TECHNOLOGIES)

1   4 Little Trees, Find Solutions AI <https://www.findsolutionai.com/4little-trees>

2   Chan, M. (2021), This AI reads children's emotions as they learn, *CNN Business*, 17 February 2021 <https://edition.cnn.com/2021/02/16/tech/emotion-recognition-ai-education-spc-intl-hnk/index.html>

3   Marketers Media, Emotion analytics market to rake in $25bn by 2023 <https://marketersmedia.com/emotion-analytics-market-to-rake-in-around-us-25-billion-by-2023-with-17-cagr/328705>

4   Somers, M. (2019), Emotion AI explained, *MIT Management Sloan School*, 8 March 2019 <https://mitsloan.mit.edu/ideas-made-to-matter/emotion-ai-explained>

5   Although how much do we read the small print, and how much do we really know when our images and videos are being used by technology companies?

6   Barrett, L.F., Adolphs, R., Marsella, S., Martinez, A.M., Pollak, S.D. (2019), Emotional expressions reconsidered: Challenges to inferring emotion from human facial movements, *Psychological Science in the Public Interest* 20(1), 1–68

7   Rhue, L. (2018), Racial Influence on Automated Perceptions of Emotions, available at SSRN <https://ssrn.com/abstract=3281765>

8   In my previous book *Sway*, Bloomsbury, 2020, I looked at voice-assistants and the gender bias that is in-built, with most of them conforming to the subservient role and expectations of women in our society. I have also discussed at length the gender and racial bias in AI, especially in facial recognition technologies.

9   Agarwal, P. (2019), It's time we faced up to AI's race problem, *Prospect*, 14 August 2019 <https://www.prospectmagazine.co.uk/science-and-technology/facial-recognition-technology-police-uk-race-gender-london-stations>

10 Richter, F. (2021), Women's representation in Big Tech, *Statista*, 1 July 2021 <https://www.statista.com/chart/4467/female-employees-at-tech-companies/>

11 PWC UK research report (2017), Women in tech: Time to close the gender gap <https://www.pwc.co.uk/women-in-technology/women-in-tech-report.pdf>

12 Domnich, A., Anbarjafari, G. (2021), Responsible AI: Gender bias assessment in emotion recognition, *ArXiv*, <http://arxiv.org/abs/2103.11436>

13 Schwemmer, C., Knight, C., Bello-Pardo, E. et al. (2020), Diagnosing gender bias in image recognition systems, *Socius: Sociological Research for a Dynamic World*

14 Amores, J., Hernandez, J., Dementyev, A., Wang, X., Maes, P. (2018), BioEssence: A wearable olfactory display that monitors cardio-respiratory information to support mental wellbeing <https://dam-prod.media.mit.edu/x/2018/05/24/bioessence-EMBC_8vyWSNB.pdf>

15 Only a concept at this stage and scientists are working on developing it. I have been unable to find any reliable information on whether it was only a prototype or if any such devices were actually made and sold.

16 Whelan, E., McDuff, D., Gleasure, R., vom Brocke, J. (2018), How emotion-sensing technology can reshape the workplace, *MIT Sloan Management Review* <https://sloanreview.mit.edu/article/how-emotion-sensing-technology-can-reshape-the-workplace/>

17 Stock trade typo costs firm $225m, *CBS News*, 9 December 2005. A trader working for Mizuho Securities Co. in Tokyo intended to sell a single share of a stock for about 610,000 yen (approximately $5,000). By mistake, he placed an order to sell 610,000 shares for 1 yen. The company was unable to cancel the order, leading to an estimated loss of $225 million <https://www.cbsnews.com/news/stock-trade-typo-costs-firm-225m/>

18 Replika <https://replika.ai/>

19 Such as kinktalk, dollforum and several boards on Reddit with less explicit content.

20 Murphy, M. (2019), This ap is trying to replicate you, *Quartz*, 29 August 2019 <https://qz.com/1698337/replika-this-app-is-trying-to-replicate-you/>

21 Lopez, F. (2015), San Francisco startup Senselabs' headset trains mental athletic performance, *SportTechie*, 20 April 2015 <https://www.sporttechie.com/san-francisco-startup-senselabs-headset-trains-mental-athletic-performance/>

22 McKendrick, J. (2018), Technology adds stress, then addresses stress – in real time, *RT Insights*, 13 February 2018 <https://www.rtinsights.com/technology-adds-stress-then-addresses-stress-in-real-time/>

23 Knight, W. (2017), Socially sensitive AI software coaches call center workers,

MIT Technology Review, 31 January 2017 <https://www.technologyreview.com/2017/01/31/154294/socially-sensitive-ai-software-coaches-call-center-workers/>

24 Breyer, P. (2021), EU-funded technology violates fundamental rights, *About Intel,* 22 April 2021 <https://aboutintel.eu/transparency-lawsuit-iborderctrl/>

25 Crockett, K.A., O'Shea, J.D., Khan, W. (2020), Automated deception detection of males and females from non-verbal facial micro-gestures, 2020 International Joint Conference on Neural Networks (IJCNN), 1–7

26 Hall, L. (2017), How we feel about robots that feel, *MIT Technology Review*, 24 October 2017 <https://www.technologyreview.com/2017/10/24/148259/how-we-feel-about-robots-that-feel/>

27 Can robots have emotions? *News Shots*, 8 October 2021 <https://thenews-shots.com/can-robots-have-emotions/>

28 Hortensius, R., Hekele, F., Crossy, E. (2018), The perception of emotion in artificial agents, *IEEE Transactions on Cognitive and Developmental Systems*

29 Reyes, M., Meza, I., Pineda, L. (2019), Robotics facial expression of anger in collaborative human–robot interaction, *International Journal of Advanced Robotic Systems* 16

30 Seaman, M.J. (2008), Becoming more (than) human: Affective posthumanisms, past and future, *Journal of Narrative Theory* 37, 246–275

31 Złotowski, J., Proudfoot, D., Yogeeswaran, K. et al. (2015), Anthropomorphism: Opportunities and challenges in human–robot interaction, *International Journal of Social Robotics* 7(3), 347–360

32 Kickstarter, Moflin: An AI pet robot with emotional capabilities <https://www.kickstarter.com/projects/vanguardindustries/moflin-an-ai-pet-robot-with-emotional-capabilities/description>

33 White, D., Galbraith, P.W. (2019), Japan's emerging emotional tech, *Anthropology News* 60(1), 6–10

34 In June 2021 the production of Pepper was paused due to weakening demand, by which time around 27,000 units had been manufactured.

35 Best, S. (2020), Lifelike sex robots that 'have a heartbeat', *Mirror*, 11 May 2020 <https://www.mirror.co.uk/tech/lifelike-sex-robots-have-heartbeat-22009064>

36 Levy, D. (2007), *Love and Sex with Robots: The Evolution of Human–Robot Relationships*, HarperCollins

37 Pearson, I. (2015), The Future of Sex: The Rise of the Robosexuals <http://graphics.bondara.com/Future_sex_report.pdf>

38 Sex dolls are defined as human-like, full-body, anatomically correct anthropomorphic dolls of different materials (e.g., rubber, plush, silicone and thermoplastic elastomer) and price ranges that are designed for sexual use. A sex robot is much like a sex doll but equipped with sensors and AI.

39 Levy, D. (2012), The ethics of robot prostitutes, in Lin, P., Abney, K., Bekey, G.A. (eds), *Robot Ethics: The Ethical and Social Implications of Robotics*, MIT Press, 223–31

40 Yeoman, I., Mars, M. (2012), Robots, men and sex tourism, *Futures* 44(4), 365–71

41 Ellen, B. (2017), Female sex robots, feel free to replace us, *The Guardian*, 3 December 2017 <https://www.theguardian.com/commentisfree/2017/dec/03/sex-robots-technology-women-artificial-intelligence>

42 Ferguson, A. (2010), *The Sex Doll: A History*, McFarland & Company

43 Knafo, D., Lo Bosco, R. (2017), *The Age of Perversion: Desire and Technology in Psychoanalysis and Culture*, Routledge/Taylor & Francis

44 Roos, B. (2005), Oskar Kokoschka's sex toy: The women and the doll who conceived the artist, *Modernism/Modernity* 12(2), 291–309

45 North, A. (2017), Women of sex tech, unite, *New York Times*, 18 August 2017 <https://www.nytimes.com/2017/08/18/nyregion/women-of-sex-tech-unite.html>

46 Valverde, S. (2012), The modern sex doll-owner: A descriptive analysis, thesis presented, California State Polytechnic <https://digitalcommons.calpoly.edu/cgi/viewcontent.cgi?article=1893&context=theses>

47 Döring, N., Mohseni, M.R., Walter, R. (2020), Design, use, and effects of sex dolls and sex robots: Scoping review, *Journal of Medical Internet Research* 22(7), e18551

48 A 2007 study from the University of Alberta found that one-third of 13-year-old boys admitted viewing porn; and a survey published by *Psychologies* magazine in the UK found that a third of 14- to 16-year-olds had first seen sexual images online when they were 10 or younger (from *The Guardian*, July 2010)

49 Dines, G. (2015), Growing up in a pornified culture, *TEDx Talk* <https://www.youtube.com/watch?v=_YpHNImNsx8>

50 Dines, G. (2010), *Pornland: How Porn Has Hijacked Our Sexuality*, Beacon Press

51 González-González, C.S., Gil-Iranzo, R.M., Paderewski-Rodríguez, P. (2021), Human–robot interaction and sexbots: A systematic literature review, *Sensors* 21(1), 216

52 A 42-year-old African-American self-proclaimed doll-lover from Michigan, Davecat has lived with RealDoll Sidore Kuroneko (nickname 'Shi-chan') since 1998 and regards her as his wife. They wear matching wedding rings inscribed with the words 'Synthetic love lasts forever'.

53 Knafo, D., Lo Bosco, R. (2017), *The Age of Perversion: Desire and Technology in Psychoanalysis and Culture*, Routledge/Taylor & Francis

54 Beck, J. (2013), Married to a doll: Why one man advocates synthetic love, *Atlantic*, 6 September 2013 <https://www.theatlantic.com/health/archive/2013/09/married-to-a-doll-why-one-man-advocates-synthetic-love/279361/>

55 Richardson, K. (2016), The asymmetrical 'relationship': Parallels between prostitution and the development of sex robots. *ACM SIGCAS Computers and Society* 45(3), 290–293

56 The Turing test, devised by Alan Turing in 1950, is a test of a machine's ability to show intelligent behaviour that is considered equivalent to that of a human, to be indistinguishable from it and even surpass it.

57 Asimov, I. (1964), Visit to the World's Fair of 2014, *New York Times*, 16 August 1964 <http://www.nytimes.com/books/97/03/23/lifetimes/asi-v-fair.html>

58 Gatebox <https://www.gatebox.ai/en/hikari>

59 White, D., Galbraith, P.W. (2019), Japan's emerging emotional tech, *Anthropology News* 60(1), 6–10 <http://dx.doi.org/10.1111/AN.1070>

60 Merish, L. (1996), Cuteness and commodity aesthetics: Tom Thumb and Shirley Temple, in R. Garland Thomson (ed.), *Freakery: Cultural Spectacles of the Extraordinary Body*, New York University Press, 185–203

61 Tu, J. (2018), Because I am small and Asian, I am fetishised by some white men, *Sydney Morning Herald*, 26 November 2018 <https://www.smh.com.au/lifestyle/life-and-relationships/because-i-am-small-and-asian-i-am-fetishised-by-some-white-men-20181126-p50ifk.html>

62 Devlin, K., Belton, O., The measure of a woman: Fembots, fact and fiction,

in S. Cave, K. Dihal, S. Dillon (eds), *AI Narratives: A History of Imaginative Thinking about Intelligent Machines*, Oxford University Press

63   Rumens, N. (2016), Postfeminism, men, masculinities and work: A research agenda for gender and organization studies scholars, *Gender, Work and Organization* 24(3), 245–259

64   Döring, N., Mohseni, M.R., Walter, R. (2020), Design, use, and effects of sex dolls and sex robots: Scoping review, *Journal of Medical Internet Research* 22(7), e18551

65   Nomura, T., Kanda, T., Suzuki, T. (2006), Experimental investigation into influence of negative attitudes toward robots on human–robot interaction, *AI and Society* 20(2), 138–150

66   Scheutz, M., Arnold, T. (2016), Are we ready for sex robots? 2016 11th ACM/IEEE International Conference on Human Robot Interaction, 351–358

67   Scheutz, M., Arnold, T. (2016), Are we ready for sex robots? 2016 11th ACM/IEEE International Conference on Human Robot Interaction, 351–358

68   Most of the marketing, as well as academic studies, is aimed at heterosexual men.

69   Nordmo, M., Næss, J.Ø., Husøy, M.F., Arnestad, M.N. (2020), Friends, lovers or nothing: Men and women differ in their perceptions of sex robots and platonic love robots, *Frontiers in Psychology* 11, 355

70   We spoke to Harmony's first beta tester, the 'artificial intelligence' s*x doll, *SamaGame* <https://samagame.com/en/we-spoke-to-harmonys-first-beta-tester-the-artificial-intelligence-sx-doll/>, last accessed 25 May 2022.

71   Morris, A. (2018), Meet the man who test drives sex robots, *Forbes*, 27 September 2018 <https://www.forbes.com/sites/andreamorris/2018/09/27/meet-the-man-who-test-drives-sex-robots/#23a831f9452d>

72   Davis, A.P. (2018), Are we ready for robot sex? *The Cut*, May 2018 <https://www.thecut.com/2018/05/sex-robots-realbotix.html>

73   Clark-Flory, T. (2017), This sex robot is designed to make you fall in love, *Vocativ*, 3 April 2017 <https://www.vocativ.com/409728/can-sex-robots-teach-us-to-be-better-humans/index.html>

74   Tay, B., Jung, Y., Park, T. (2014), When stereotypes meet robots: The double-edge sword of robot gender and personality in human–robot interaction, *Computers in Human Behavior* 38, 75–84

75 Eyssel, F., Hegel, F. (2012), (S)he's got the look: Gender stereotyping of robots, *Journal of Applied Social Psychology* 42(9), 2213–2230

76 Trovato, G., Lopez, A., Paredes, R., Cuellar, F. (2017), Security and guidance: Two roles for a humanoid robot in an interaction experiment, in *Proceedings of 26th IEEE International Symposium on Robot and Human Interactive Communication*, 230–235

77 Giger, J.-C., Piçarra, N., Alves-Oliveira, P., Oliveira, R., Arriaga, P. (2019), Humanization of robots: Is it really such a good idea? *Human Behavior and Emerging Technologies* 1(2), 111–123

78 Hopping, C. (2015), Campaign calls for ban of AI sex robots, *IT Pro*, 18 September 2015 <https://www.itpro.co.uk/strategy/25290/campaign-calls-for-ban-of-ai-sex-robots>

79 Article 19 (2021), Emotional entanglement: China's emotion recognition market and its implications for human rights <https://www.article19.org/wp-content/uploads/2021/01/ER-Tech-China-Report.pdf>

80 Haraway, D. (1991), A cyborg manifesto: Science, technology, and socialist-feminism in the late twentieth century, in *Simians, Cyborgs and Women: The Reinvention of Nature*, Routledge, 149–181

81 Kakoudaki, D. (2014), *Anatomy of a Robot: Literature, Cinema, and the Cultural Work of Artificial People*, Rutgers University Press

EPILOGUE: EMOTIONAL UTOPIA

1 Abbott, E.A. (1884), *Flatland: A Romance in Many Dimensions*, Seeley & Co, 97

2 Roberson, D., Davies, I., Davidoff, J. (2000), Color categories are not universal: Replications and new evidence from a stone-age culture, *Journal of Experimental Psychology: General*, 129(3), 369–398

3 And this rumination can be a vicious cycle.

4 Barrett, L.F., Bliss-Moreau, E. (2009), She's emotional. He's having a bad day: Attributional explanations for emotion stereotypes, *Emotion* 9(5), 649–658

5 Shields, S.A. (1991), Gender in the psychology of emotion: A selective research review, in K.I. Strongman (ed.), *International Review of Studies on Emotion*, vol. 1, Wiley, 227–245

6 David, Y.B., Idan, O. (2018), 'We don't have to talk about how I feel':

Emotionality as a tool of resistance in political discourse among Israeli students – a gendered socio-linguistic perspective, *International Feminist Journal of Politics* 21(2), 1–24

7   Tufail, Z., Polletta, F. (2015), The gendering of emotional flexibility: Why angry women are both admired and devalued in debt settlement firms, *Gender & Society* 29(4), 484–508

8   Weigard, A., Loviska, A.M., Beltz, A.M. (2021), Little evidence for sex or ovarian hormone influences on affective variability, *Scientific Reports* 11, 20925

9   We might assume that there would be some confirmation bias, so we more readily see compassionate and nurturing behaviour from women in leadership positions. But this is not the case. Since there is a dissociation between 'woman' and 'leader', women are judged and penalised more because they are seen as violating the gender norms when in leadership positions. Men have more leeway. And haven't we seen this again and again!

10 Louise Bourgeois, *Arch of Hysteria* (1993), Sotheby's catalogue, *Contemporary Art Evening Auction 2019* <https://www.sothebys.com/en/auctions/ecatalogue/2019/contemporary-art-evening-auction-n10069/lot.10.html>

11 Turner, C. (2012), Analysing Louise Bourgeois, *The Guardian*, 6 April 2012 <https://www.theguardian.com/artanddesign/2012/apr/06/louise-bourgeois-freud>

12 *Arch of Hysteria*, 1993. Bronze, polished patina. Collection The Easton Foundation, New York

13 Exhibition catalogue (1997), *Louise Bourgeois: Blue Days and Pink Days*, Fondazione Prada, Milan, 214

14 Louise Bourgeois, cited in exhibition catalogue (2003), *The Body Transformed*, National Gallery of Canada, Ottawa, 18

15 Nixon, M. (2005), *Fantastic Reality: Louise Bourgeois and a Story of Modern Art*, MIT Press. Mignon Nixon's book explores the connections between Bourgeois's work and psychoanalytic theory in an extraordinarily profound and illuminating way.

16 Crosbie, S. (2014), Why the world needs to be a bit more hysterical, blog post, 25 February 2014 <http://www.shan-crosbie.com/blog/2014/2/25/why-the-world-needs-to-be-a-bit-more-hysterical>

INDEX

INDEX